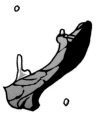

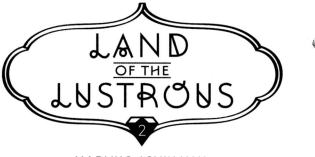

LAND
OF THE
LUSTROUS
2

HARUKO ICHIKAWA

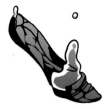

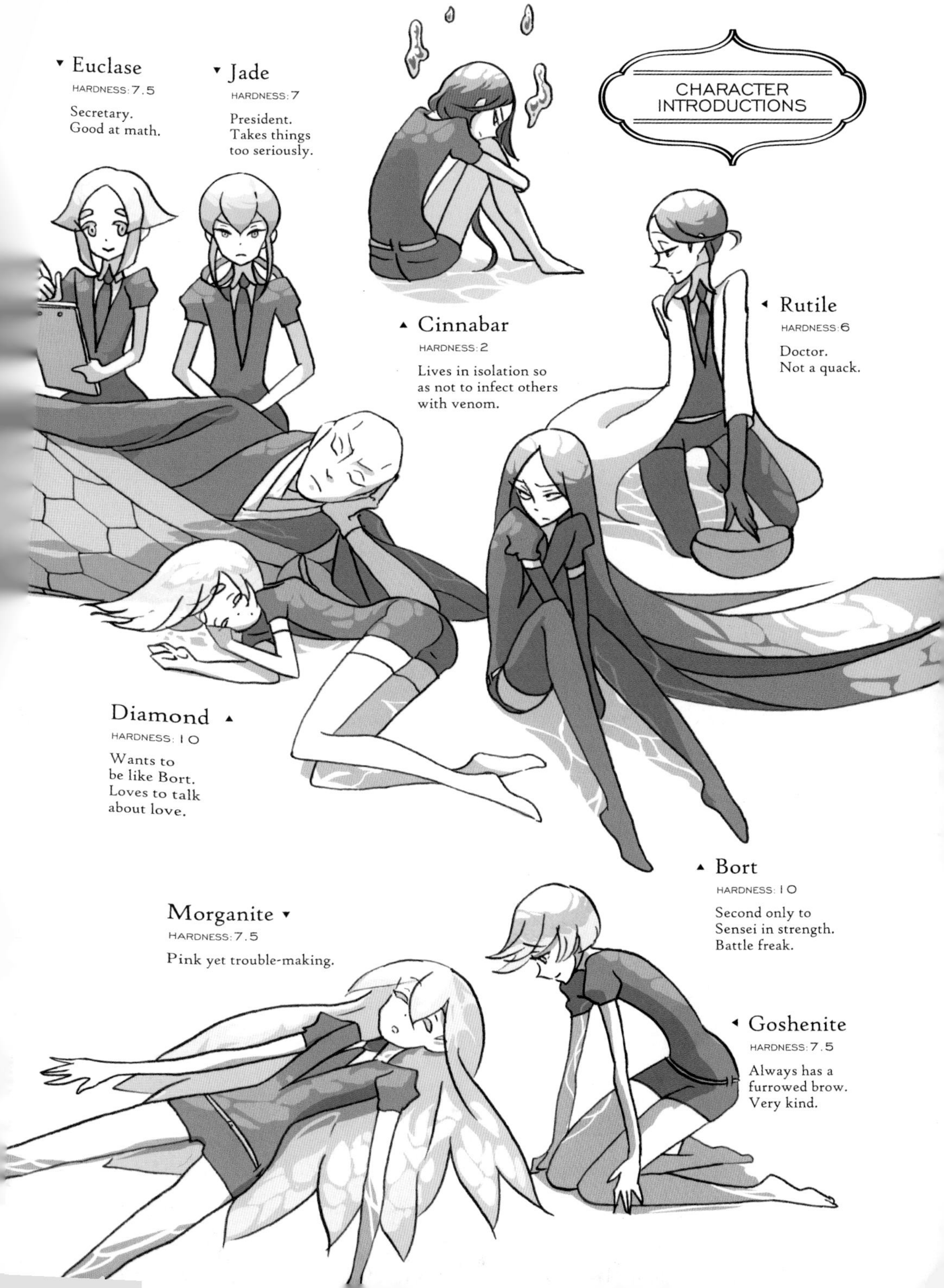
CHARACTER INTRODUCTIONS
▼ Euclase
HARDNESS: 7.5
Secretary. Good at math.
▼ Jade
HARDNESS: 7
President. Takes things too seriously.
▲ Cinnabar
HARDNESS: 2
Lives in isolation so as not to infect others with venom.
◀ Rutile
HARDNESS: 6
Doctor. Not a quack.
Diamond ▲
HARDNESS: 10
Wants to be like Bort. Loves to talk about love.
▲ Bort
HARDNESS: 10
Second only to Sensei in strength. Battle freak.
Morganite ▼
HARDNESS: 7.5
Pink yet trouble-making.
◀ Goshenite
HARDNESS: 7.5
Always has a furrowed brow. Very kind.

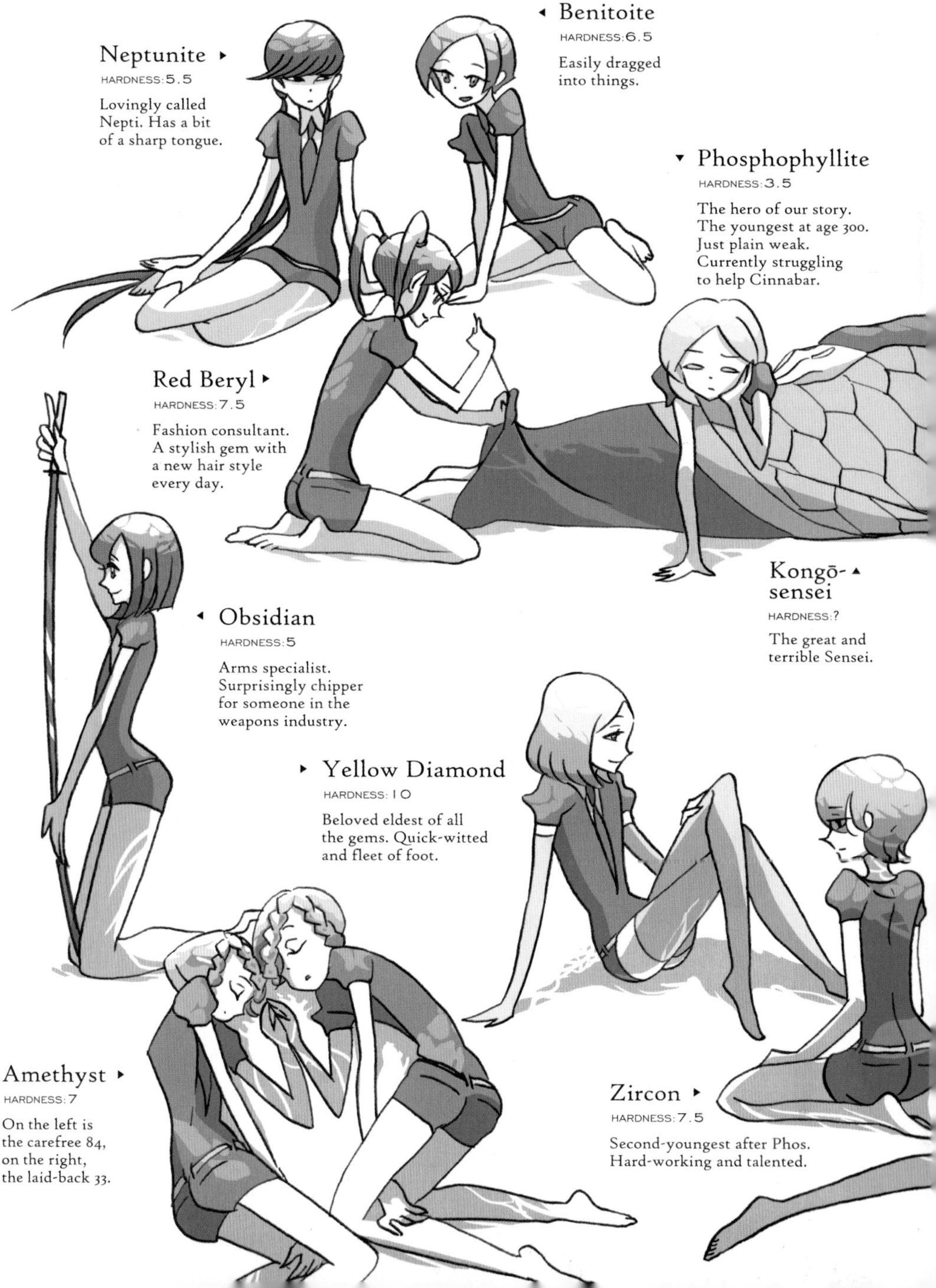
Benitoite
HARDNESS: 6.5
Easily dragged into things.
Neptunite
HARDNESS: 5.5
Lovingly called Nepti. Has a bit of a sharp tongue.
Phosphophyllite
HARDNESS: 3.5
The hero of our story. The youngest at age 300. Just plain weak. Currently struggling to help Cinnabar.
Red Beryl
HARDNESS: 7.5
Fashion consultant. A stylish gem with a new hair style every day.
Kongō-sensei
HARDNESS: ?
The great and terrible Sensei.
Obsidian
HARDNESS: 5
Arms specialist. Surprisingly chipper for someone in the weapons industry.
Yellow Diamond
HARDNESS: 10
Beloved eldest of all the gems. Quick-witted and fleet of foot.
Zircon
HARDNESS: 7.5
Second-youngest after Phos. Hard-working and talented.
Amethyst
HARDNESS: 7
On the left is the carefree 84, on the right, the laid-back 33.

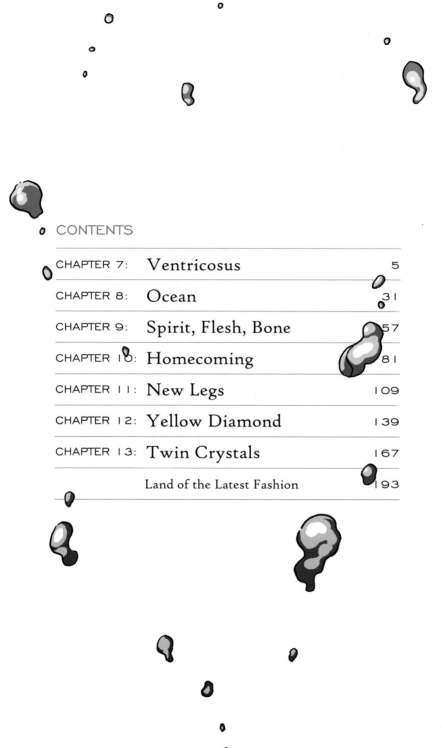

CONTENTS

CHAPTER 7:

Ventricosus

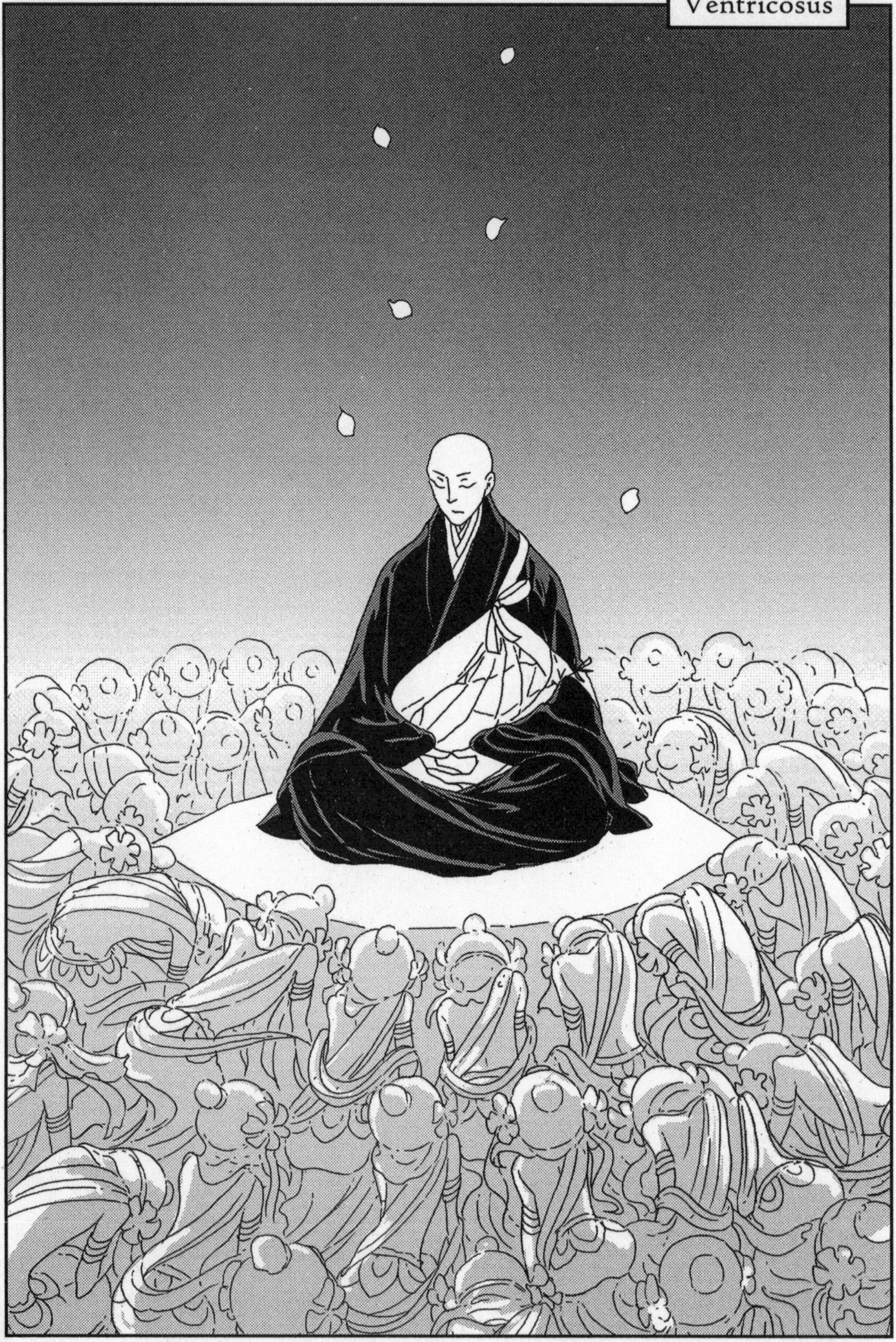

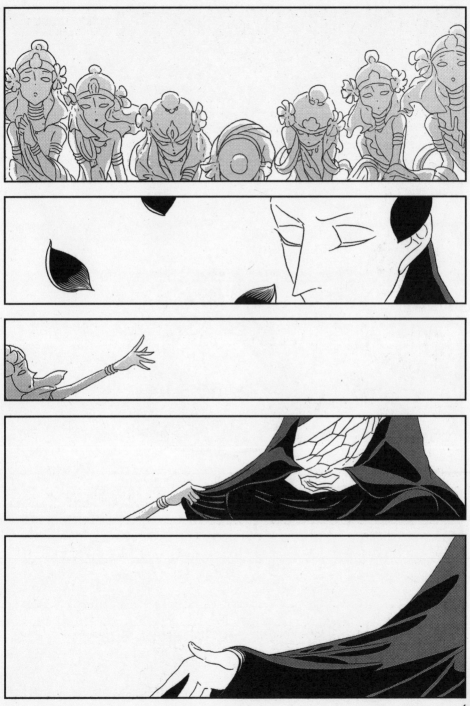

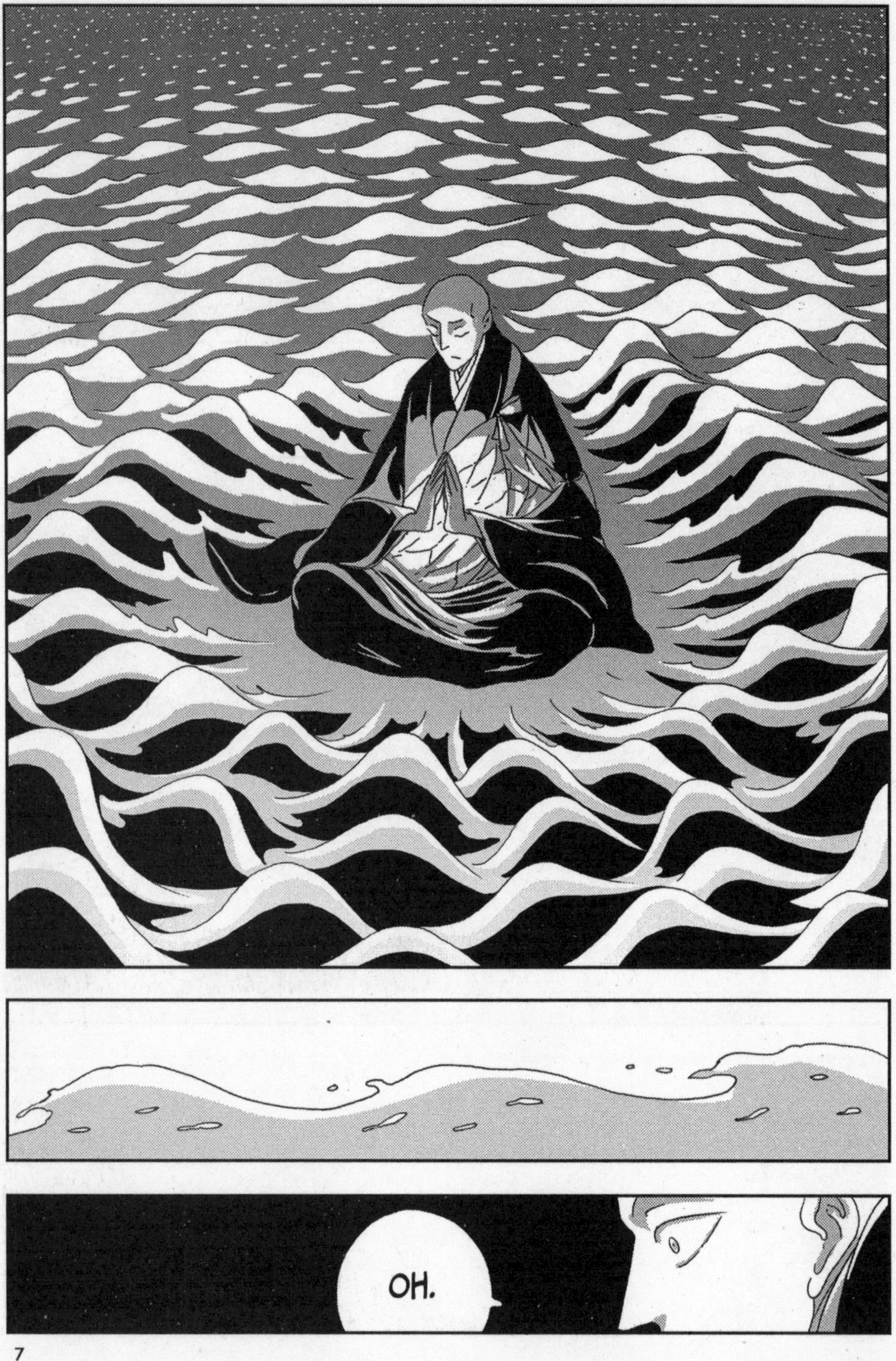
OH.

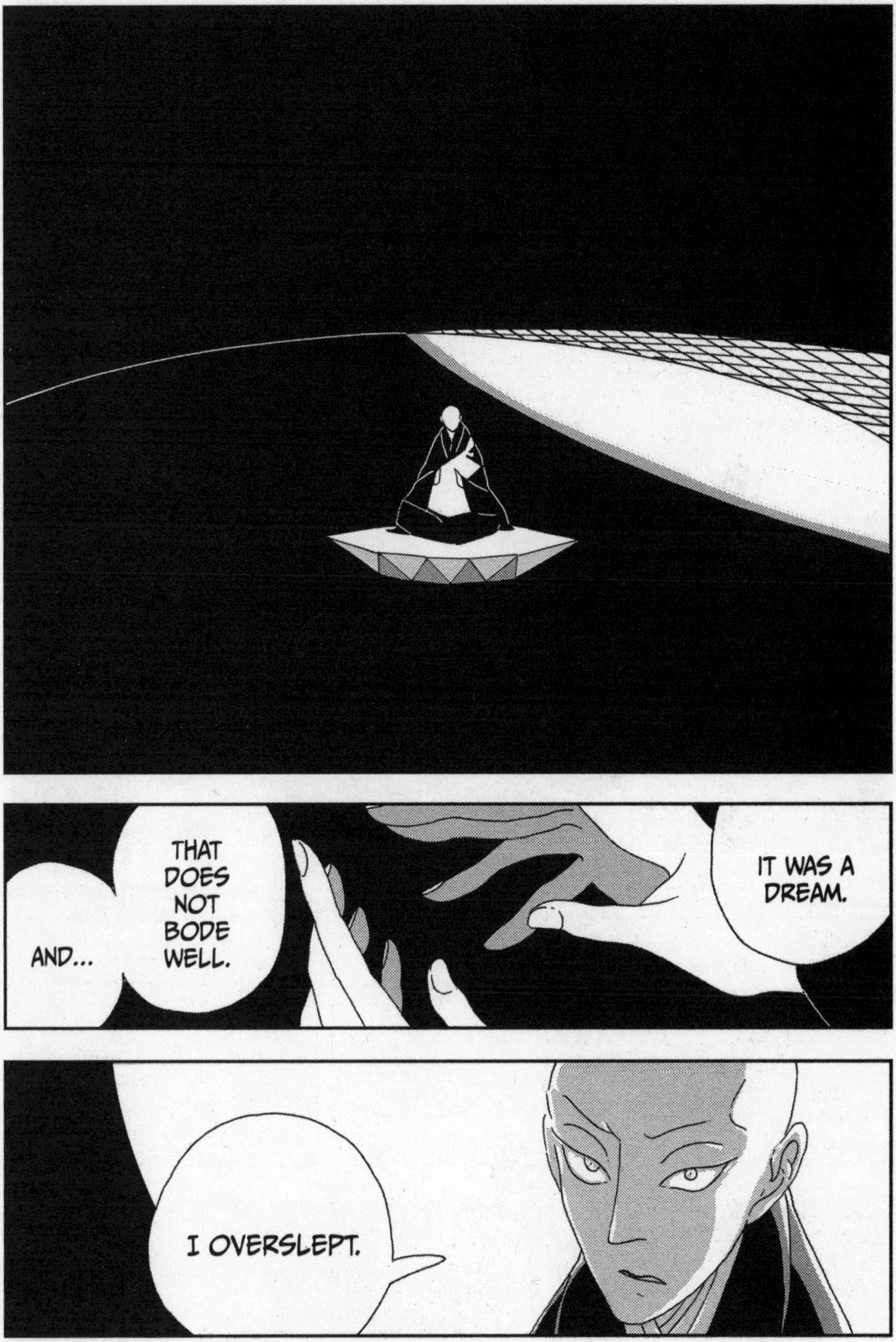
IT WAS A DREAM.
THAT DOES NOT BODE WELL.
AND...
I OVERSLEPT.

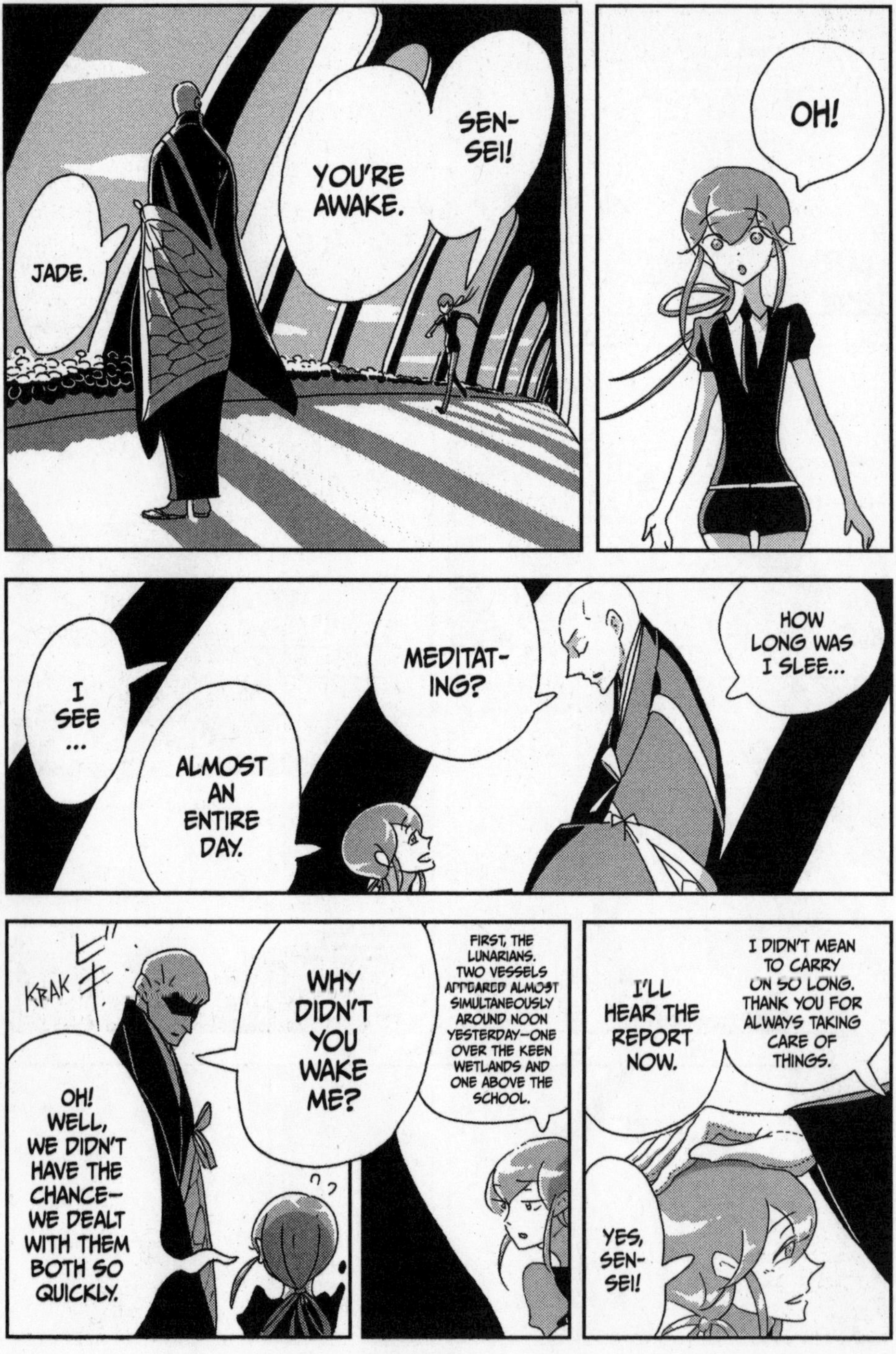
OH!
SEN-SEI!
YOU'RE AWAKE.
JADE.
HOW LONG WAS I SLEE...
MEDITAT-ING?
ALMOST AN ENTIRE DAY.
I SEE ...
I DIDN'T MEAN TO CARRY ON SO LONG. THANK YOU FOR ALWAYS TAKING CARE OF THINGS.
I'LL HEAR THE REPORT NOW.
YES, SEN-SEI!
FIRST, THE LUNARIANS. TWO VESSELS APPEARED ALMOST SIMULTANEOUSLY AROUND NOON YESTERDAY—ONE OVER THE KEEN WETLANDS AND ONE ABOVE THE SCHOOL.
KRAK
WHY DIDN'T YOU WAKE ME?
OH! WELL, WE DIDN'T HAVE THE CHANCE—WE DEALT WITH THEM BOTH SO QUICKLY.

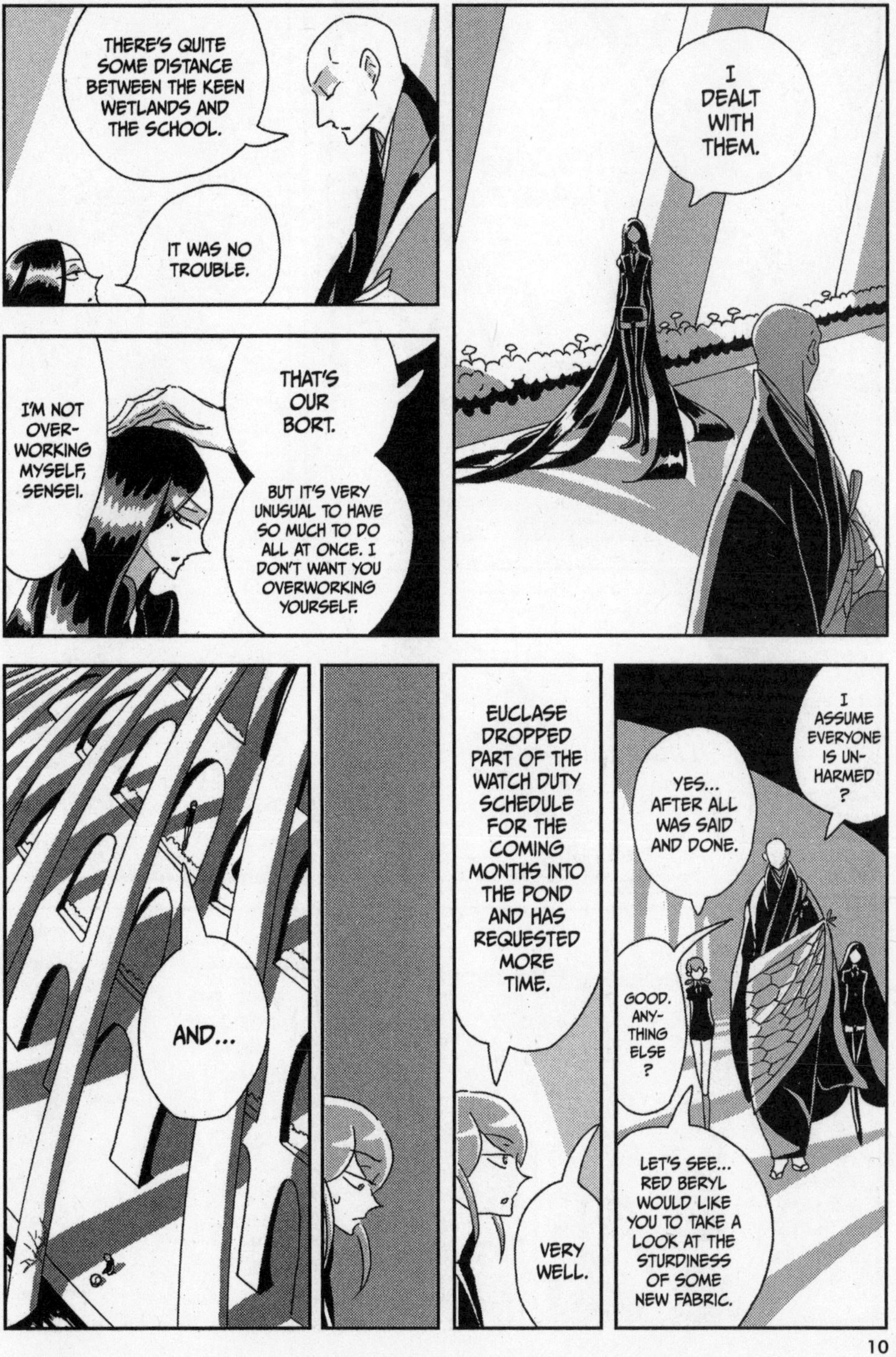
I DEALT WITH THEM.
THERE'S QUITE SOME DISTANCE BETWEEN THE KEEN WETLANDS AND THE SCHOOL.
IT WAS NO TROUBLE.
THAT'S OUR BORT.
BUT IT'S VERY UNUSUAL TO HAVE SO MUCH TO DO ALL AT ONCE. I DON'T WANT YOU OVERWORKING YOURSELF.
I'M NOT OVER-WORKING MYSELF, SENSEI.
I ASSUME EVERYONE IS UN-HARMED ?
YES... AFTER ALL WAS SAID AND DONE.
GOOD. ANY-THING ELSE ?
LET'S SEE... RED BERYL WOULD LIKE YOU TO TAKE A LOOK AT THE STURDINESS OF SOME NEW FABRIC.
EUCLASE DROPPED PART OF THE WATCH DUTY SCHEDULE FOR THE COMING MONTHS INTO THE POND AND HAS REQUESTED MORE TIME.
VERY WELL.
AND...

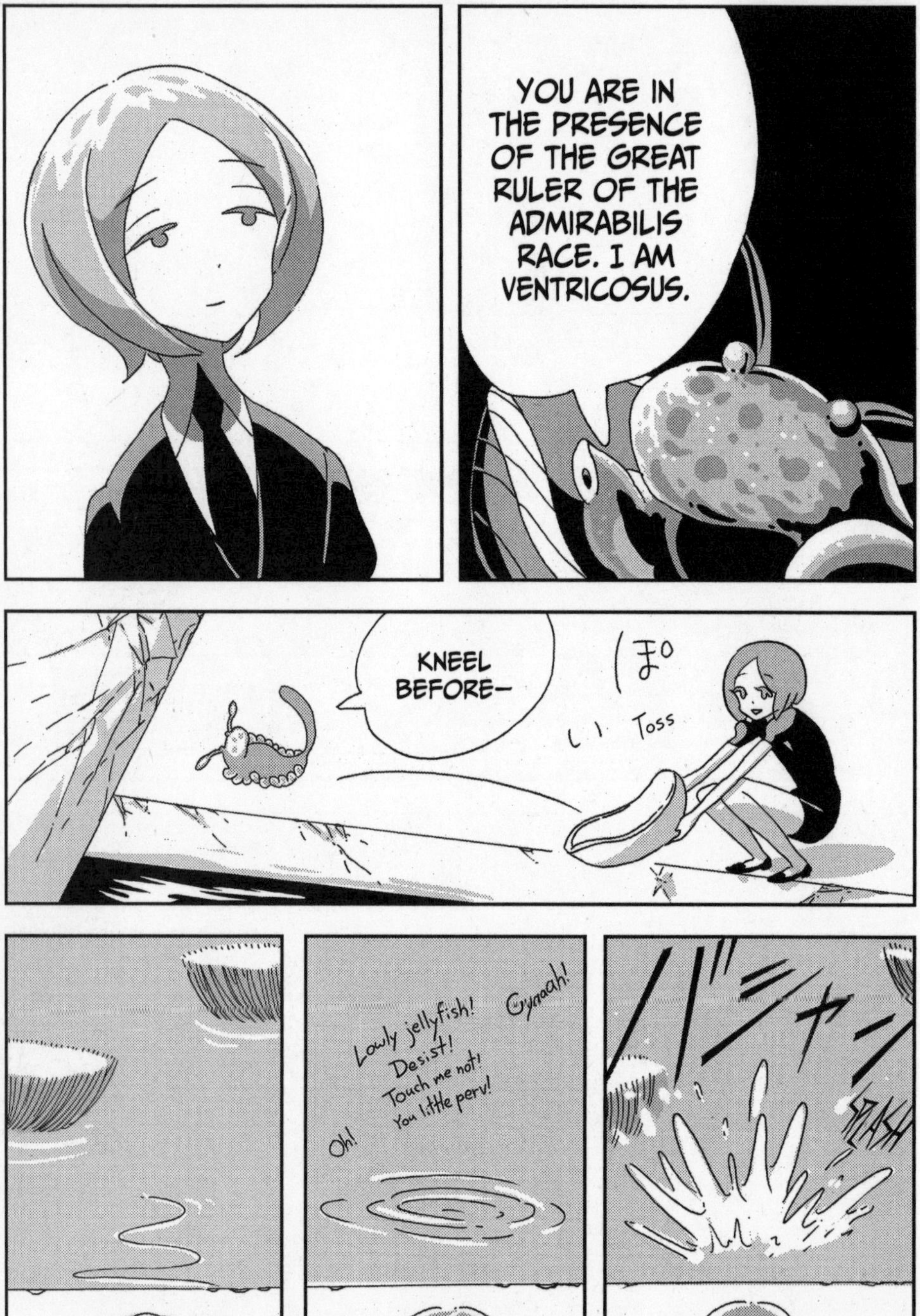
YOU ARE IN THE PRESENCE OF THE GREAT RULER OF THE ADMIRABILIS RACE. I AM VENTRICOSUS.
KNEEL BEFORE–
Toss
SPLASH
Gyaaah!
Lowly jellyfish! Desist! Touch me not! You little perv!
Oh!

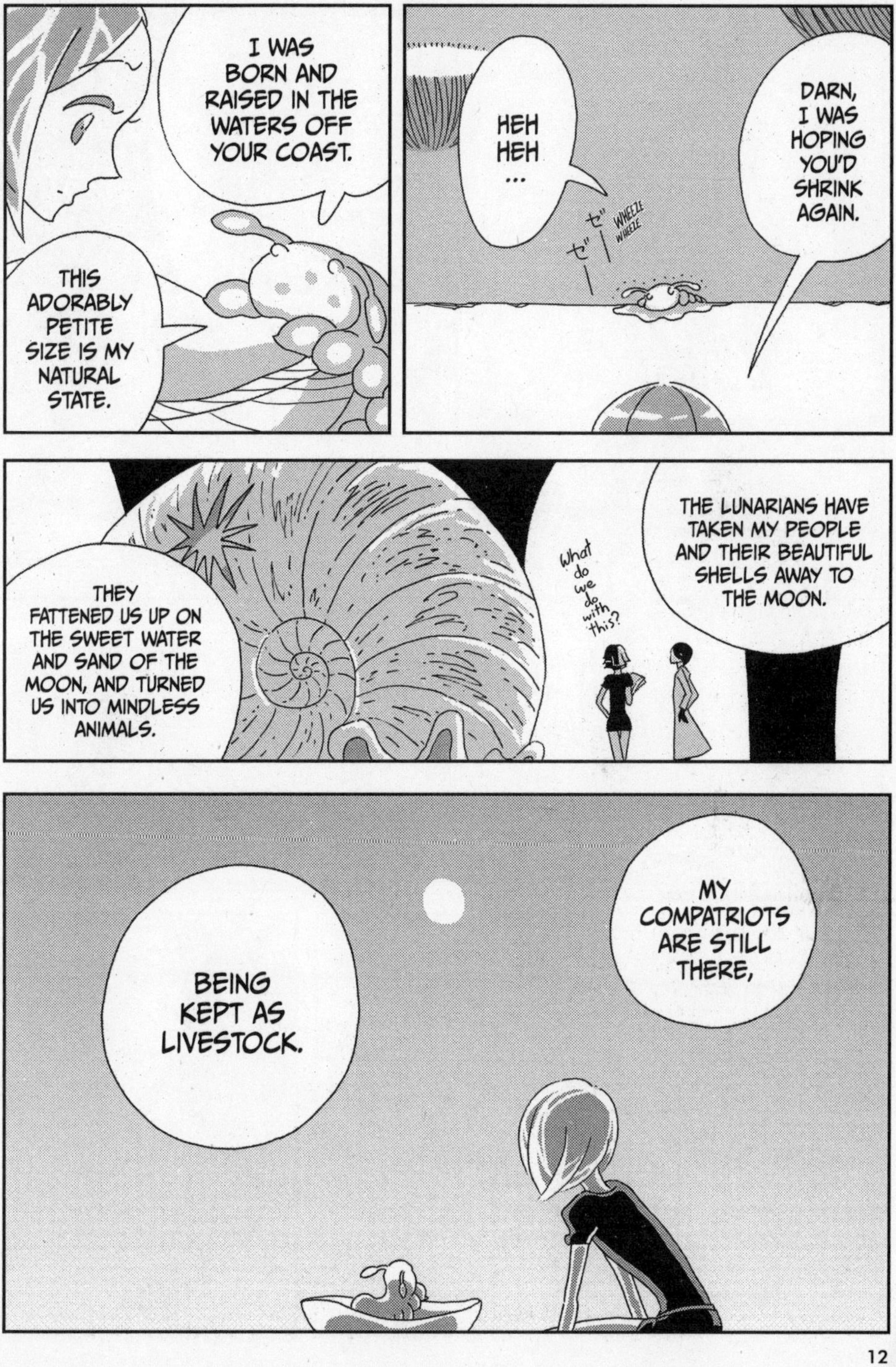
DARN, I WAS HOPING YOU'D SHRINK AGAIN.
HEH HEH ...
WHEEZE WHEEZE
ぜー ぜー
I WAS BORN AND RAISED IN THE WATERS OFF YOUR COAST.
THIS ADORABLY PETITE SIZE IS MY NATURAL STATE.
THE LUNARIANS HAVE TAKEN MY PEOPLE AND THEIR BEAUTIFUL SHELLS AWAY TO THE MOON.
What do we do with this?
THEY FATTENED US UP ON THE SWEET WATER AND SAND OF THE MOON, AND TURNED US INTO MINDLESS ANIMALS.
MY COMPATRIOTS ARE STILL THERE,
BEING KEPT AS LIVESTOCK.

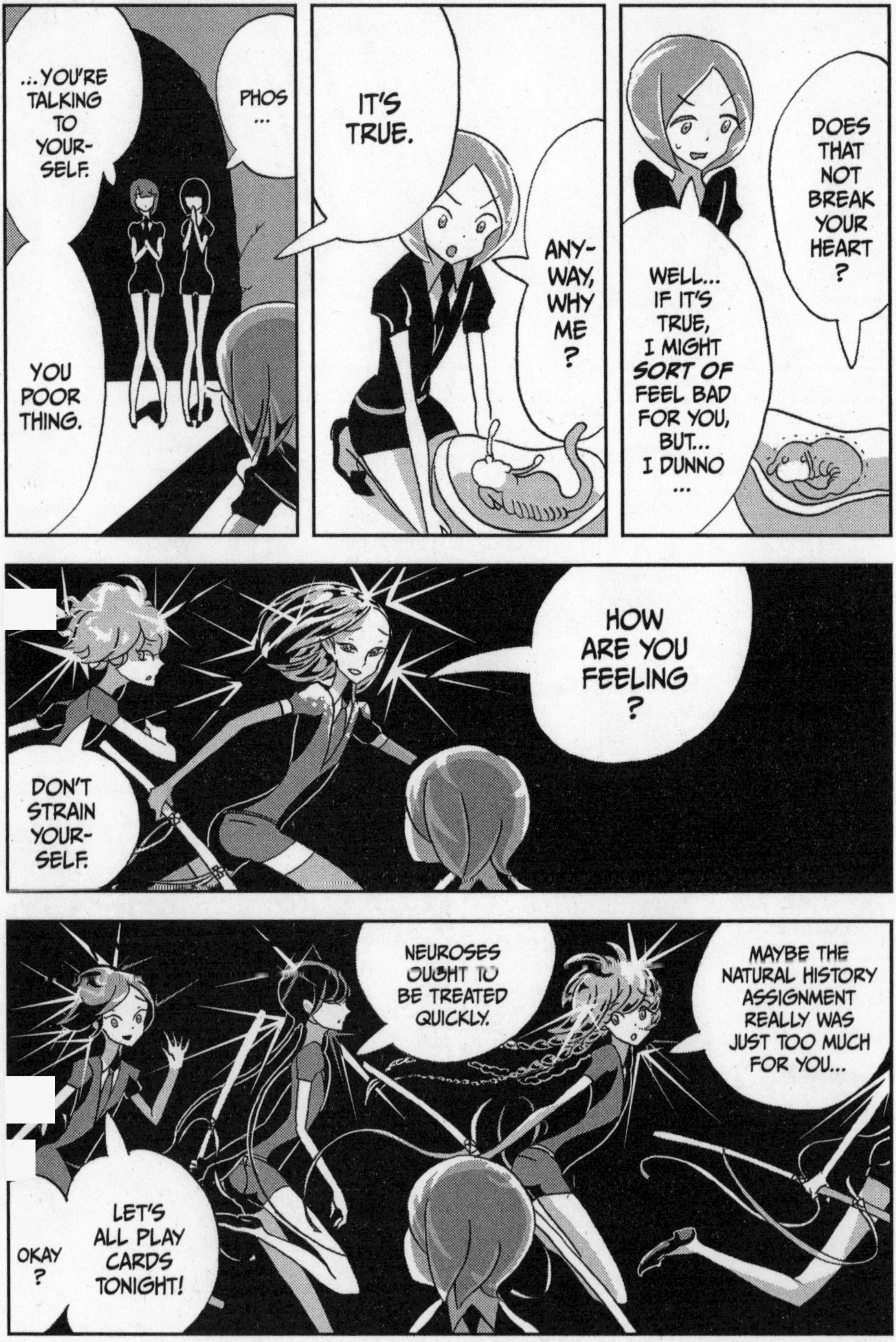
DOES THAT NOT BREAK YOUR HEART?
WELL... IF IT'S TRUE, I MIGHT *SORT OF* FEEL BAD FOR YOU, BUT... I DUNNO...
IT'S TRUE.
ANYWAY, WHY ME?
PHOS...
...YOU'RE TALKING TO YOURSELF.
YOU POOR THING.
HOW ARE YOU FEELING?
DON'T STRAIN YOURSELF.
MAYBE THE NATURAL HISTORY ASSIGNMENT REALLY WAS JUST TOO MUCH FOR YOU...
NEUROSES OUGHT TO BE TREATED QUICKLY.
LET'S ALL PLAY CARDS TONIGHT!
OKAY?

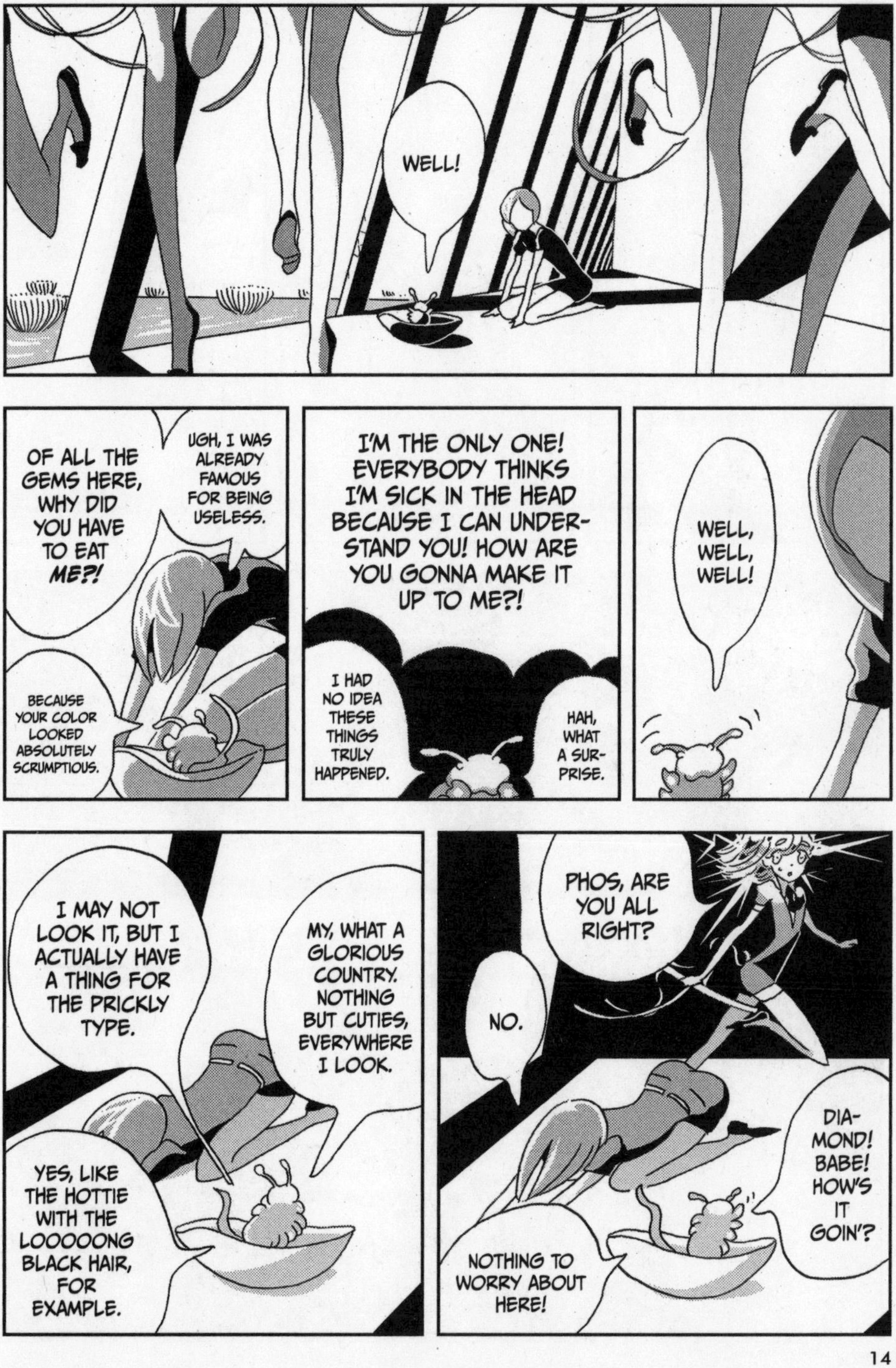
WELL!
WELL, WELL, WELL!
I'M THE ONLY ONE! EVERYBODY THINKS I'M SICK IN THE HEAD BECAUSE I CAN UNDER-STAND YOU! HOW ARE YOU GONNA MAKE IT UP TO ME?!
HAH, WHAT A SUR-PRISE.
I HAD NO IDEA THESE THINGS TRULY HAPPENED.
UGH, I WAS ALREADY FAMOUS FOR BEING USELESS.
OF ALL THE GEMS HERE, WHY DID YOU HAVE TO EAT *ME?!*
BECAUSE YOUR COLOR LOOKED ABSOLUTELY SCRUMPTIOUS.
PHOS, ARE YOU ALL RIGHT?
NO.
DIA-MOND! BABE! HOW'S IT GOIN'?
NOTHING TO WORRY ABOUT HERE!
MY, WHAT A GLORIOUS COUNTRY. NOTHING BUT CUTIES, EVERYWHERE I LOOK.
I MAY NOT LOOK IT, BUT I ACTUALLY HAVE A THING FOR THE PRICKLY TYPE.
YES, LIKE THE HOTTIE WITH THE LOOOOOONG BLACK HAIR, FOR EXAMPLE.

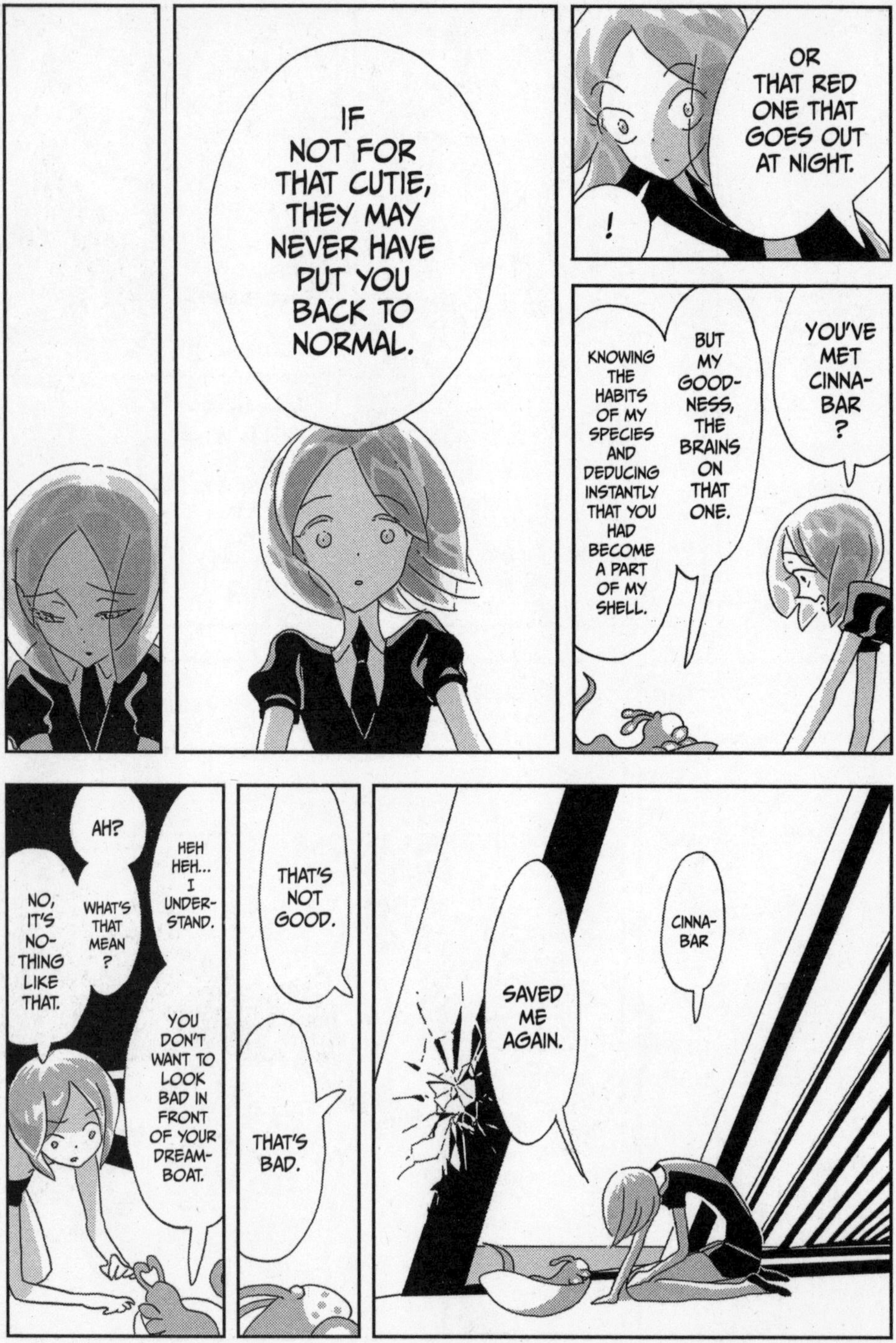
OR THAT RED ONE THAT GOES OUT AT NIGHT.
!
YOU'VE MET CINNA-BAR?
BUT MY GOOD-NESS, THE BRAINS ON THAT ONE.
KNOWING THE HABITS OF MY SPECIES AND DEDUCING INSTANTLY THAT YOU HAD BECOME A PART OF MY SHELL.
IF NOT FOR THAT CUTIE, THEY MAY NEVER HAVE PUT YOU BACK TO NORMAL.
CINNA-BAR
SAVED ME AGAIN.
THAT'S NOT GOOD.
THAT'S BAD.
HEH HEH... I UNDER-STAND.
AH?
WHAT'S THAT MEAN?
NO, IT'S NO-THING LIKE THAT.
YOU DON'T WANT TO LOOK BAD IN FRONT OF YOUR DREAM-BOAT.

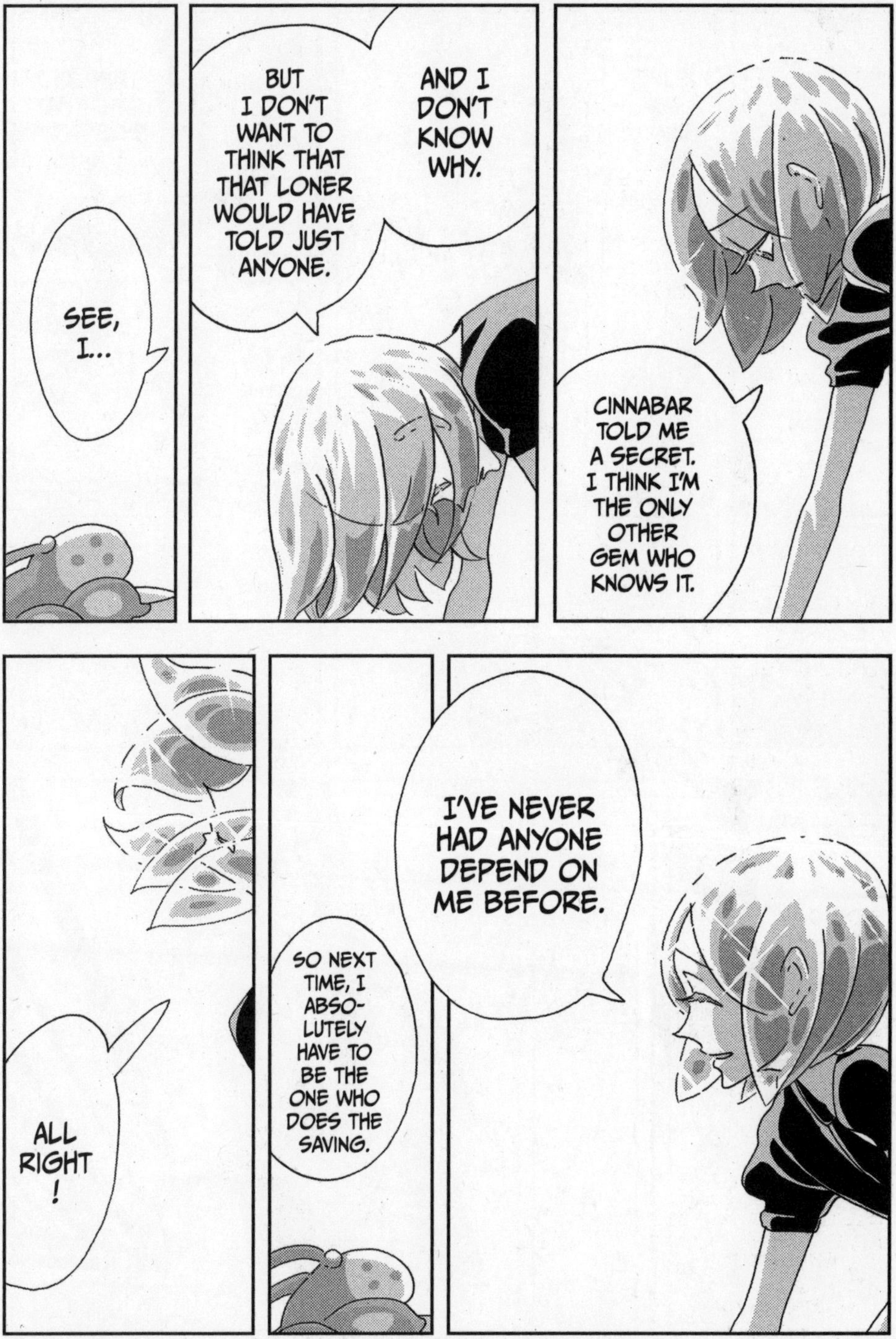
CINNABAR TOLD ME A SECRET. I THINK I'M THE ONLY OTHER GEM WHO KNOWS IT.
AND I DON'T KNOW WHY.
BUT I DON'T WANT TO THINK THAT THAT LONER WOULD HAVE TOLD JUST ANYONE.
SEE, I...
I'VE NEVER HAD ANYONE DEPEND ON ME BEFORE.
SO NEXT TIME, I ABSO-LUTELY HAVE TO BE THE ONE WHO DOES THE SAVING.
ALL RIGHT!

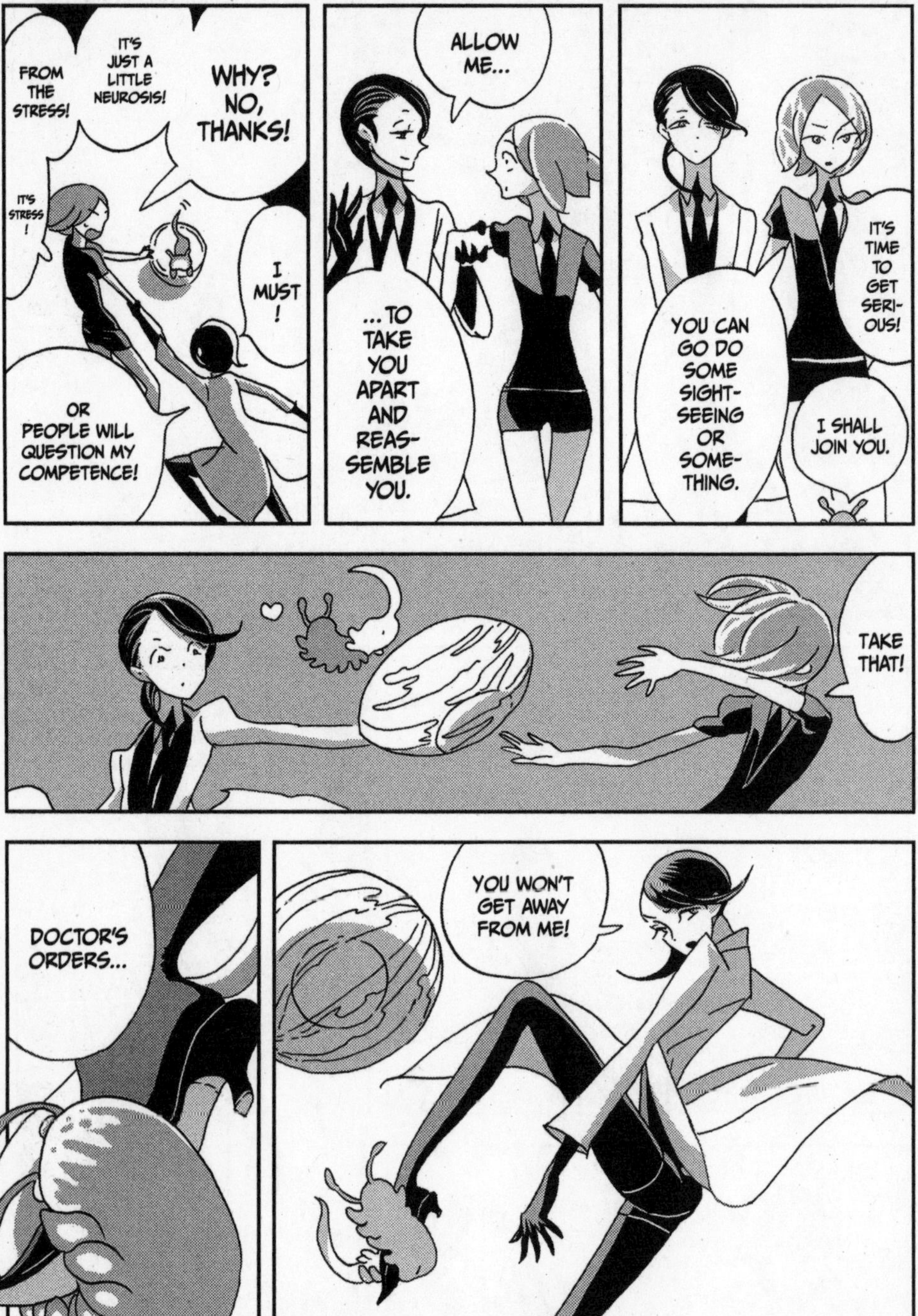
IT'S TIME TO GET SERI-OUS!
YOU CAN GO DO SOME SIGHT-SEEING OR SOME-THING.
I SHALL JOIN YOU.
ALLOW ME...
...TO TAKE YOU APART AND REAS-SEMBLE YOU.
WHY? NO, THANKS!
IT'S JUST A LITTLE NEUROSIS!
FROM THE STRESS!
I MUST!
IT'S STRESS!
OR PEOPLE WILL QUESTION MY COMPETENCE!
TAKE THAT!
YOU WON'T GET AWAY FROM ME!
DOCTOR'S ORDERS...

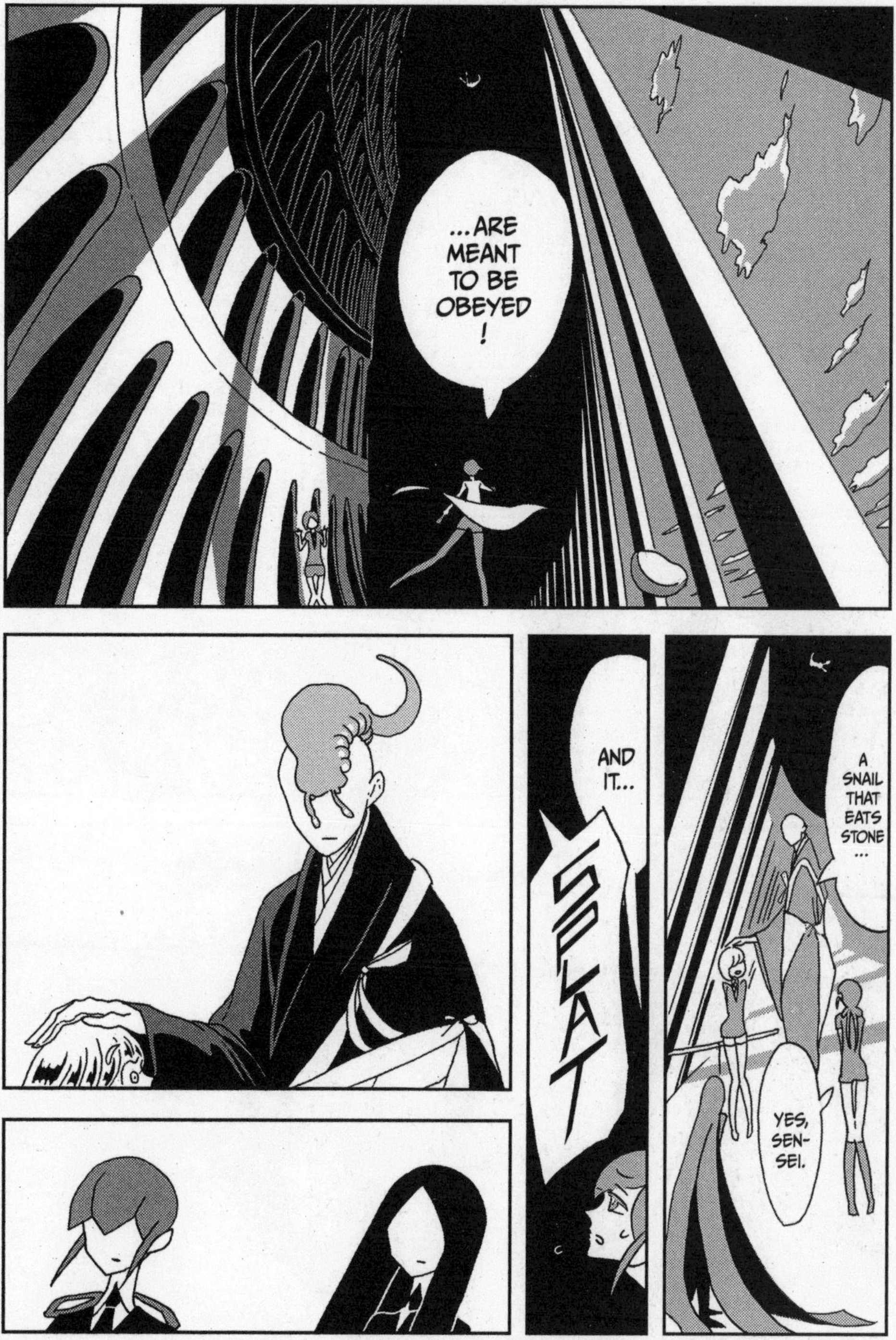
...ARE MEANT TO BE OBEYED !
A SNAIL THAT EATS STONE ...
YES, SEN-SEI.
AND IT...
SPLAT

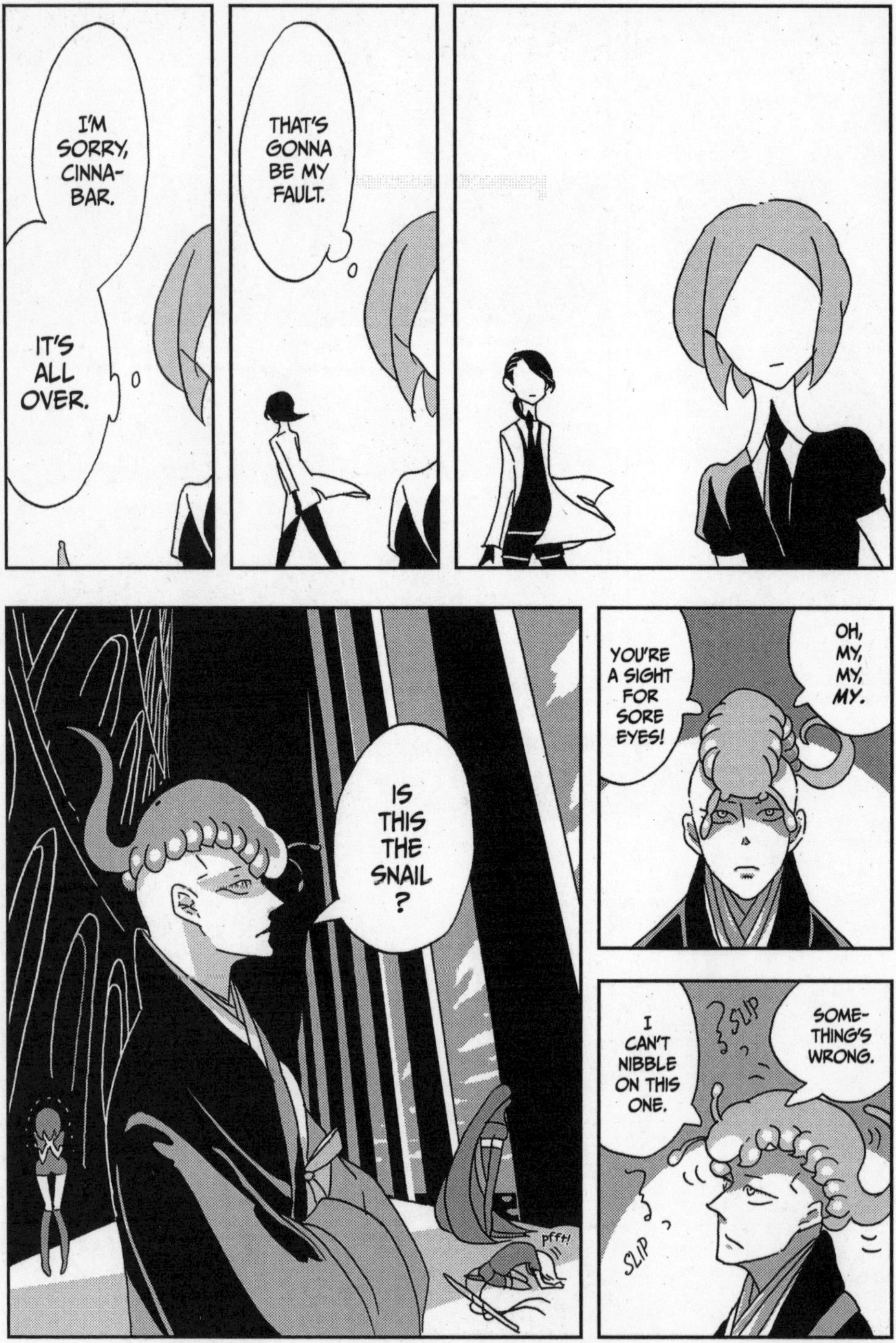
THAT'S GONNA BE MY FAULT.
I'M SORRY, CINNA-BAR.
IT'S ALL OVER.
OH, MY, MY, MY.
YOU'RE A SIGHT FOR SORE EYES!
SOME-THING'S WRONG.
SLIP
I CAN'T NIBBLE ON THIS ONE.
SLIP
IS THIS THE SNAIL?
pfft!

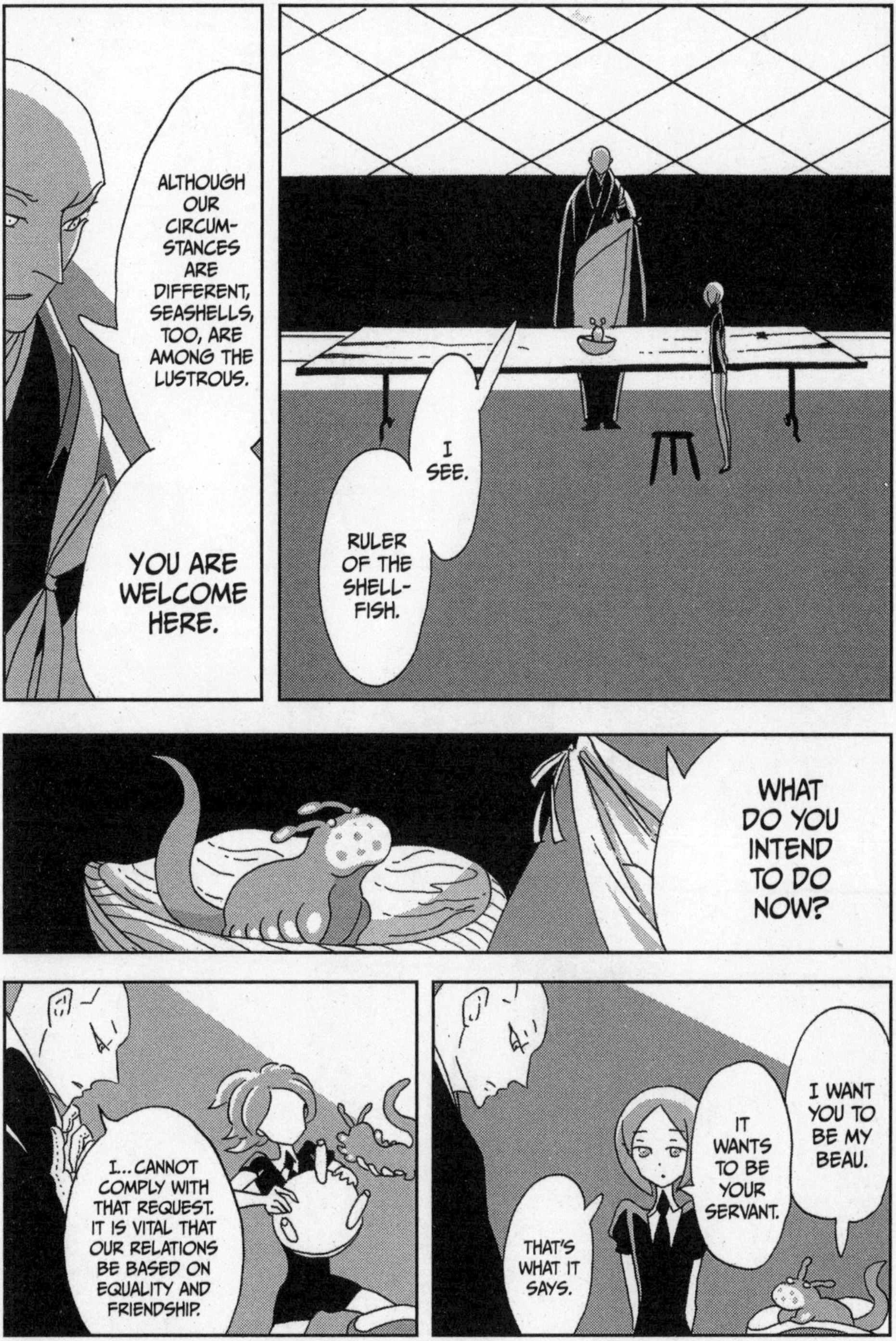
I SEE.
RULER OF THE SHELL-FISH.
ALTHOUGH OUR CIRCUM-STANCES ARE DIFFERENT, SEASHELLS, TOO, ARE AMONG THE LUSTROUS.
YOU ARE WELCOME HERE.
WHAT DO YOU INTEND TO DO NOW?
I WANT YOU TO BE MY BEAU.
IT WANTS TO BE YOUR SERVANT.
THAT'S WHAT IT SAYS.
I...CANNOT COMPLY WITH THAT REQUEST. IT IS VITAL THAT OUR RELATIONS BE BASED ON EQUALITY AND FRIENDSHIP.

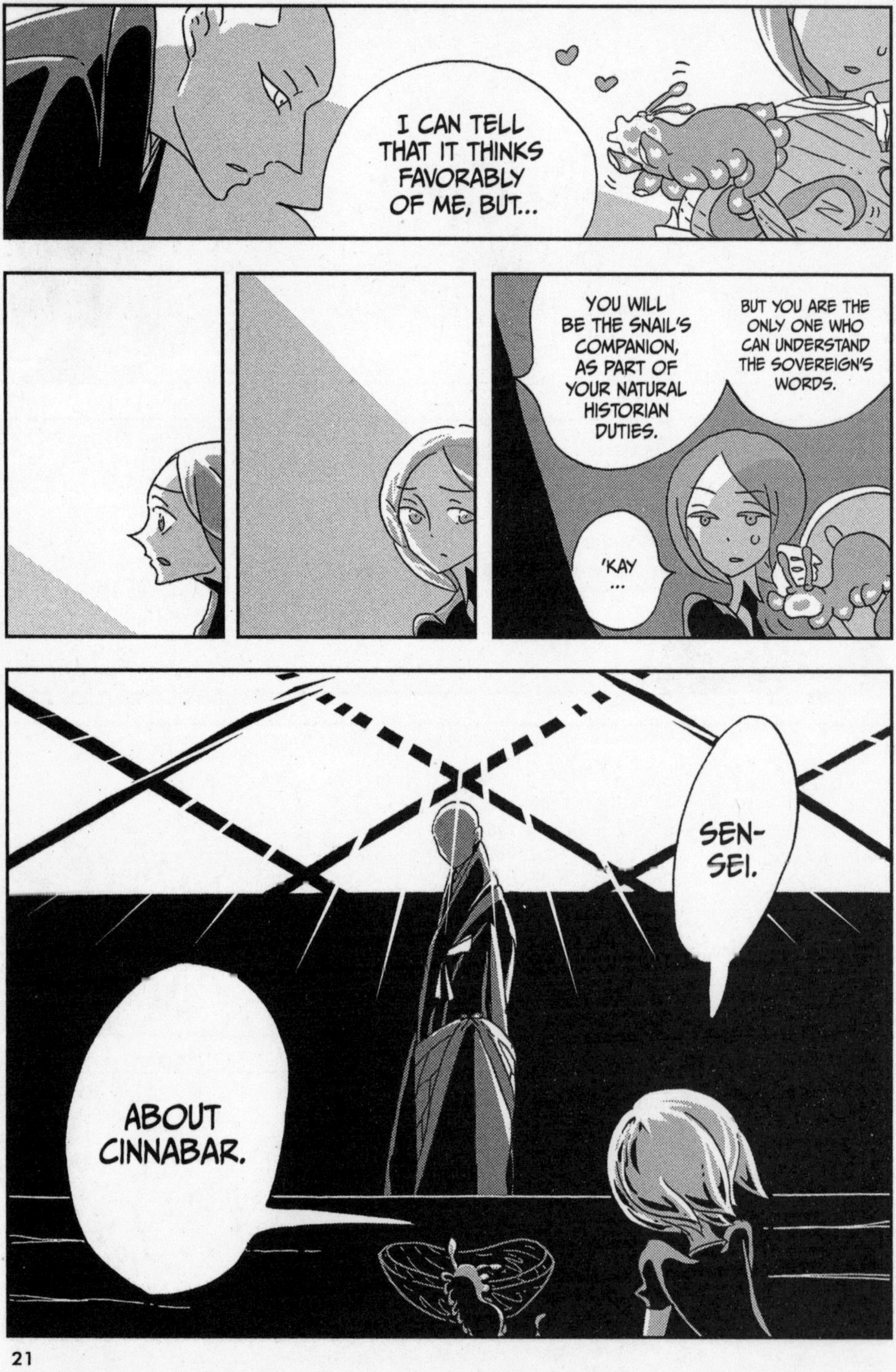
I CAN TELL THAT IT THINKS FAVORABLY OF ME, BUT...
BUT YOU ARE THE ONLY ONE WHO CAN UNDERSTAND THE SOVEREIGN'S WORDS.
YOU WILL BE THE SNAIL'S COMPANION, AS PART OF YOUR NATURAL HISTORIAN DUTIES.
'KAY ...
SEN-SEI.
ABOUT CINNABAR.

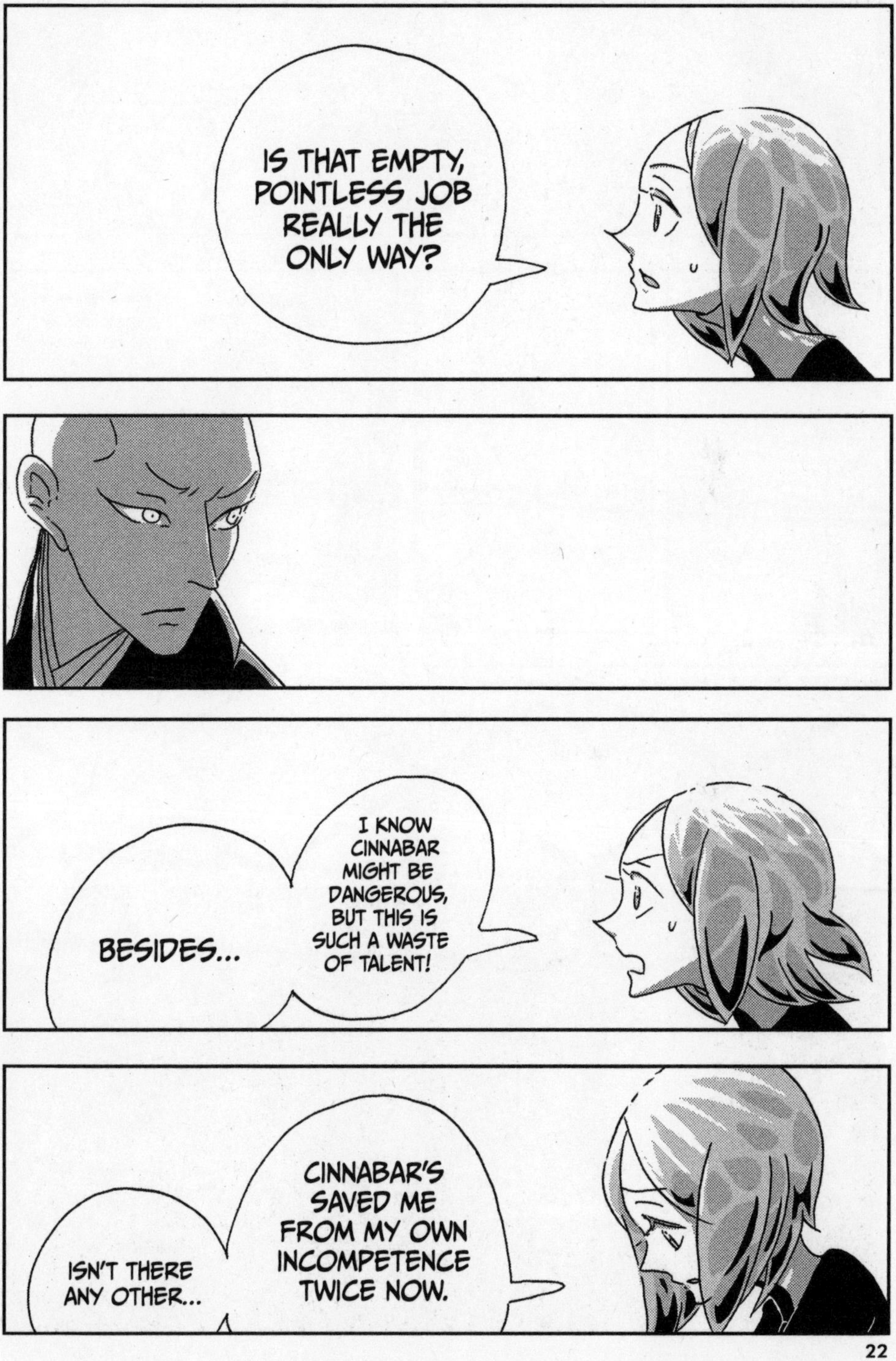
IS THAT EMPTY, POINTLESS JOB REALLY THE ONLY WAY?
I KNOW CINNABAR MIGHT BE DANGEROUS, BUT THIS IS SUCH A WASTE OF TALENT!
BESIDES...
CINNABAR'S SAVED ME FROM MY OWN INCOMPETENCE TWICE NOW.
ISN'T THERE ANY OTHER...

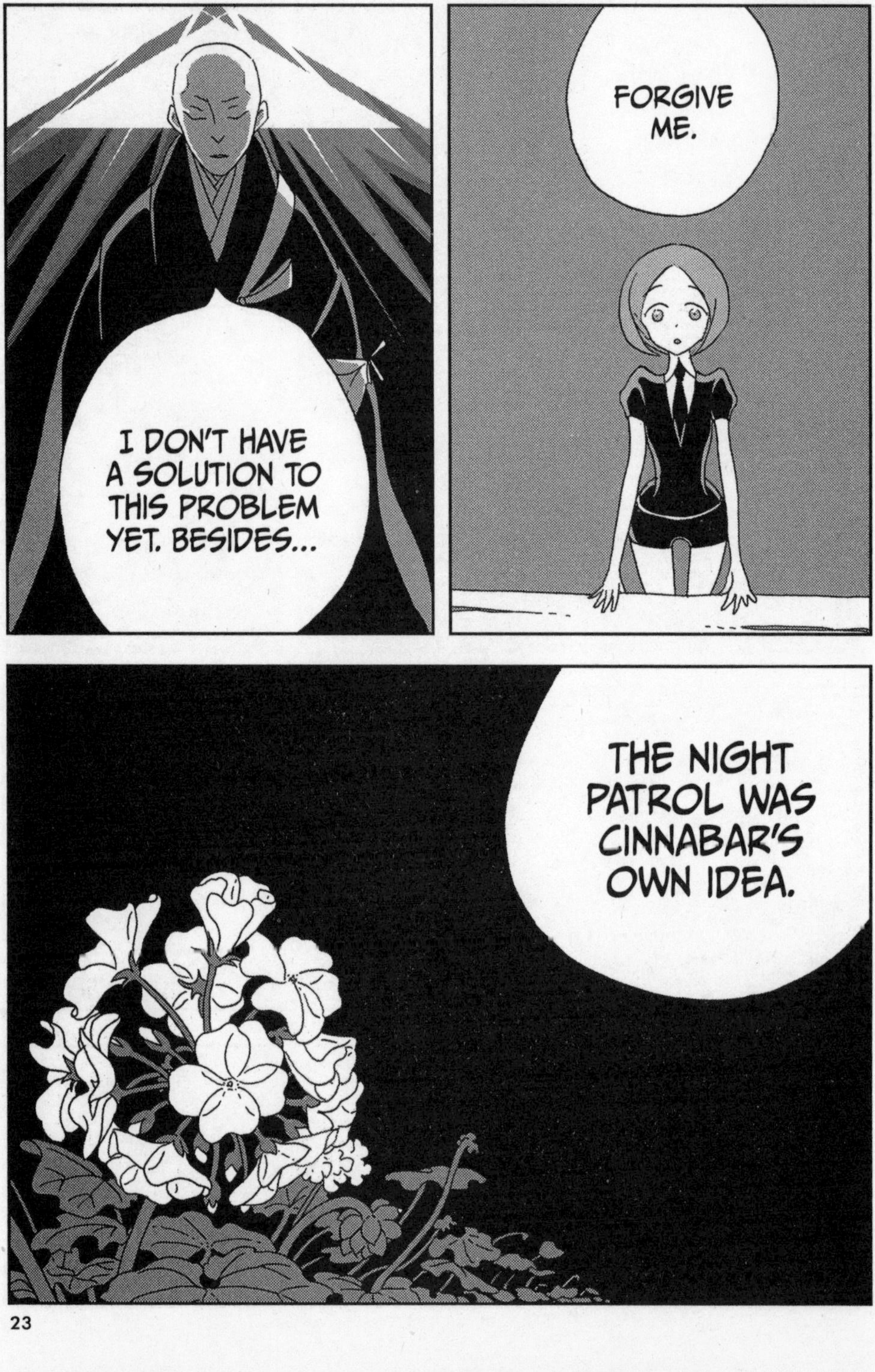
FORGIVE ME.
I DON'T HAVE A SOLUTION TO THIS PROBLEM YET. BESIDES...
THE NIGHT PATROL WAS CINNABAR'S OWN IDEA.

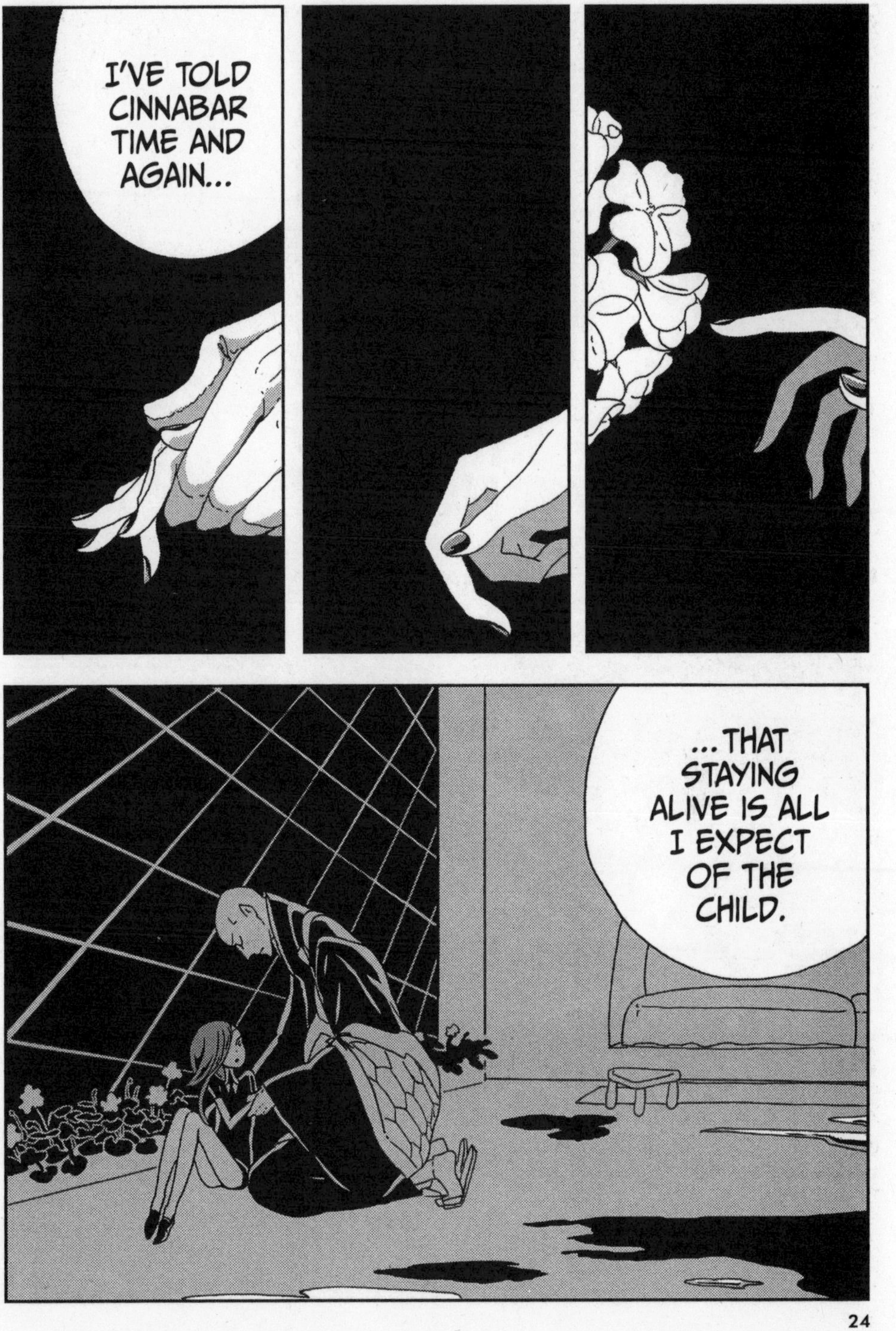
I'VE TOLD CINNABAR TIME AND AGAIN...
...THAT STAYING ALIVE IS ALL I EXPECT OF THE CHILD.

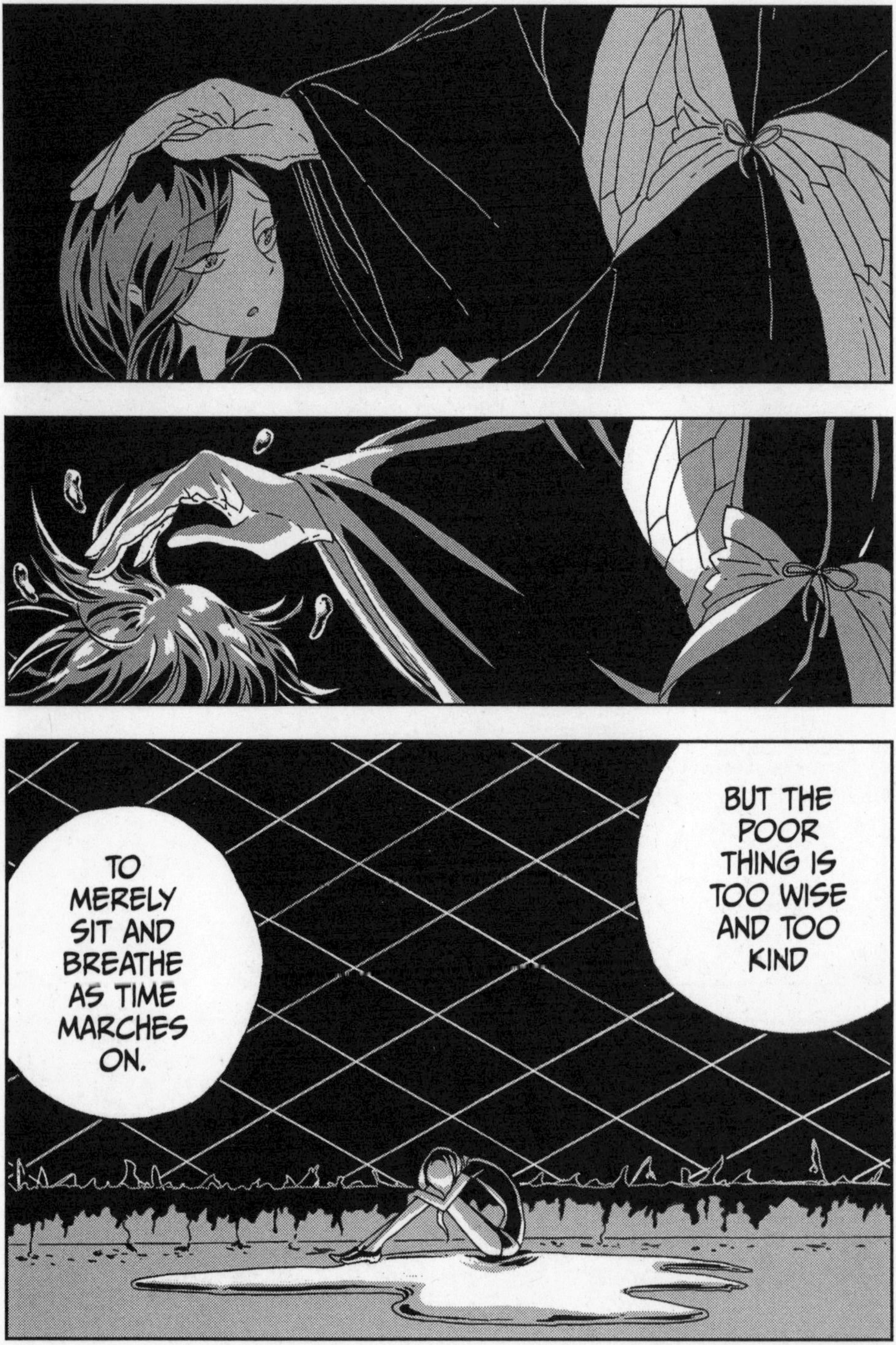
BUT THE POOR THING IS TOO WISE AND TOO KIND
TO MERELY SIT AND BREATHE AS TIME MARCHES ON.

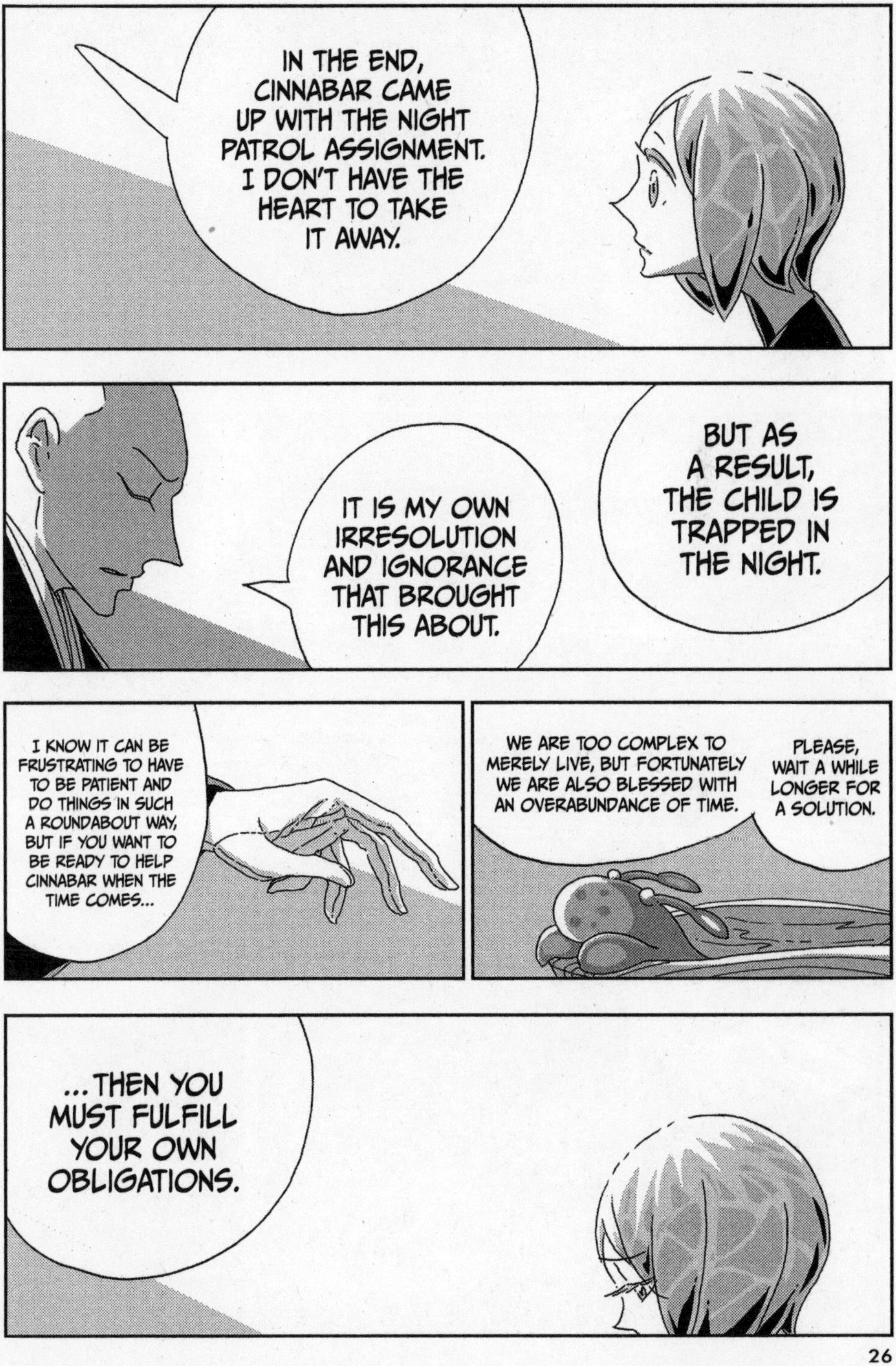
IN THE END, CINNABAR CAME UP WITH THE NIGHT PATROL ASSIGNMENT. I DON'T HAVE THE HEART TO TAKE IT AWAY.
BUT AS A RESULT, THE CHILD IS TRAPPED IN THE NIGHT.
IT IS MY OWN IRRESOLUTION AND IGNORANCE THAT BROUGHT THIS ABOUT.
PLEASE, WAIT A WHILE LONGER FOR A SOLUTION.
WE ARE TOO COMPLEX TO MERELY LIVE, BUT FORTUNATELY WE ARE ALSO BLESSED WITH AN OVERABUNDANCE OF TIME.
I KNOW IT CAN BE FRUSTRATING TO HAVE TO BE PATIENT AND DO THINGS IN SUCH A ROUNDABOUT WAY, BUT IF YOU WANT TO BE READY TO HELP CINNABAR WHEN THE TIME COMES...
...THEN YOU MUST FULFILL YOUR OWN OBLIGATIONS.

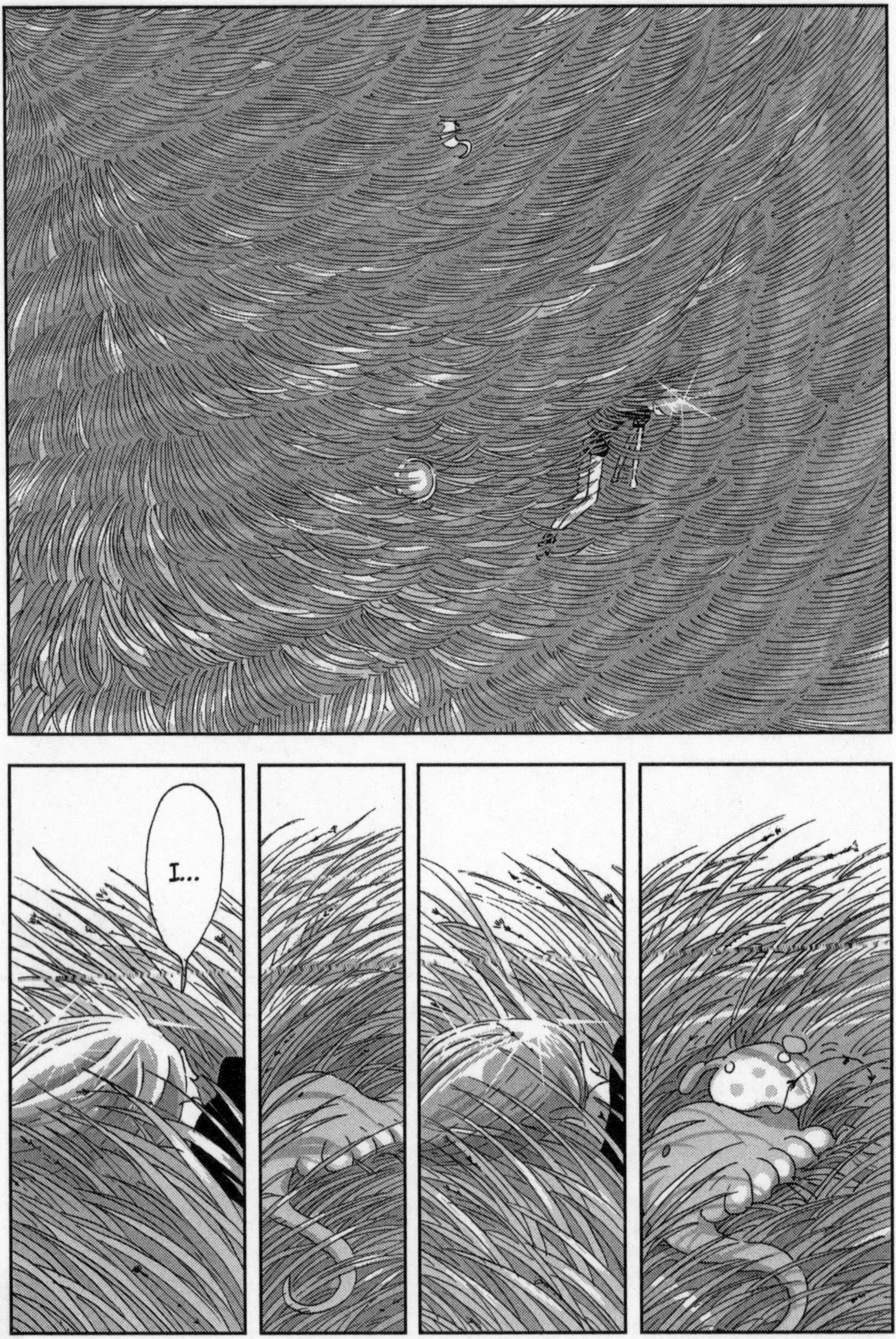
I...

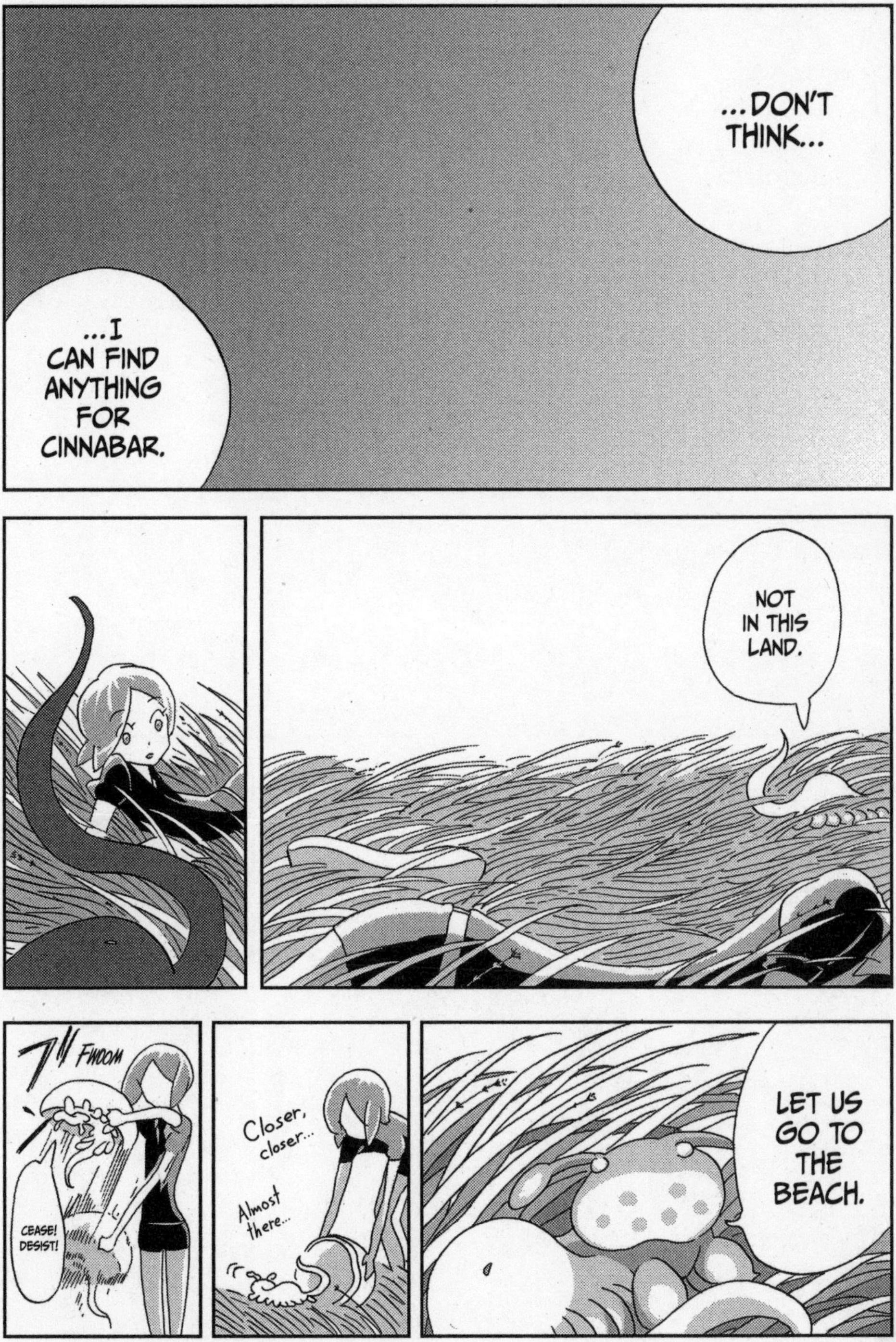
...DON'T THINK...
...I CAN FIND ANYTHING FOR CINNABAR.
NOT IN THIS LAND.
LET US GO TO THE BEACH.
Closer, closer...
Almost there...
FWOOM
CEASE! DESIST!

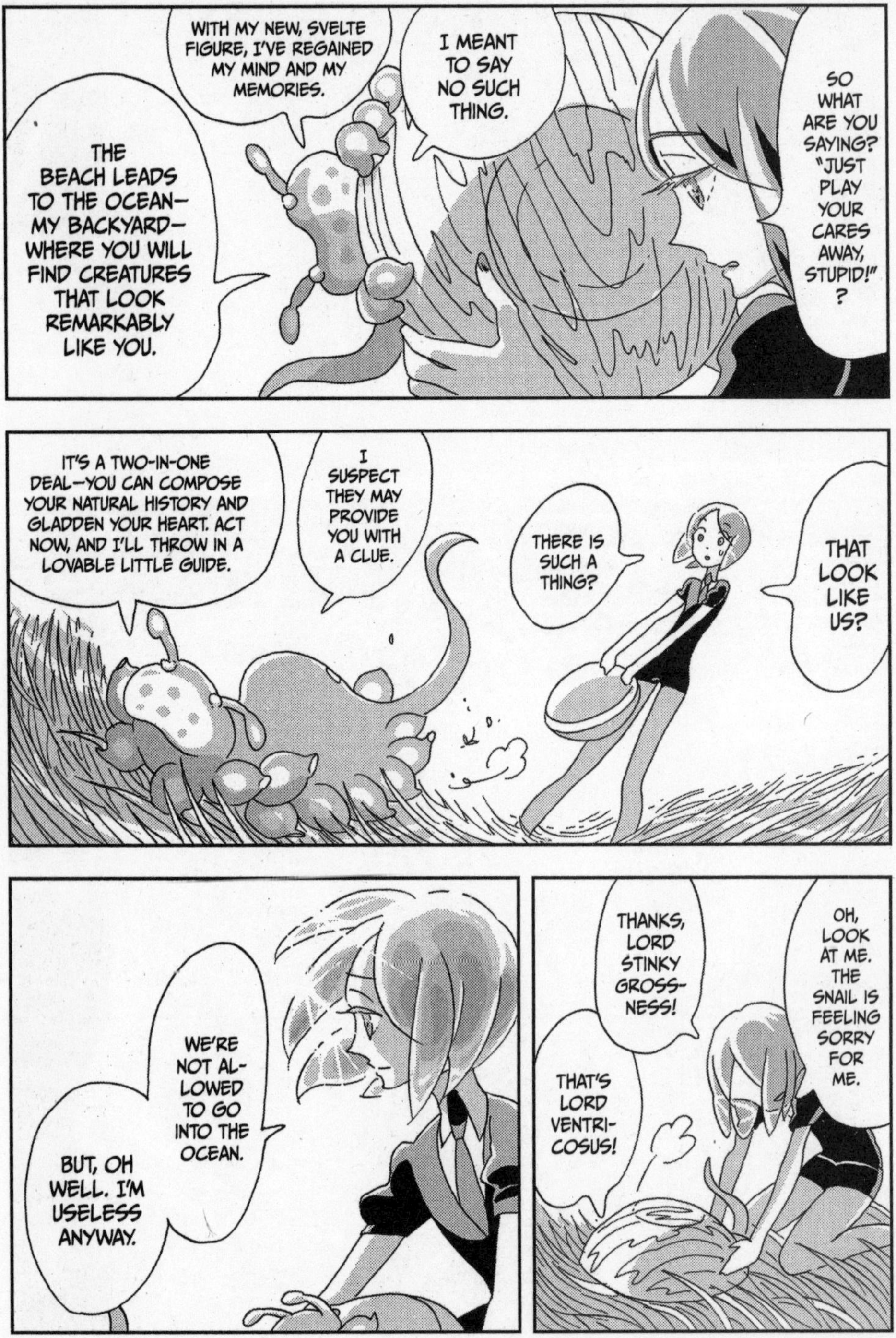
SO WHAT ARE YOU SAYING? "JUST PLAY YOUR CARES AWAY, STUPID!"?
I MEANT TO SAY NO SUCH THING.
WITH MY NEW, SVELTE FIGURE, I'VE REGAINED MY MIND AND MY MEMORIES.
THE BEACH LEADS TO THE OCEAN—MY BACKYARD—WHERE YOU WILL FIND CREATURES THAT LOOK REMARKABLY LIKE YOU.
THAT LOOK LIKE US?
THERE IS SUCH A THING?
I SUSPECT THEY MAY PROVIDE YOU WITH A CLUE.
IT'S A TWO-IN-ONE DEAL—YOU CAN COMPOSE YOUR NATURAL HISTORY AND GLADDEN YOUR HEART. ACT NOW, AND I'LL THROW IN A LOVABLE LITTLE GUIDE.
OH, LOOK AT ME. THE SNAIL IS FEELING SORRY FOR ME.
THANKS, LORD STINKY GROSS-NESS!
THAT'S LORD VENTRI-COSUS!
WE'RE NOT AL-LOWED TO GO INTO THE OCEAN.
BUT, OH WELL. I'M USELESS ANYWAY.

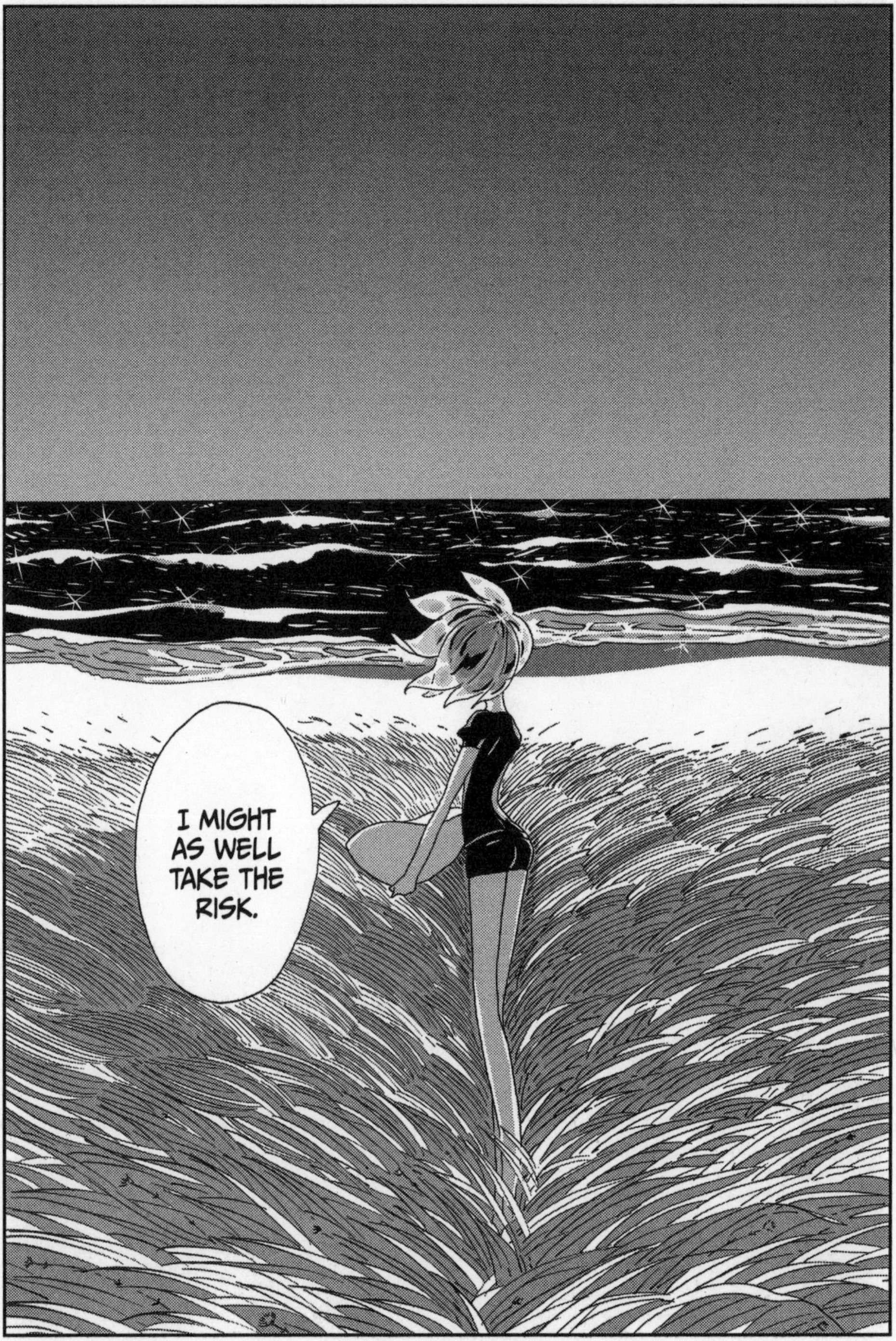
I MIGHT AS WELL TAKE THE RISK.

CHAPTER 7: Ventricosus END

CHAPTER 8:

Ocean

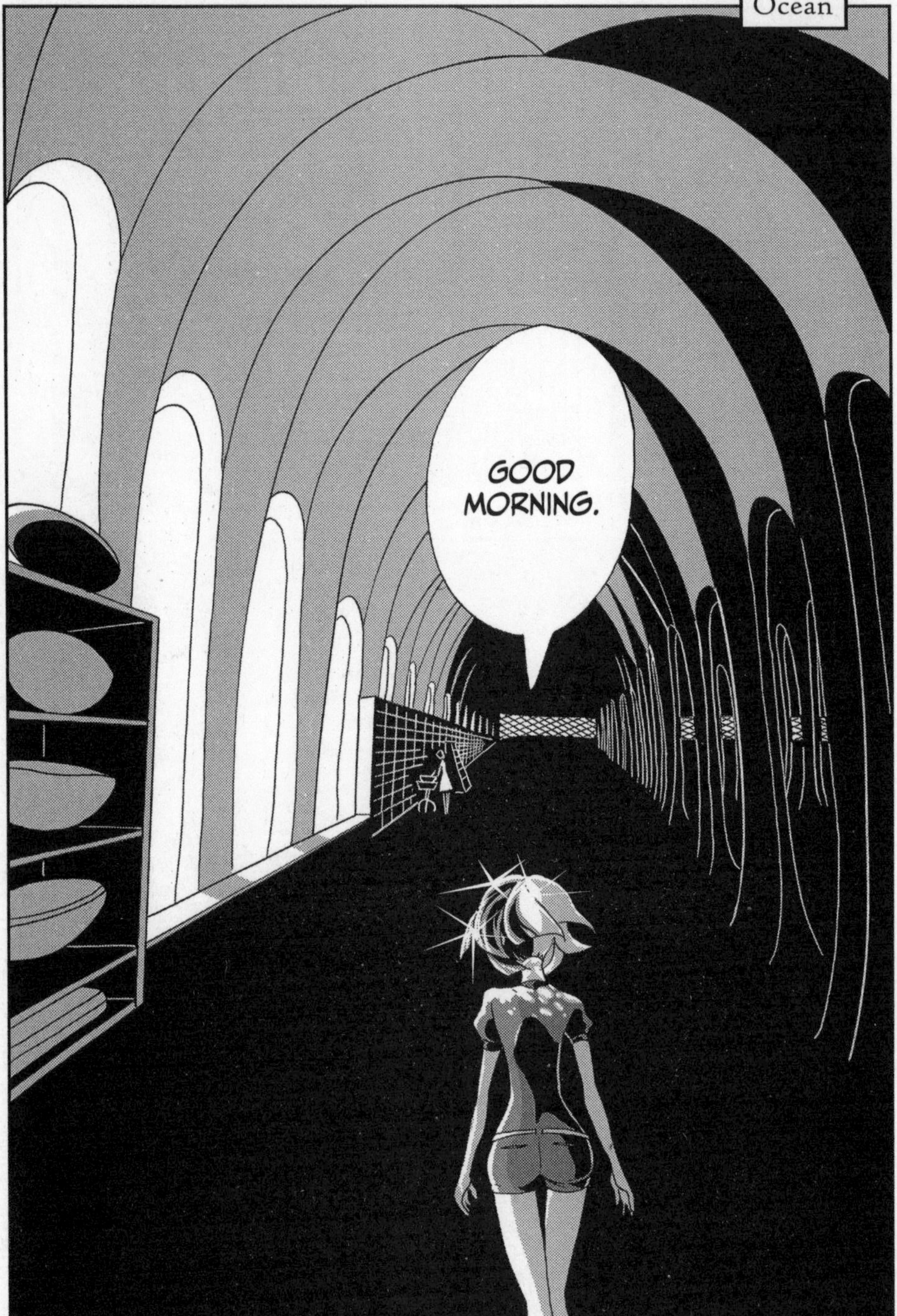
GOOD MORNING.

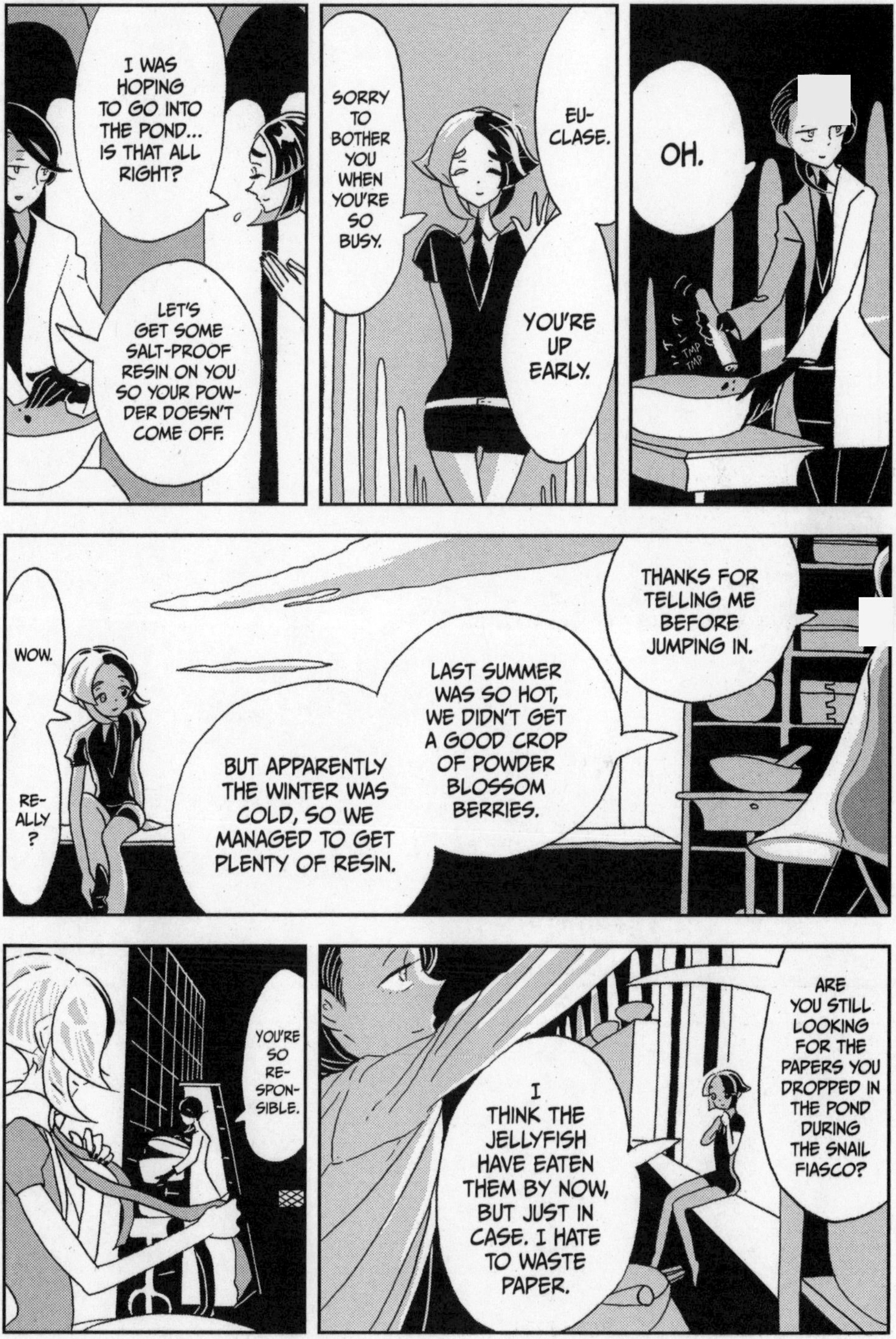
OH.
TMP TMP
EU-CLASE.
SORRY TO BOTHER YOU WHEN YOU'RE SO BUSY.
YOU'RE UP EARLY.
I WAS HOPING TO GO INTO THE POND... IS THAT ALL RIGHT?
LET'S GET SOME SALT-PROOF RESIN ON YOU SO YOUR POW-DER DOESN'T COME OFF.
THANKS FOR TELLING ME BEFORE JUMPING IN.
LAST SUMMER WAS SO HOT, WE DIDN'T GET A GOOD CROP OF POWDER BLOSSOM BERRIES.
BUT APPARENTLY THE WINTER WAS COLD, SO WE MANAGED TO GET PLENTY OF RESIN.
WOW.
RE-ALLY?
ARE YOU STILL LOOKING FOR THE PAPERS YOU DROPPED IN THE POND DURING THE SNAIL FIASCO?
I THINK THE JELLYFISH HAVE EATEN THEM BY NOW, BUT JUST IN CASE. I HATE TO WASTE PAPER.
YOU'RE SO RE-SPON-SIBLE.

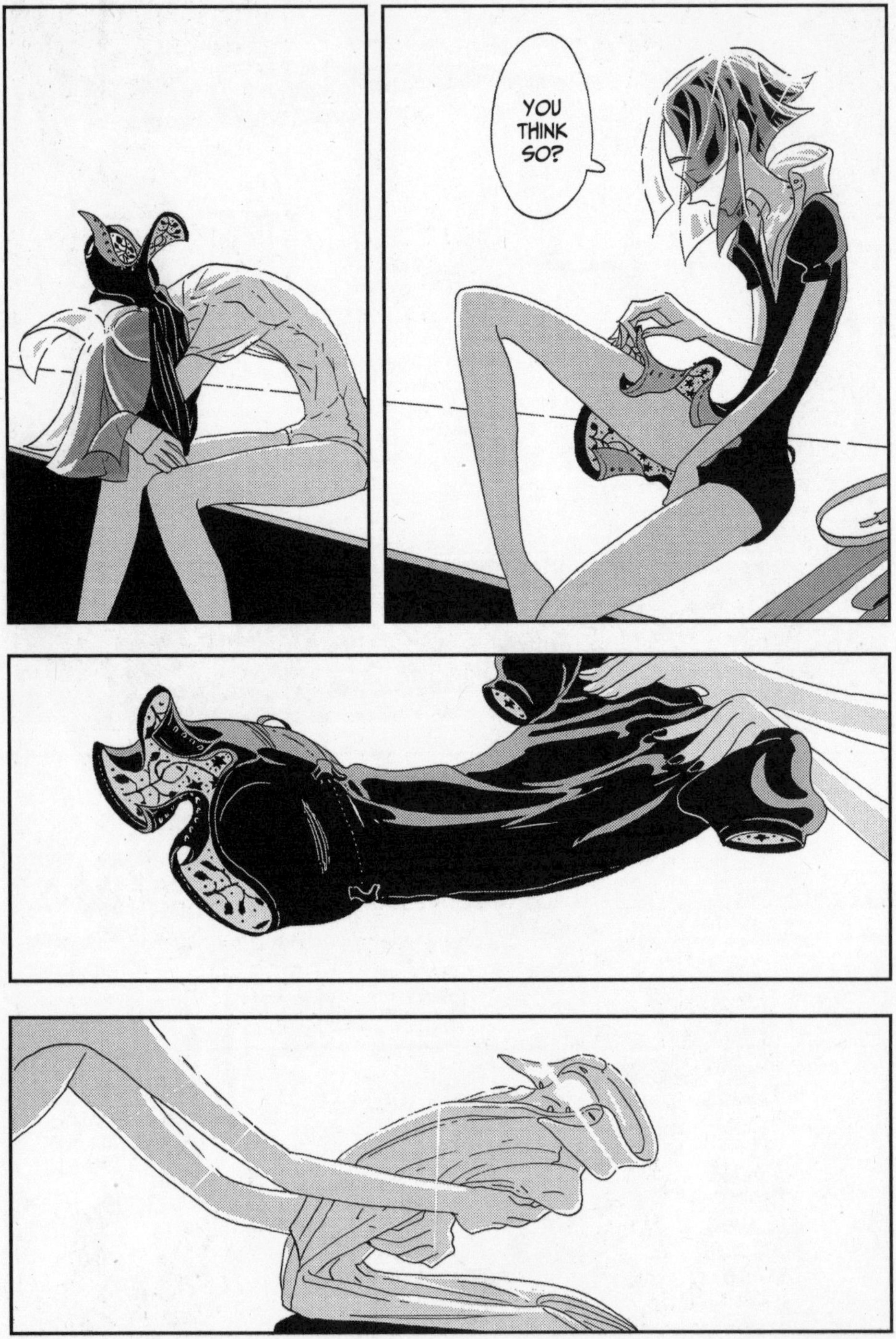
YOU THINK SO?

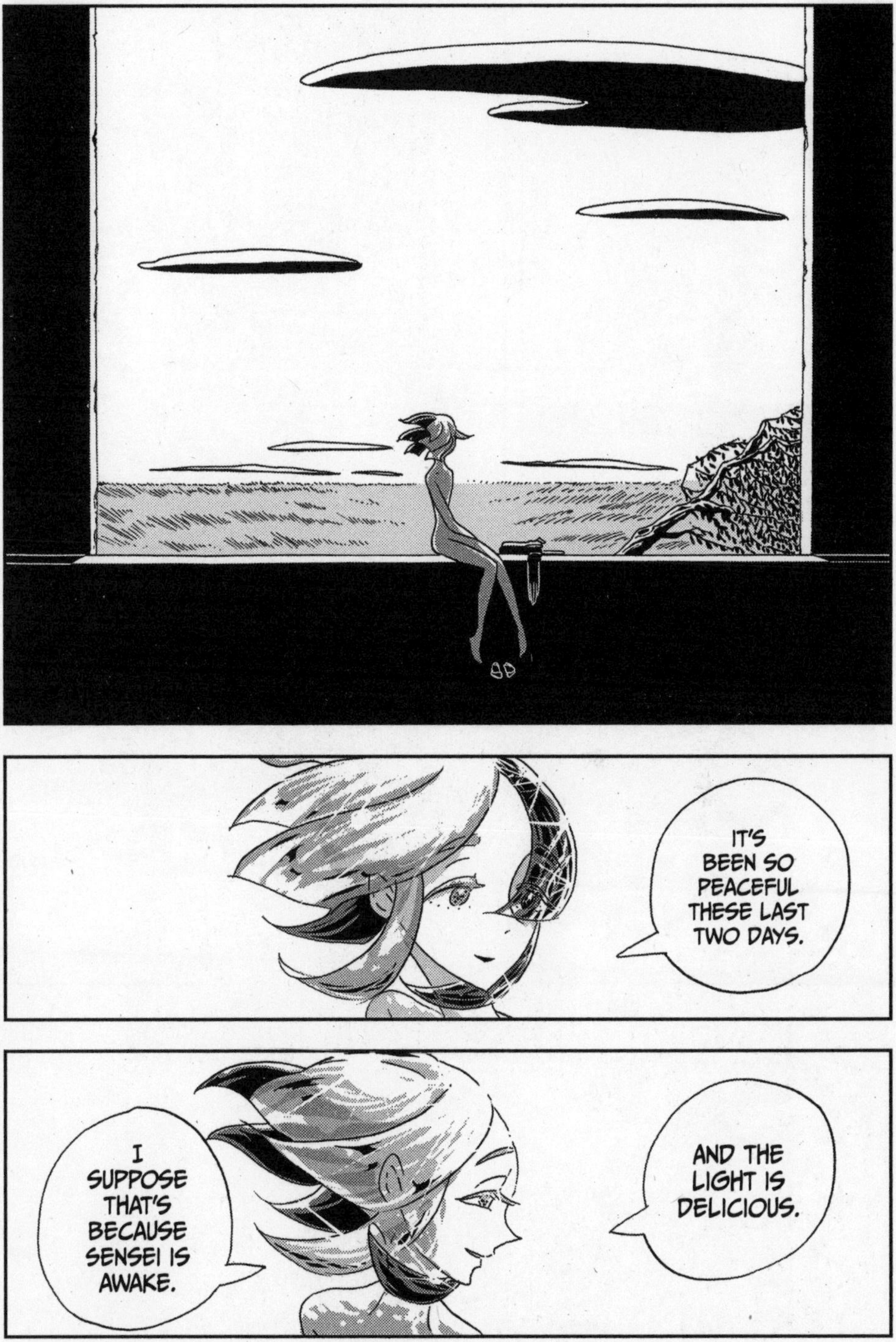
IT'S BEEN SO PEACEFUL THESE LAST TWO DAYS.
AND THE LIGHT IS DELICIOUS.
I SUPPOSE THAT'S BECAUSE SENSEI IS AWAKE.

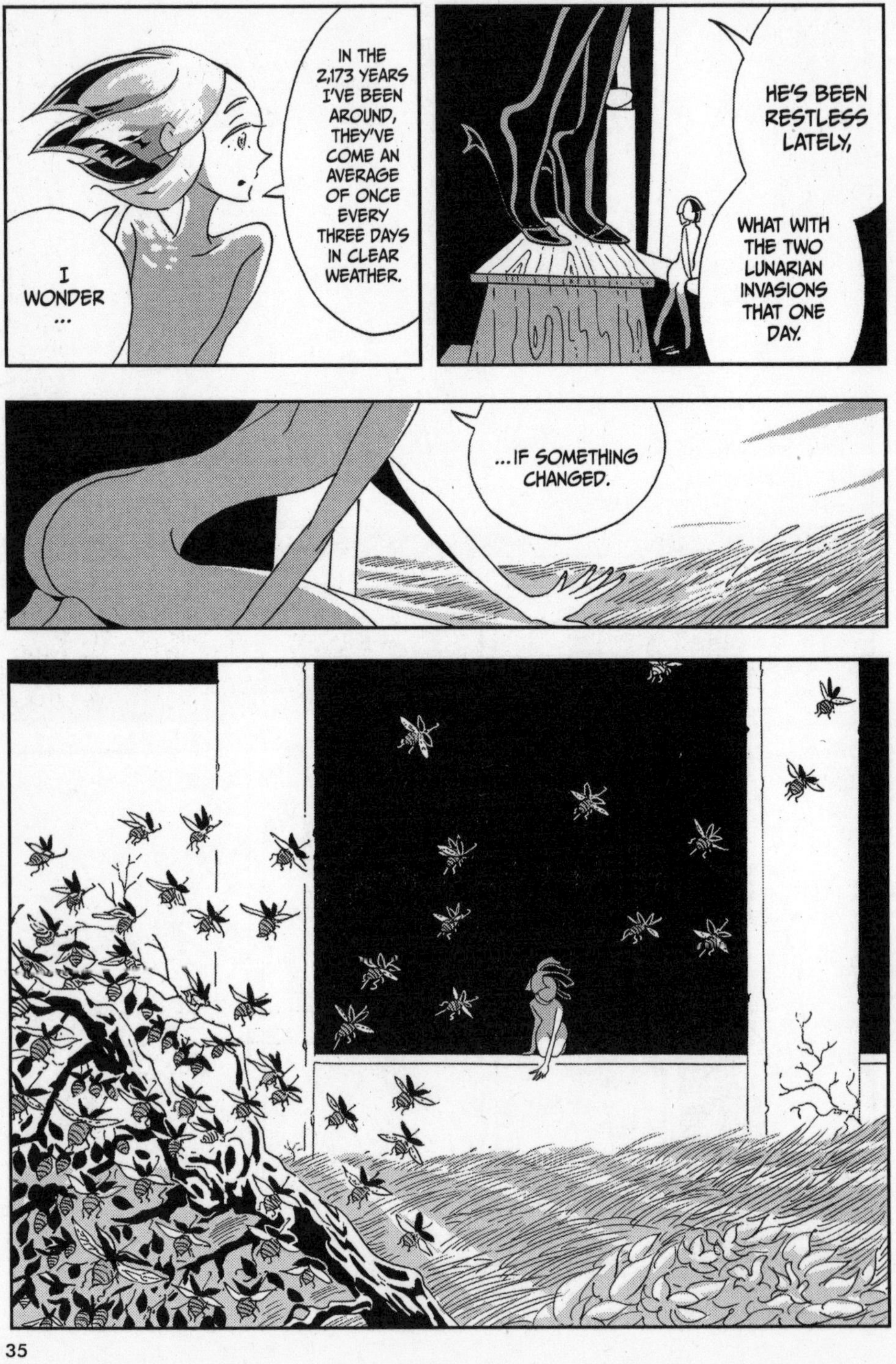
HE'S BEEN RESTLESS LATELY,
WHAT WITH THE TWO LUNARIAN INVASIONS THAT ONE DAY.
IN THE 2,173 YEARS I'VE BEEN AROUND, THEY'VE COME AN AVERAGE OF ONCE EVERY THREE DAYS IN CLEAR WEATHER.
I WONDER ...
...IF SOMETHING CHANGED.

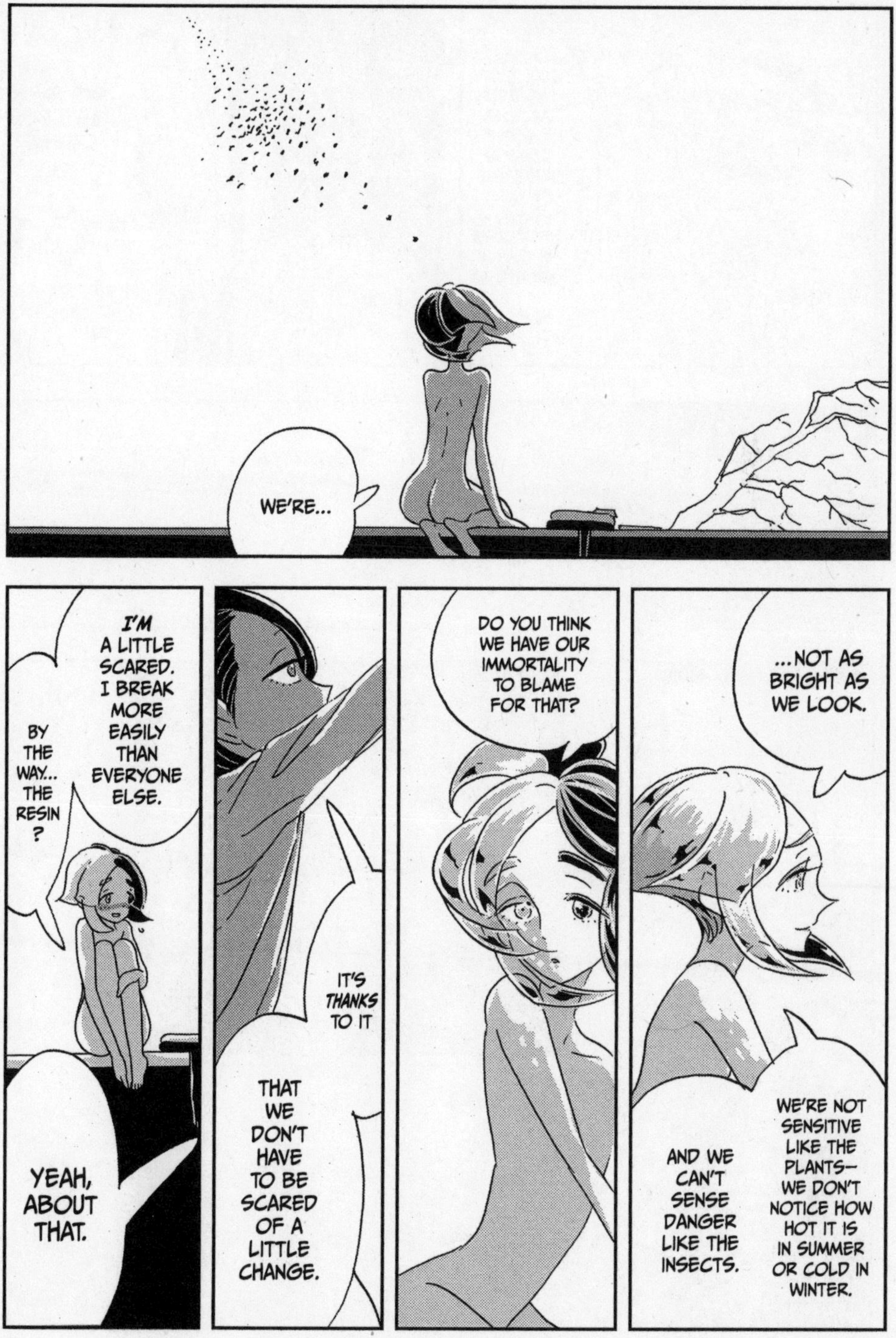
WE'RE...
...NOT AS BRIGHT AS WE LOOK.
WE'RE NOT SENSITIVE LIKE THE PLANTS— WE DON'T NOTICE HOW HOT IT IS IN SUMMER OR COLD IN WINTER.
AND WE CAN'T SENSE DANGER LIKE THE INSECTS.
DO YOU THINK WE HAVE OUR IMMORTALITY TO BLAME FOR THAT?
IT'S *THANKS* TO IT
THAT WE DON'T HAVE TO BE SCARED OF A LITTLE CHANGE.
I'M A LITTLE SCARED. I BREAK MORE EASILY THAN EVERYONE ELSE.
BY THE WAY... THE RESIN?
YEAH, ABOUT THAT.

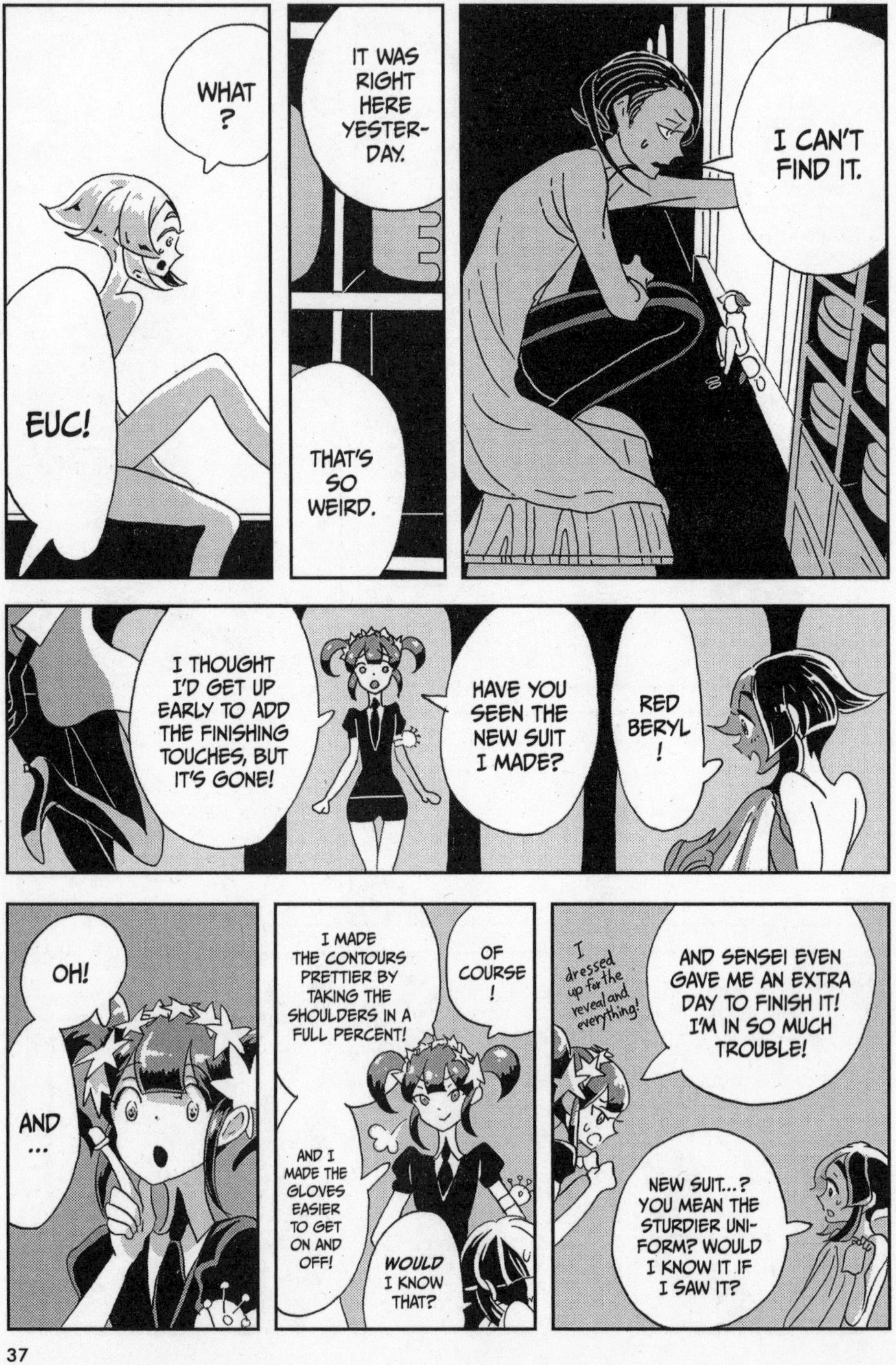
I CAN'T FIND IT.
IT WAS RIGHT HERE YESTER-DAY.
THAT'S SO WEIRD.
WHAT?
EUC!
RED BERYL!
HAVE YOU SEEN THE NEW SUIT I MADE?
I THOUGHT I'D GET UP EARLY TO ADD THE FINISHING TOUCHES, BUT IT'S GONE!
AND SENSEI EVEN GAVE ME AN EXTRA DAY TO FINISH IT! I'M IN SO MUCH TROUBLE!
I dressed up for the reveal and everything!
NEW SUIT...? YOU MEAN THE STURDIER UNI-FORM? WOULD I KNOW IT IF I SAW IT?
OF COURSE!
I MADE THE CONTOURS PRETTIER BY TAKING THE SHOULDERS IN A FULL PERCENT!
AND I MADE THE GLOVES EASIER TO GET ON AND OFF!
WOULD I KNOW THAT?
OH!
AND ...

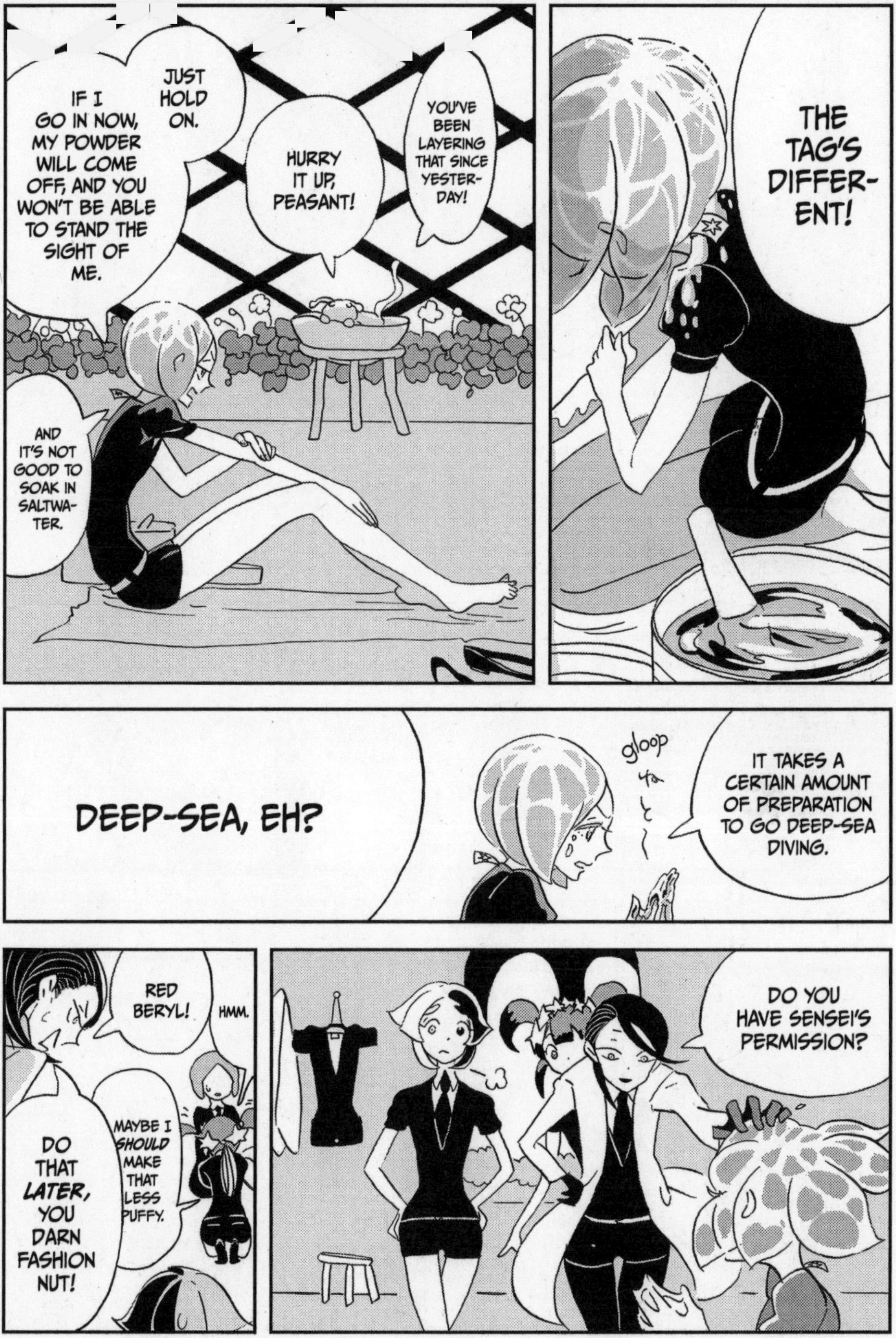
THE TAG'S DIFFERENT!
YOU'VE BEEN LAYERING THAT SINCE YESTERDAY!
HURRY IT UP, PEASANT!
JUST HOLD ON.
IF I GO IN NOW, MY POWDER WILL COME OFF, AND YOU WON'T BE ABLE TO STAND THE SIGHT OF ME.
AND IT'S NOT GOOD TO SOAK IN SALTWATER.
IT TAKES A CERTAIN AMOUNT OF PREPARATION TO GO DEEP-SEA DIVING.
gloop
DEEP-SEA, EH?
DO YOU HAVE SENSEI'S PERMISSION?
HMM.
RED BERYL!
MAYBE I *SHOULD* MAKE THAT LESS PUFFY.
DO THAT *LATER*, YOU DARN FASHION NUT!

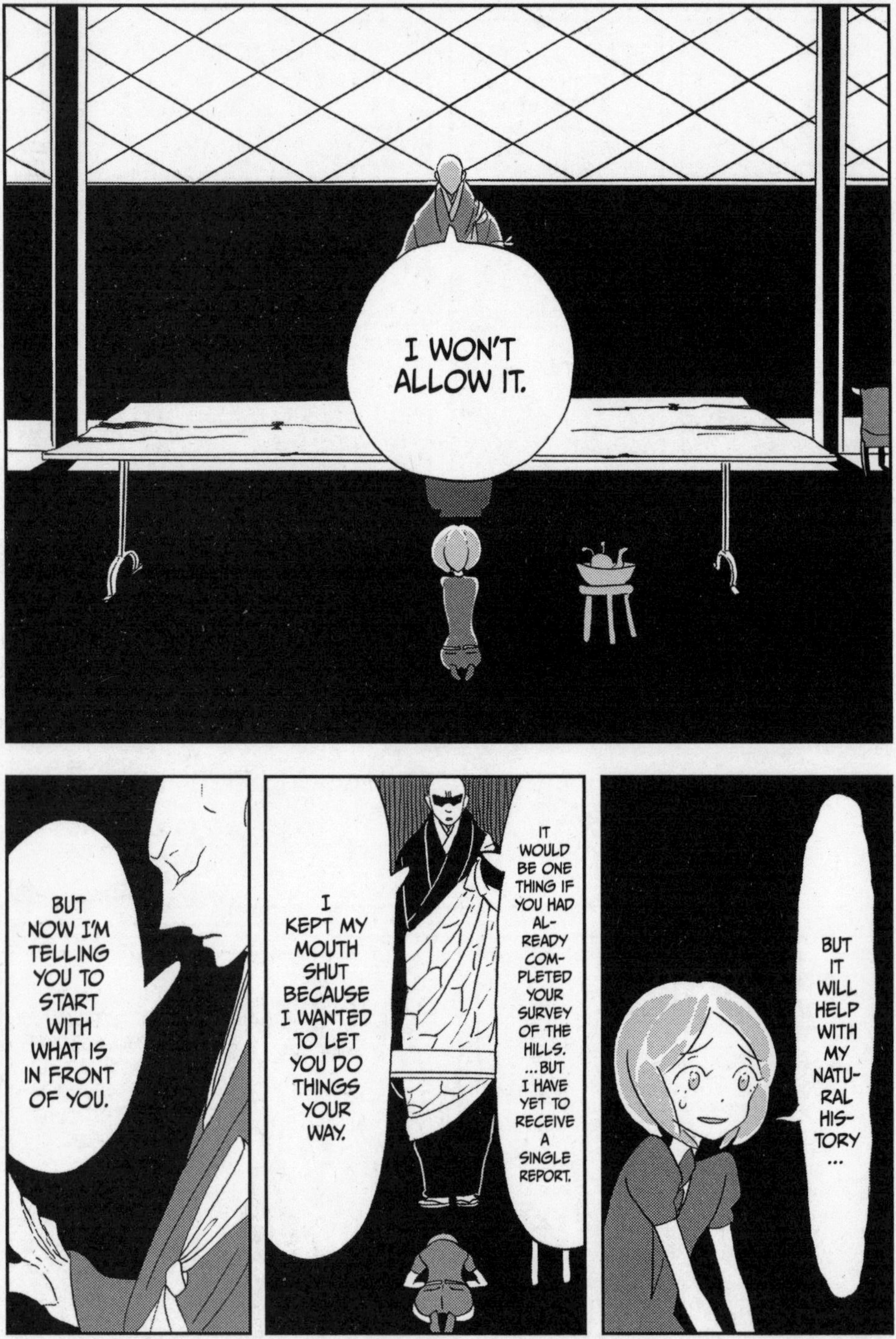
I WON'T ALLOW IT.
BUT IT WILL HELP WITH MY NATURAL HISTORY...
IT WOULD BE ONE THING IF YOU HAD ALREADY COMPLETED YOUR SURVEY OF THE HILLS. ...BUT I HAVE YET TO RECEIVE A SINGLE REPORT.
I KEPT MY MOUTH SHUT BECAUSE I WANTED TO LET YOU DO THINGS YOUR WAY.
BUT NOW I'M TELLING YOU TO START WITH WHAT IS IN FRONT OF YOU.

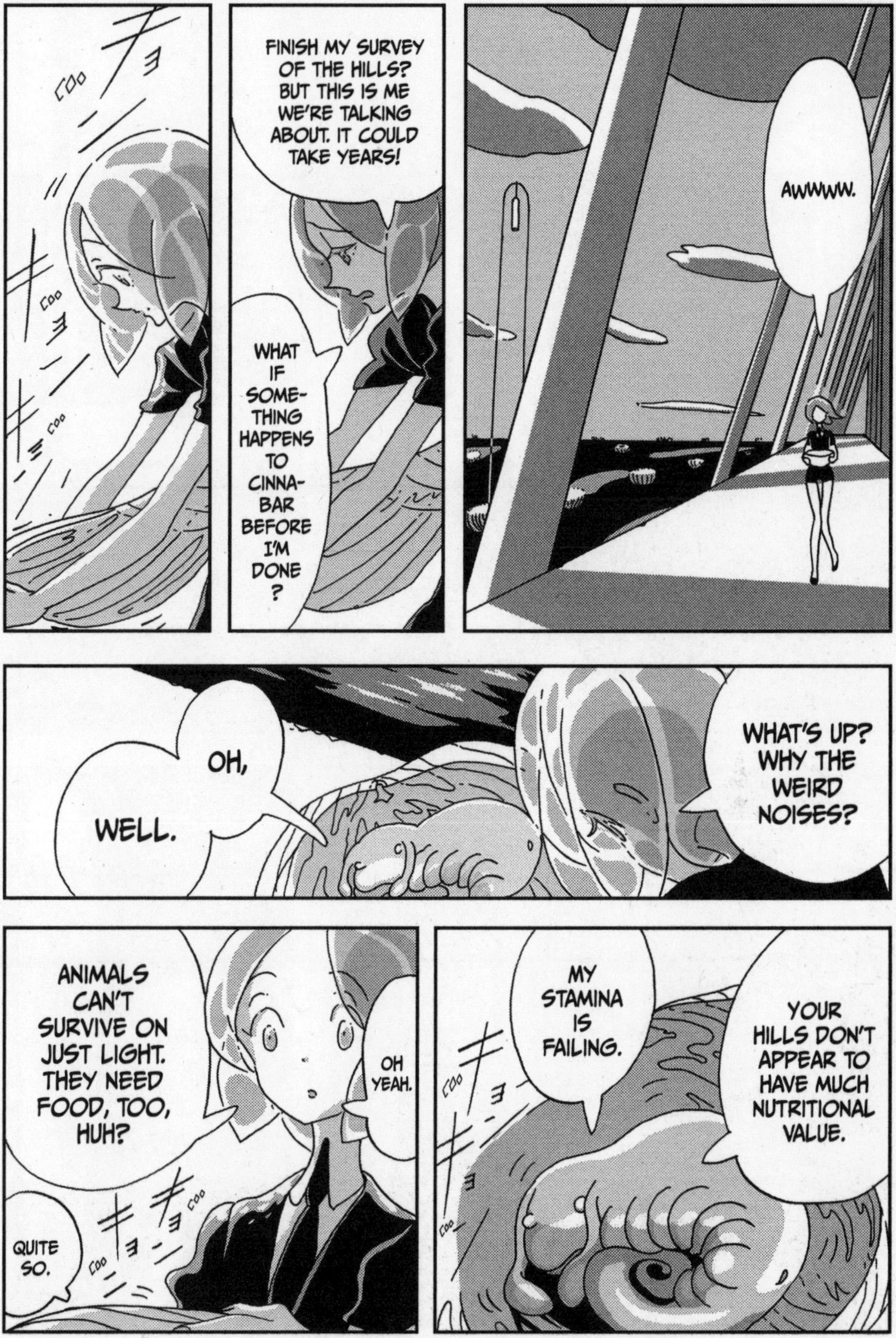
AWWWW.
FINISH MY SURVEY OF THE HILLS? BUT THIS IS ME WE'RE TALKING ABOUT. IT COULD TAKE YEARS!
WHAT IF SOME-THING HAPPENS TO CINNA-BAR BEFORE I'M DONE?
COO
COO
COO
WHAT'S UP? WHY THE WEIRD NOISES?
OH,
WELL.
YOUR HILLS DON'T APPEAR TO HAVE MUCH NUTRITIONAL VALUE.
MY STAMINA IS FAILING.
COO
COO
OH YEAH.
ANIMALS CAN'T SURVIVE ON JUST LIGHT. THEY NEED FOOD, TOO, HUH?
COO
COO
QUITE SO.

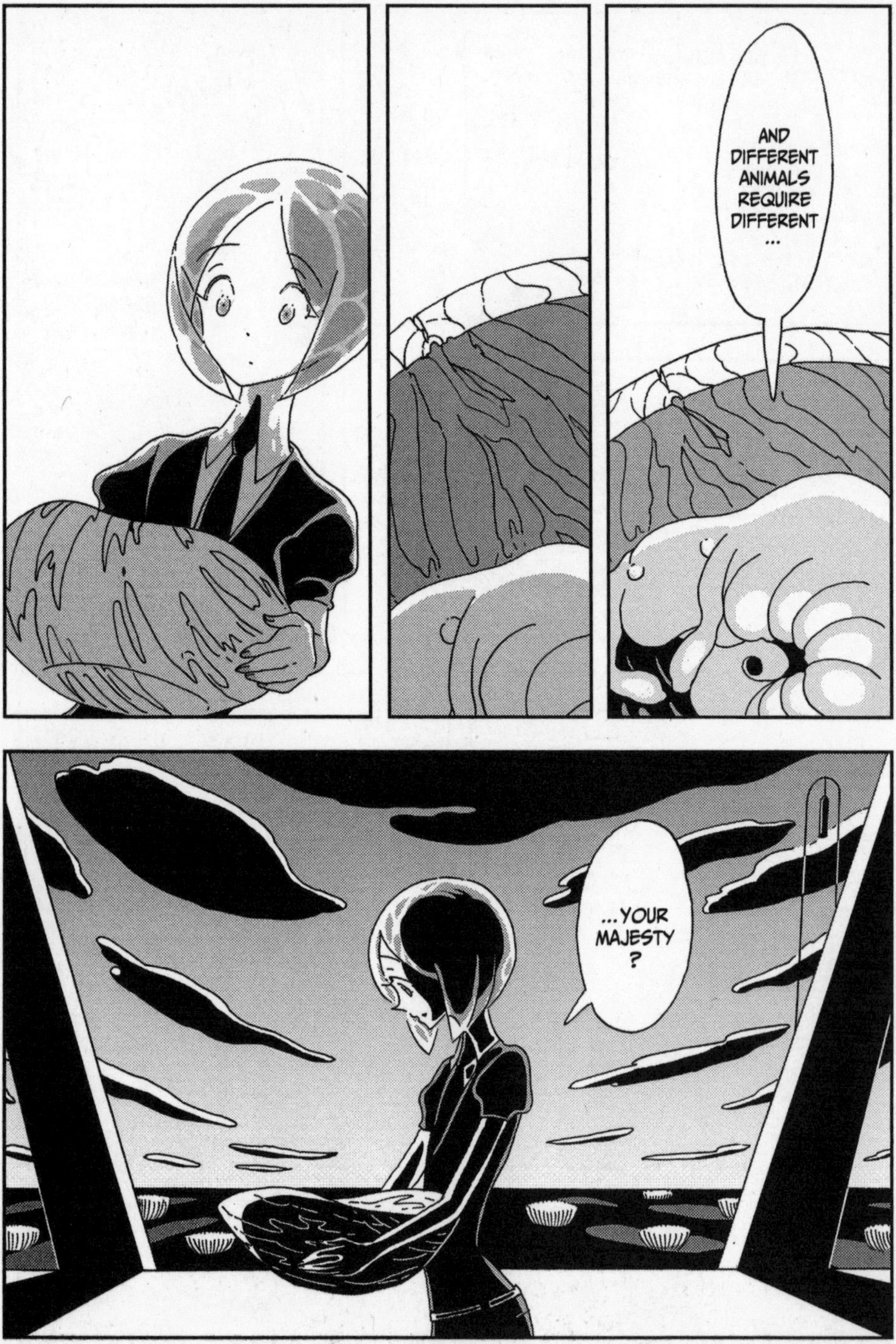
AND DIFFERENT ANIMALS REQUIRE DIFFERENT ...
...YOUR MAJESTY ?

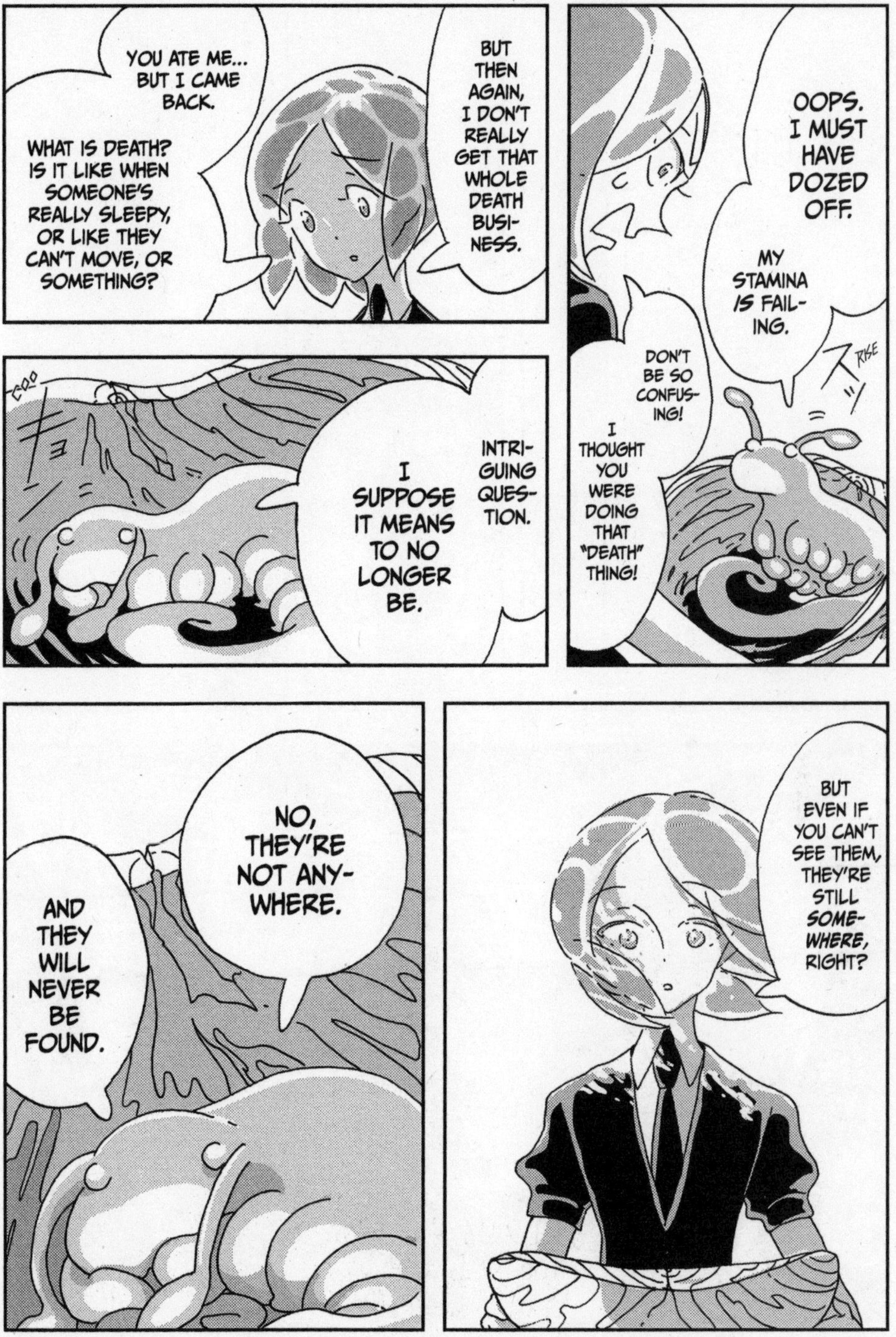
OOPS. I MUST HAVE DOZED OFF.
MY STAMINA *IS* FAILING.
RISE
DON'T BE SO CONFUSING!
I THOUGHT YOU WERE DOING THAT "DEATH" THING!
BUT THEN AGAIN, I DON'T REALLY GET THAT WHOLE DEATH BUSINESS.
YOU ATE ME... BUT I CAME BACK.
WHAT IS DEATH? IS IT LIKE WHEN SOMEONE'S REALLY SLEEPY, OR LIKE THEY CAN'T MOVE, OR SOMETHING?
INTRIGUING QUESTION.
I SUPPOSE IT MEANS TO NO LONGER BE.
COO
BUT EVEN IF YOU CAN'T SEE THEM, THEY'RE STILL *SOMEWHERE*, RIGHT?
NO, THEY'RE NOT ANYWHERE.
AND THEY WILL NEVER BE FOUND.

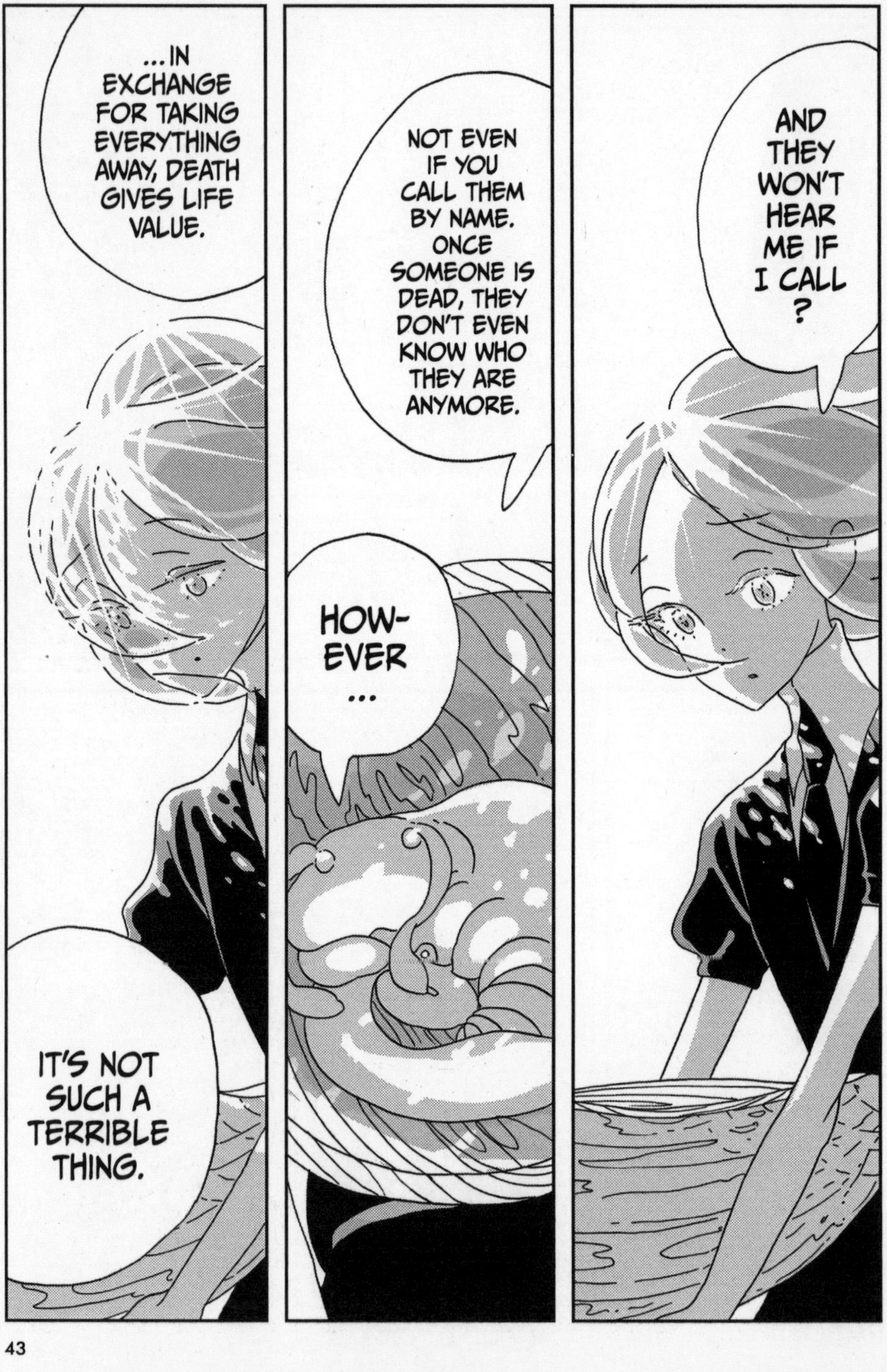
AND THEY WON'T HEAR ME IF I CALL ?
NOT EVEN IF YOU CALL THEM BY NAME. ONCE SOMEONE IS DEAD, THEY DON'T EVEN KNOW WHO THEY ARE ANYMORE.
HOW-EVER ...
...IN EXCHANGE FOR TAKING EVERYTHING AWAY, DEATH GIVES LIFE VALUE.
IT'S NOT SUCH A TERRIBLE THING.

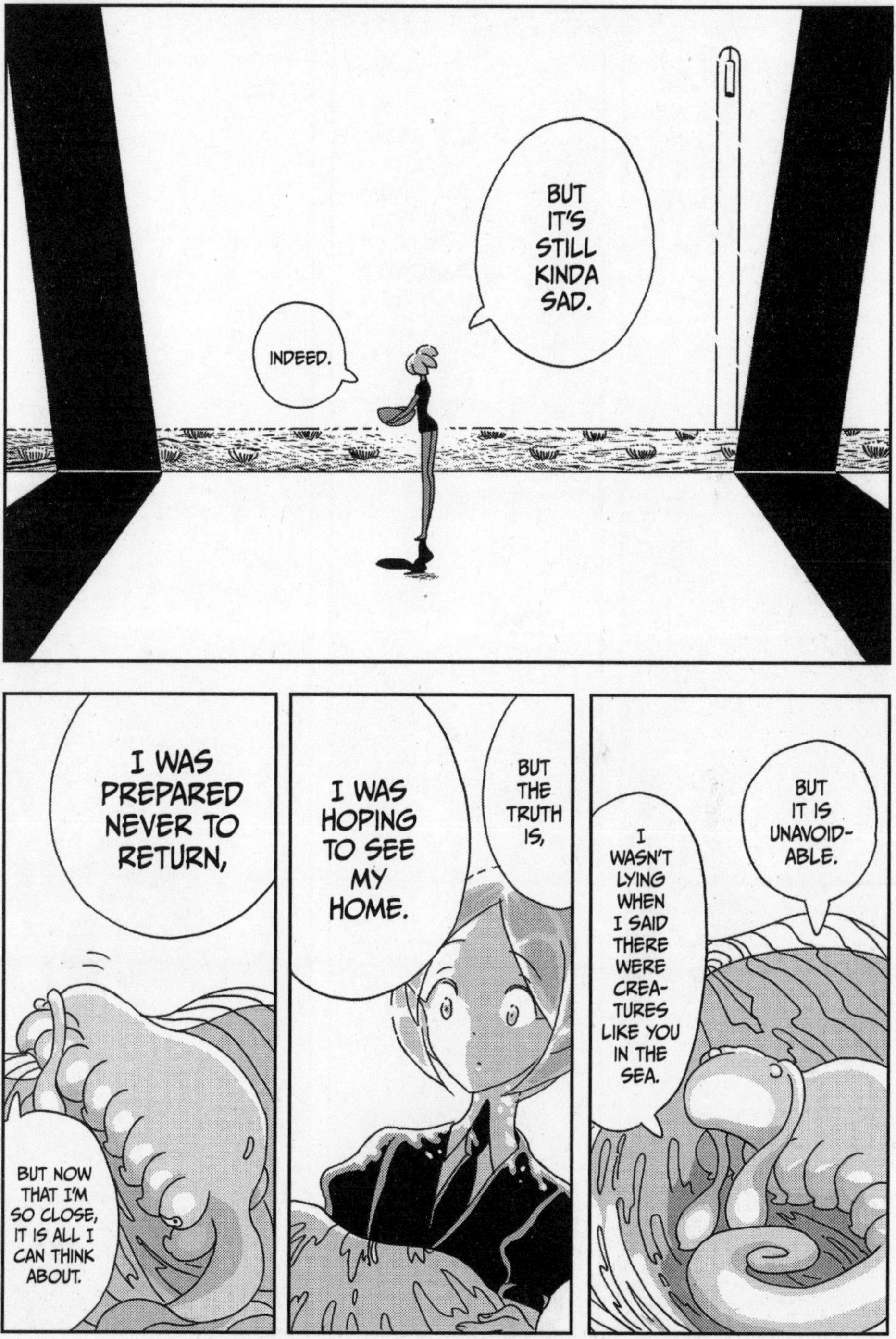
BUT IT'S STILL KINDA SAD.
INDEED.
BUT IT IS UNAVOIDABLE.
I WASN'T LYING WHEN I SAID THERE WERE CREATURES LIKE YOU IN THE SEA.
BUT THE TRUTH IS,
I WAS HOPING TO SEE MY HOME.
I WAS PREPARED NEVER TO RETURN,
BUT NOW THAT I'M SO CLOSE, IT IS ALL I CAN THINK ABOUT.

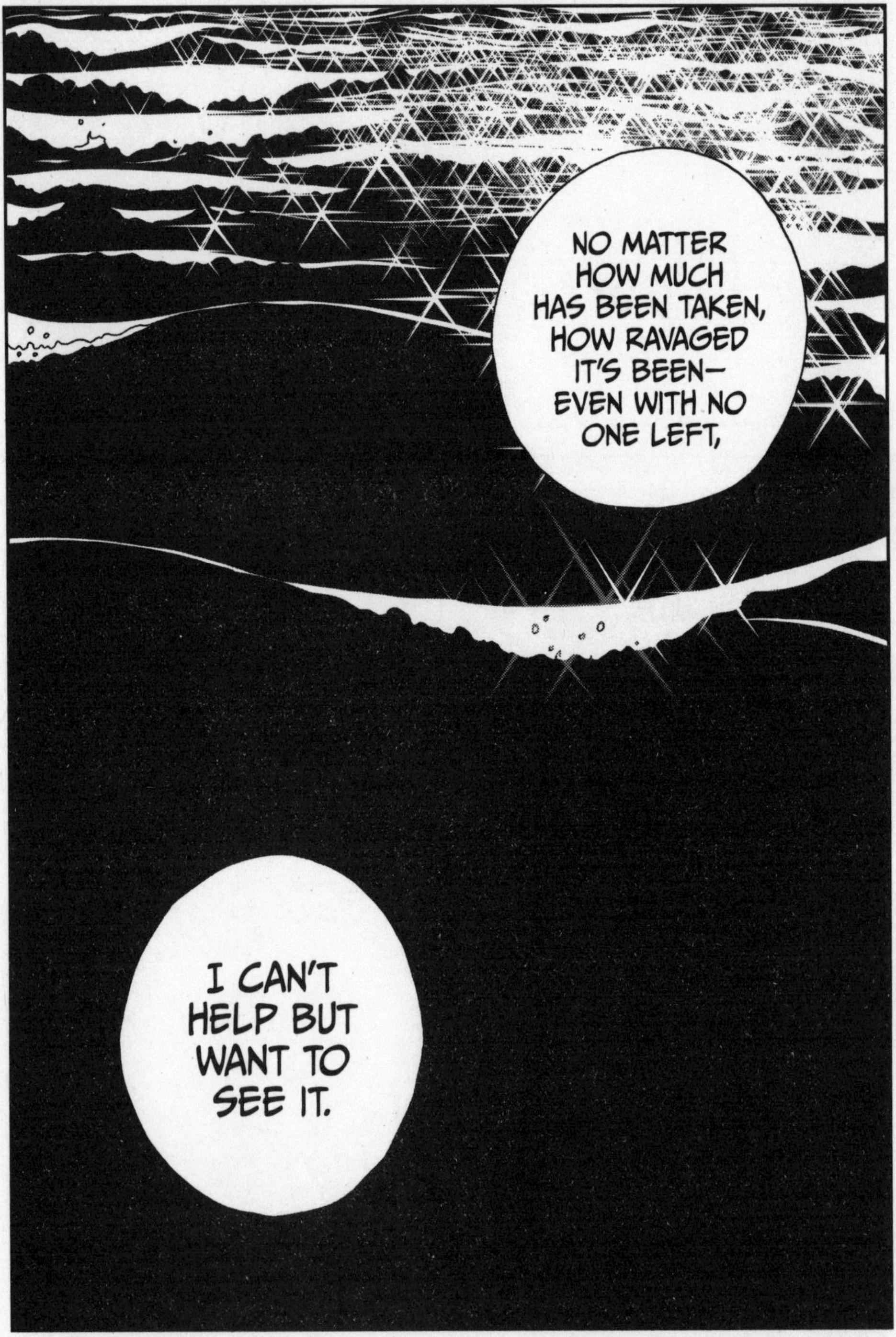
NO MATTER HOW MUCH HAS BEEN TAKEN, HOW RAVAGED IT'S BEEN— EVEN WITH NO ONE LEFT,
I CAN'T HELP BUT WANT TO SEE IT.

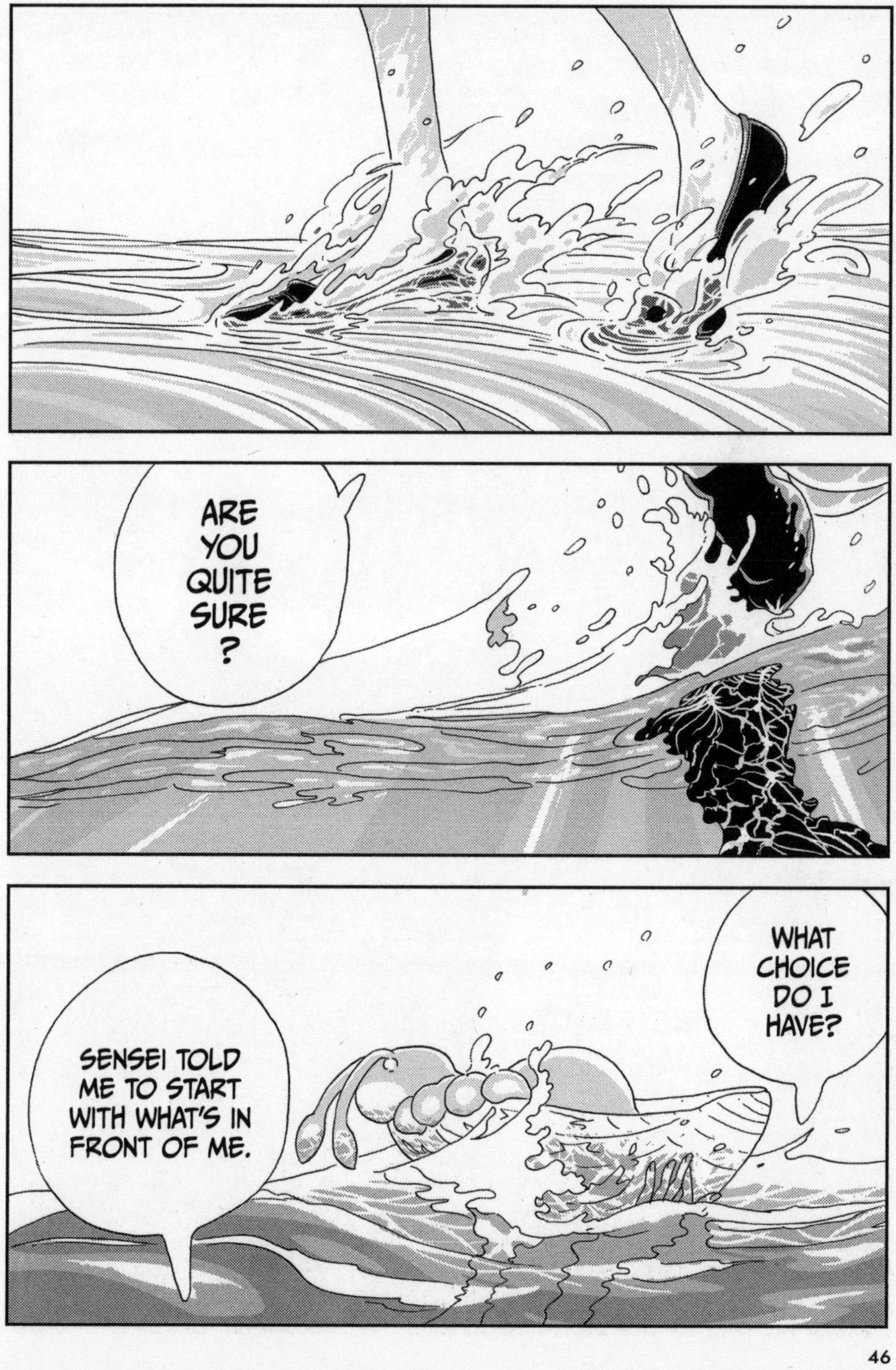
ARE YOU QUITE SURE ?
WHAT CHOICE DO I HAVE?
SENSEI TOLD ME TO START WITH WHAT'S IN FRONT OF ME.

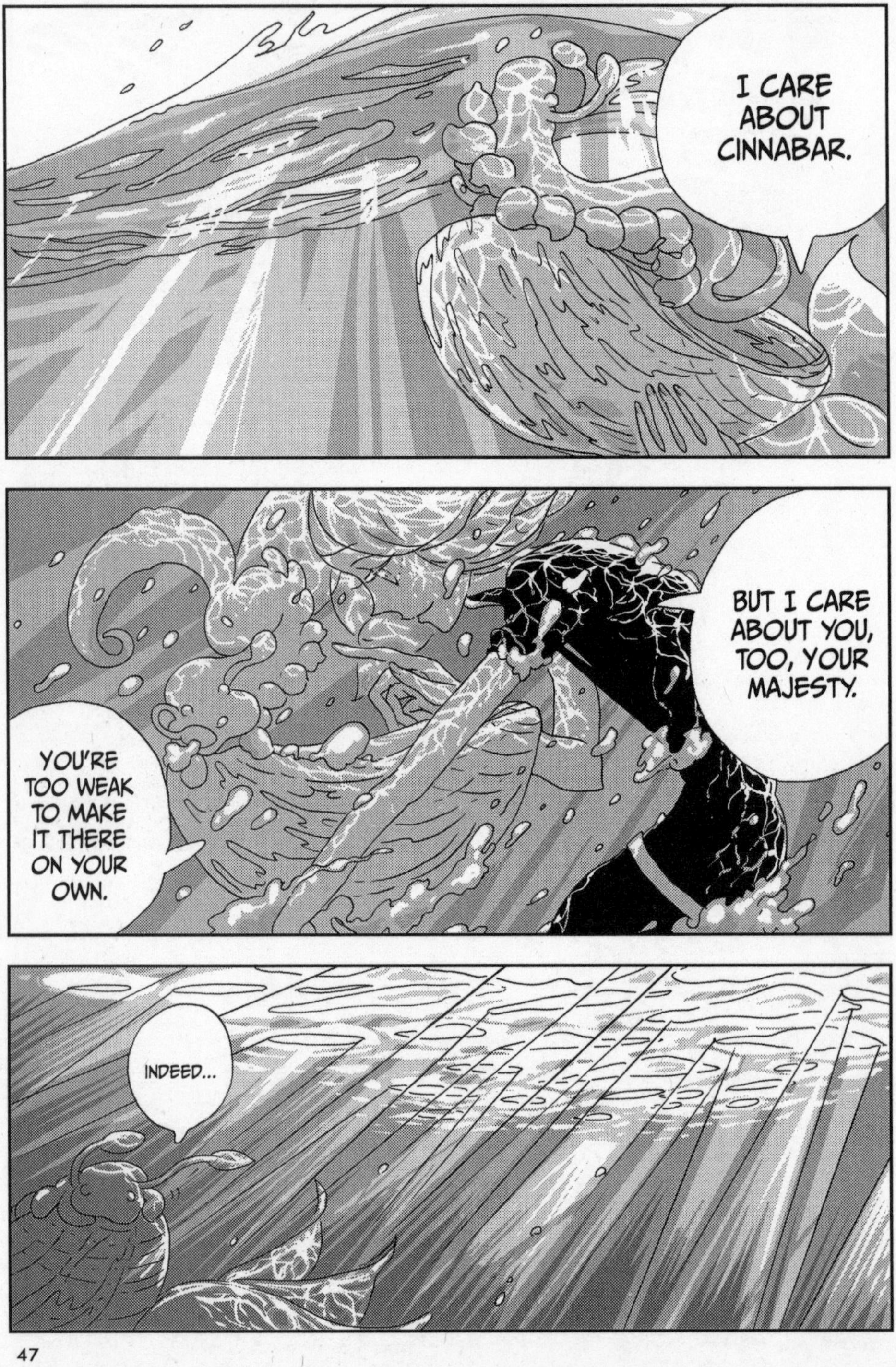
I CARE ABOUT CINNABAR.
BUT I CARE ABOUT YOU, TOO, YOUR MAJESTY.
YOU'RE TOO WEAK TO MAKE IT THERE ON YOUR OWN.
INDEED...

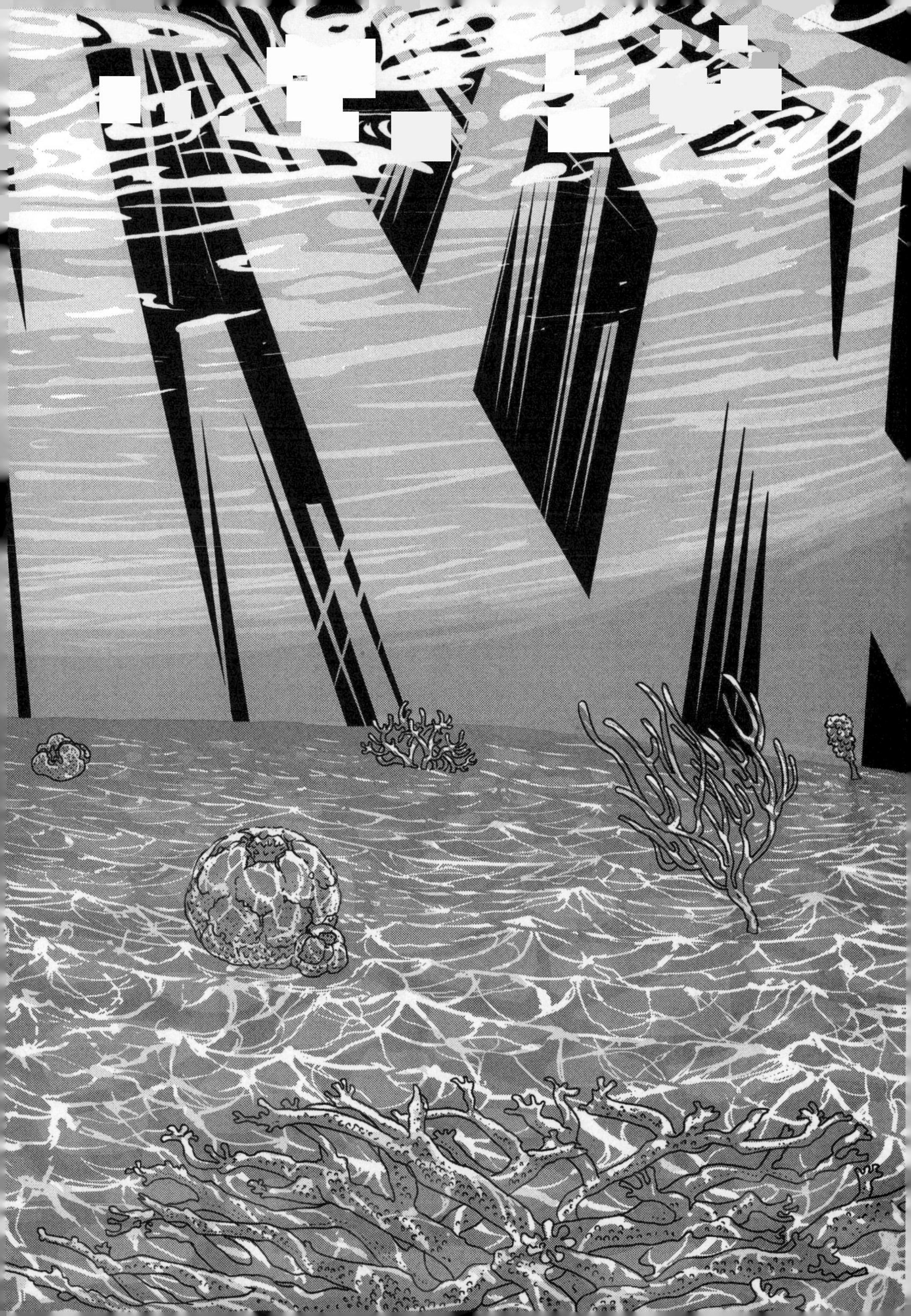

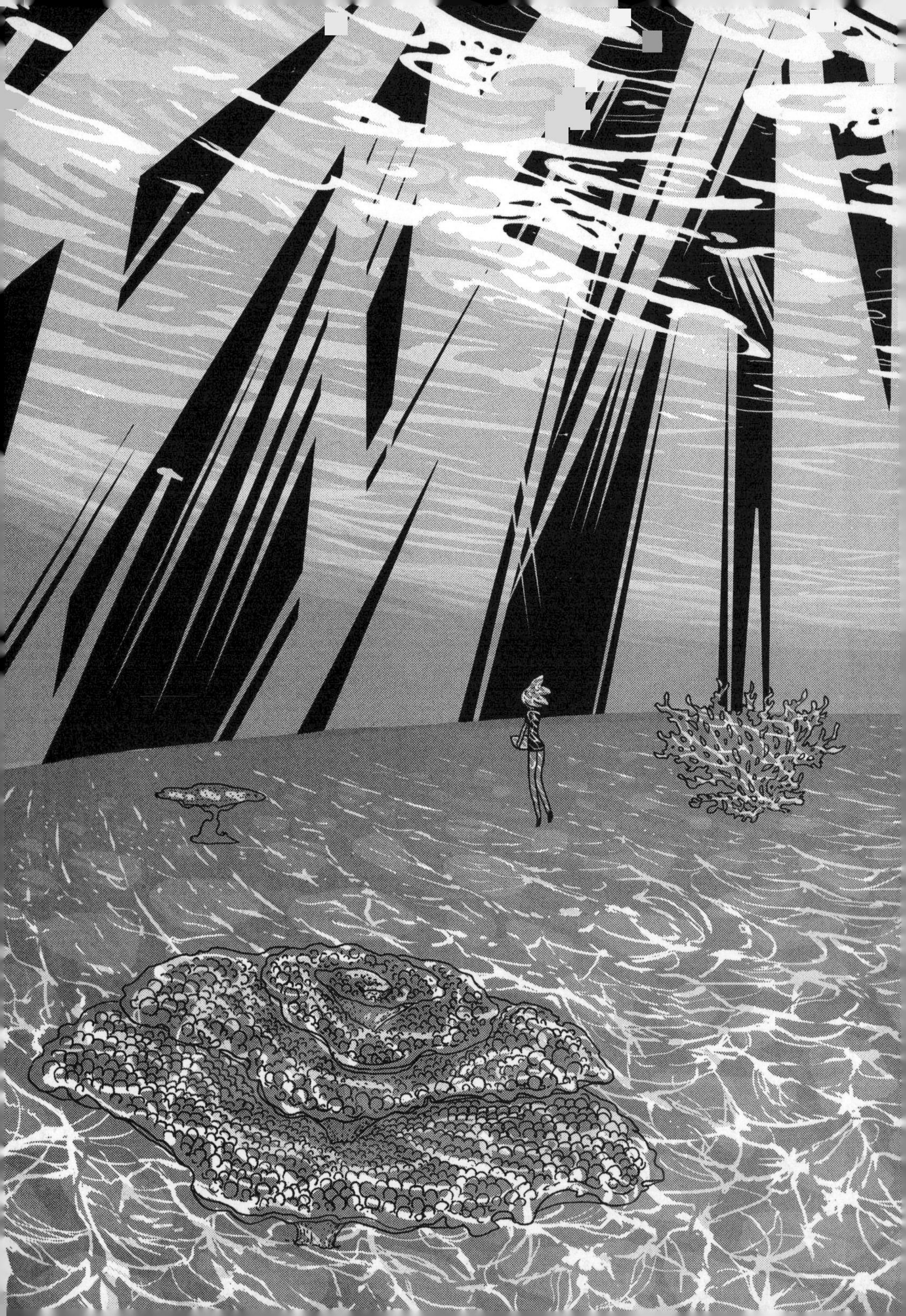

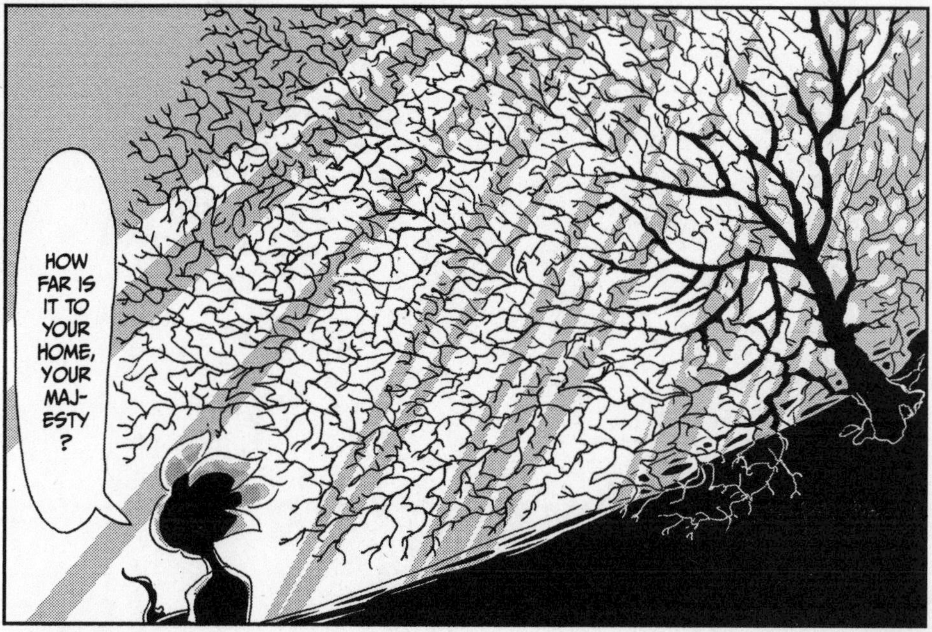
HOW FAR IS IT TO YOUR HOME, YOUR MAJ-ESTY?

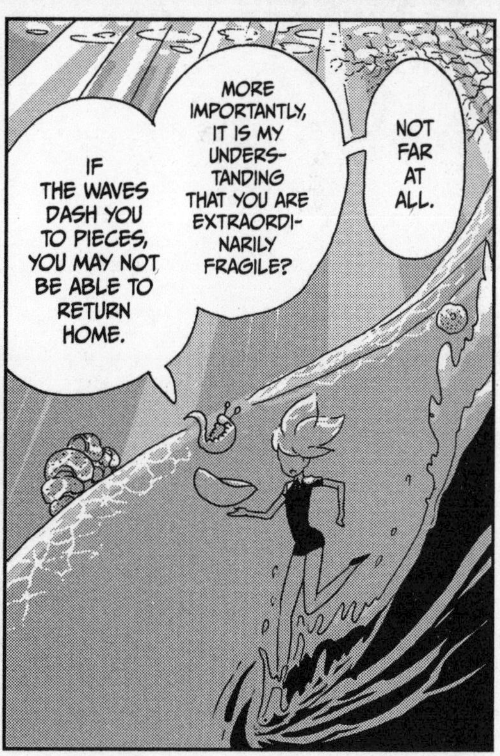
NOT FAR AT ALL.
MORE IMPORTANTLY, IT IS MY UNDERS-TANDING THAT YOU ARE EXTRAORDI-NARILY FRAGILE?
IF THE WAVES DASH YOU TO PIECES, YOU MAY NOT BE ABLE TO RETURN HOME.

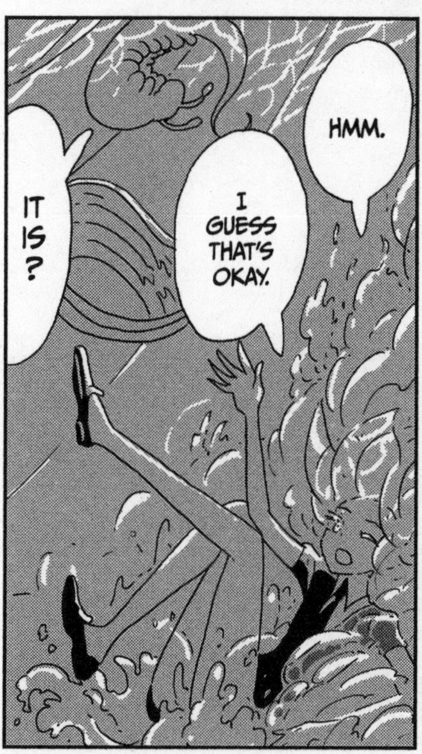
HMM.
I GUESS THAT'S OKAY.
IT IS?

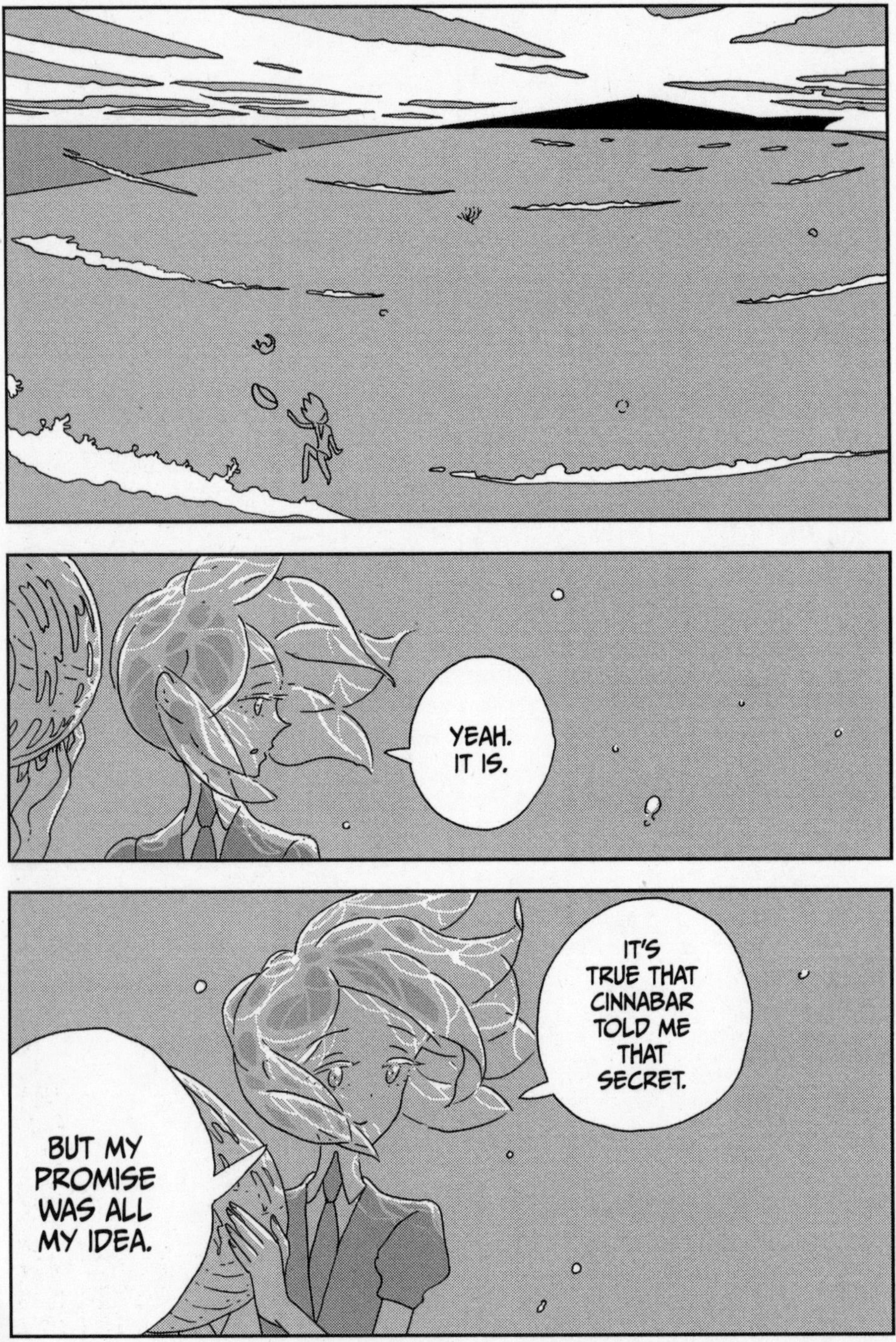
YEAH. IT IS.
IT'S TRUE THAT CINNABAR TOLD ME THAT SECRET.
BUT MY PROMISE WAS ALL MY IDEA.

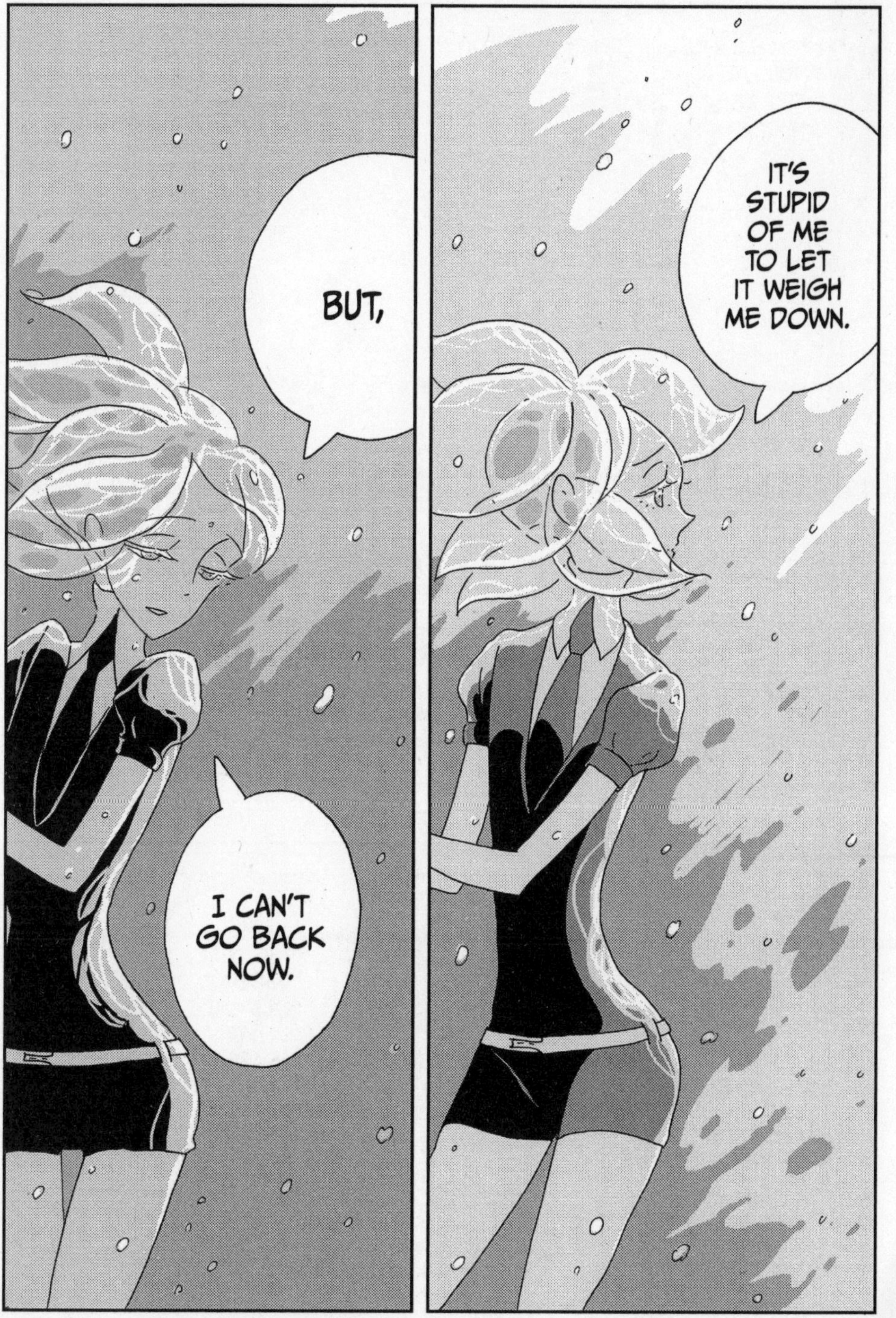
IT'S STUPID OF ME TO LET IT WEIGH ME DOWN.
BUT,
I CAN'T GO BACK NOW.

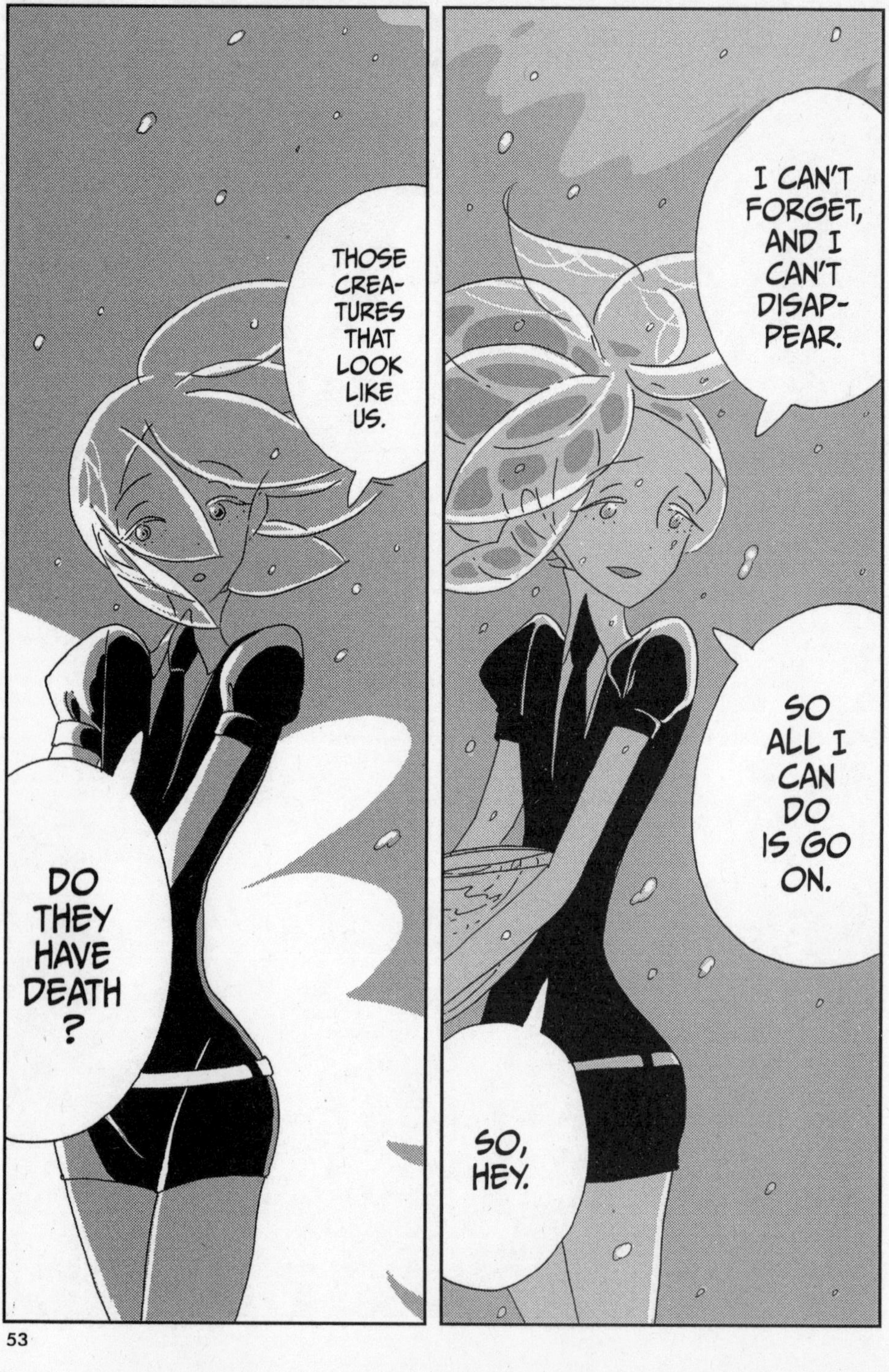
I CAN'T FORGET, AND I CAN'T DISAP-PEAR.
SO ALL I CAN DO IS GO ON.
SO, HEY.
THOSE CREA-TURES THAT LOOK LIKE US.
DO THEY HAVE DEATH?

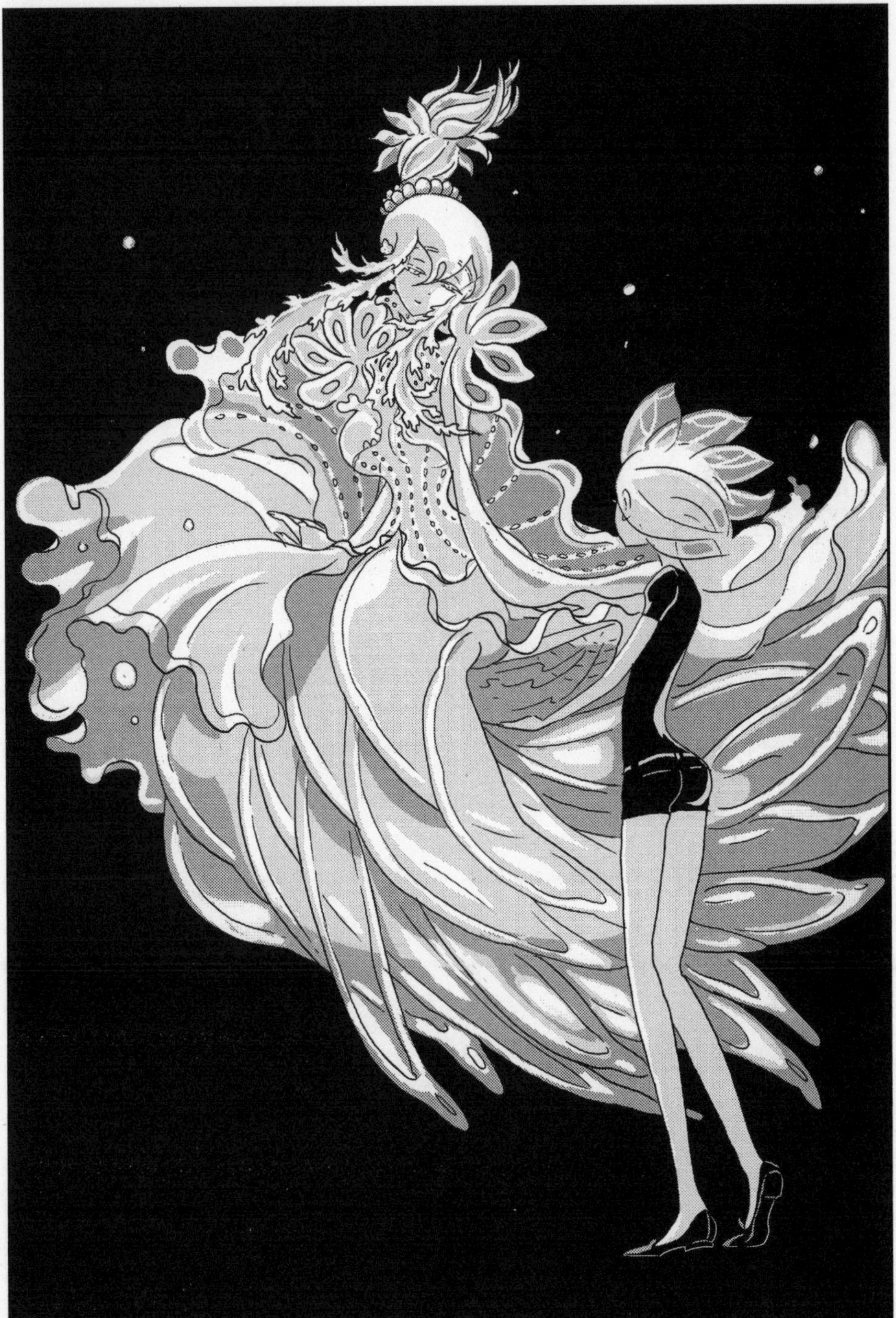

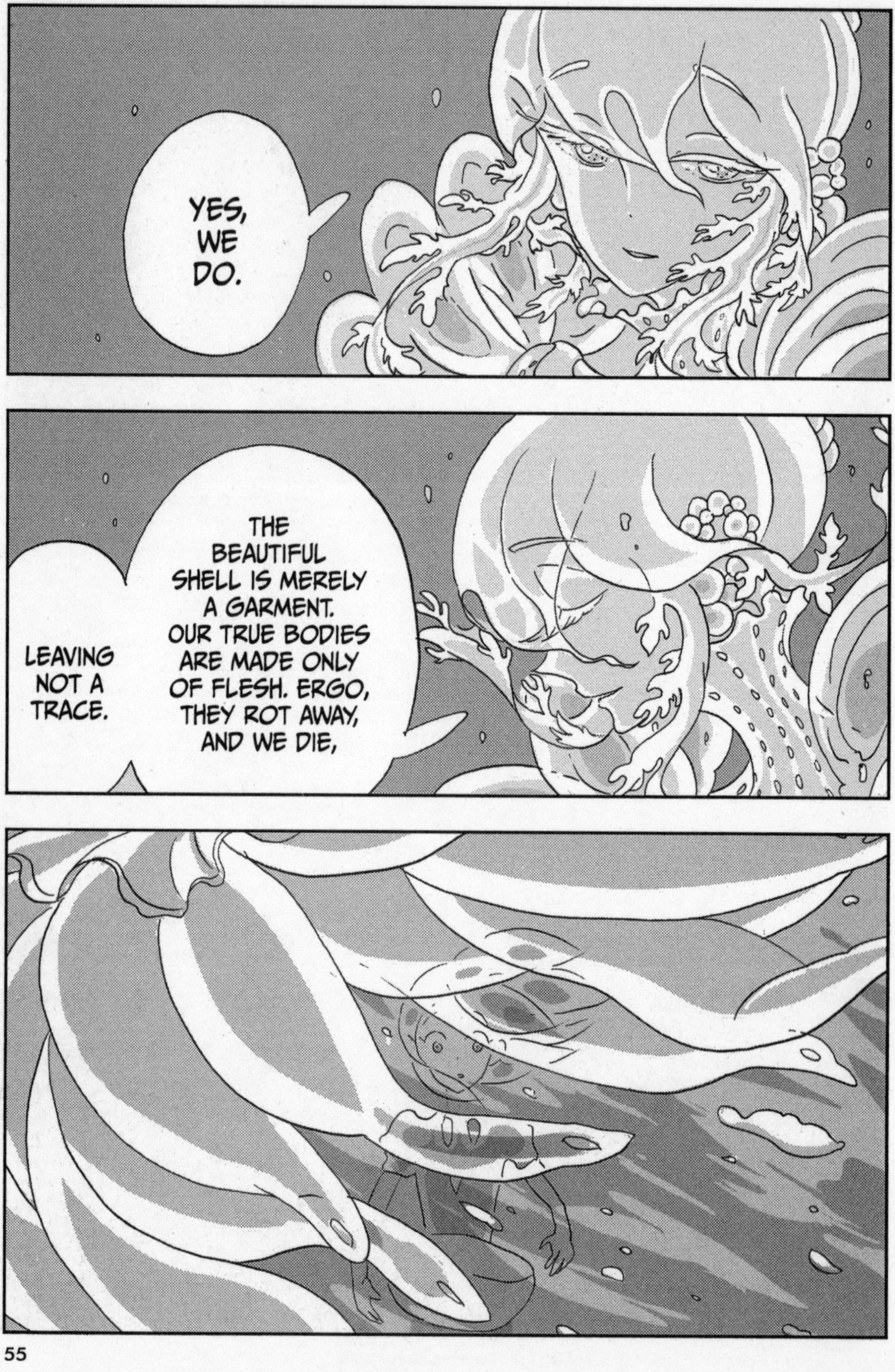
YES, WE DO.
THE BEAUTIFUL SHELL IS MERELY A GARMENT. OUR TRUE BODIES ARE MADE ONLY OF FLESH. ERGO, THEY ROT AWAY, AND WE DIE,
LEAVING NOT A TRACE.

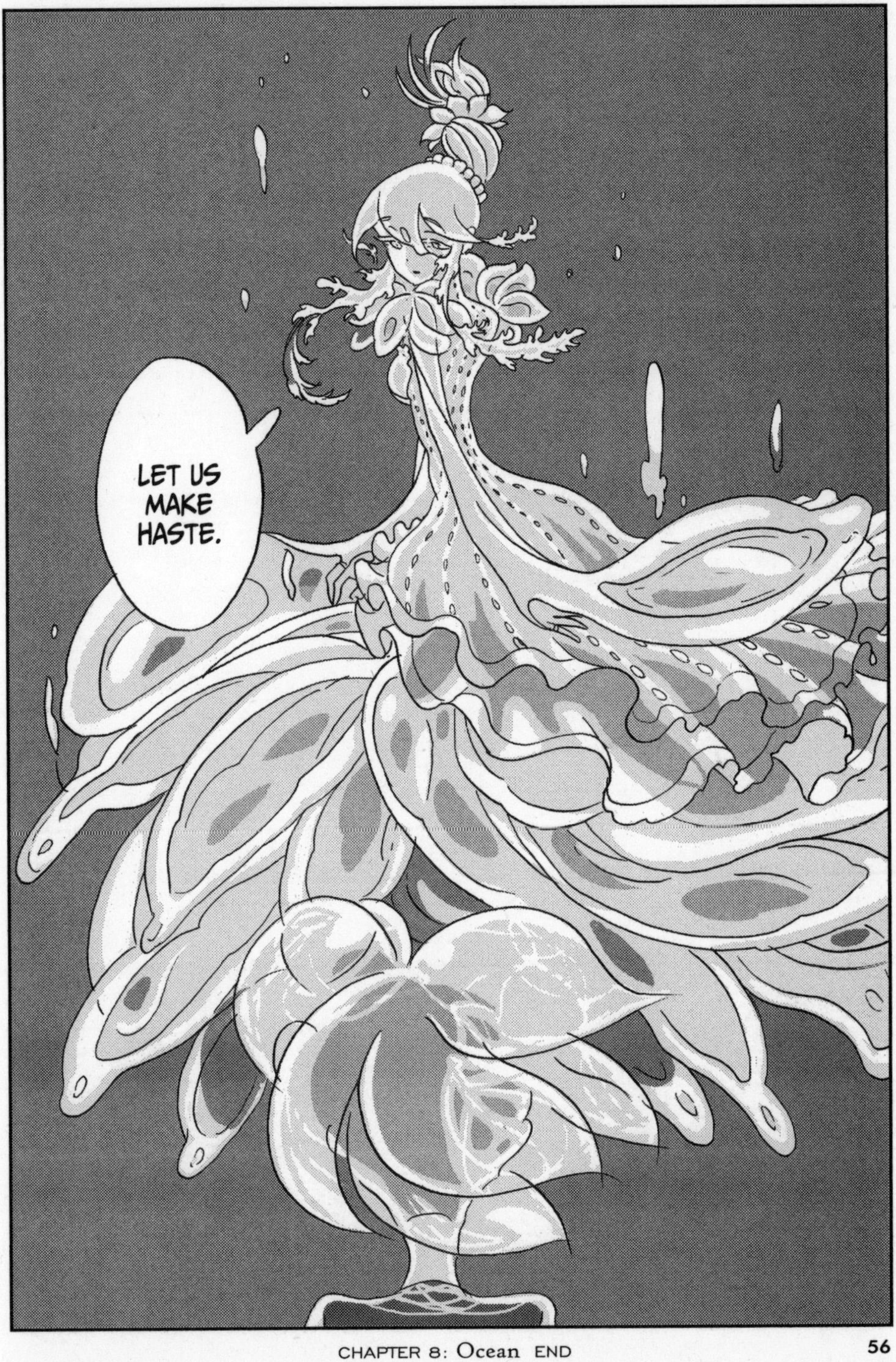
LET US MAKE HASTE.

CHAPTER 8: Ocean END

CHAPTER 9:

Spirit, Flesh, Bone

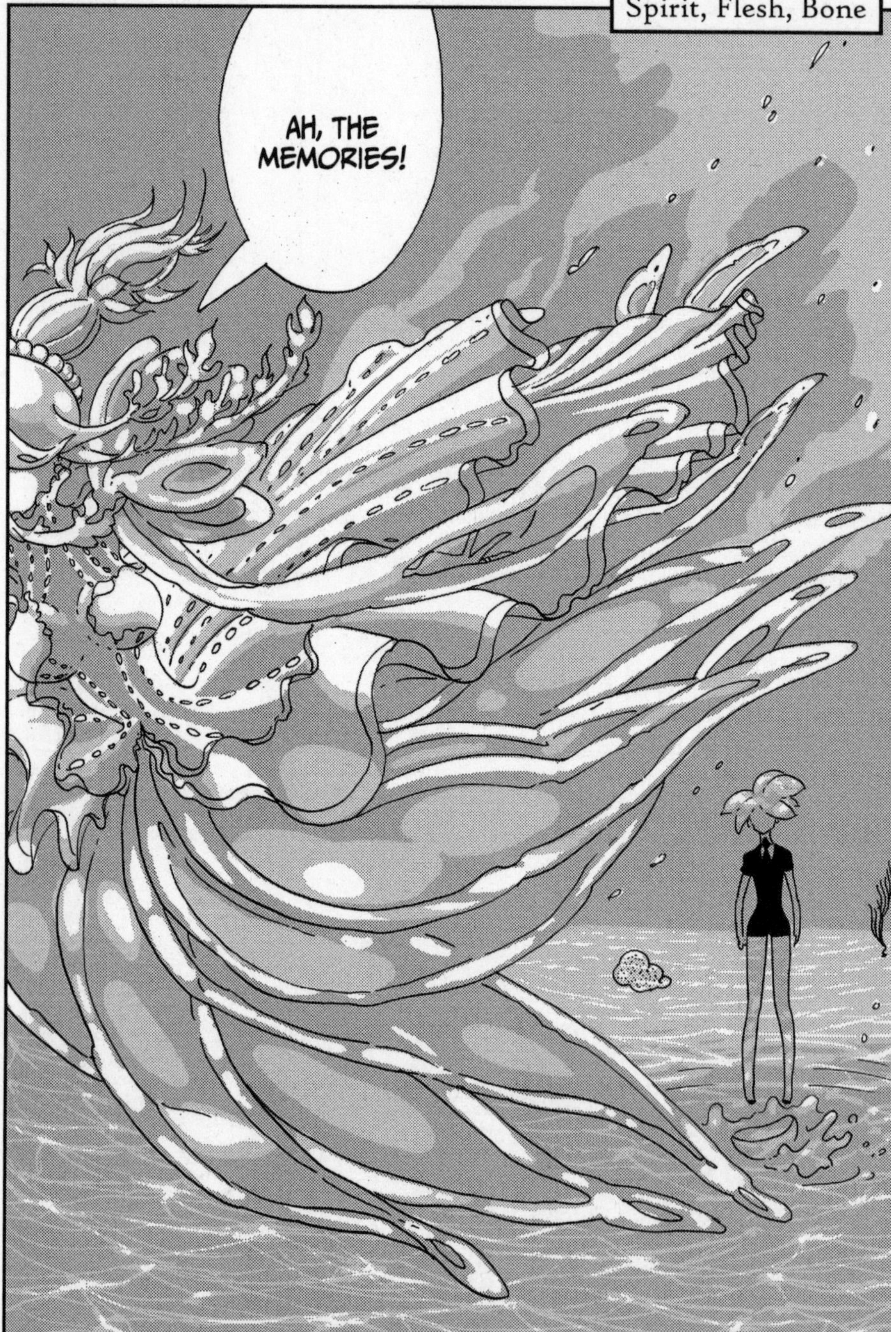
AH, THE MEMORIES!

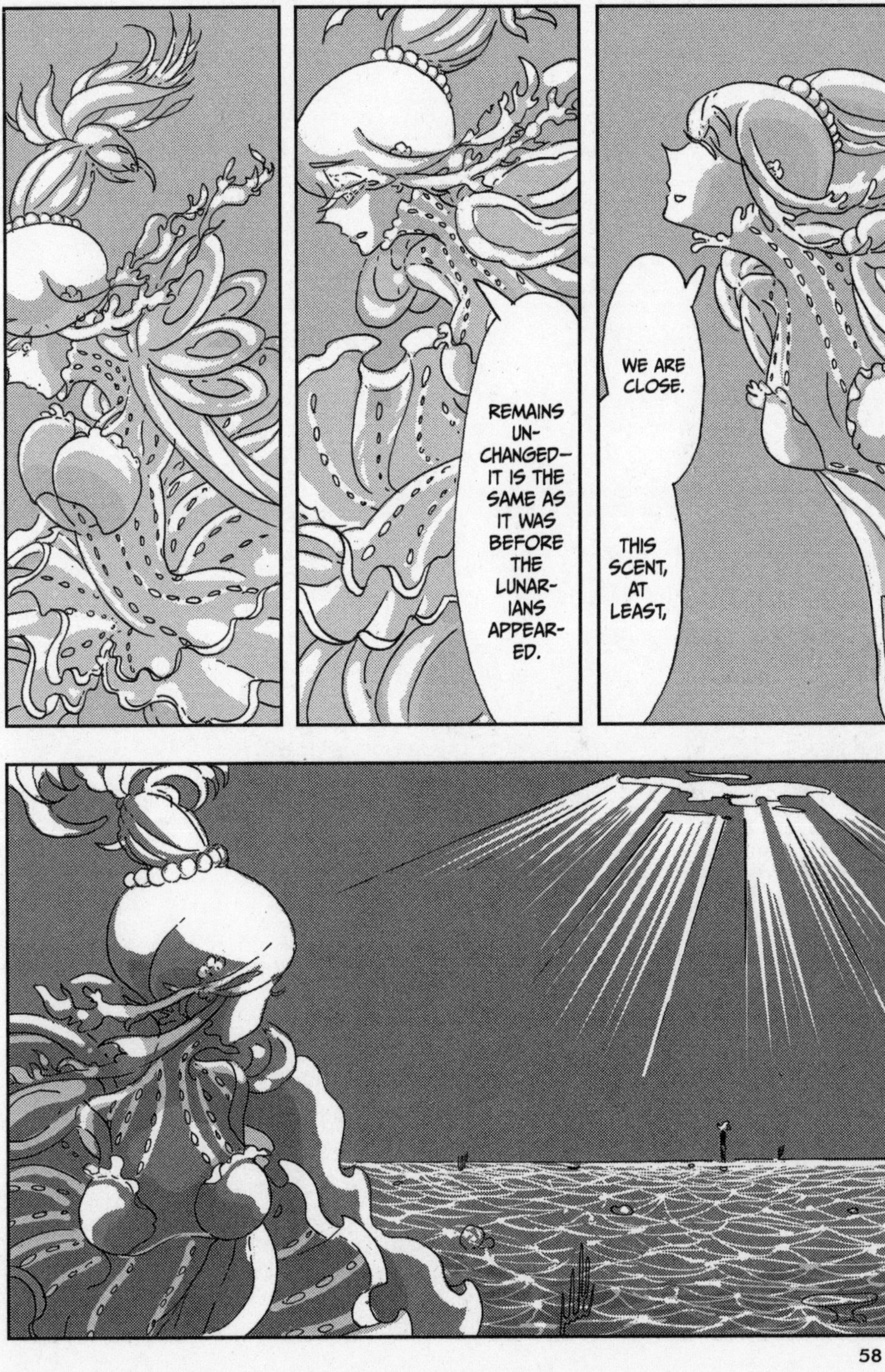
WE ARE CLOSE.
THIS SCENT, AT LEAST,
REMAINS UNCHANGED—IT IS THE SAME AS IT WAS BEFORE THE LUNARIANS APPEARED.

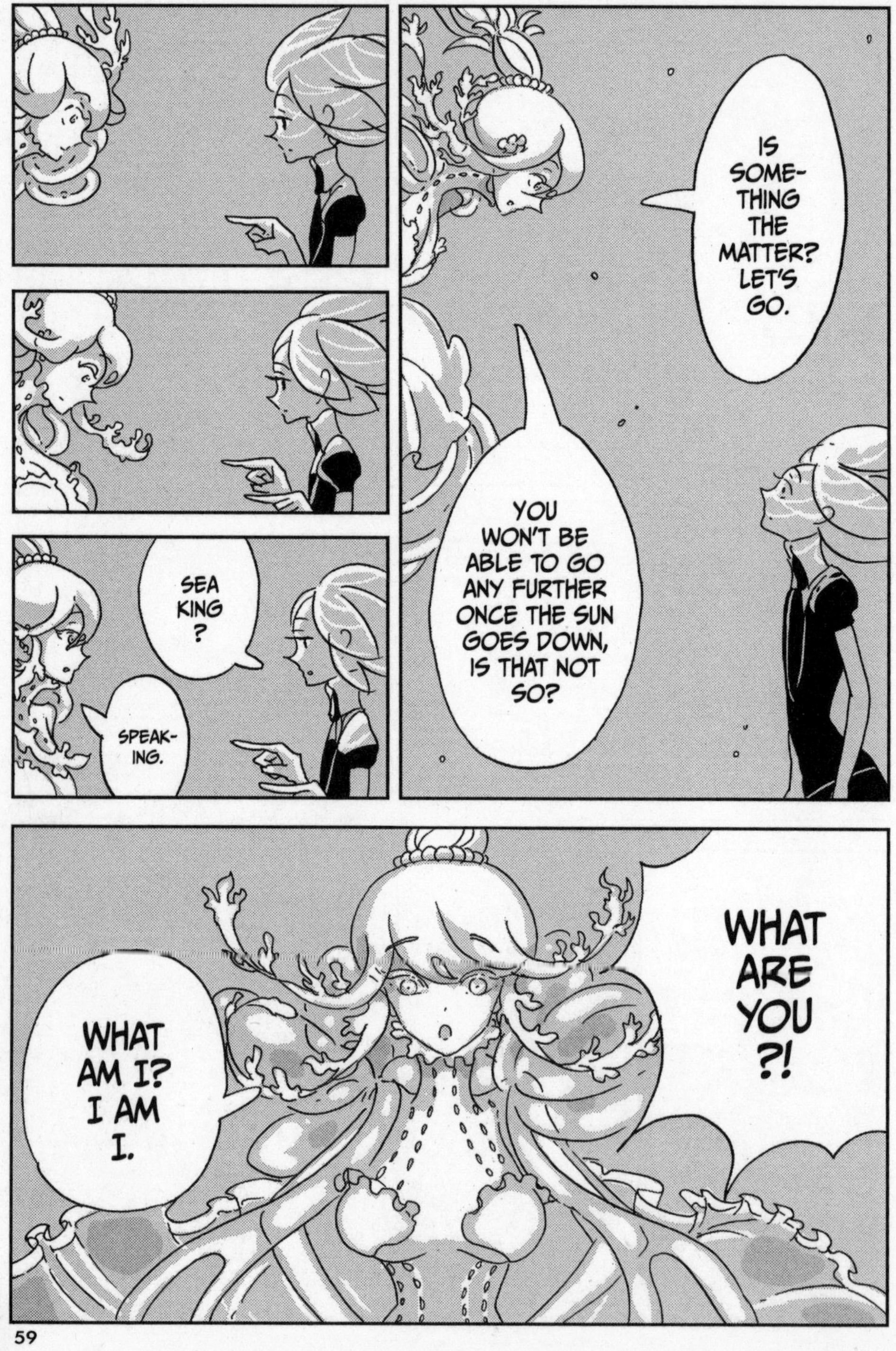
IS SOMETHING THE MATTER? LET'S GO.
YOU WON'T BE ABLE TO GO ANY FURTHER ONCE THE SUN GOES DOWN, IS THAT NOT SO?
SEA KING?
SPEAKING.
WHAT ARE YOU?!
WHAT AM I? I AM I.

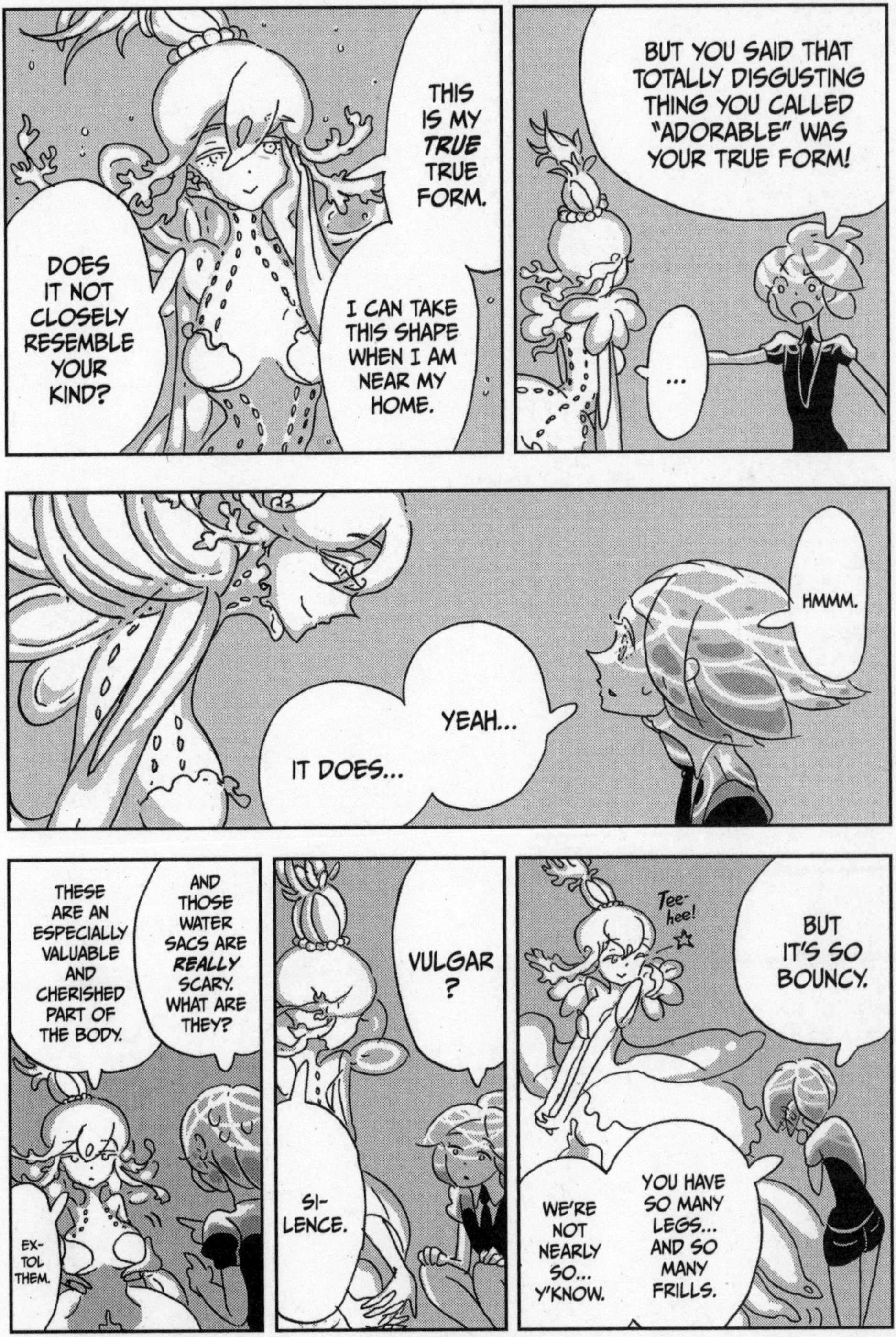
BUT YOU SAID THAT TOTALLY DISGUSTING THING YOU CALLED "ADORABLE" WAS YOUR TRUE FORM!
...
THIS IS MY TRUE TRUE FORM.
I CAN TAKE THIS SHAPE WHEN I AM NEAR MY HOME.
DOES IT NOT CLOSELY RESEMBLE YOUR KIND?
HMMM.
YEAH...
IT DOES...
Tee-hee!
BUT IT'S SO BOUNCY.
YOU HAVE SO MANY LEGS... AND SO MANY FRILLS.
WE'RE NOT NEARLY SO... Y'KNOW.
VULGAR?
SI-LENCE.
AND THOSE WATER SACS ARE REALLY SCARY. WHAT ARE THEY?
THESE ARE AN ESPECIALLY VALUABLE AND CHERISHED PART OF THE BODY.
EX-TOL THEM.

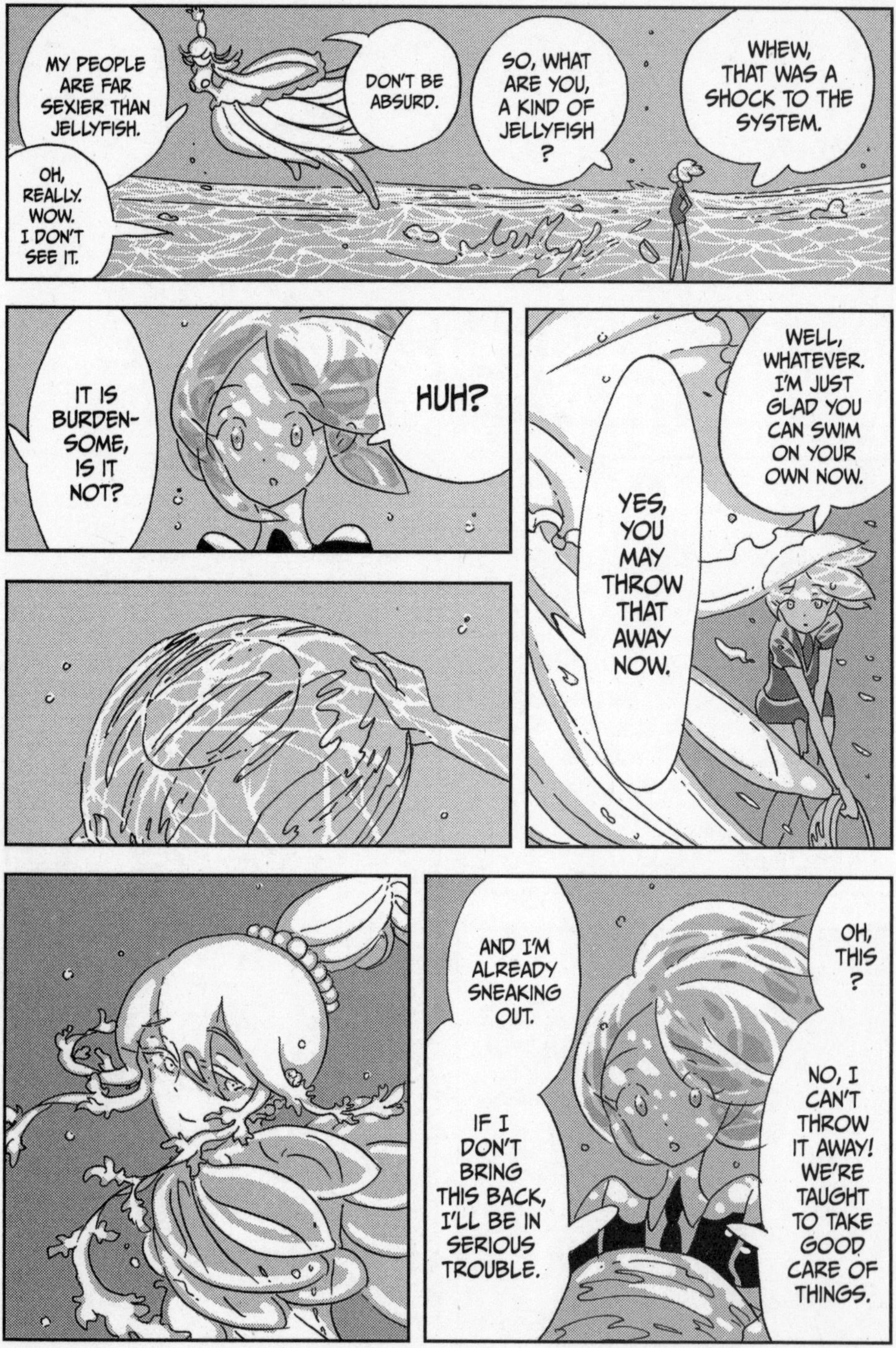
WHEW, THAT WAS A SHOCK TO THE SYSTEM.
SO, WHAT ARE YOU, A KIND OF JELLYFISH?
DON'T BE ABSURD.
MY PEOPLE ARE FAR SEXIER THAN JELLYFISH.
OH, REALLY. WOW. I DON'T SEE IT.
WELL, WHATEVER. I'M JUST GLAD YOU CAN SWIM ON YOUR OWN NOW.
YES, YOU MAY THROW THAT AWAY NOW.
HUH?
IT IS BURDEN-SOME, IS IT NOT?
OH, THIS?
NO, I CAN'T THROW IT AWAY! WE'RE TAUGHT TO TAKE GOOD CARE OF THINGS.
AND I'M ALREADY SNEAKING OUT.
IF I DON'T BRING THIS BACK, I'LL BE IN SERIOUS TROUBLE.

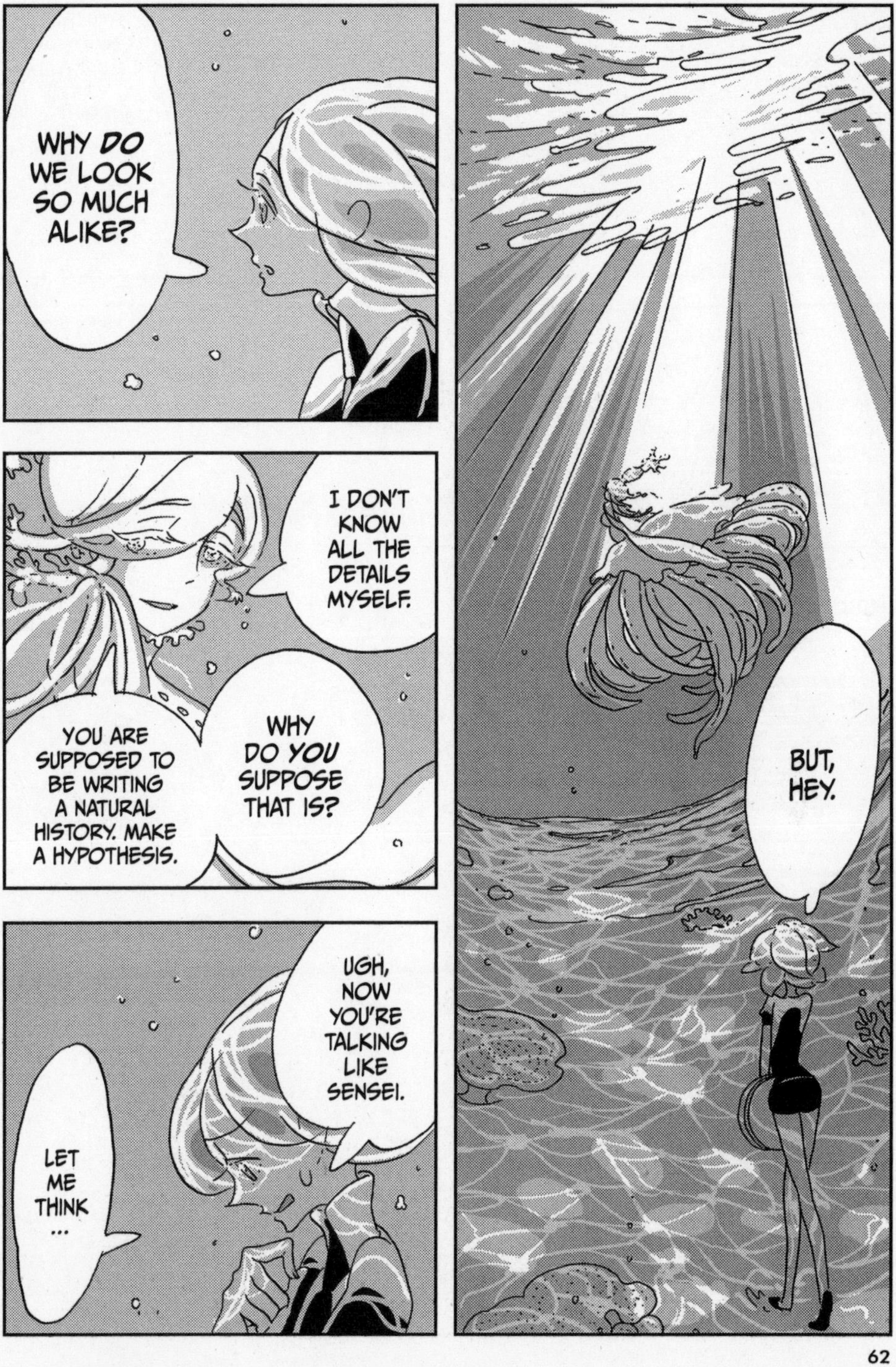
BUT, HEY.
WHY DO WE LOOK SO MUCH ALIKE?
I DON'T KNOW ALL THE DETAILS MYSELF.
WHY DO YOU SUPPOSE THAT IS?
YOU ARE SUPPOSED TO BE WRITING A NATURAL HISTORY. MAKE A HYPOTHESIS.
UGH, NOW YOU'RE TALKING LIKE SENSEI.
LET ME THINK ...

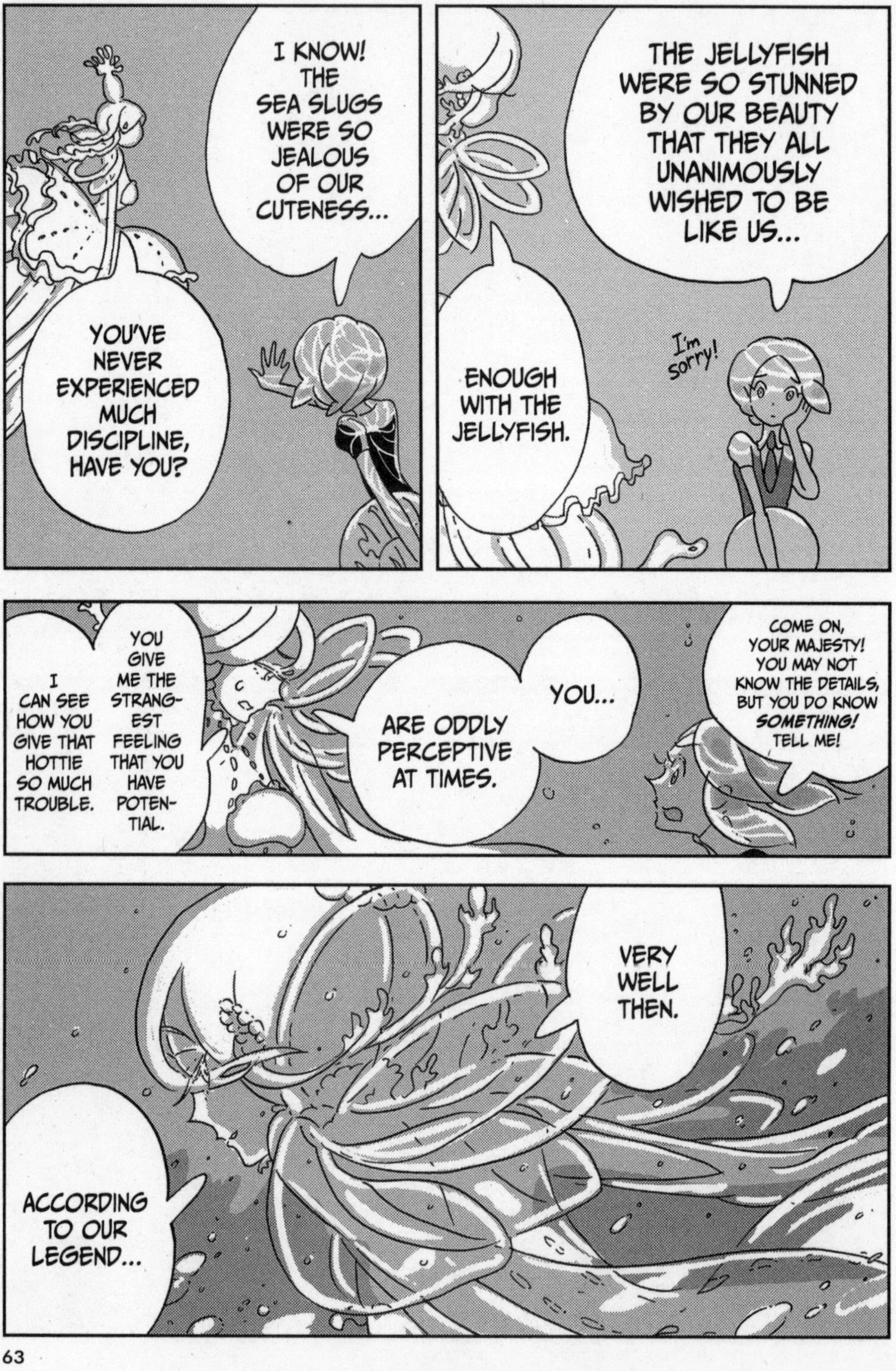
THE JELLYFISH WERE SO STUNNED BY OUR BEAUTY THAT THEY ALL UNANIMOUSLY WISHED TO BE LIKE US...
I'm sorry!
ENOUGH WITH THE JELLYFISH.
I KNOW! THE SEA SLUGS WERE SO JEALOUS OF OUR CUTENESS...
YOU'VE NEVER EXPERIENCED MUCH DISCIPLINE, HAVE YOU?
COME ON, YOUR MAJESTY! YOU MAY NOT KNOW THE DETAILS, BUT YOU DO KNOW *SOMETHING!* TELL ME!
YOU...
ARE ODDLY PERCEPTIVE AT TIMES.
YOU GIVE ME THE STRANG-EST FEELING THAT YOU HAVE POTEN-TIAL.
I CAN SEE HOW YOU GIVE THAT HOTTIE SO MUCH TROUBLE.
VERY WELL THEN.
ACCORDING TO OUR LEGEND...

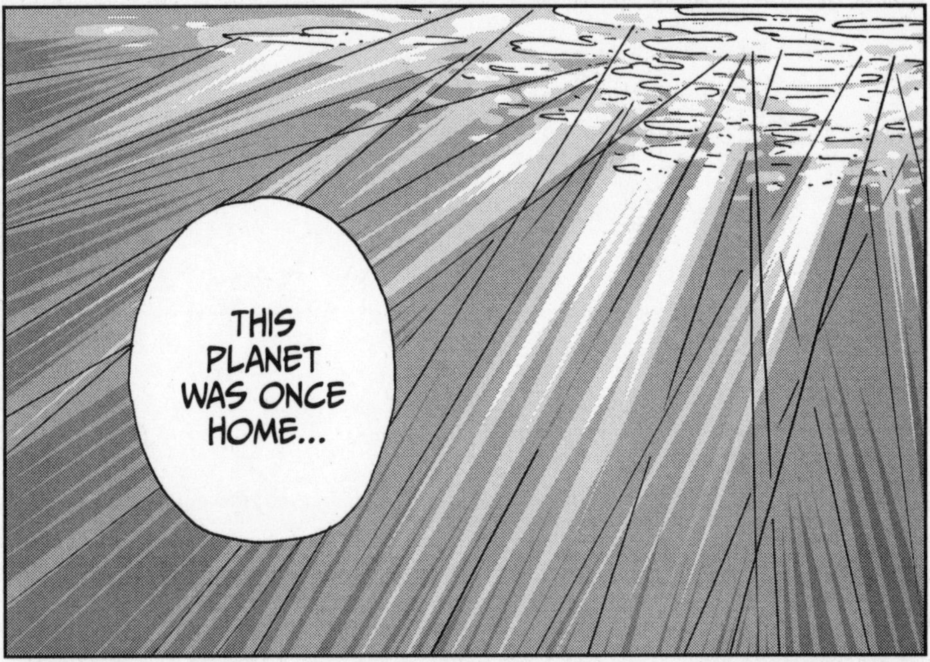
THIS PLANET WAS ONCE HOME...

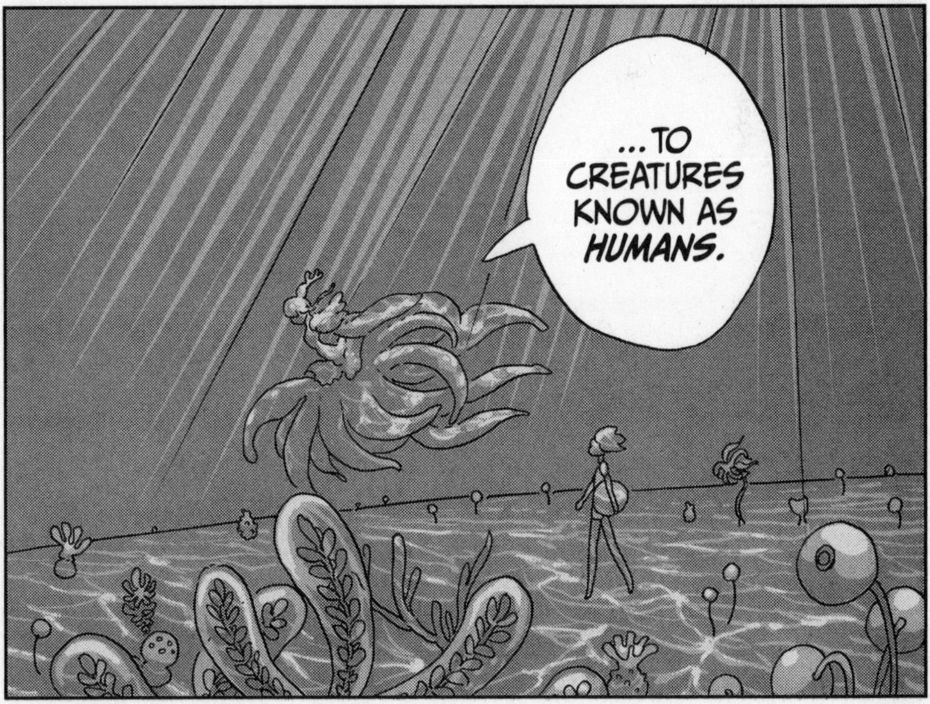
...TO CREATURES KNOWN AS *HUMANS.*

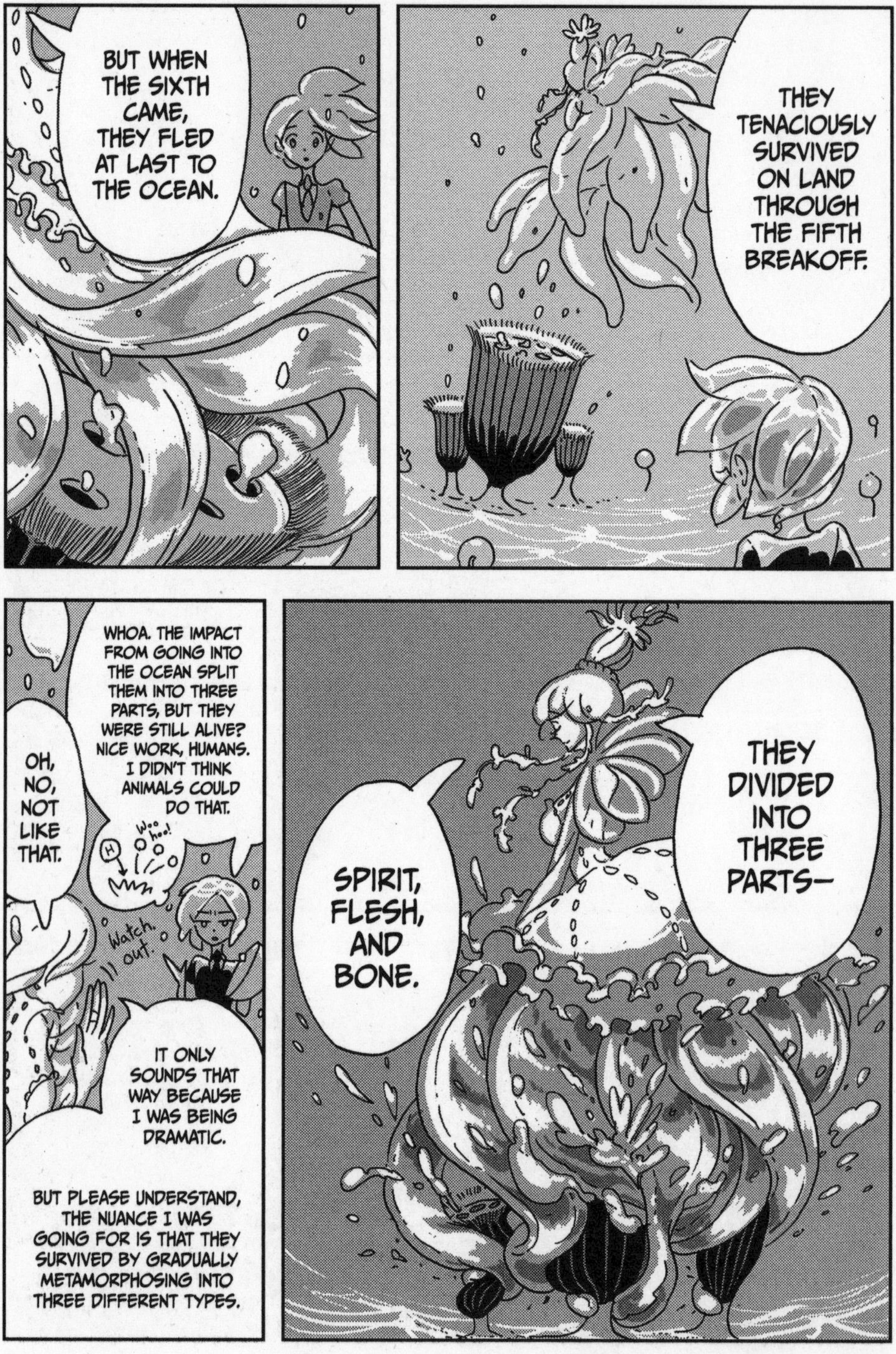
THEY TENACIOUSLY SURVIVED ON LAND THROUGH THE FIFTH BREAKOFF.
BUT WHEN THE SIXTH CAME, THEY FLED AT LAST TO THE OCEAN.
THEY DIVIDED INTO THREE PARTS—
SPIRIT, FLESH, AND BONE.
WHOA. THE IMPACT FROM GOING INTO THE OCEAN SPLIT THEM INTO THREE PARTS, BUT THEY WERE STILL ALIVE? NICE WORK, HUMANS. I DIDN'T THINK ANIMALS COULD DO THAT.
Woo hoo!
H
OH, NO, NOT LIKE THAT.
Watch. out.
IT ONLY SOUNDS THAT WAY BECAUSE I WAS BEING DRAMATIC.
BUT PLEASE UNDERSTAND, THE NUANCE I WAS GOING FOR IS THAT THEY SURVIVED BY GRADUALLY METAMORPHOSING INTO THREE DIFFERENT TYPES.

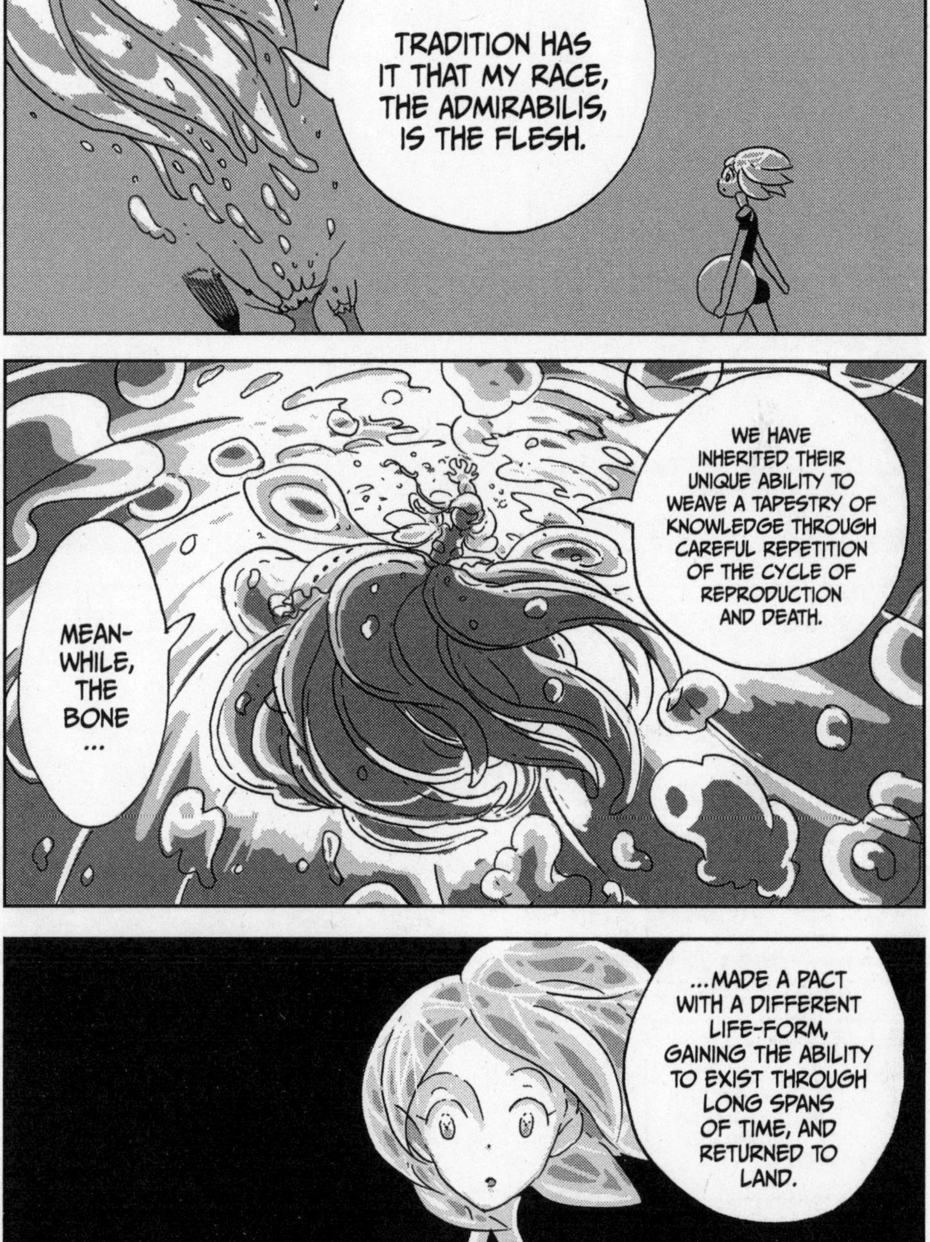
TRADITION HAS IT THAT MY RACE, THE ADMIRABILIS, IS THE FLESH.
WE HAVE INHERITED THEIR UNIQUE ABILITY TO WEAVE A TAPESTRY OF KNOWLEDGE THROUGH CAREFUL REPETITION OF THE CYCLE OF REPRODUCTION AND DEATH.
MEAN-WHILE, THE BONE ...
...MADE A PACT WITH A DIFFERENT LIFE-FORM, GAINING THE ABILITY TO EXIST THROUGH LONG SPANS OF TIME, AND RETURNED TO LAND.

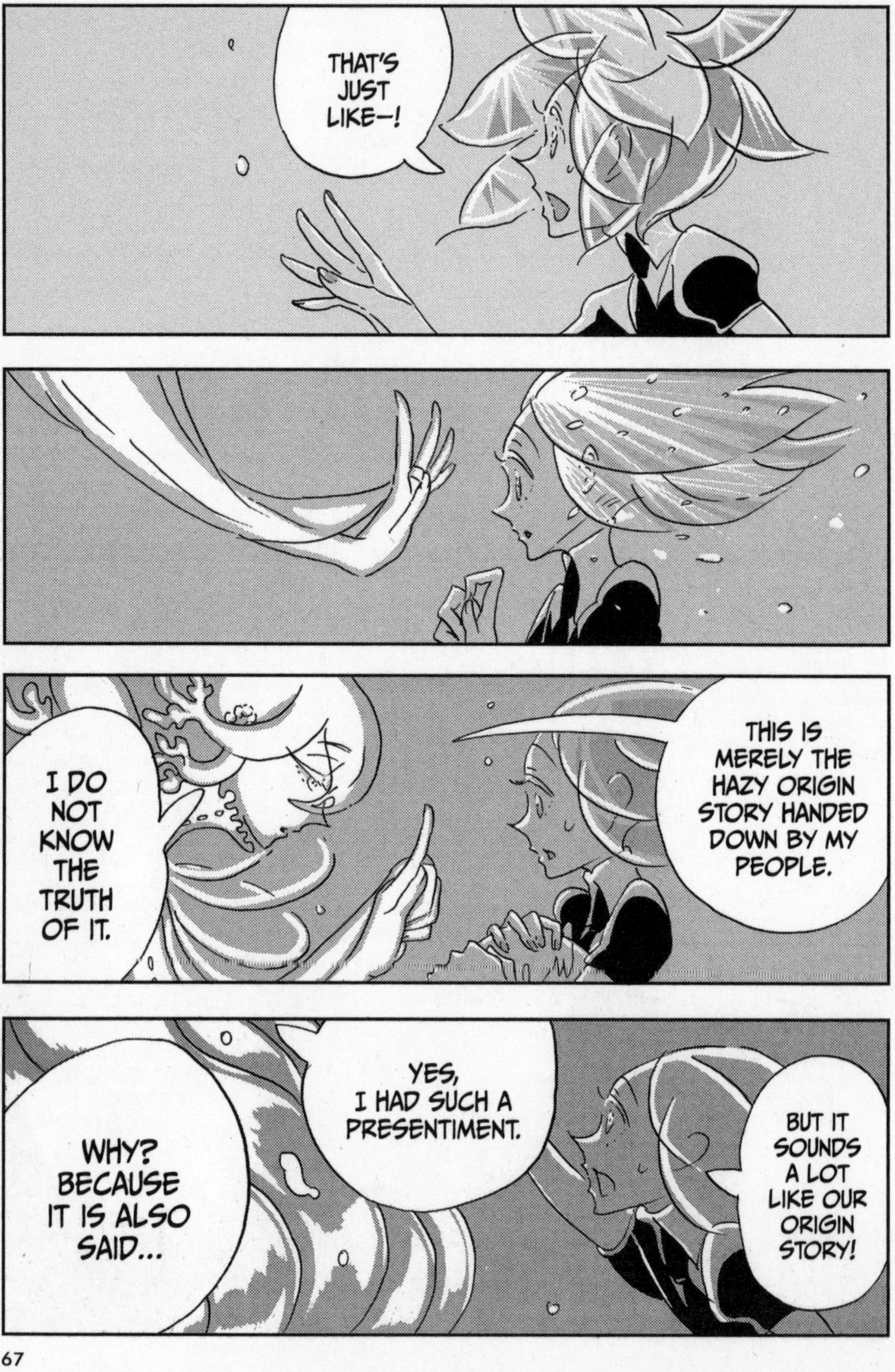
THAT'S JUST LIKE–!
THIS IS MERELY THE HAZY ORIGIN STORY HANDED DOWN BY MY PEOPLE.
I DO NOT KNOW THE TRUTH OF IT.
BUT IT SOUNDS A LOT LIKE OUR ORIGIN STORY!
YES, I HAD SUCH A PRESENTIMENT.
WHY? BECAUSE IT IS ALSO SAID...

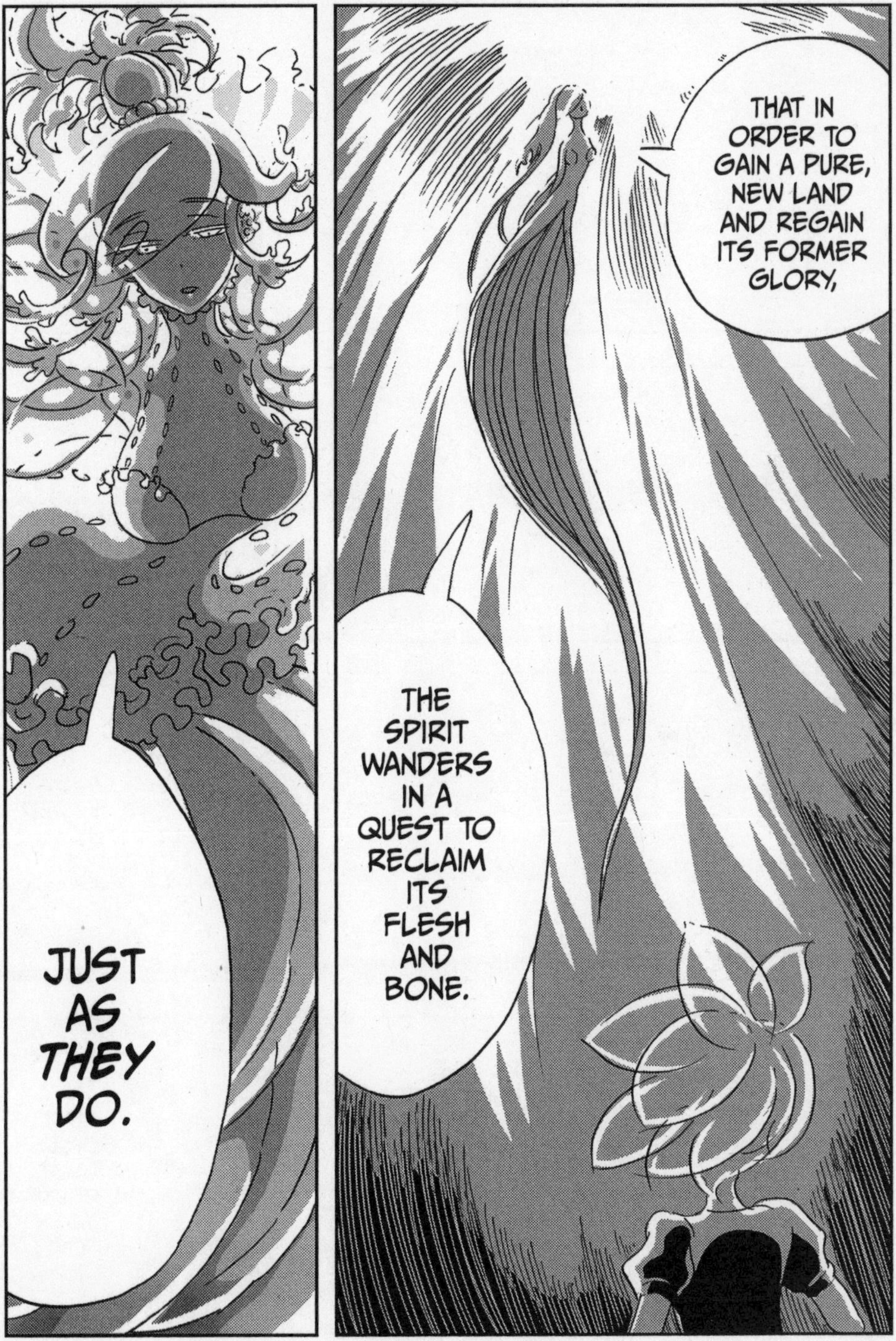
THAT IN ORDER TO GAIN A PURE, NEW LAND AND REGAIN ITS FORMER GLORY,
THE SPIRIT WANDERS IN A QUEST TO RECLAIM ITS FLESH AND BONE.
JUST AS THEY DO.

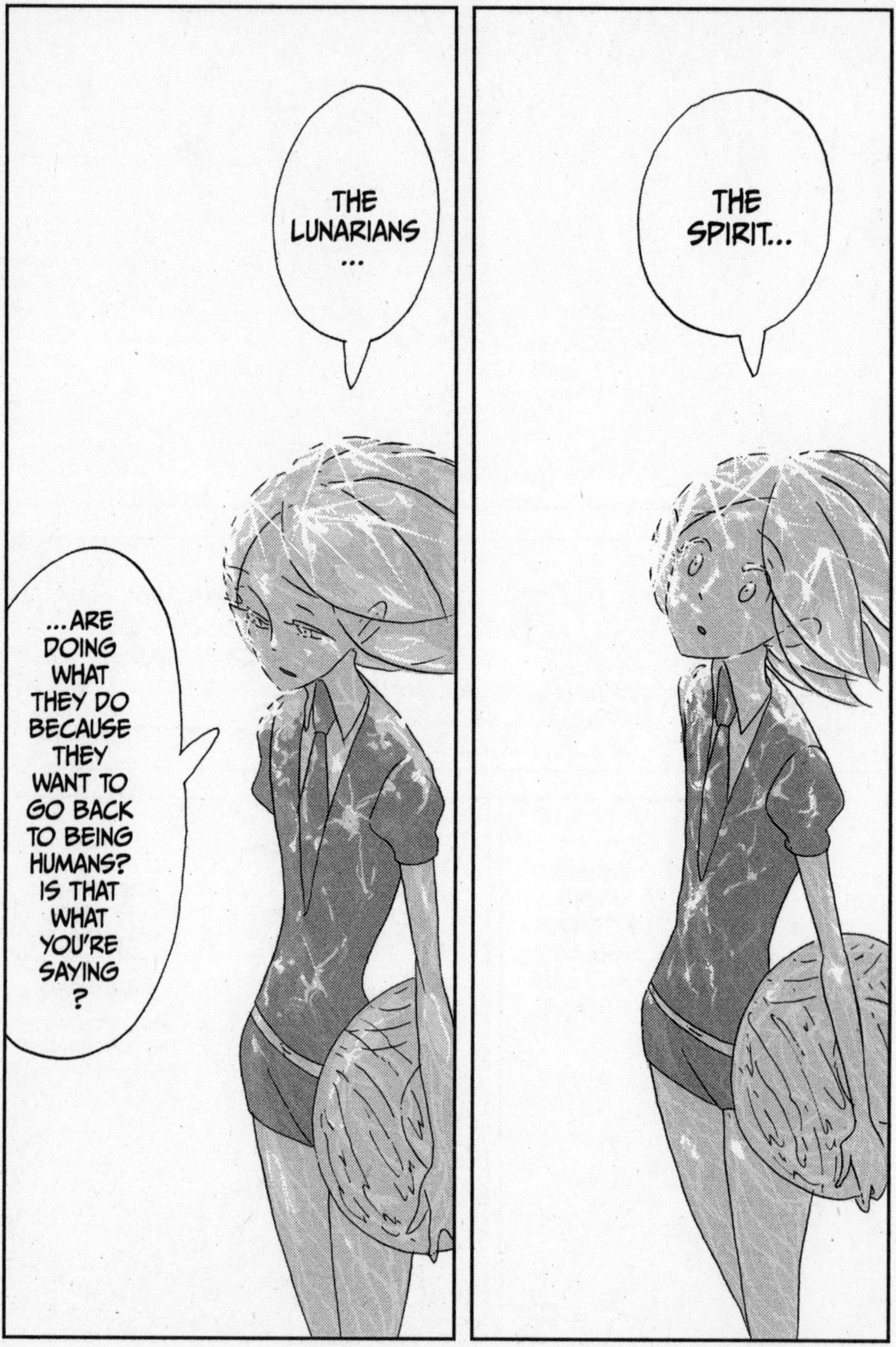
THE SPIRIT...
THE LUNARIANS ...
...ARE DOING WHAT THEY DO BECAUSE THEY WANT TO GO BACK TO BEING HUMANS? IS THAT WHAT YOU'RE SAYING ?

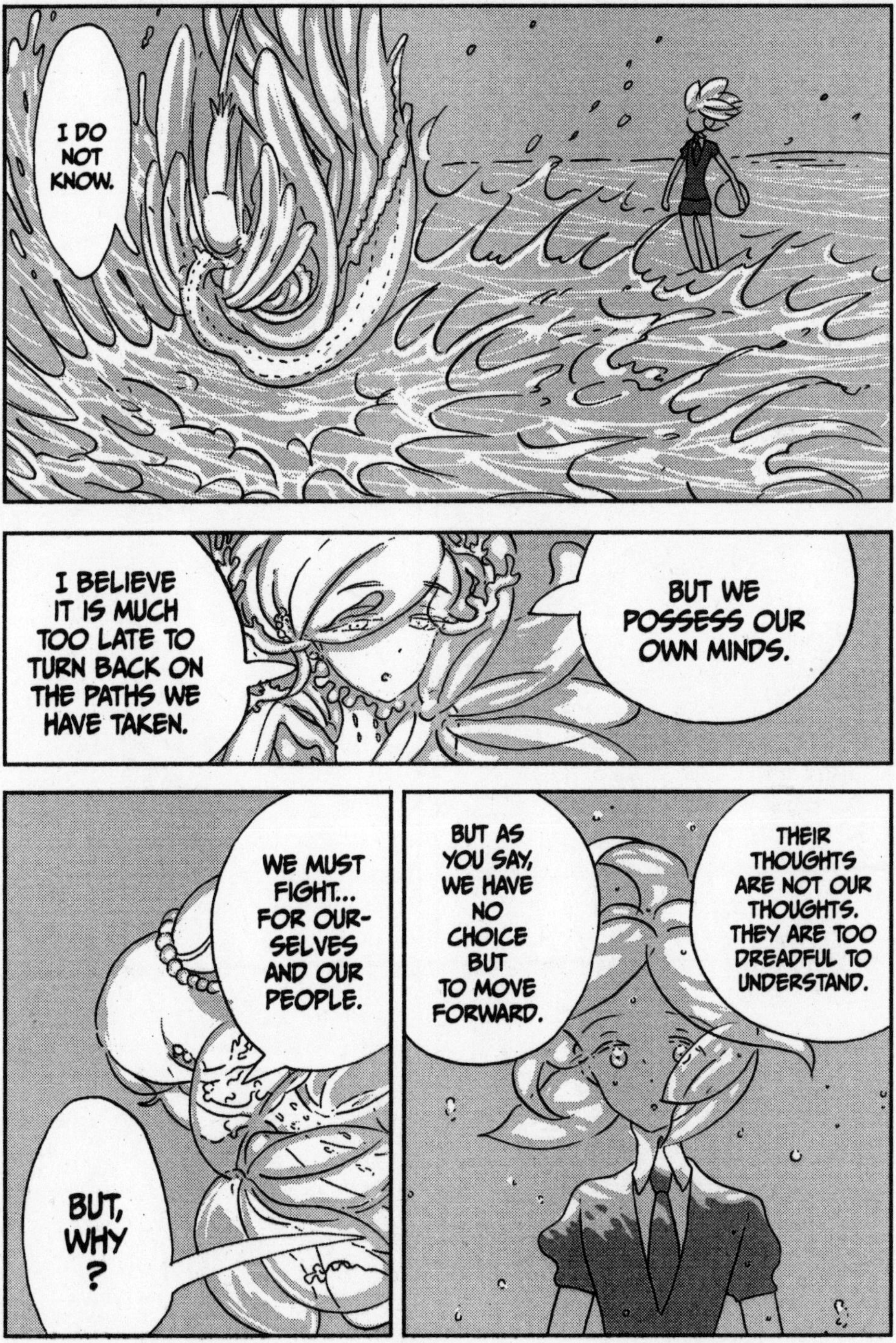
I DO NOT KNOW.
BUT WE POSSESS OUR OWN MINDS.
I BELIEVE IT IS MUCH TOO LATE TO TURN BACK ON THE PATHS WE HAVE TAKEN.
THEIR THOUGHTS ARE NOT OUR THOUGHTS. THEY ARE TOO DREADFUL TO UNDERSTAND.
BUT AS YOU SAY, WE HAVE NO CHOICE BUT TO MOVE FORWARD.
WE MUST FIGHT... FOR OUR-SELVES AND OUR PEOPLE.
BUT, WHY ?

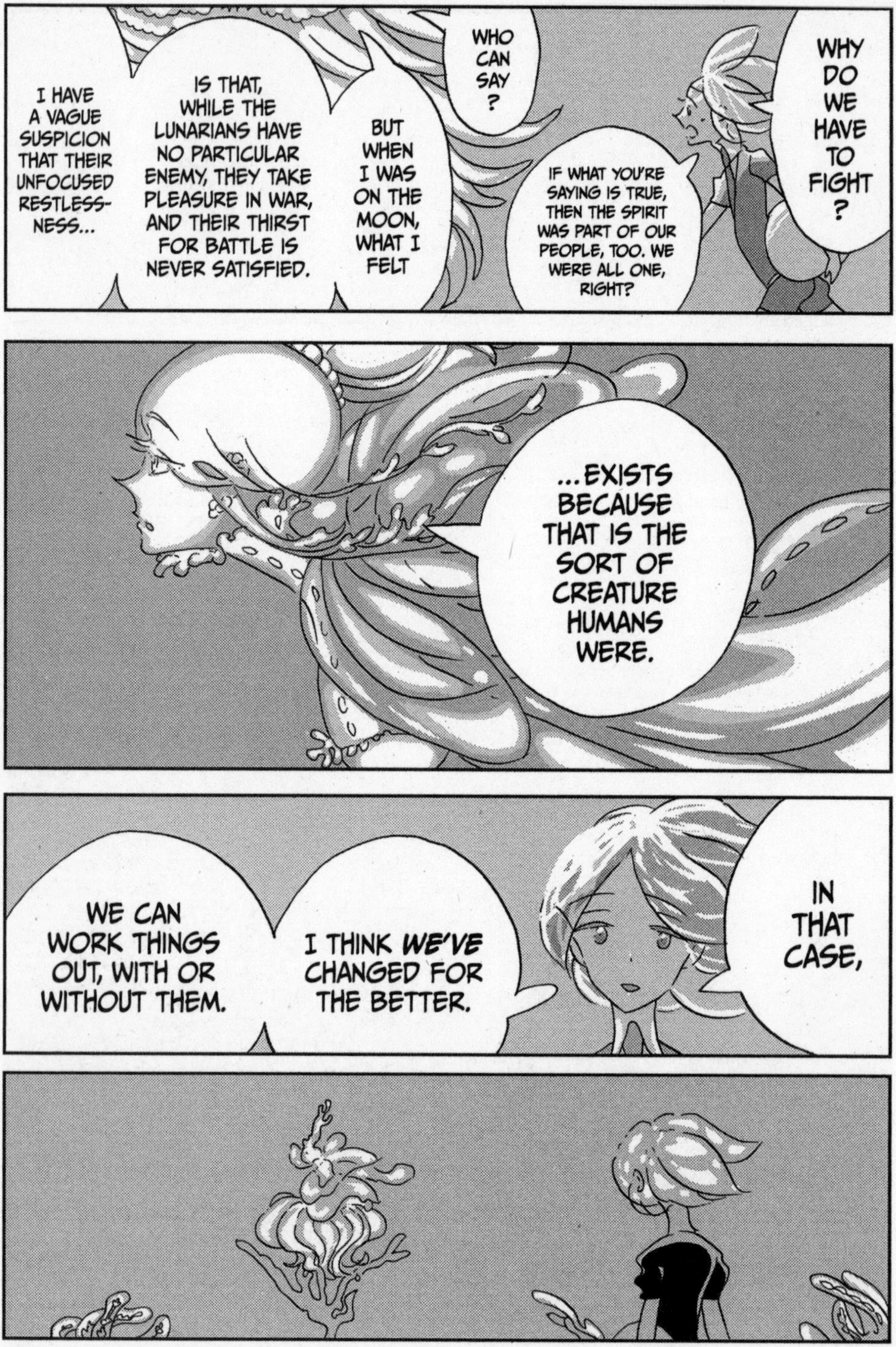
WHY DO WE HAVE TO FIGHT?
IF WHAT YOU'RE SAYING IS TRUE, THEN THE SPIRIT WAS PART OF OUR PEOPLE, TOO. WE WERE ALL ONE, RIGHT?
WHO CAN SAY?
BUT WHEN I WAS ON THE MOON, WHAT I FELT
IS THAT, WHILE THE LUNARIANS HAVE NO PARTICULAR ENEMY, THEY TAKE PLEASURE IN WAR, AND THEIR THIRST FOR BATTLE IS NEVER SATISFIED.
I HAVE A VAGUE SUSPICION THAT THEIR UNFOCUSED RESTLESS-NESS...
...EXISTS BECAUSE THAT IS THE SORT OF CREATURE HUMANS WERE.
IN THAT CASE,
I THINK *WE'VE* CHANGED FOR THE BETTER.
WE CAN WORK THINGS OUT, WITH OR WITHOUT THEM.

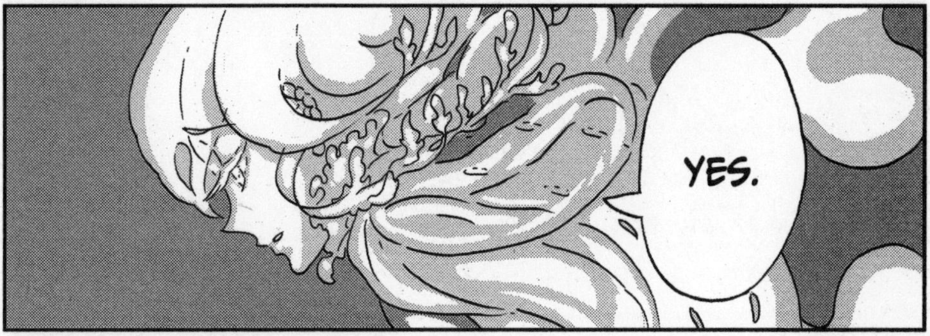
YES.

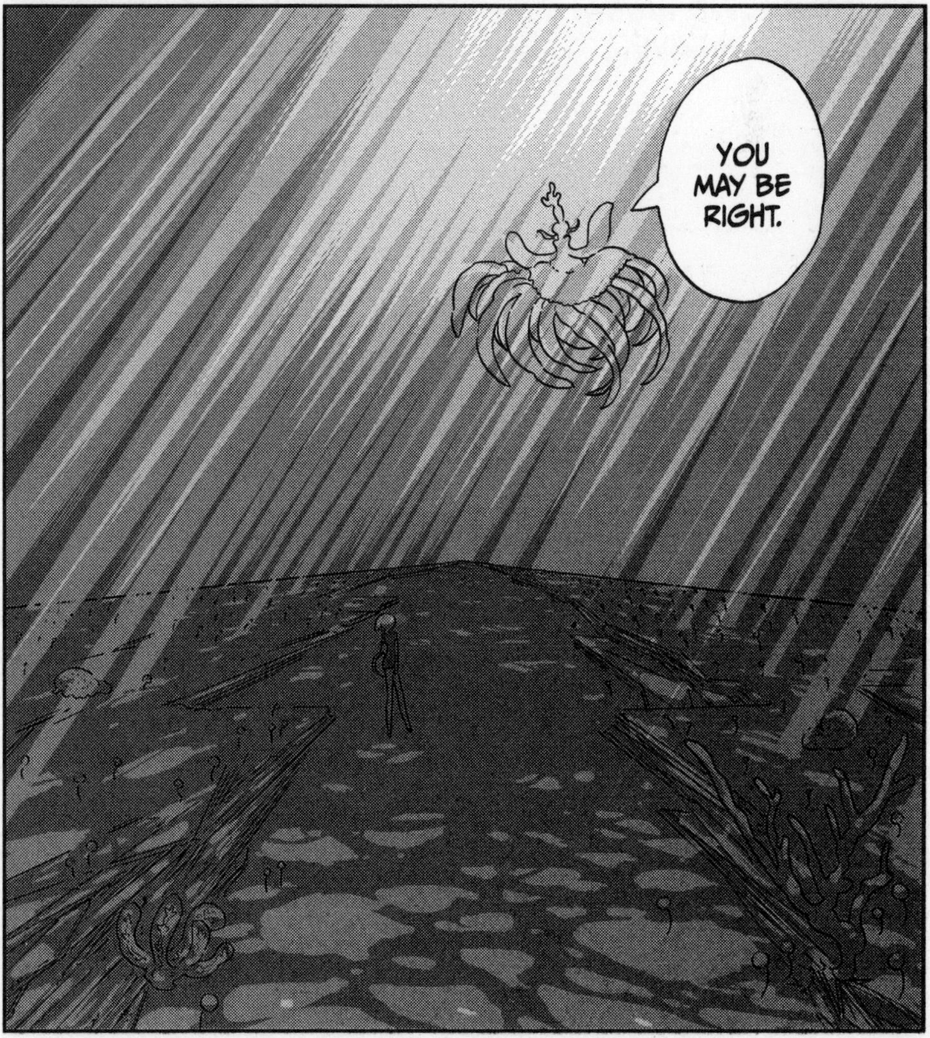
YOU MAY BE RIGHT.

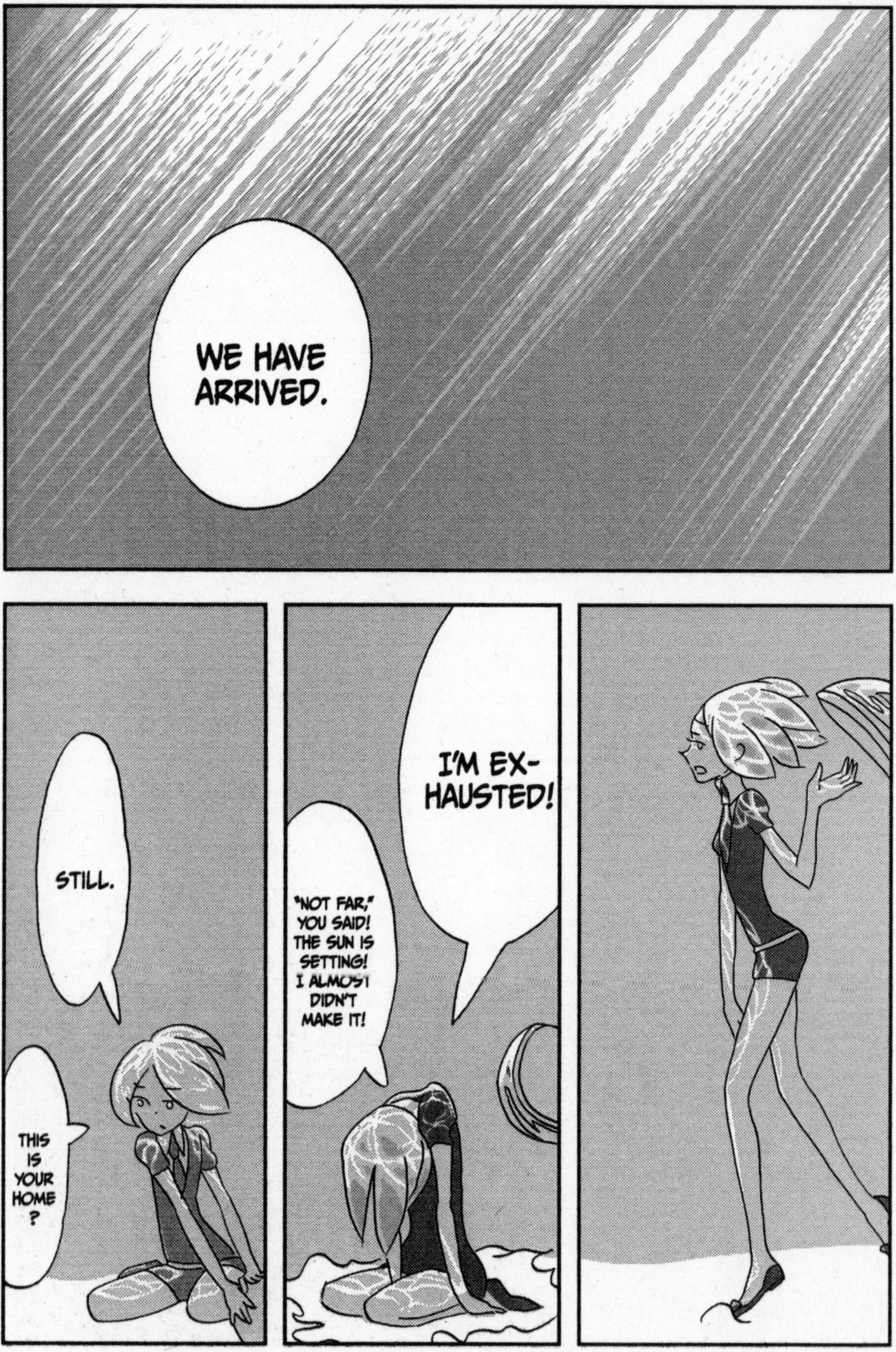
WE HAVE ARRIVED.
I'M EX-HAUSTED!
"NOT FAR," YOU SAID! THE SUN IS SETTING! I ALMOST DIDN'T MAKE IT!
STILL.
THIS IS YOUR HOME?

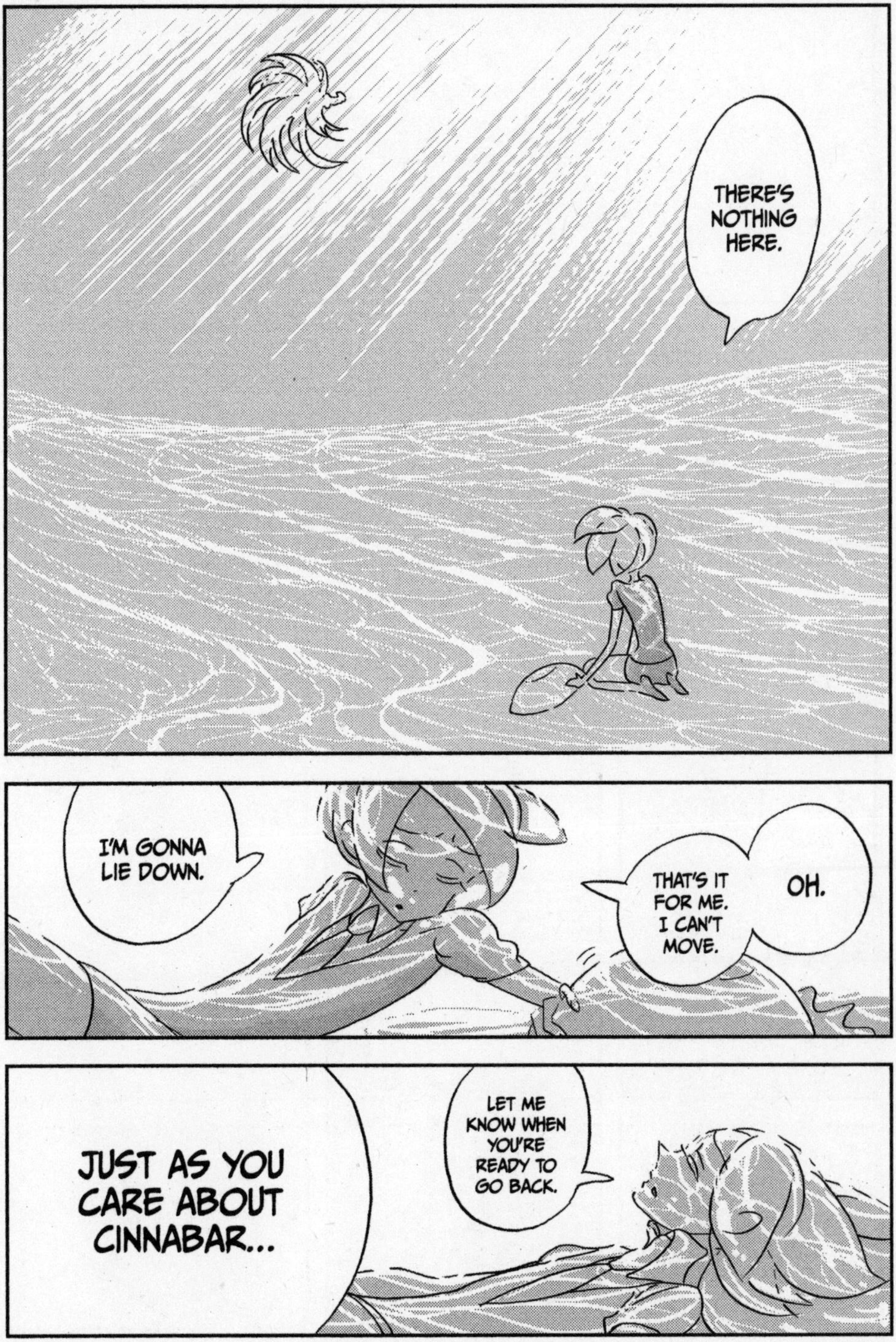
THERE'S NOTHING HERE.
OH.
THAT'S IT FOR ME. I CAN'T MOVE.
I'M GONNA LIE DOWN.
LET ME KNOW WHEN YOU'RE READY TO GO BACK.
JUST AS YOU CARE ABOUT CINNABAR...

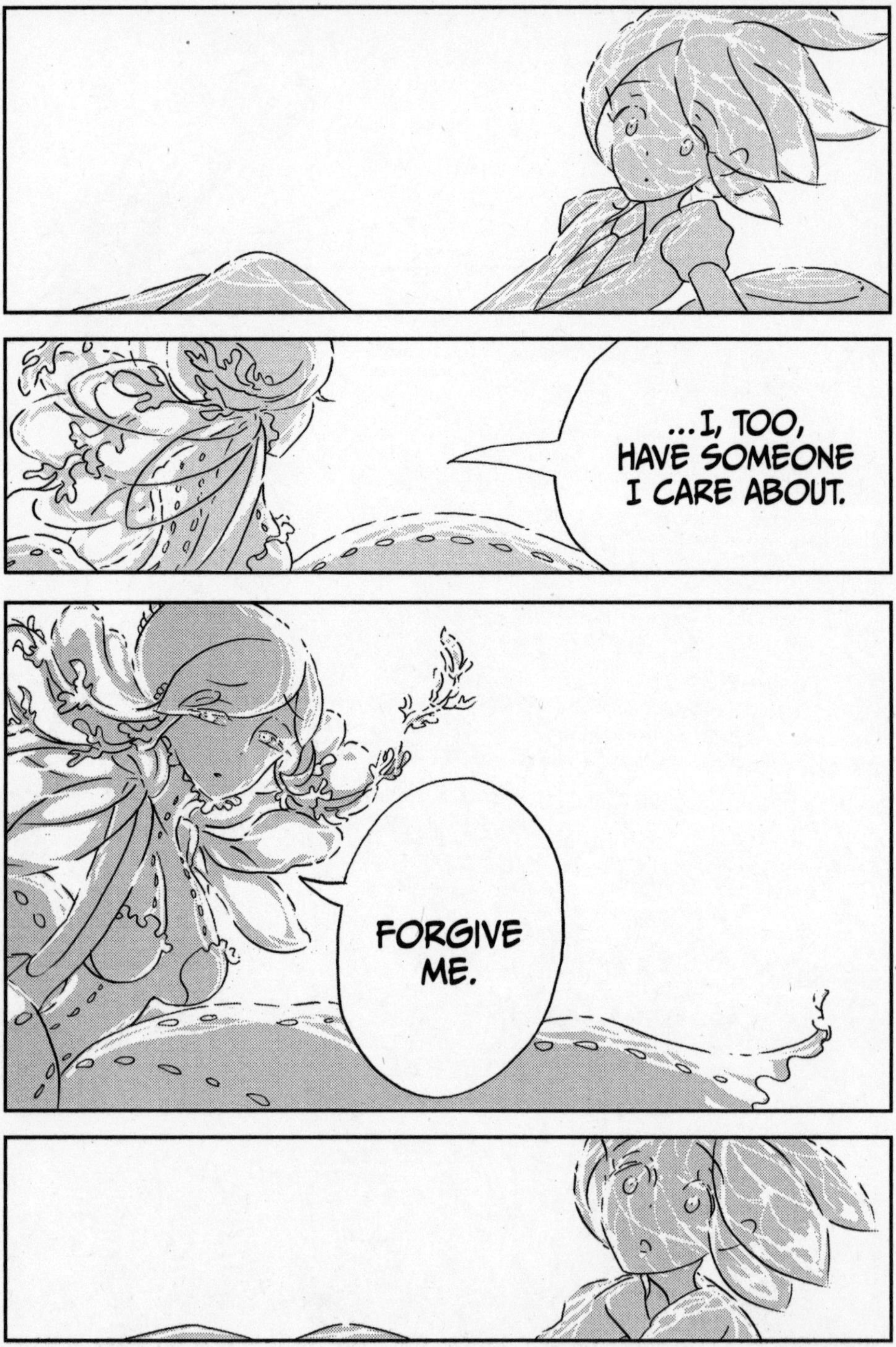
...I, TOO, HAVE SOMEONE I CARE ABOUT.
FORGIVE ME.

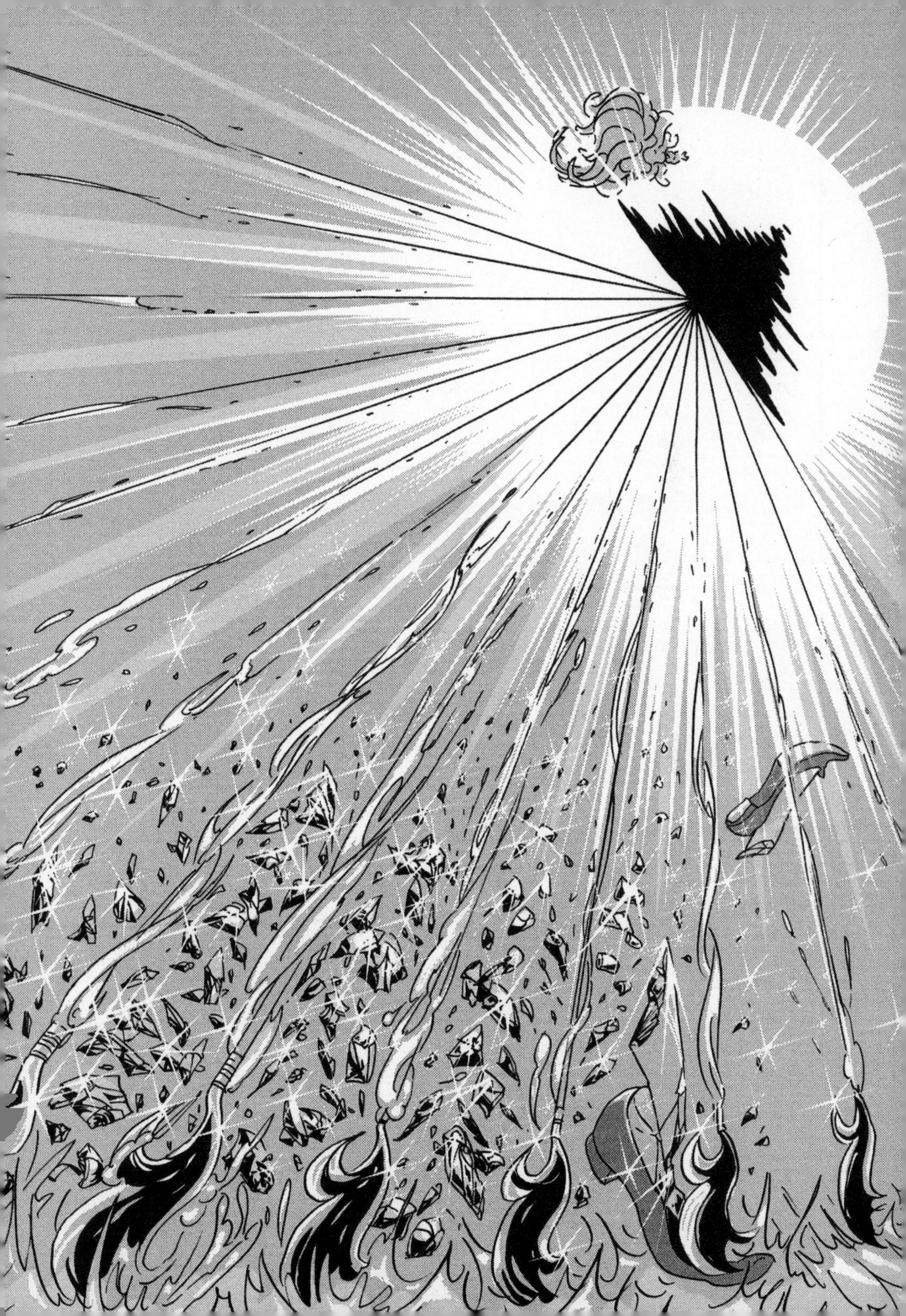

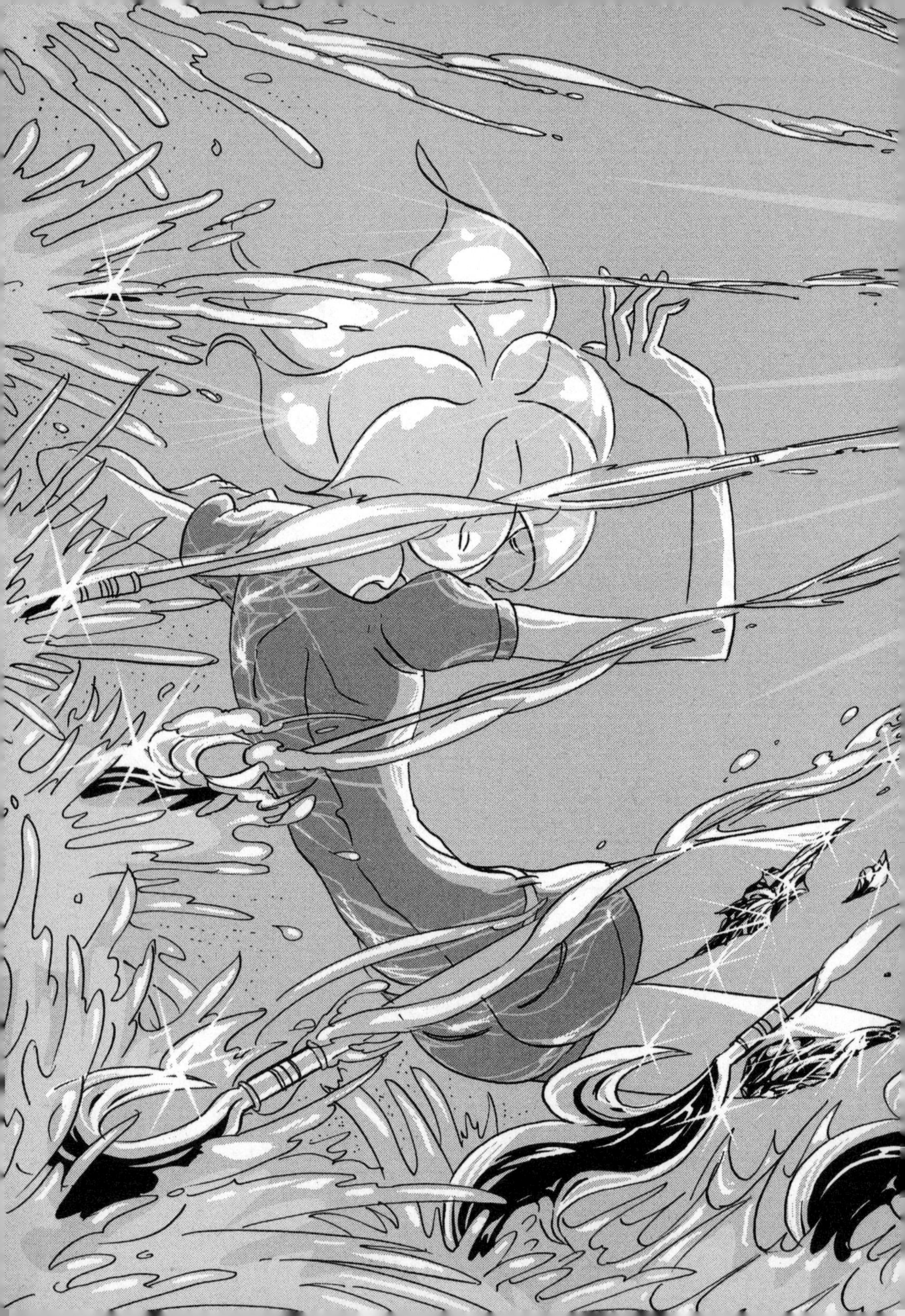

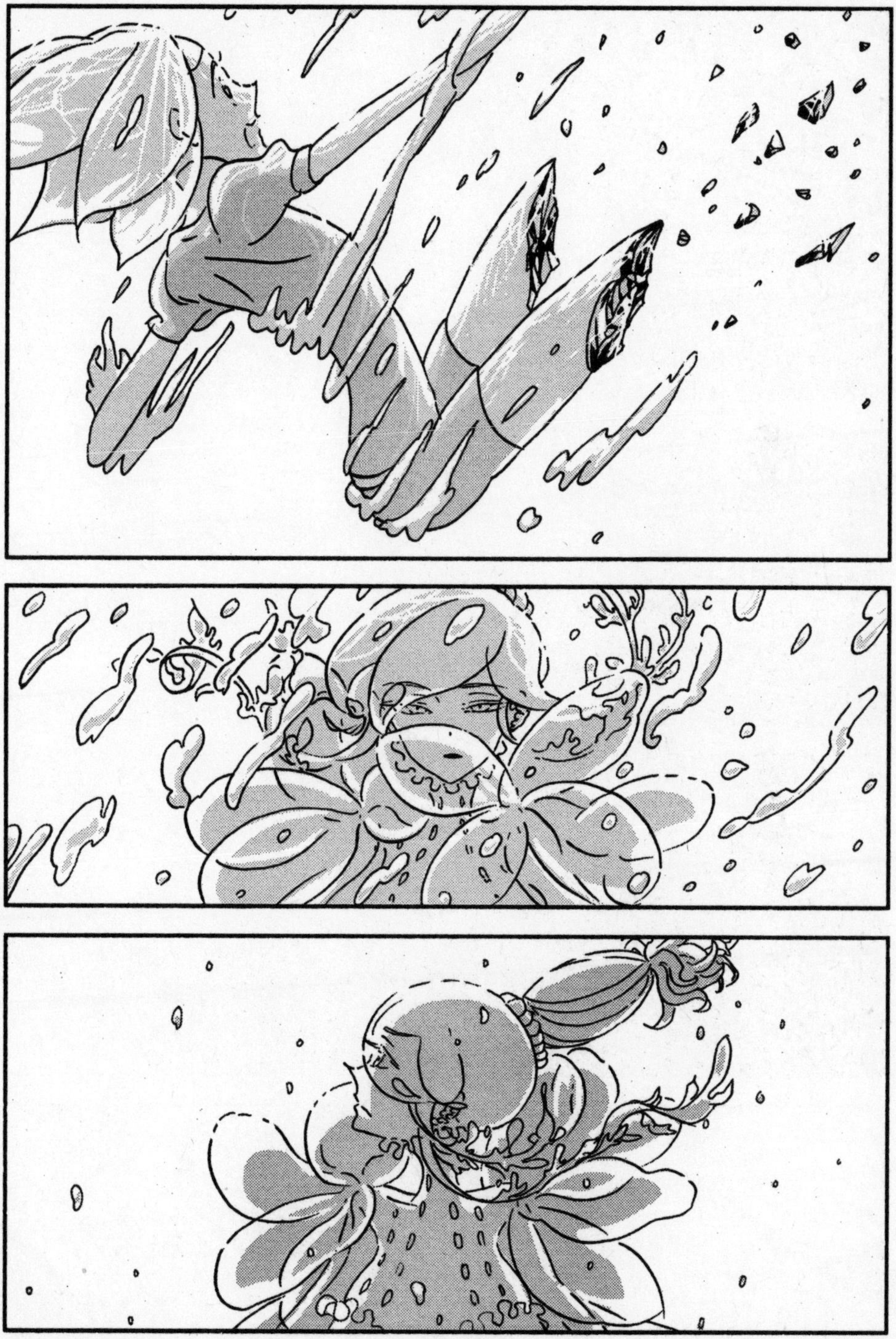

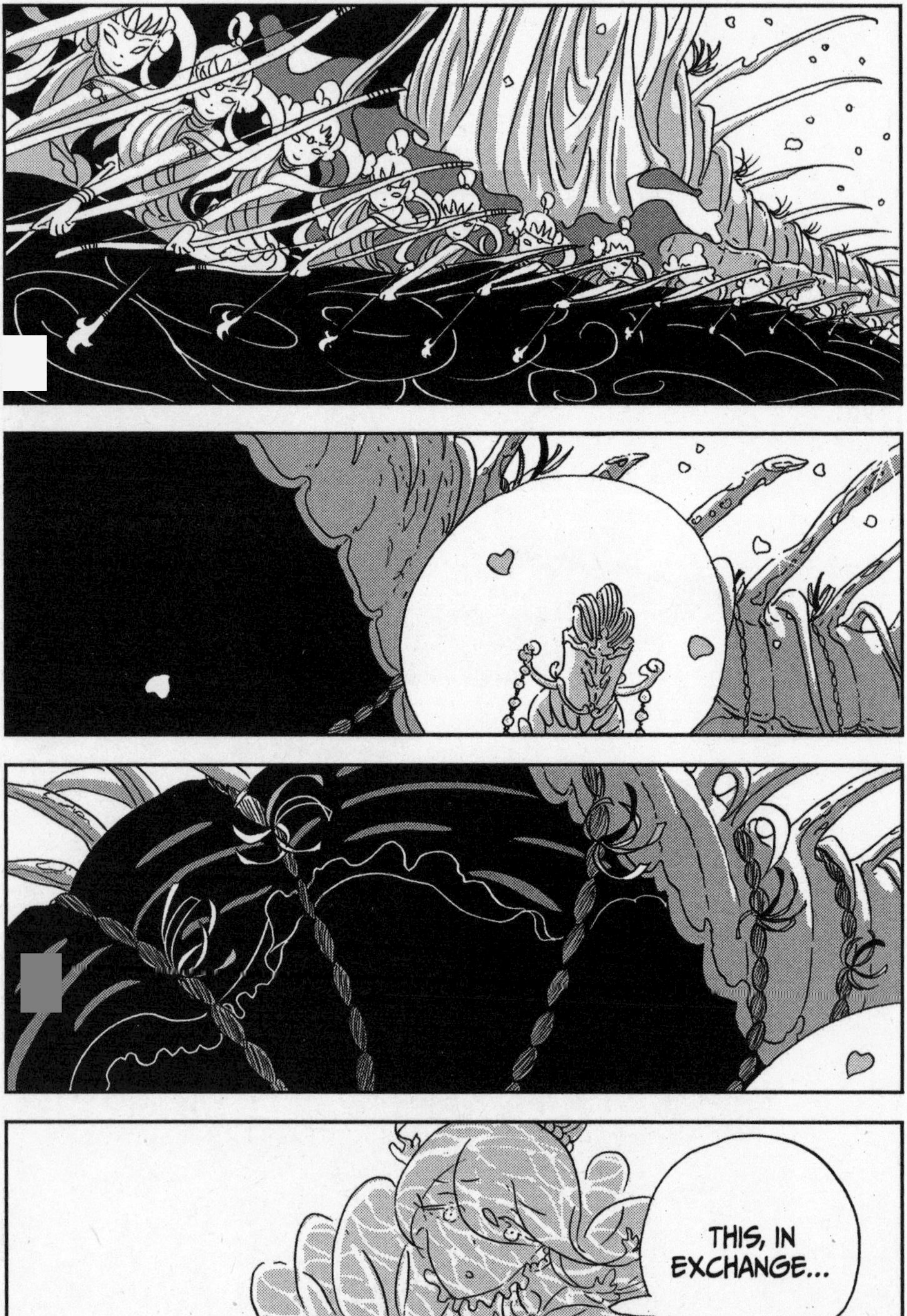
THIS, IN EXCHANGE...

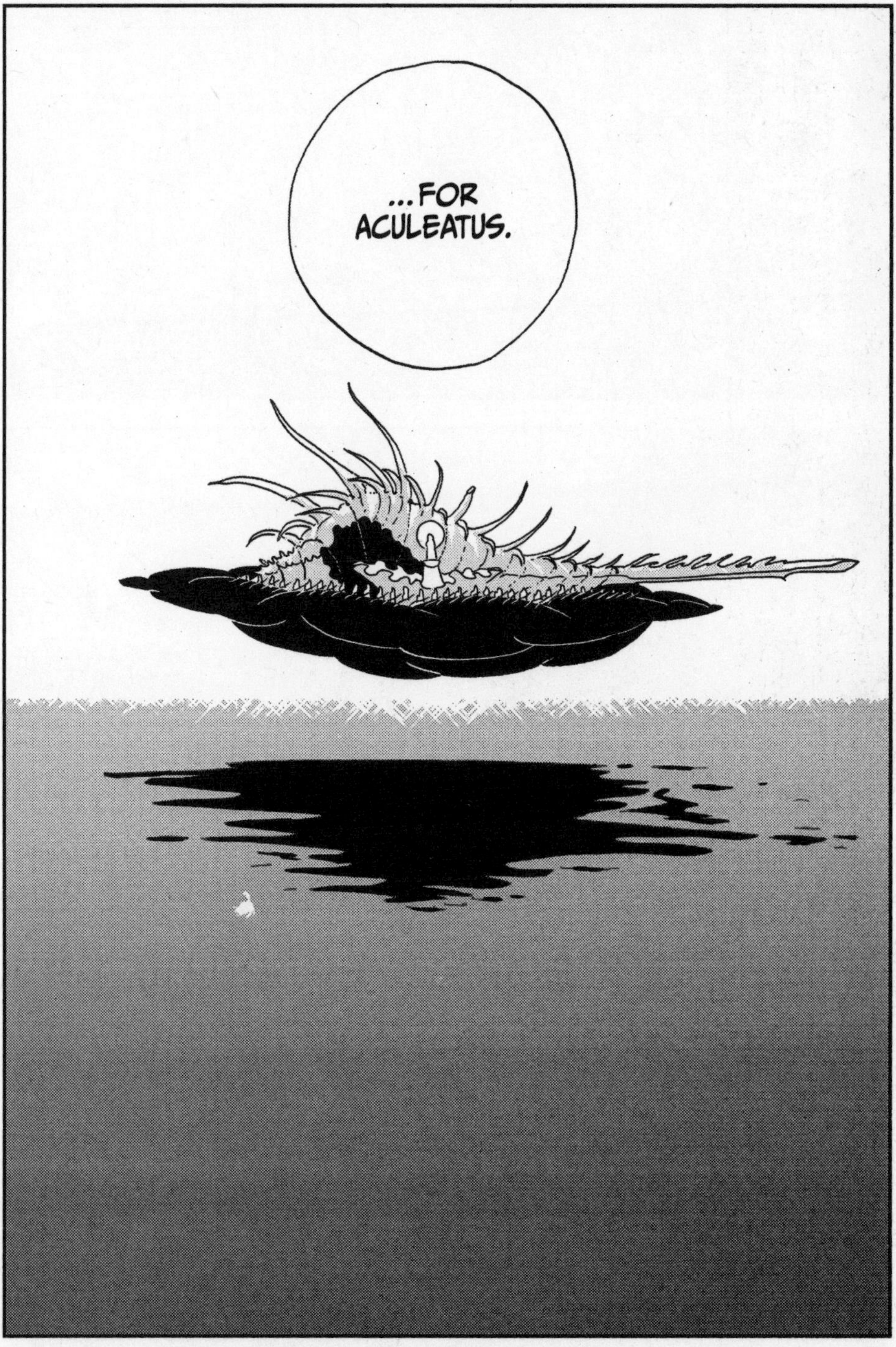
...FOR ACULEATUS.

CHAPTER 9: Spirit, Flesh, Bone END

CHAPTER 10:

Homecoming

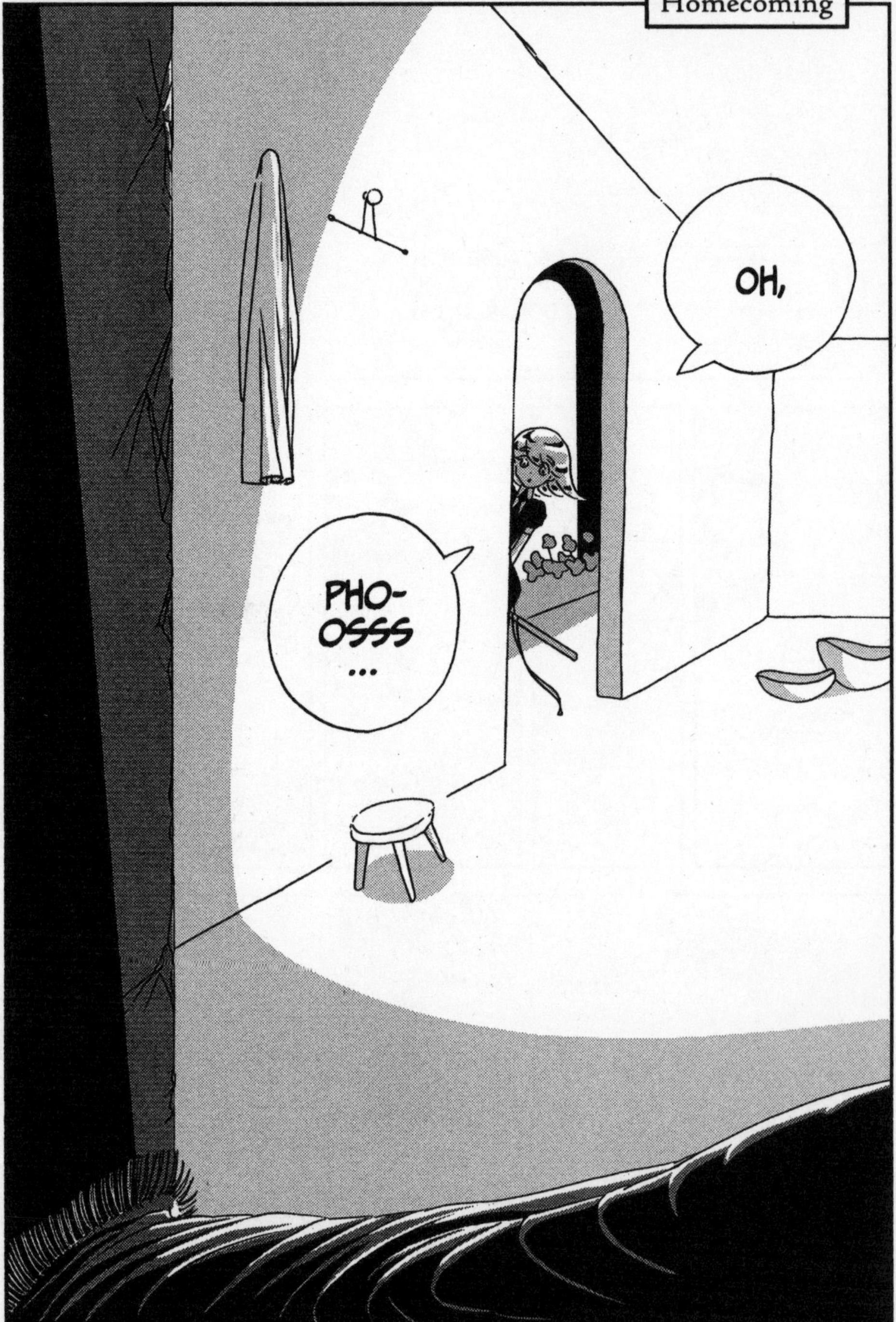
OH,
PHO-OSSS...

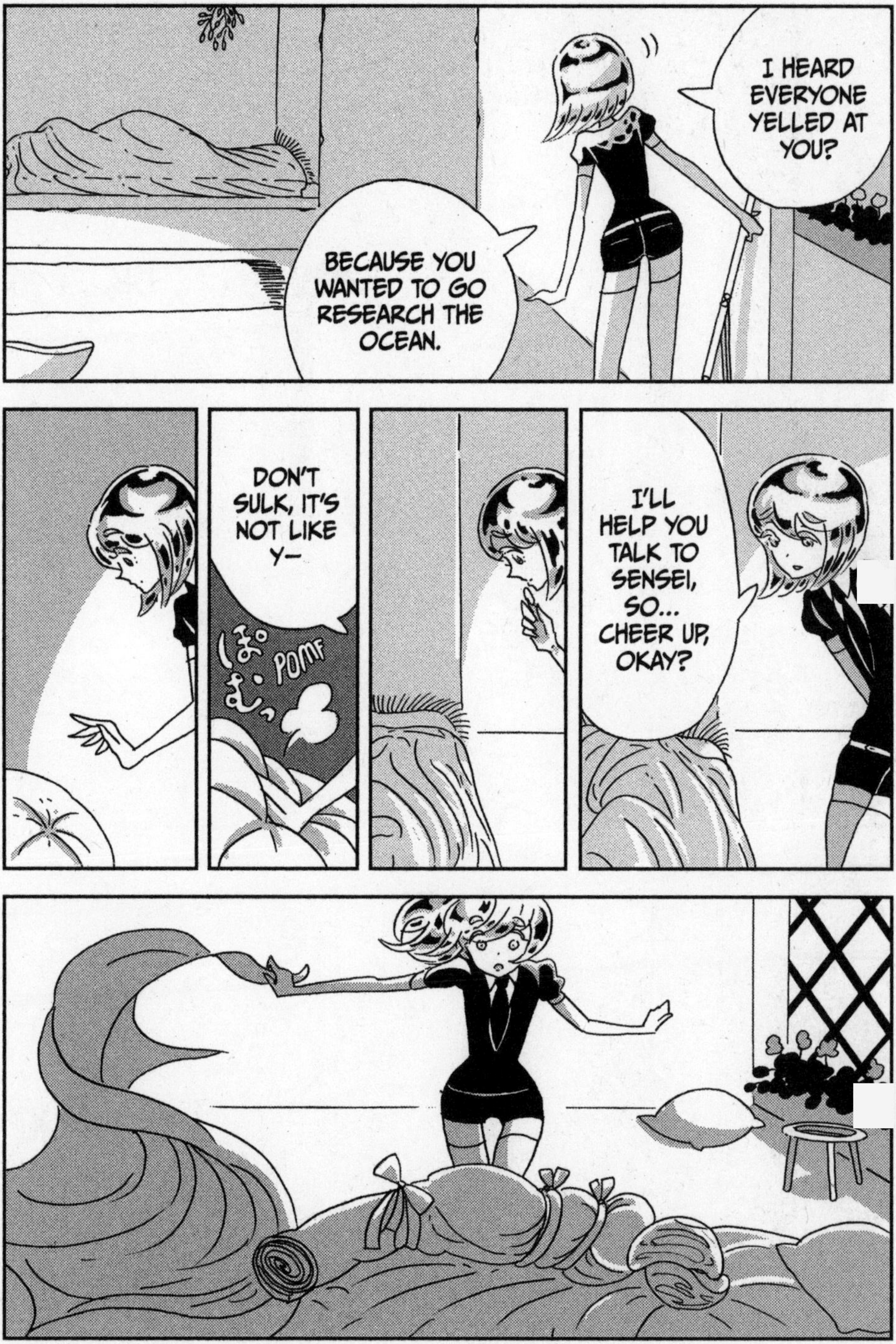
I HEARD EVERYONE YELLED AT YOU?
BECAUSE YOU WANTED TO GO RESEARCH THE OCEAN.
I'LL HELP YOU TALK TO SENSEI, SO... CHEER UP, OKAY?
DON'T SULK, IT'S NOT LIKE Y—
ぽむっ
POMF

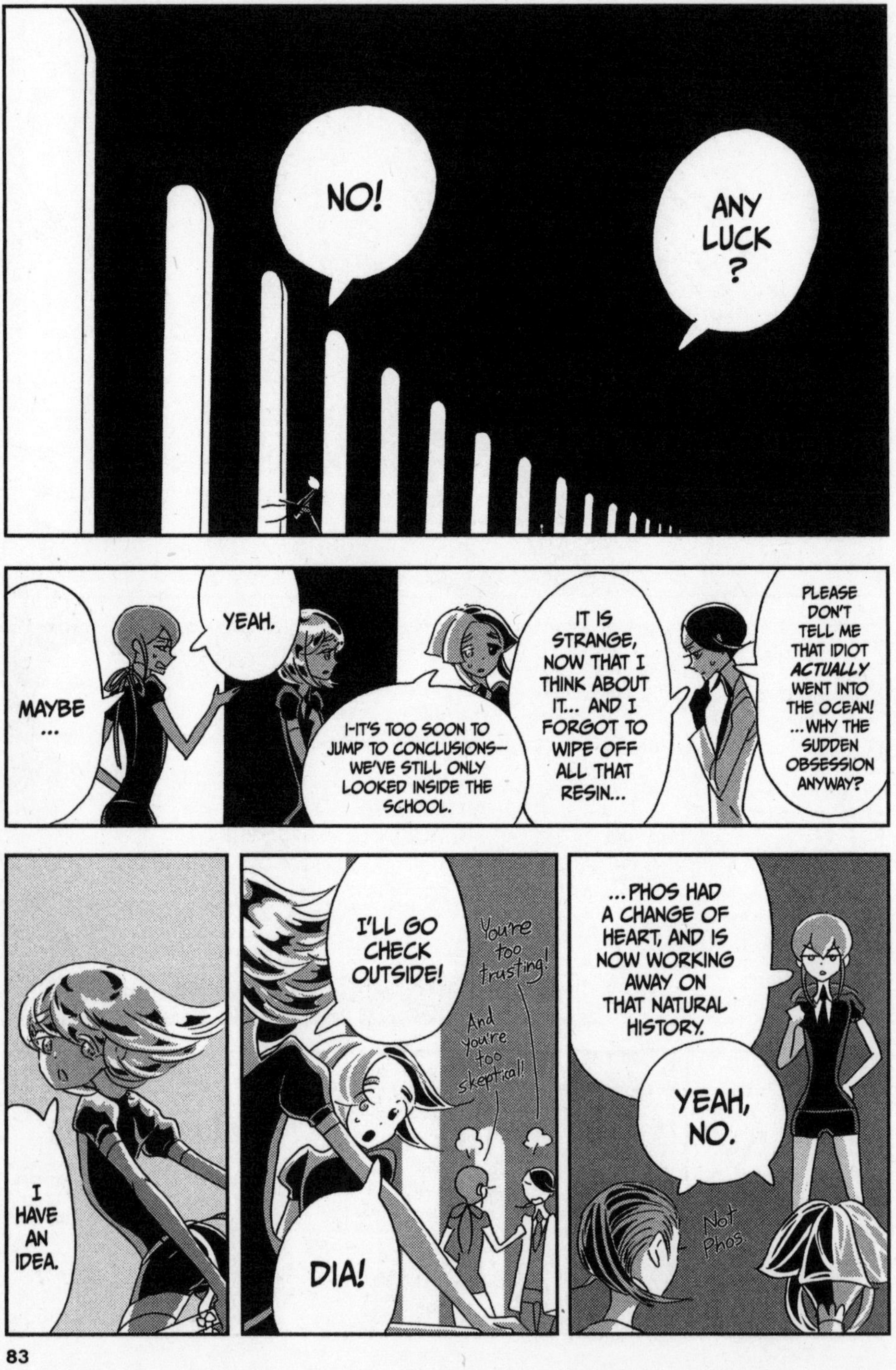
ANY LUCK ?
NO!
PLEASE DON'T TELL ME THAT IDIOT ACTUALLY WENT INTO THE OCEAN! ...WHY THE SUDDEN OBSESSION ANYWAY?
IT IS STRANGE, NOW THAT I THINK ABOUT IT... AND I FORGOT TO WIPE OFF ALL THAT RESIN...
I-IT'S TOO SOON TO JUMP TO CONCLUSIONS— WE'VE STILL ONLY LOOKED INSIDE THE SCHOOL.
YEAH.
MAYBE ...
...PHOS HAD A CHANGE OF HEART, AND IS NOW WORKING AWAY ON THAT NATURAL HISTORY.
YEAH, NO.
Not Phos
I'LL GO CHECK OUTSIDE!
You're too trusting!
And you're too skeptical!
DIA!
I HAVE AN IDEA.

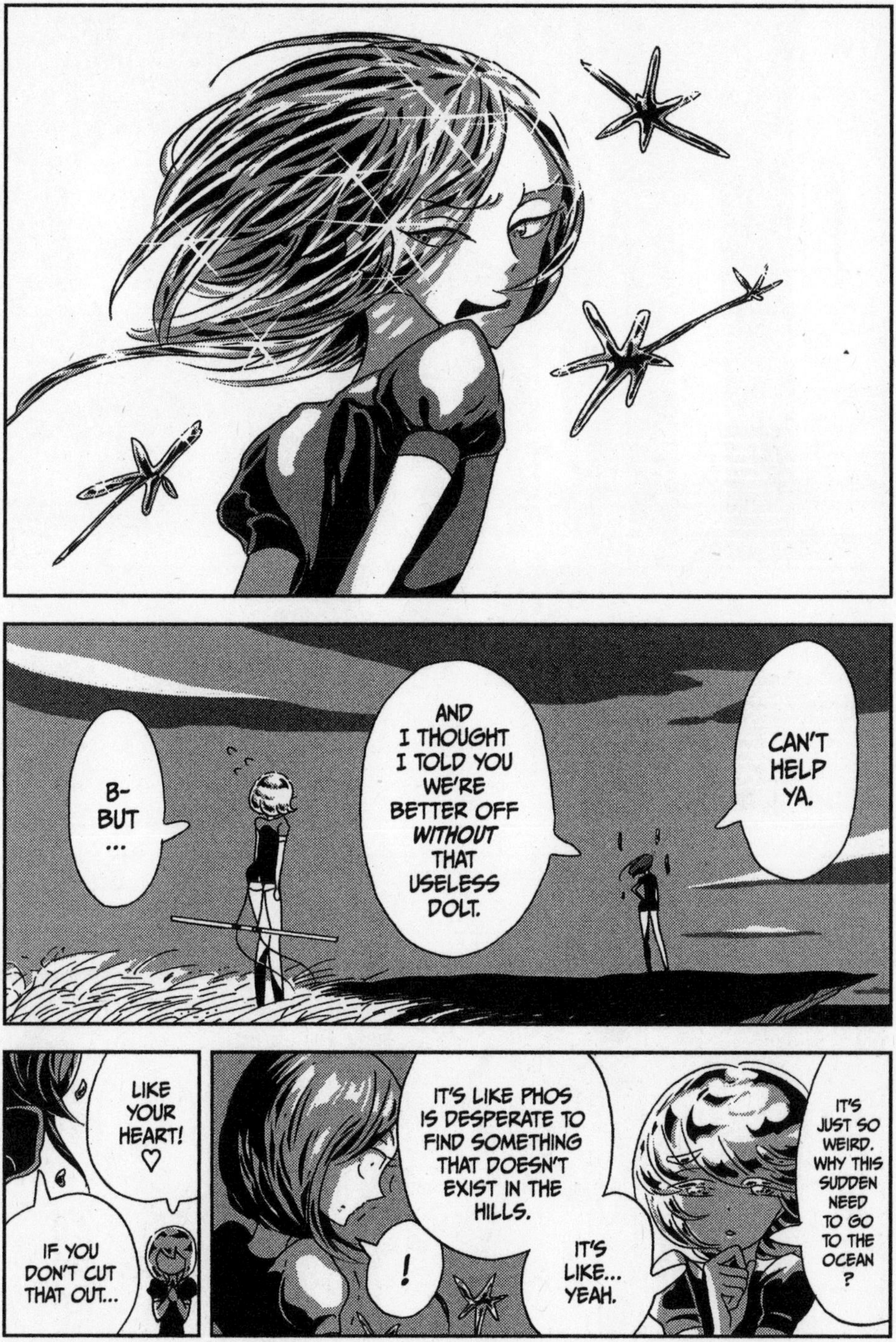
CAN'T HELP YA.
AND I THOUGHT I TOLD YOU WE'RE BETTER OFF *WITHOUT* THAT USELESS DOLT.
B-BUT ...
IT'S JUST SO WEIRD. WHY THIS SUDDEN NEED TO GO TO THE OCEAN?
IT'S LIKE PHOS IS DESPERATE TO FIND SOMETHING THAT DOESN'T EXIST IN THE HILLS.
IT'S LIKE... YEAH.
!
LIKE YOUR HEART! ♡
IF YOU DON'T CUT THAT OUT...

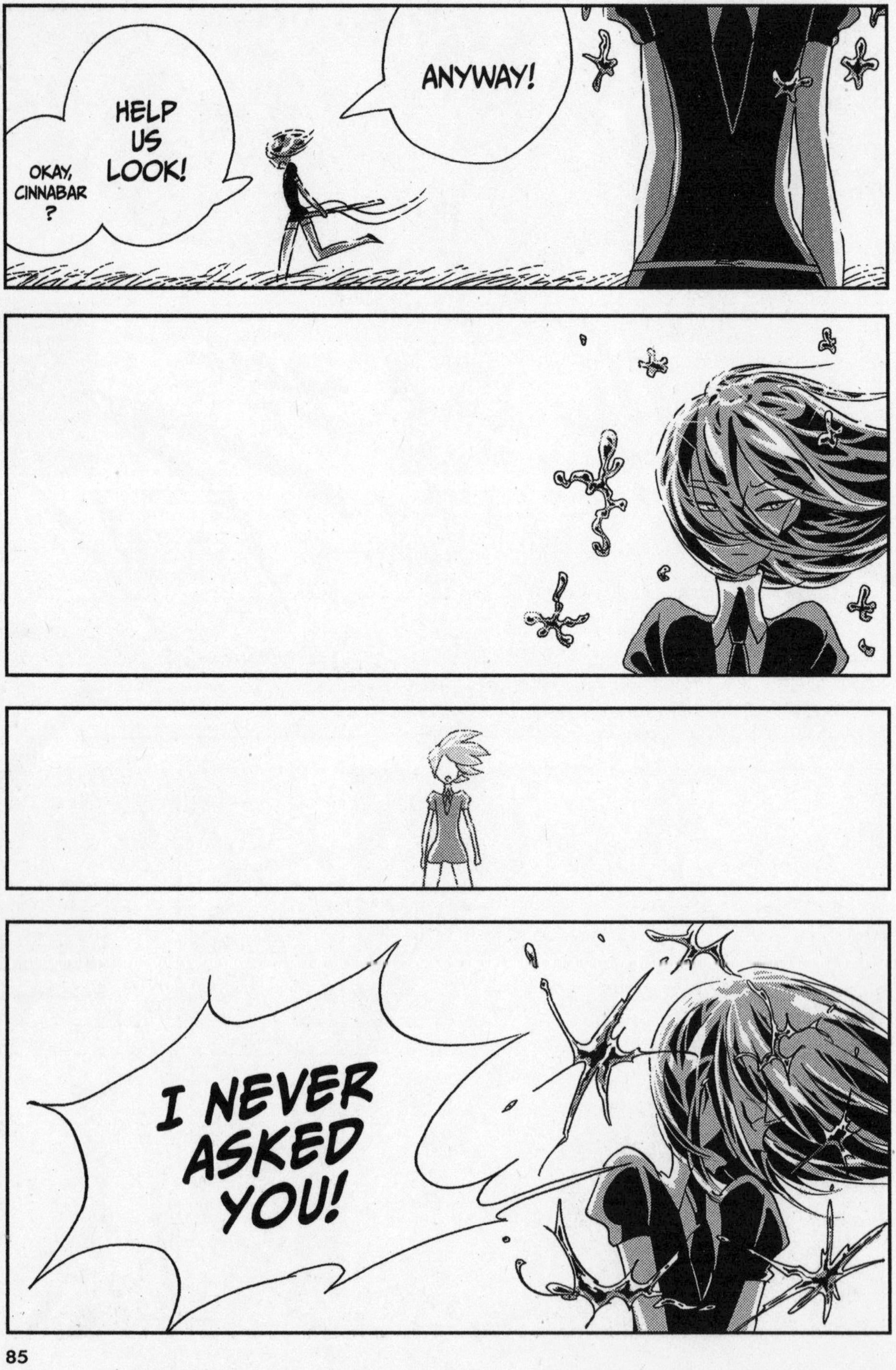

ANYWAY!
HELP US LOOK!
OKAY, CINNABAR?
I NEVER ASKED YOU!

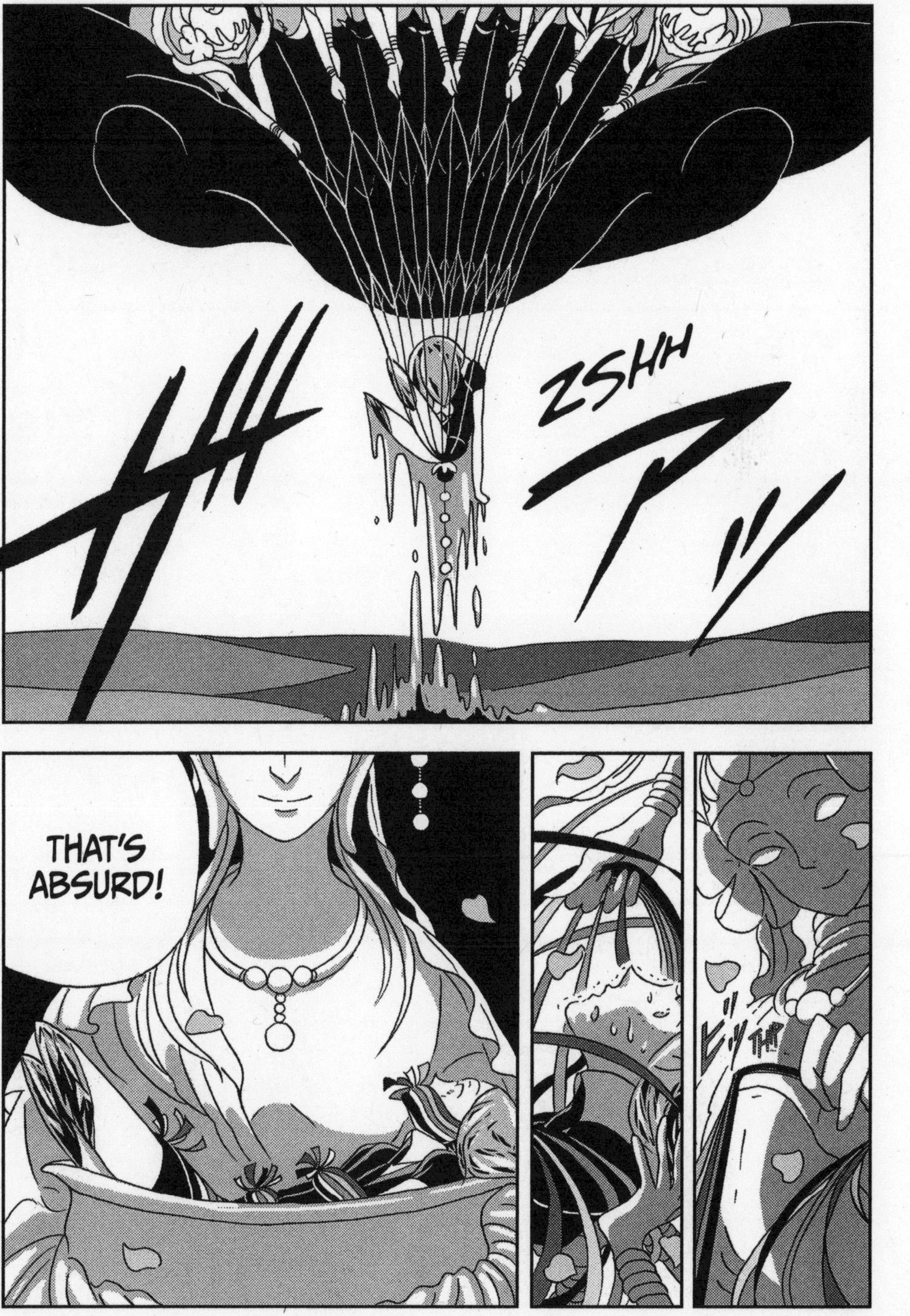
ZSHH
ザアッ
ビッ
THP
THAT'S ABSURD!

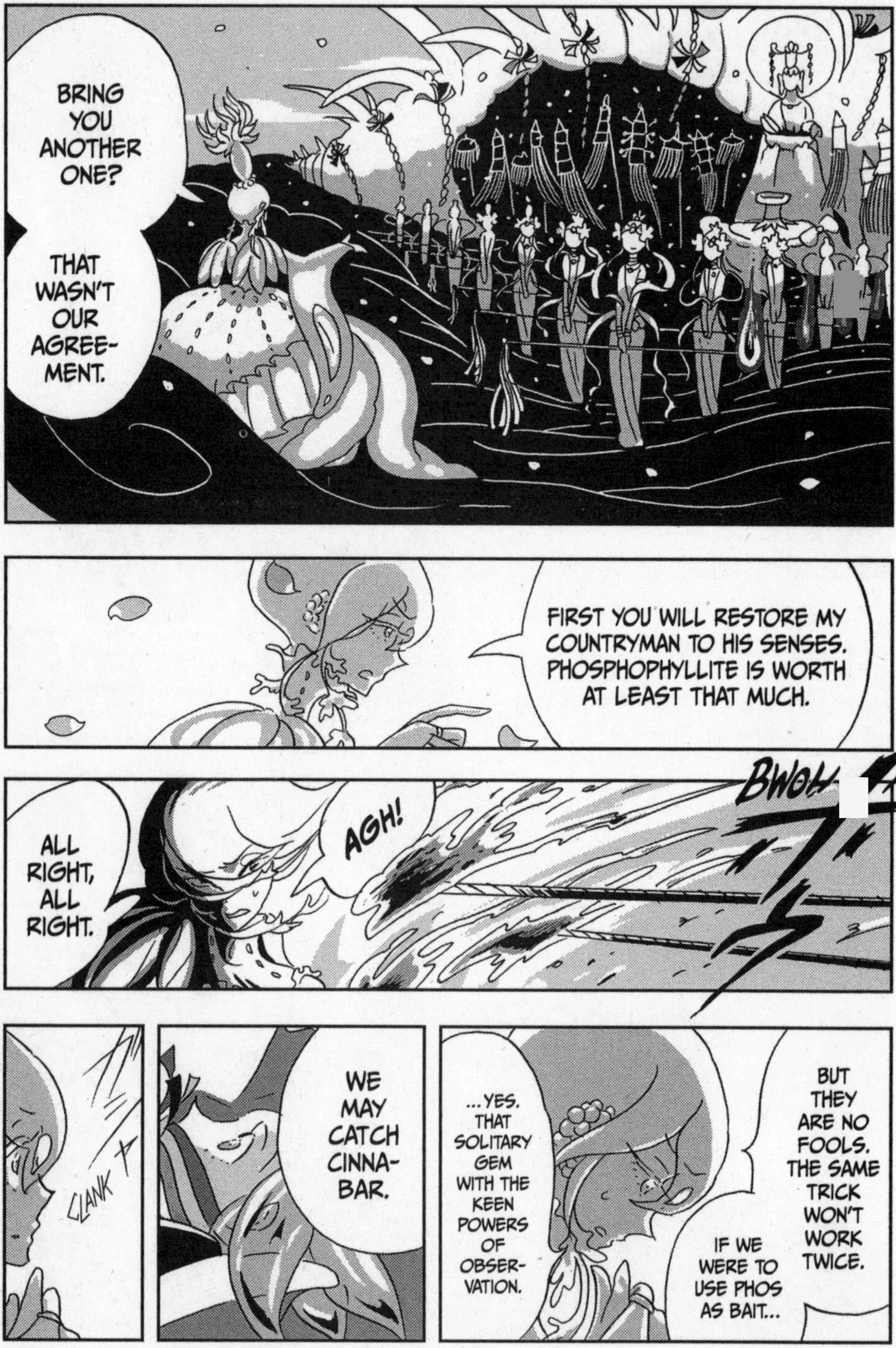
BRING YOU ANOTHER ONE?
THAT WASN'T OUR AGREE-MENT.
FIRST YOU WILL RESTORE MY COUNTRYMAN TO HIS SENSES. PHOSPHOPHYLLITE IS WORTH AT LEAST THAT MUCH.
BWOH
AGH!
ALL RIGHT, ALL RIGHT.
BUT THEY ARE NO FOOLS. THE SAME TRICK WON'T WORK TWICE.
IF WE WERE TO USE PHOS AS BAIT...
...YES. THAT SOLITARY GEM WITH THE KEEN POWERS OF OBSER-VATION.
WE MAY CATCH CINNA-BAR.
CLANK

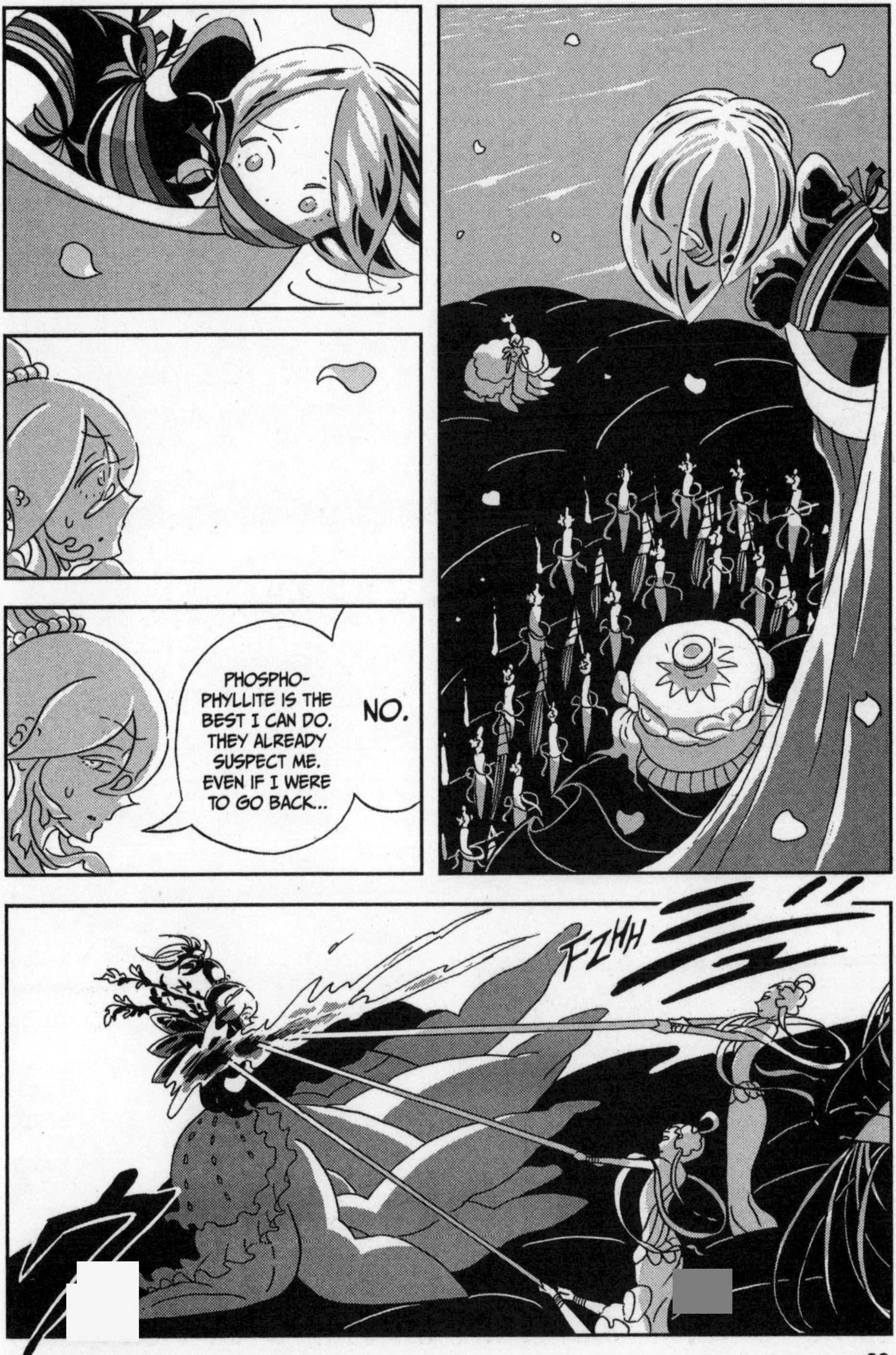
NO.
PHOSPHO-PHYLLITE IS THE BEST I CAN DO. THEY ALREADY SUSPECT ME. EVEN IF I WERE TO GO BACK...
FZHH

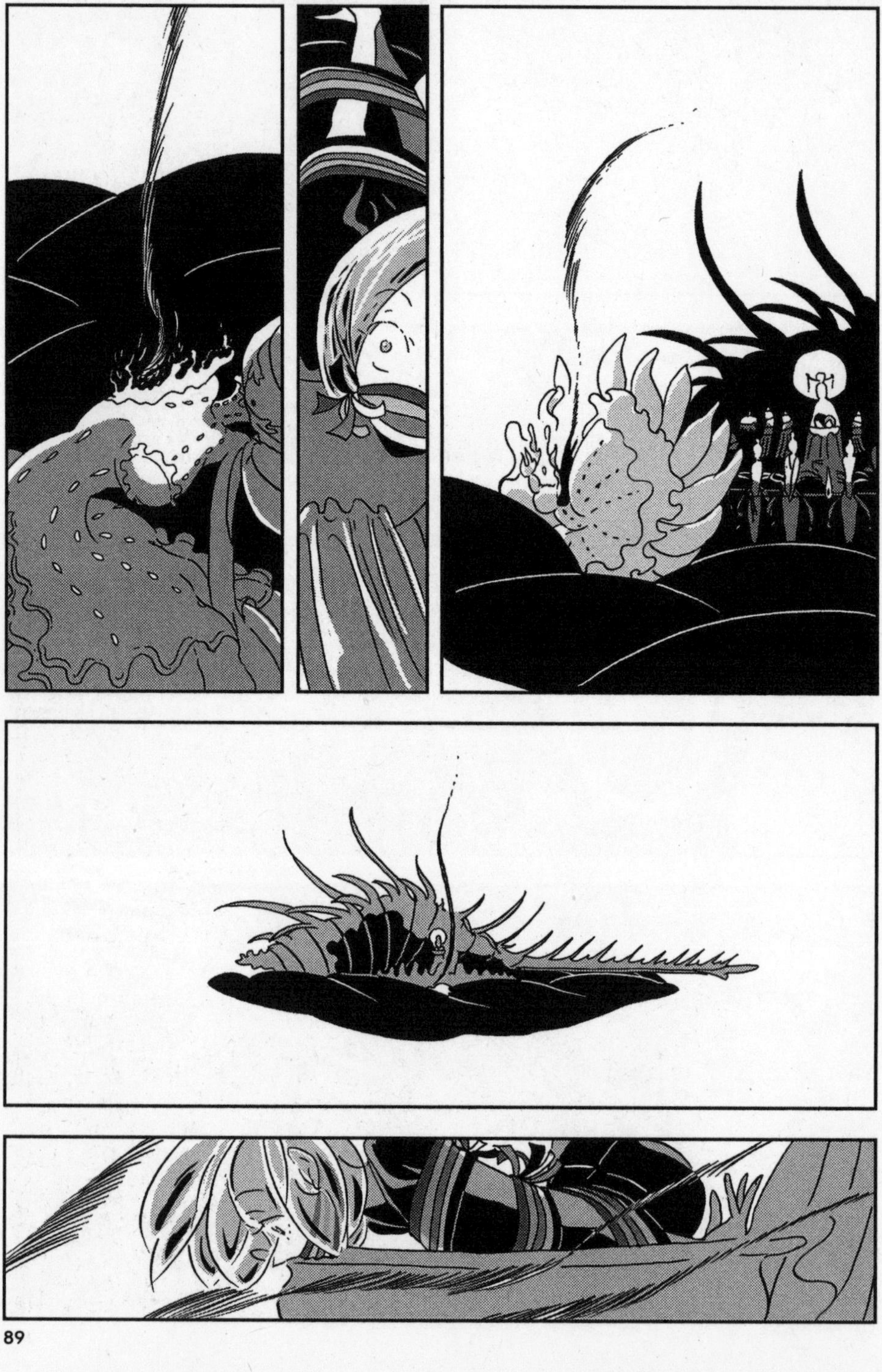

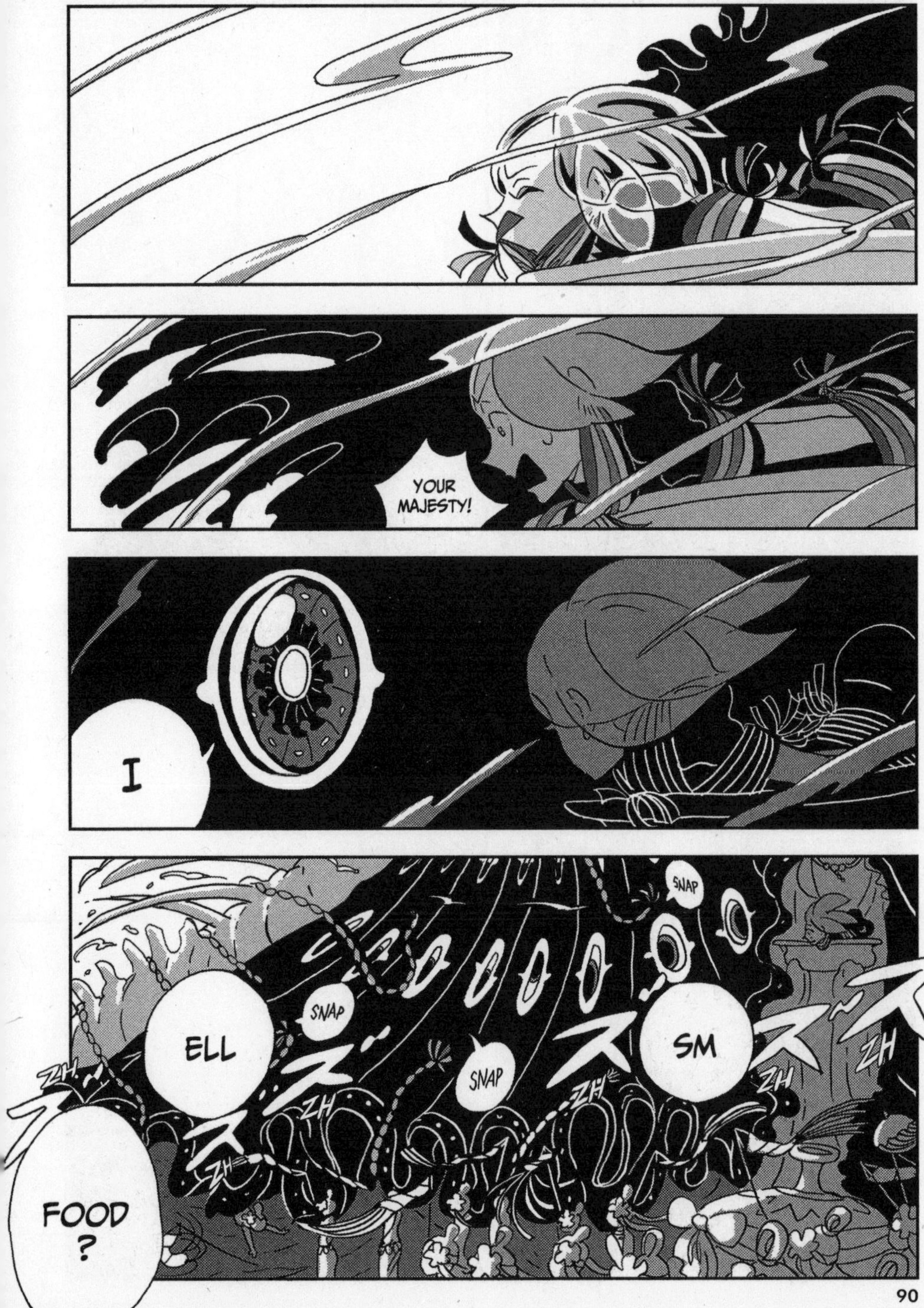
YOUR MAJESTY!
I
SNAP
ZH
SM
ZH
SNAP
ZH
ELL
SNAP
ZH
ZH
FOOD
?

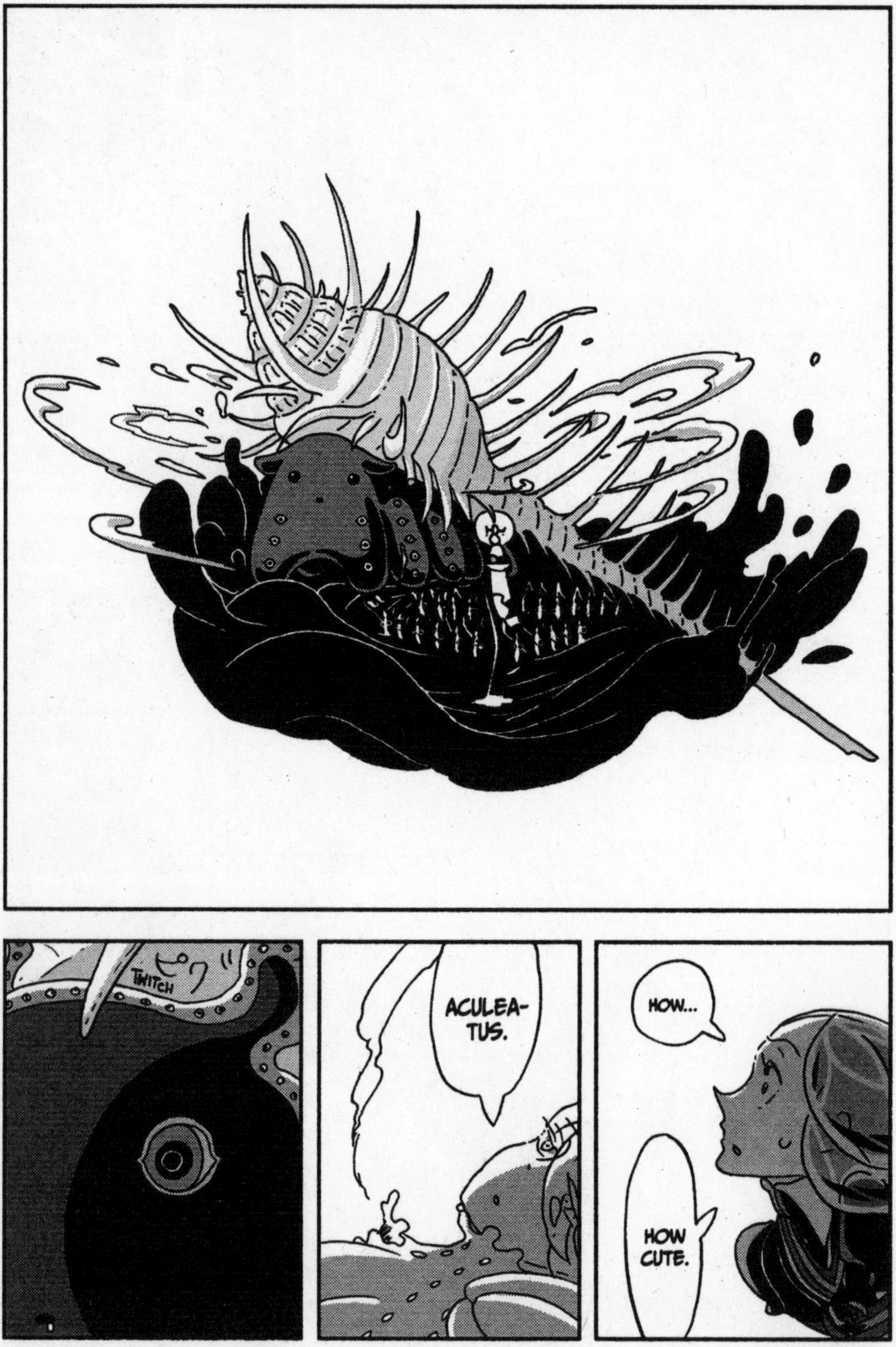
HOW...
HOW CUTE.
ACULEA-TUS.
TWITCH

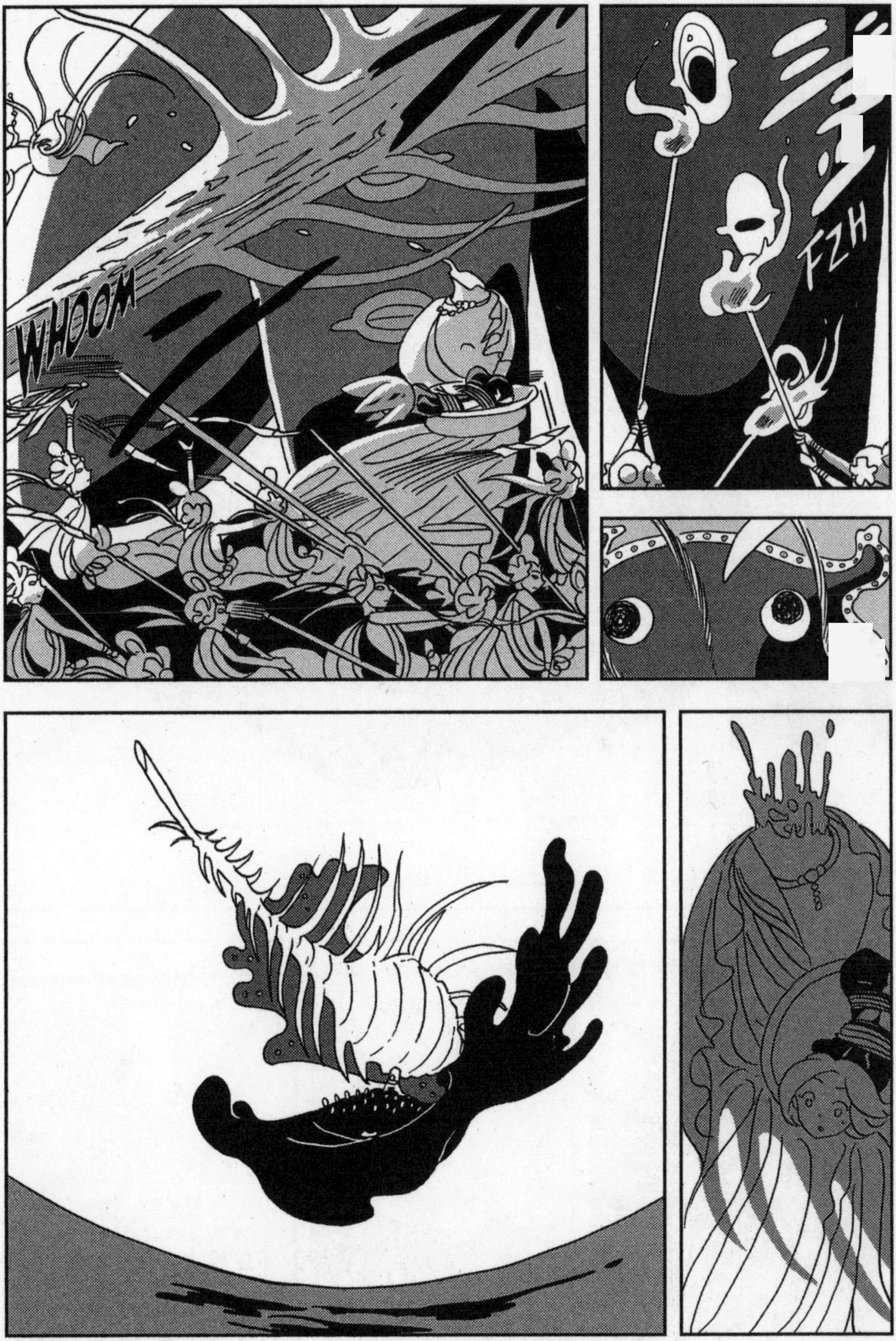
FZH
WHOOM

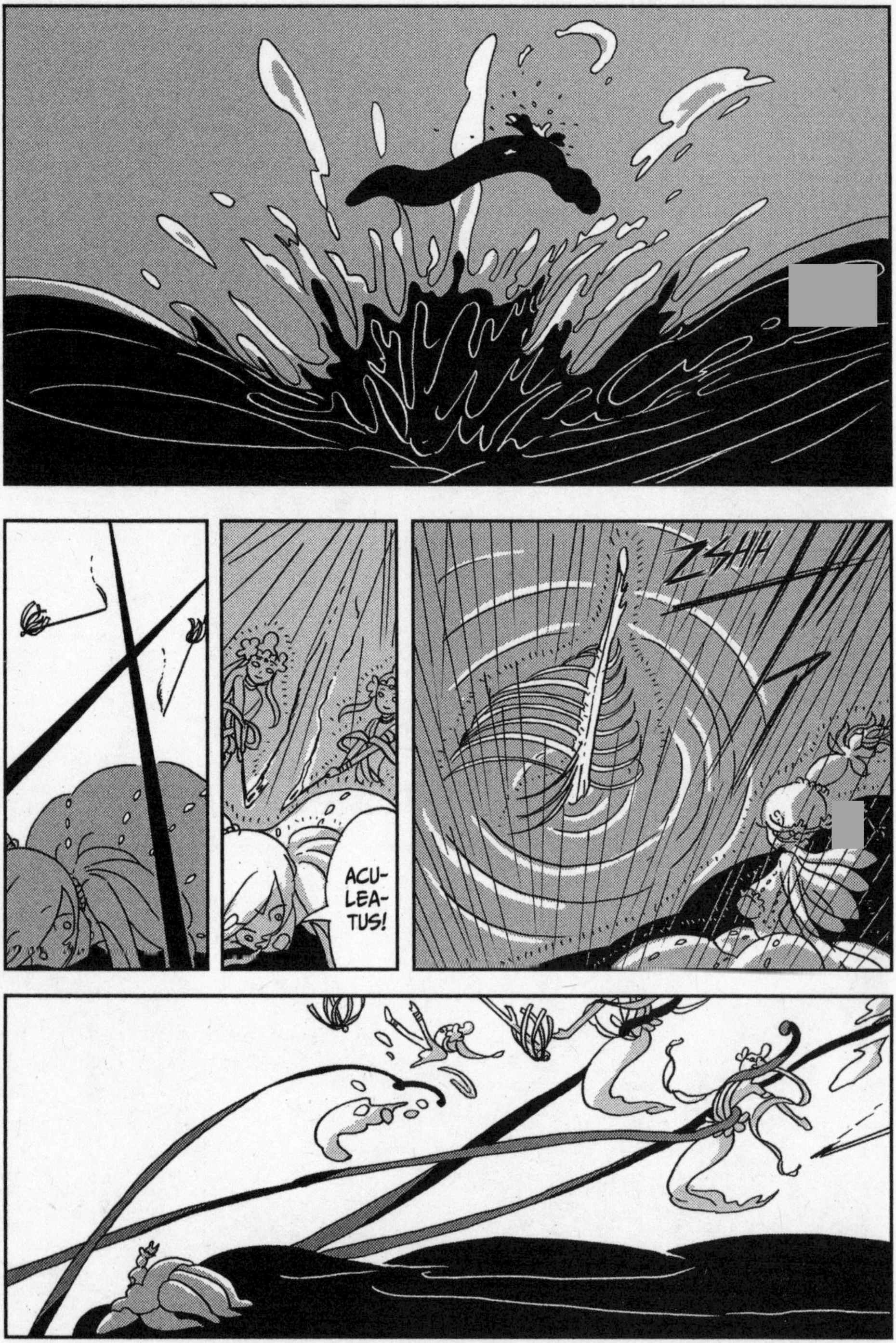
ZSHH
ACU-LEA-TUS!

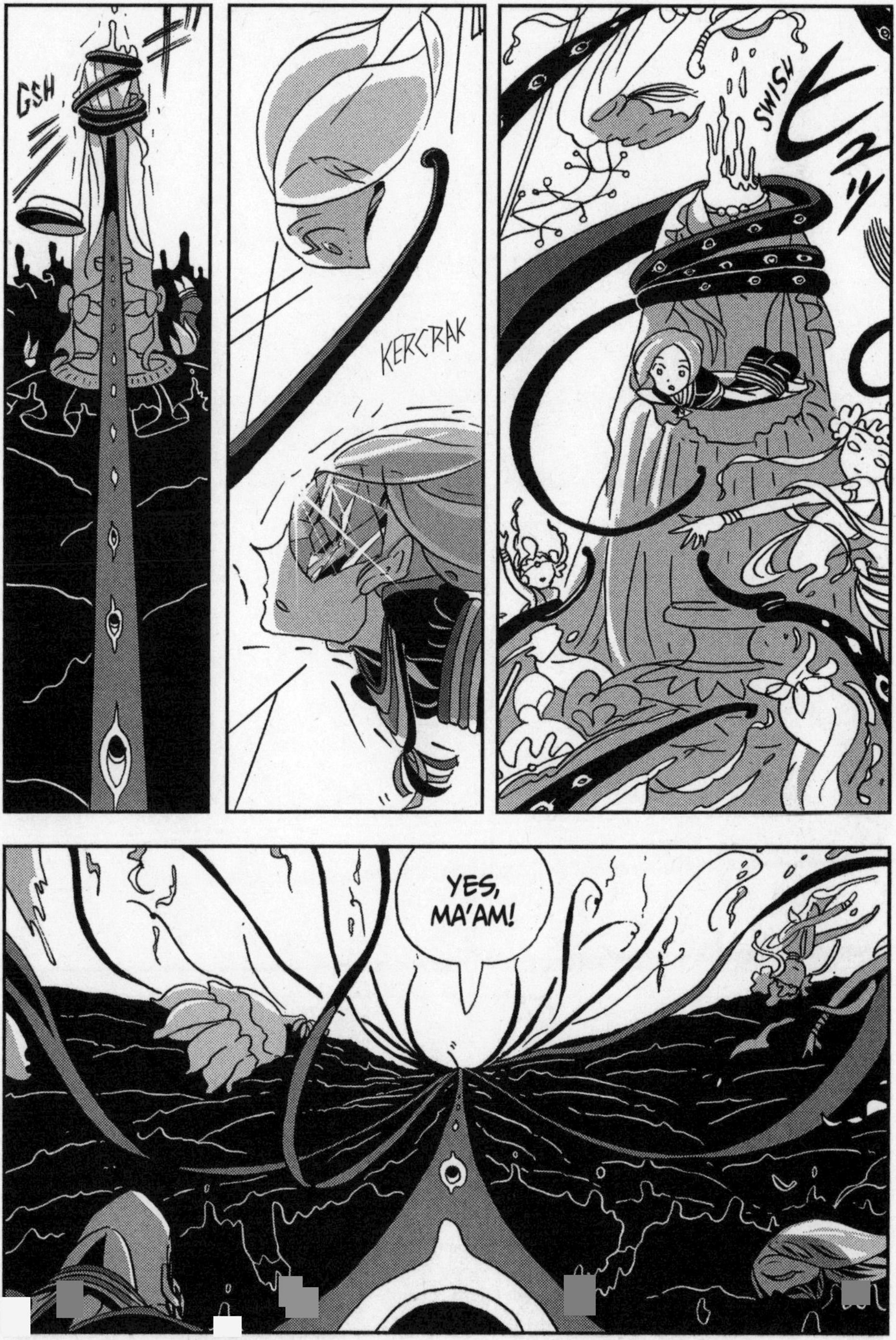
SWISH
KERCRAK
GSH
YES, MA'AM!

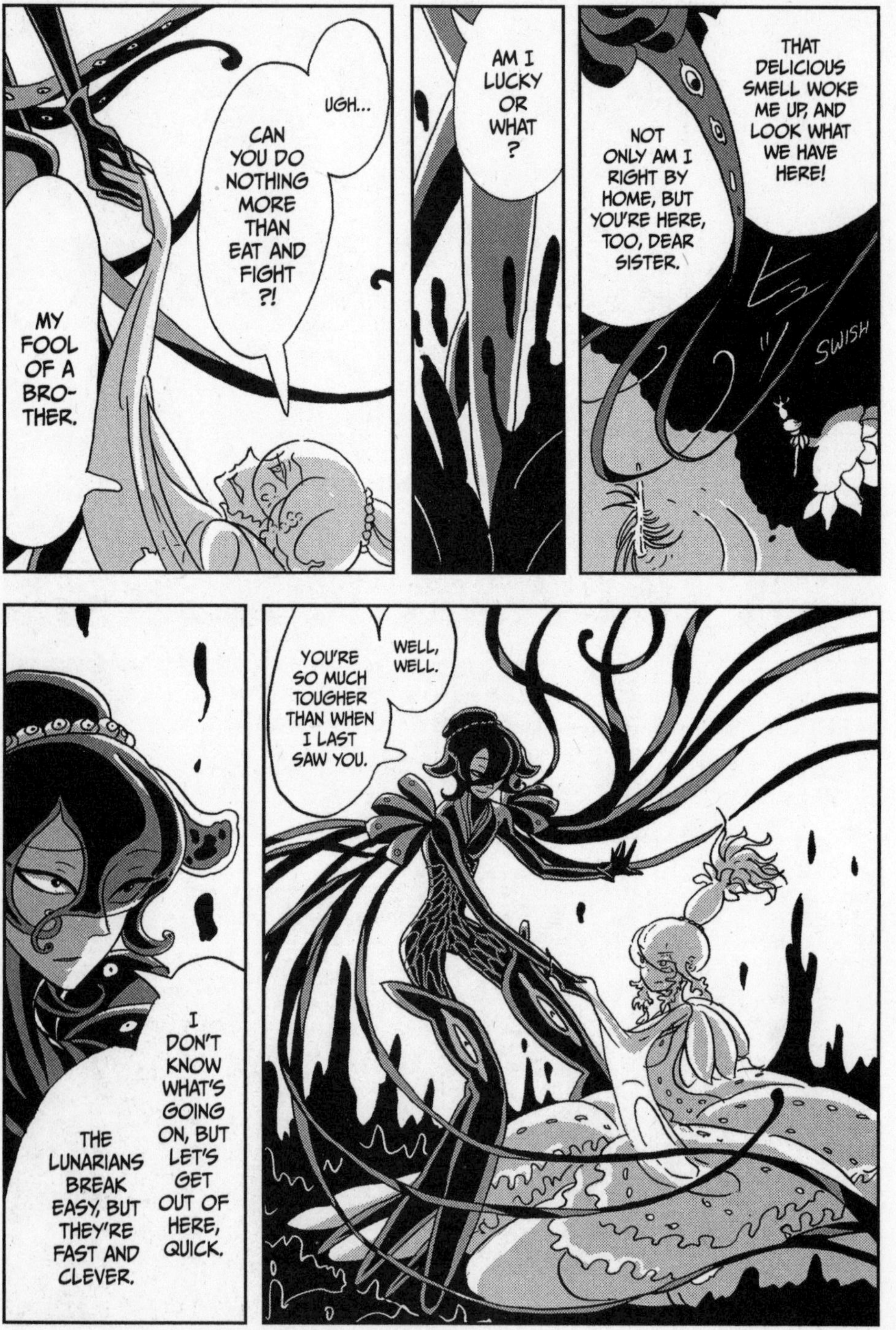
THAT DELICIOUS SMELL WOKE ME UP, AND LOOK WHAT WE HAVE HERE!
NOT ONLY AM I RIGHT BY HOME, BUT YOU'RE HERE, TOO, DEAR SISTER.
SWISH
AM I LUCKY OR WHAT?
UGH...
CAN YOU DO NOTHING MORE THAN EAT AND FIGHT?!
MY FOOL OF A BRO-THER.
WELL, WELL.
YOU'RE SO MUCH TOUGHER THAN WHEN I LAST SAW YOU.
I DON'T KNOW WHAT'S GOING ON, BUT LET'S GET OUT OF HERE, QUICK.
THE LUNARIANS BREAK EASY, BUT THEY'RE FAST AND CLEVER.

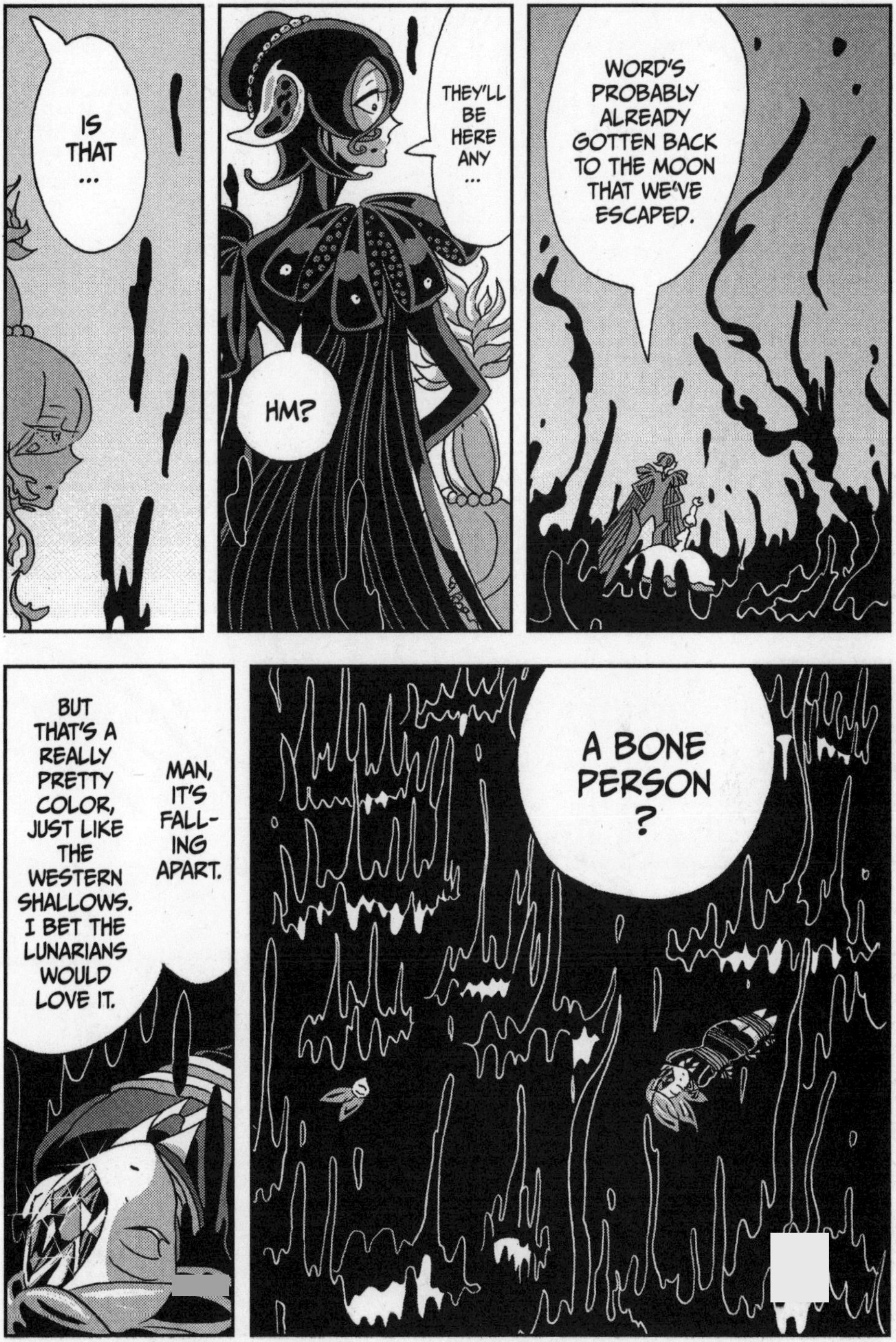
WORD'S PROBABLY ALREADY GOTTEN BACK TO THE MOON THAT WE'VE ESCAPED.
THEY'LL BE HERE ANY ...
HM?
IS THAT ...
A BONE PERSON ?
MAN, IT'S FALL-ING APART.
BUT THAT'S A REALLY PRETTY COLOR, JUST LIKE THE WESTERN SHALLOWS. I BET THE LUNARIANS WOULD LOVE IT.

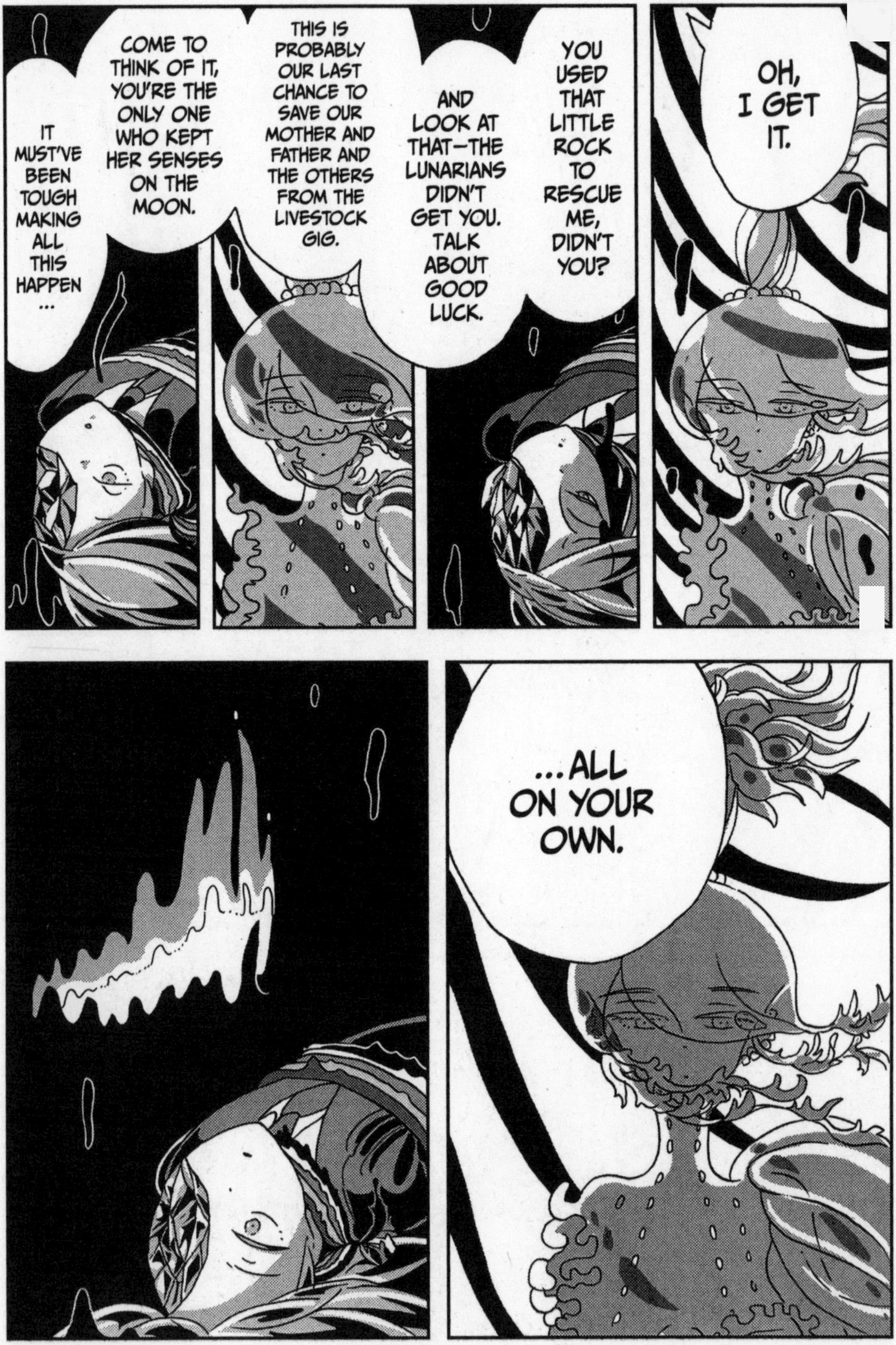
OH, I GET IT.
YOU USED THAT LITTLE ROCK TO RESCUE ME, DIDN'T YOU?
AND LOOK AT THAT—THE LUNARIANS DIDN'T GET YOU. TALK ABOUT GOOD LUCK.
THIS IS PROBABLY OUR LAST CHANCE TO SAVE OUR MOTHER AND FATHER AND THE OTHERS FROM THE LIVESTOCK GIG.
COME TO THINK OF IT, YOU'RE THE ONLY ONE WHO KEPT HER SENSES ON THE MOON.
IT MUST'VE BEEN TOUGH MAKING ALL THIS HAPPEN ...
...ALL ON YOUR OWN.

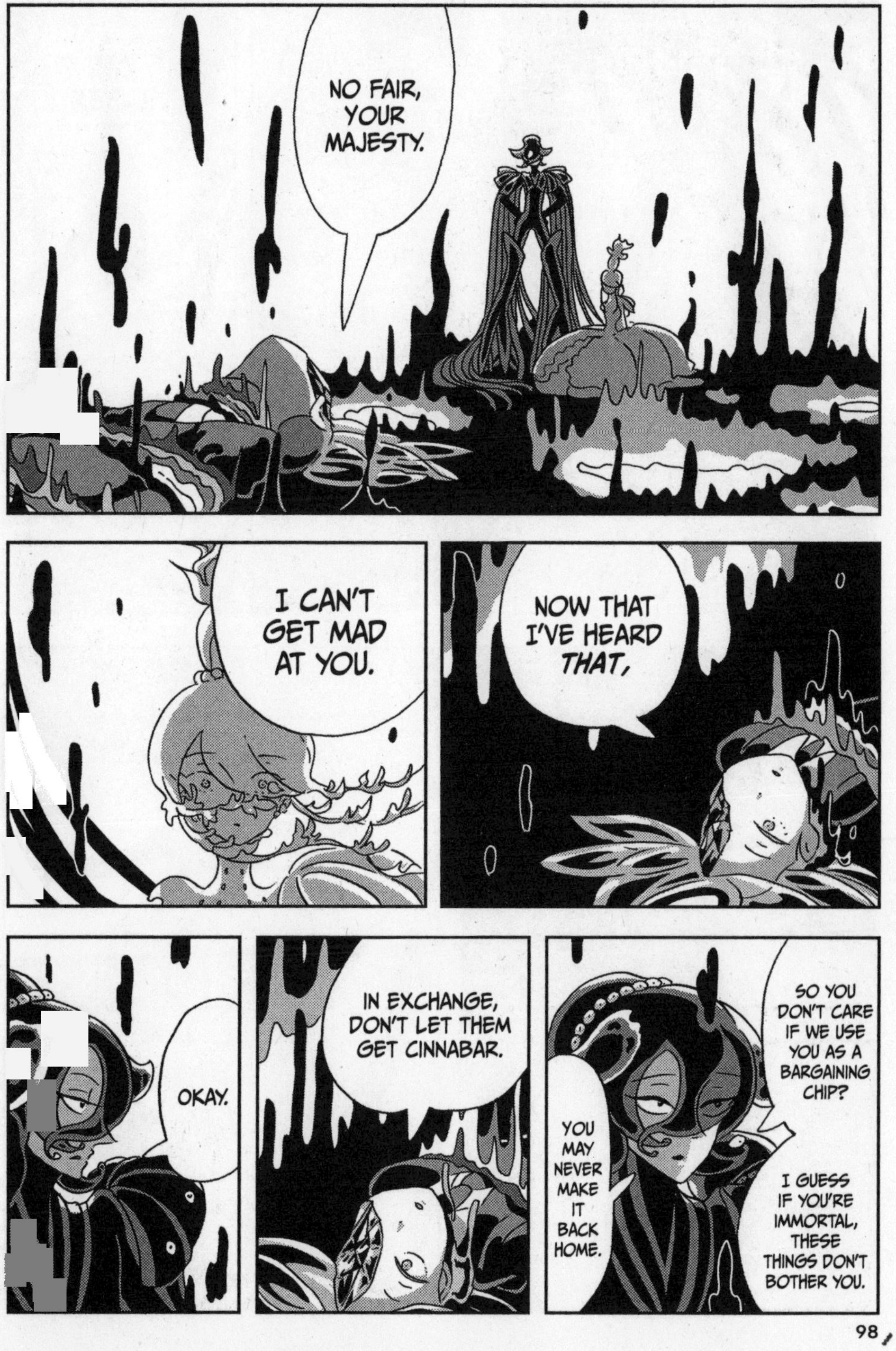
NO FAIR, YOUR MAJESTY.
NOW THAT I'VE HEARD *THAT,*
I CAN'T GET MAD AT YOU.
SO YOU DON'T CARE IF WE USE YOU AS A BARGAINING CHIP?
I GUESS IF YOU'RE IMMORTAL, THESE THINGS DON'T BOTHER YOU.
YOU MAY NEVER MAKE IT BACK HOME.
IN EXCHANGE, DON'T LET THEM GET CINNABAR.
OKAY.

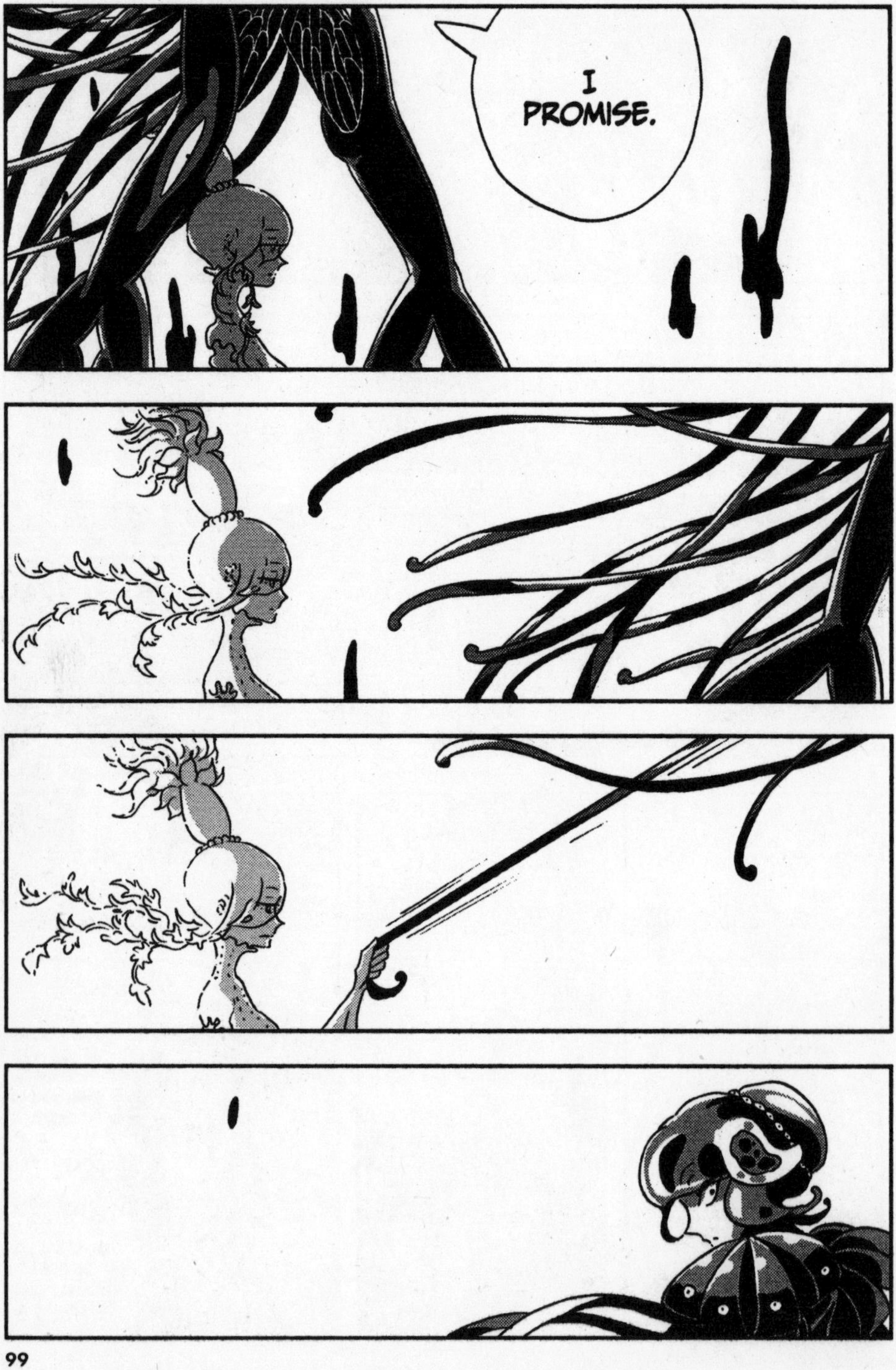
I PROMISE.

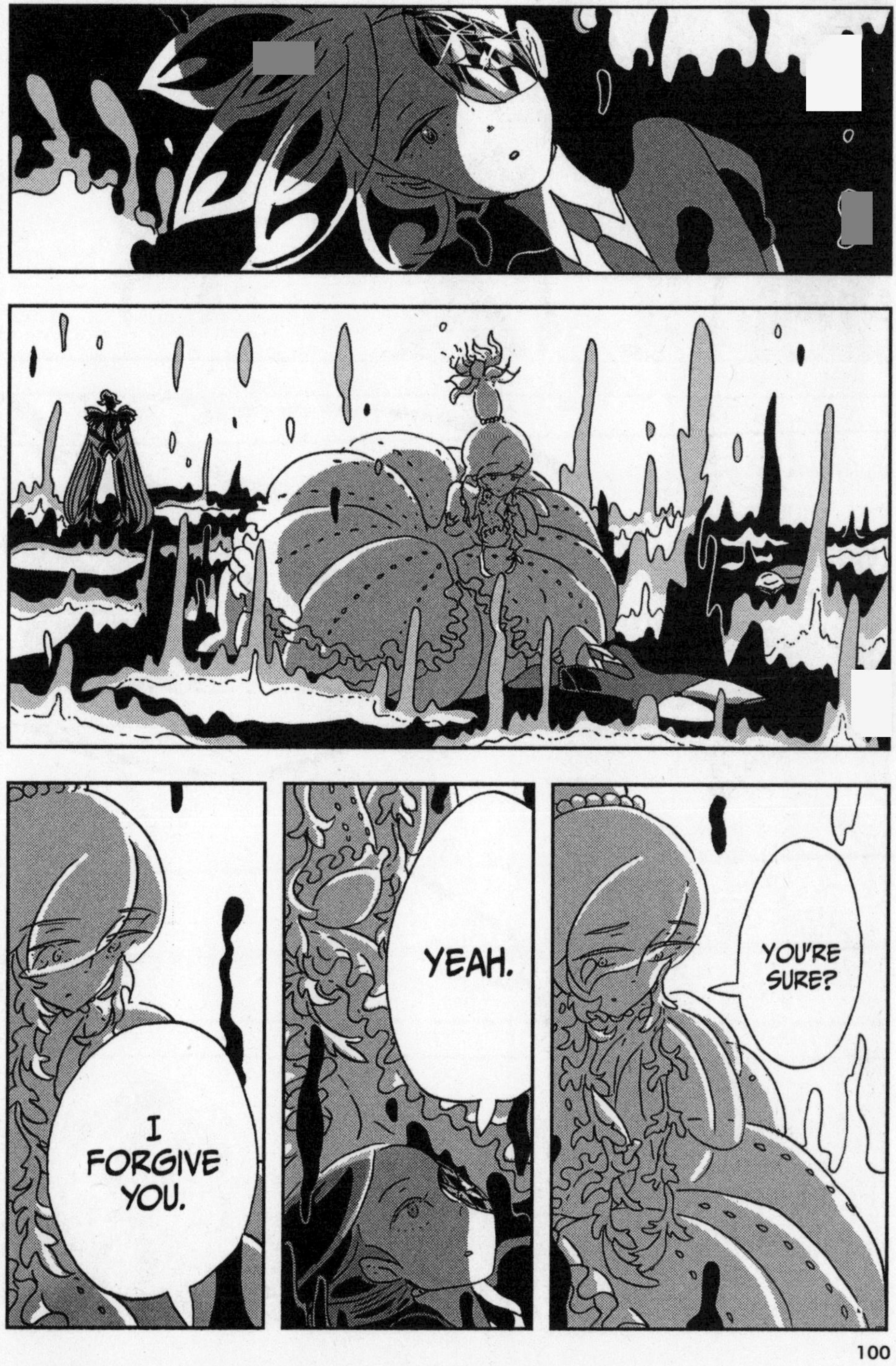
YOU'RE SURE?
YEAH.
I FORGIVE YOU.

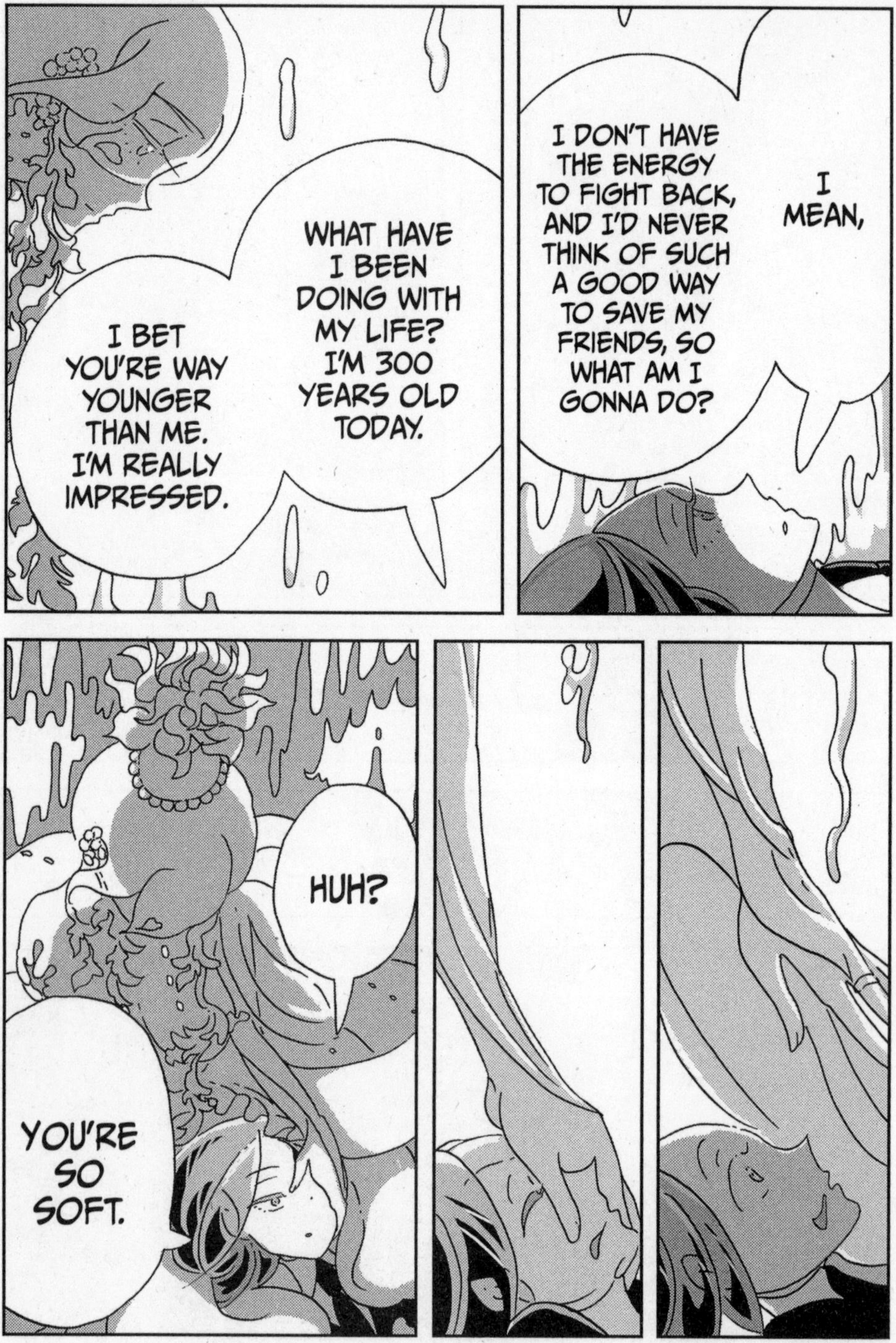
I MEAN,
I DON'T HAVE THE ENERGY TO FIGHT BACK, AND I'D NEVER THINK OF SUCH A GOOD WAY TO SAVE MY FRIENDS, SO WHAT AM I GONNA DO?
WHAT HAVE I BEEN DOING WITH MY LIFE? I'M 300 YEARS OLD TODAY.
I BET YOU'RE WAY YOUNGER THAN ME. I'M REALLY IMPRESSED.
HUH?
YOU'RE SO SOFT.

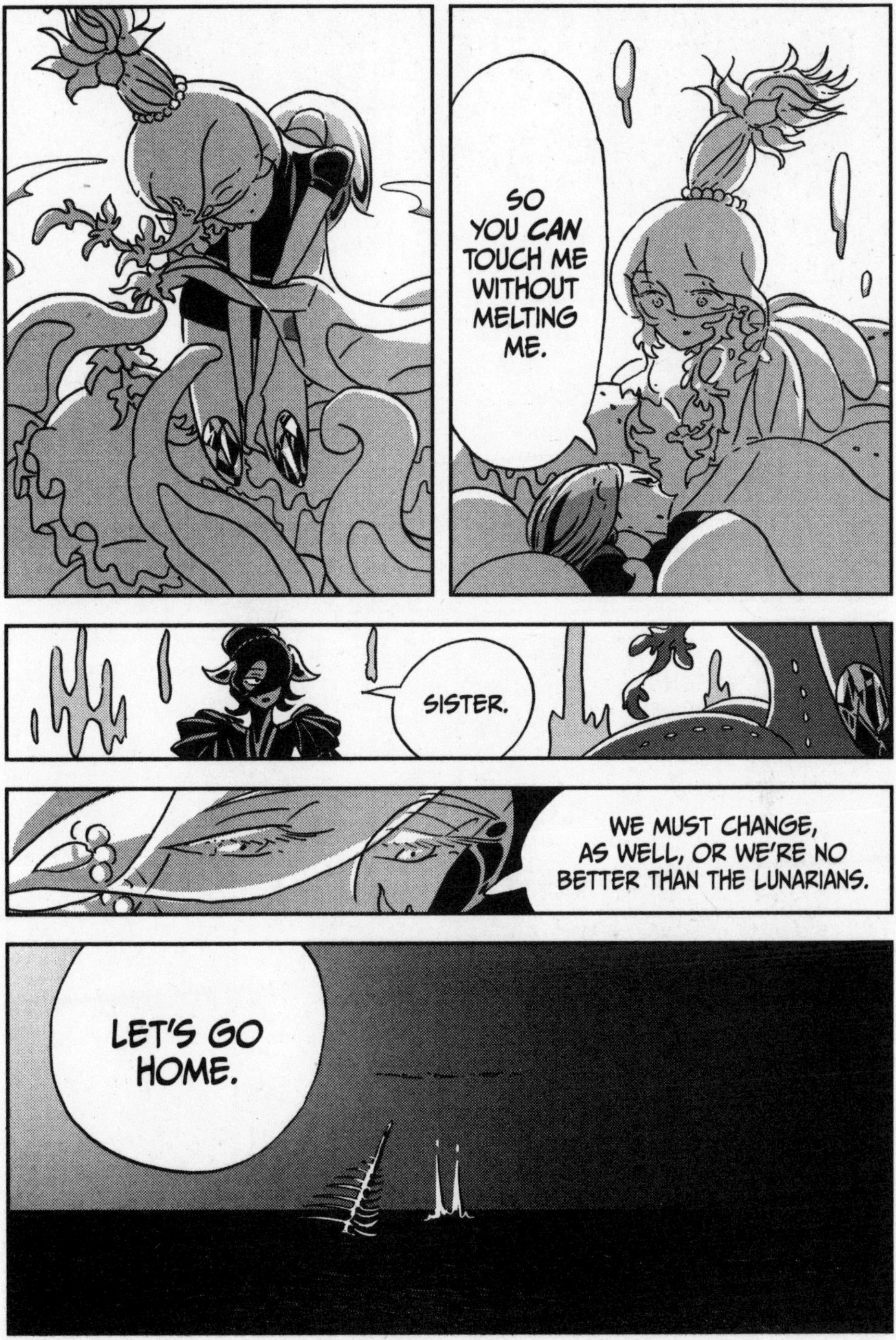
SO YOU CAN TOUCH ME WITHOUT MELTING ME.
SISTER.
WE MUST CHANGE, AS WELL, OR WE'RE NO BETTER THAN THE LUNARIANS.
LET'S GO HOME.

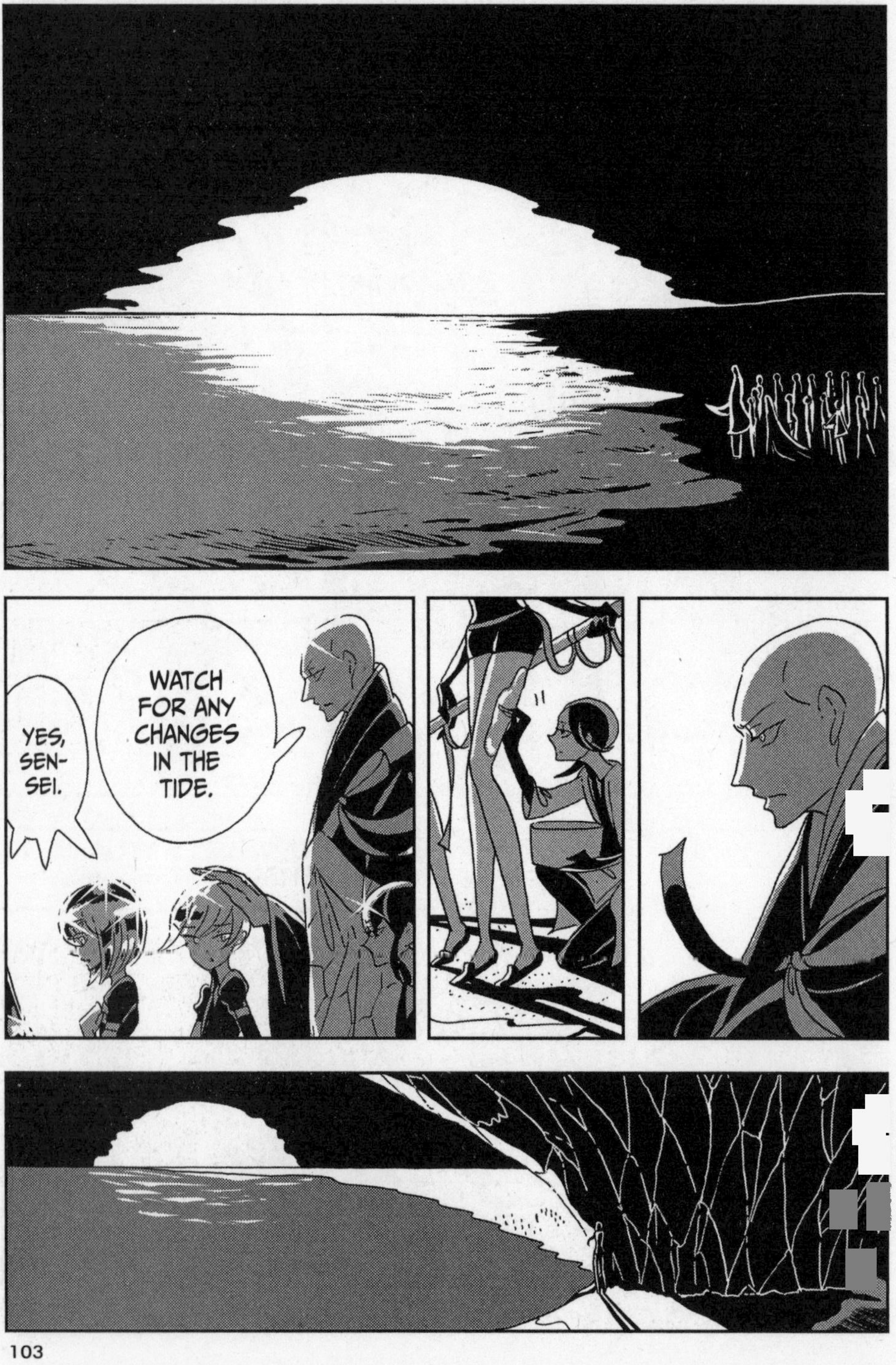
WATCH FOR ANY CHANGES IN THE TIDE.
YES, SEN-SEI.

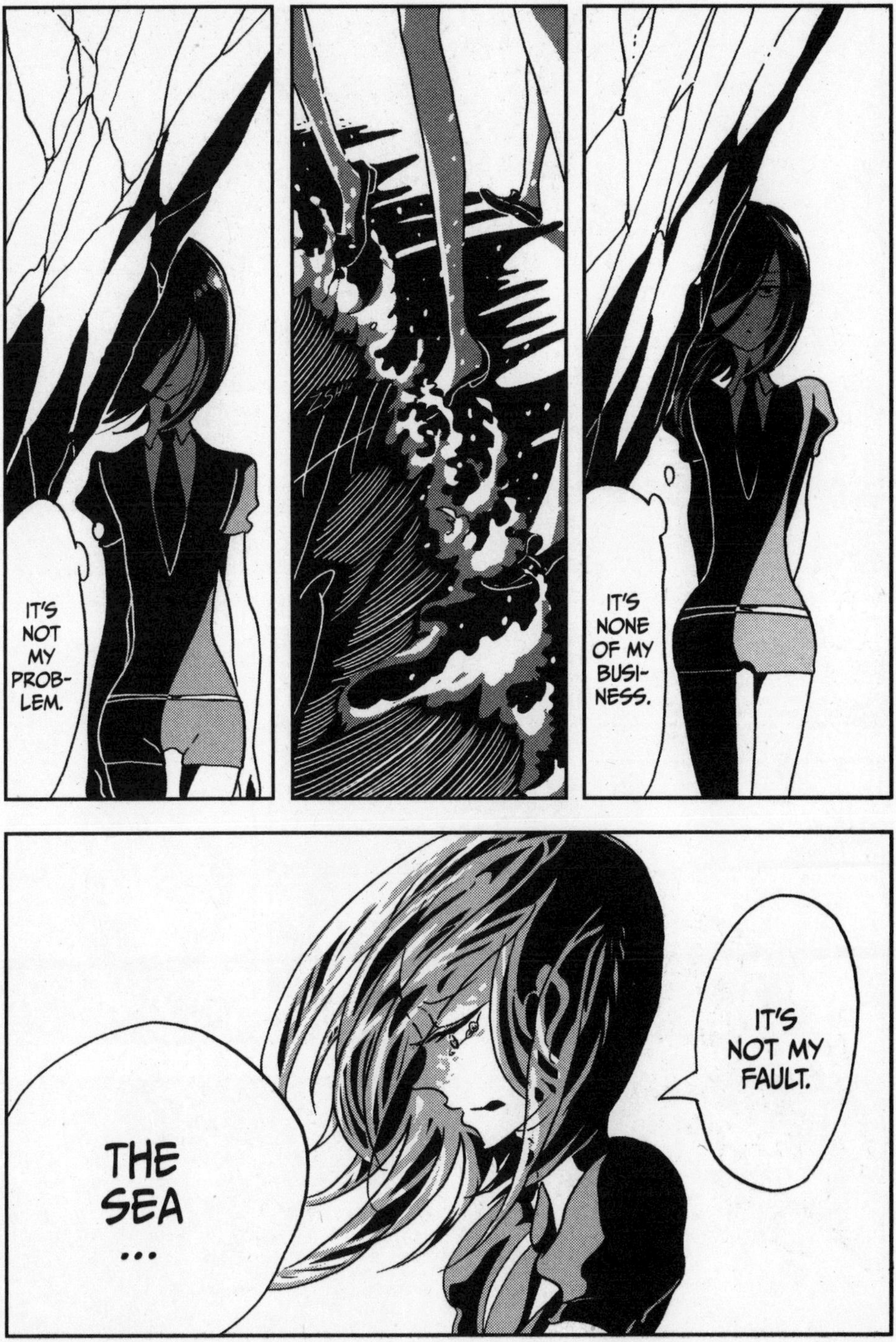
IT'S NONE OF MY BUSI- NESS.
IT'S NOT MY PROB- LEM.
IT'S NOT MY FAULT.
THE SEA ...

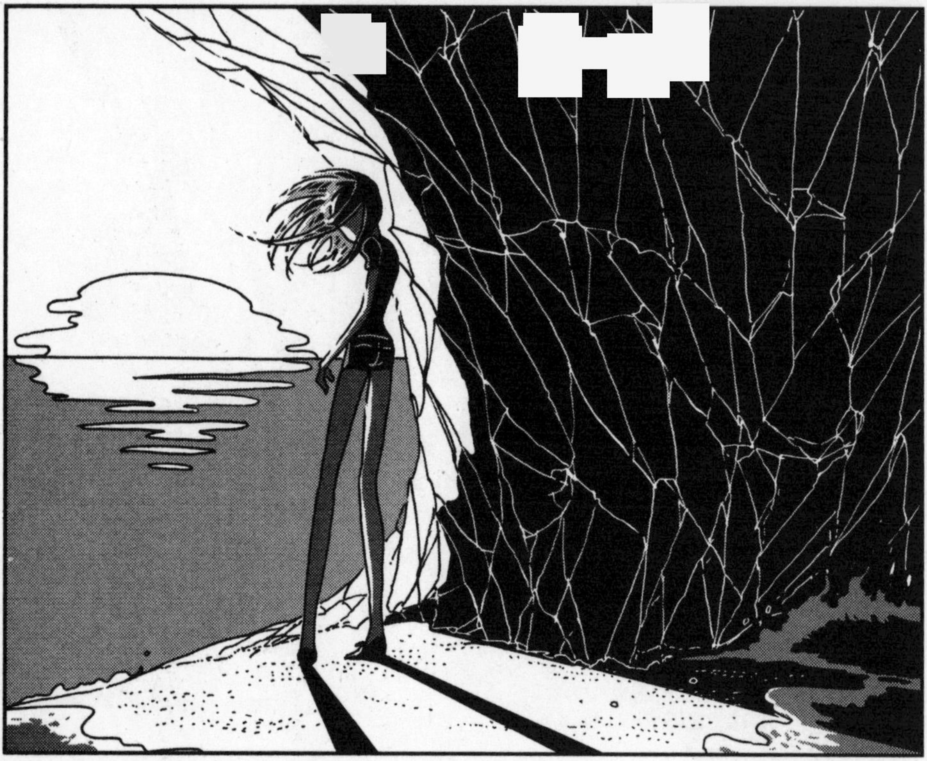

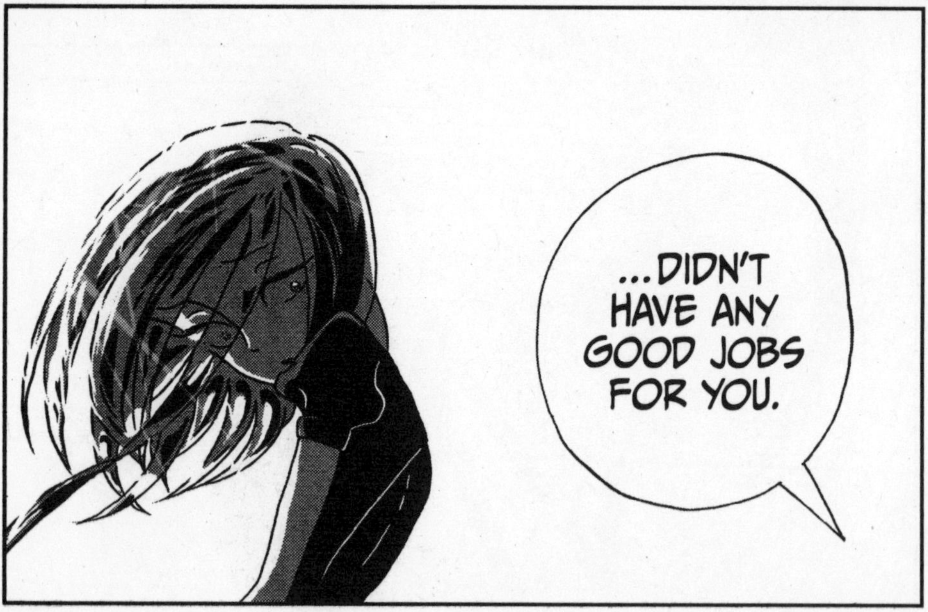
...DIDN'T HAVE ANY GOOD JOBS FOR YOU.

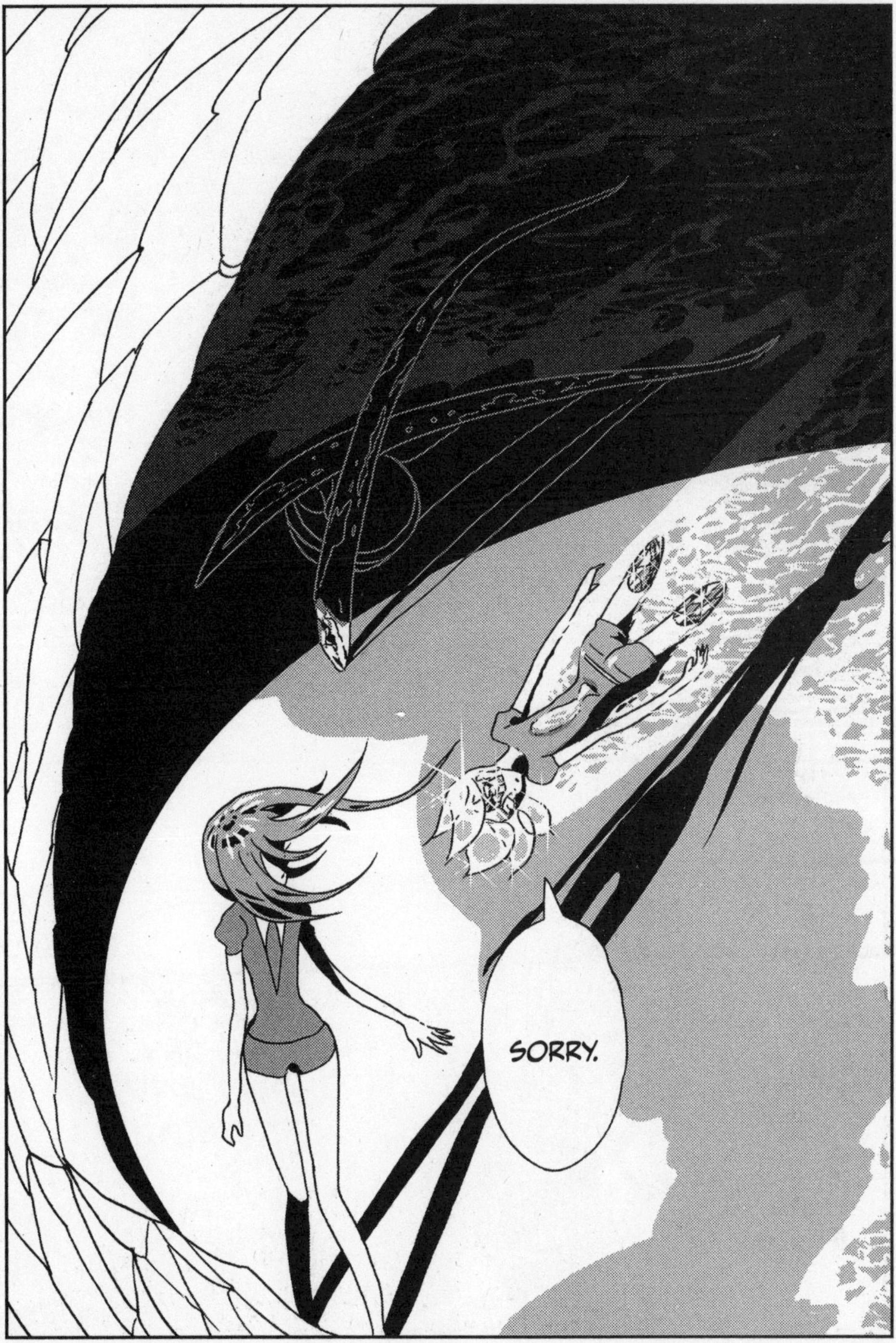
SORRY.

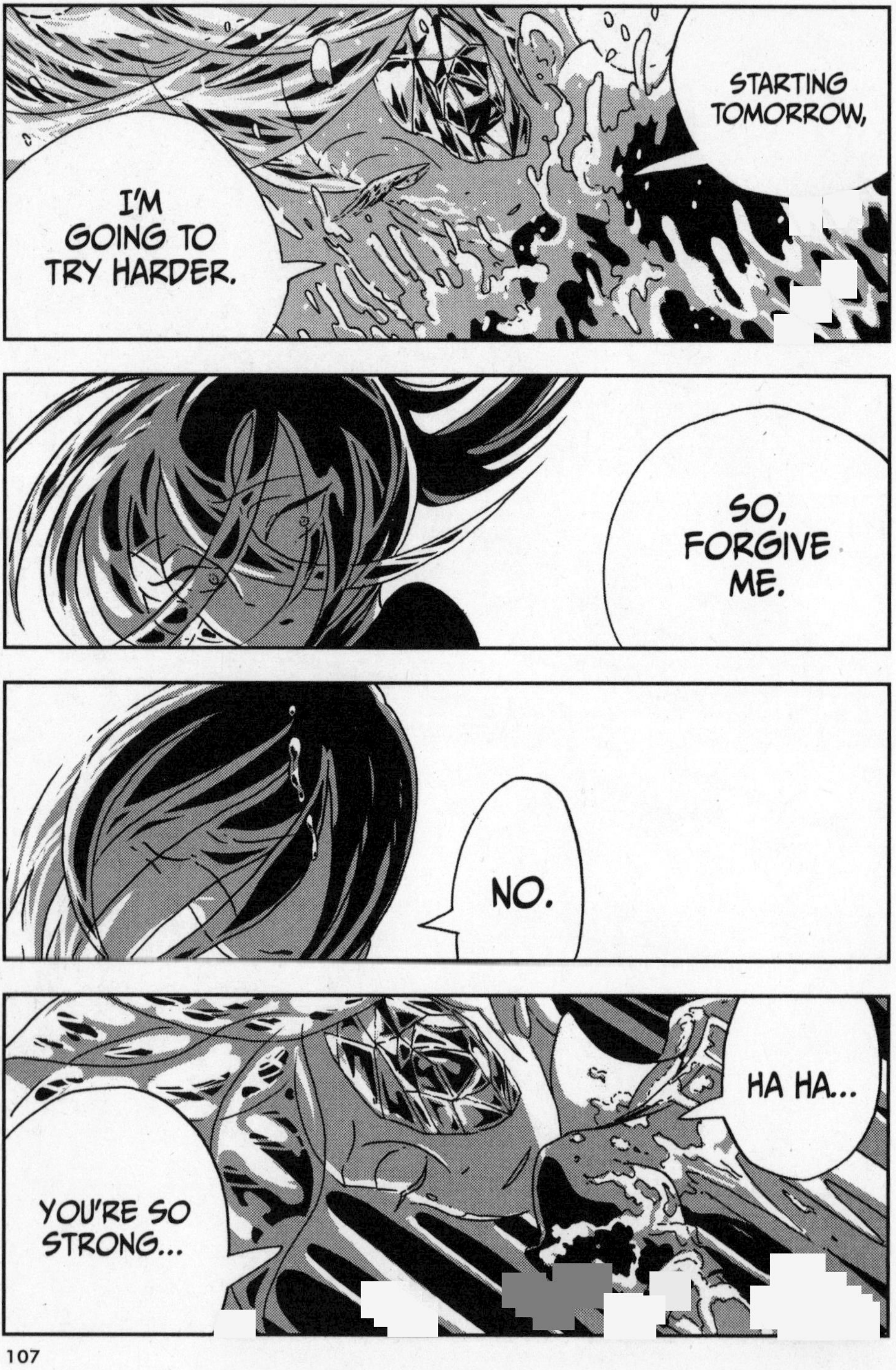
STARTING TOMORROW,
I'M GOING TO TRY HARDER.
SO, FORGIVE ME.
NO.
HA HA...
YOU'RE SO STRONG...

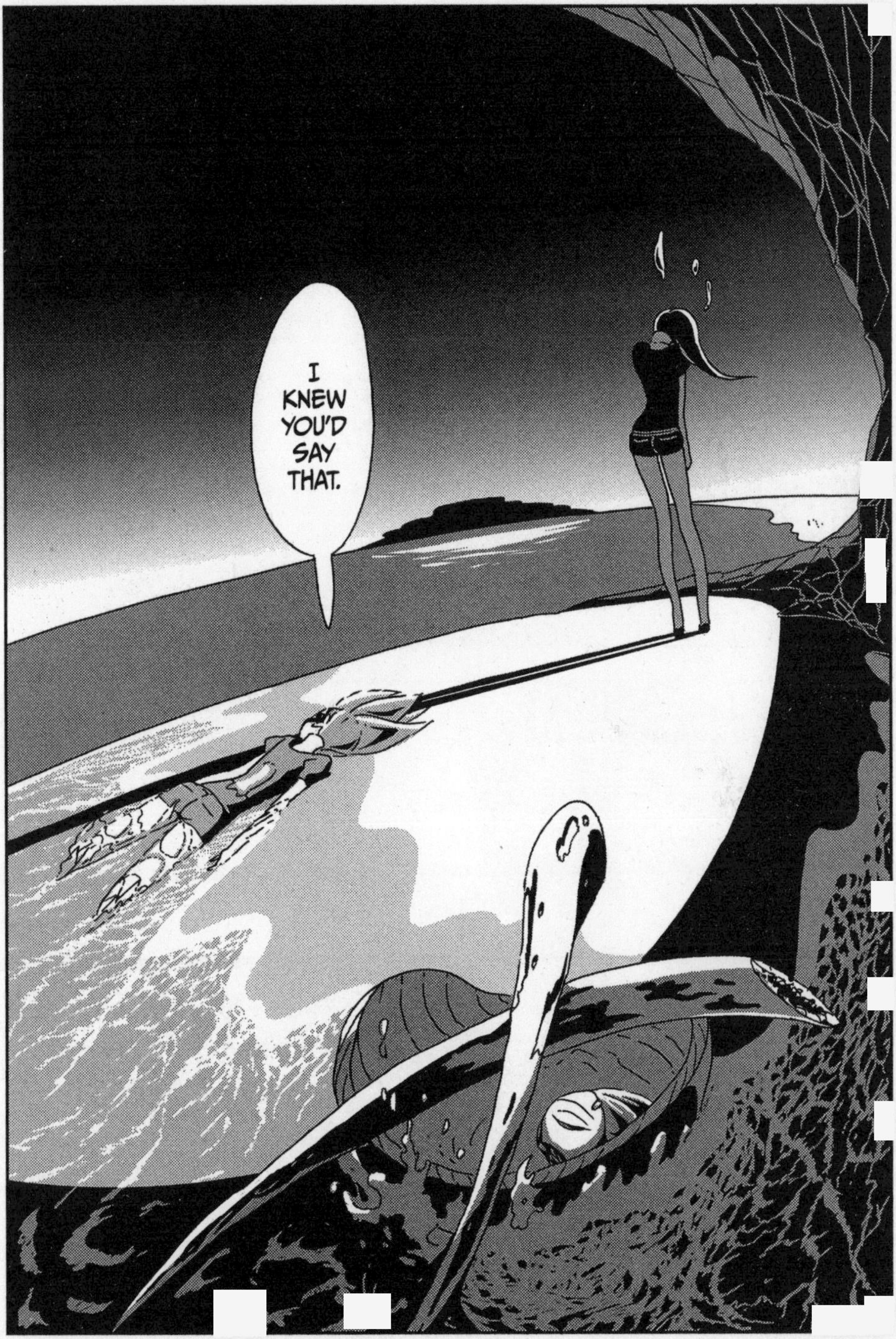
I KNEW YOU'D SAY THAT.

CHAPTER 10: Homecoming END

CHAPTER 11:

New Legs

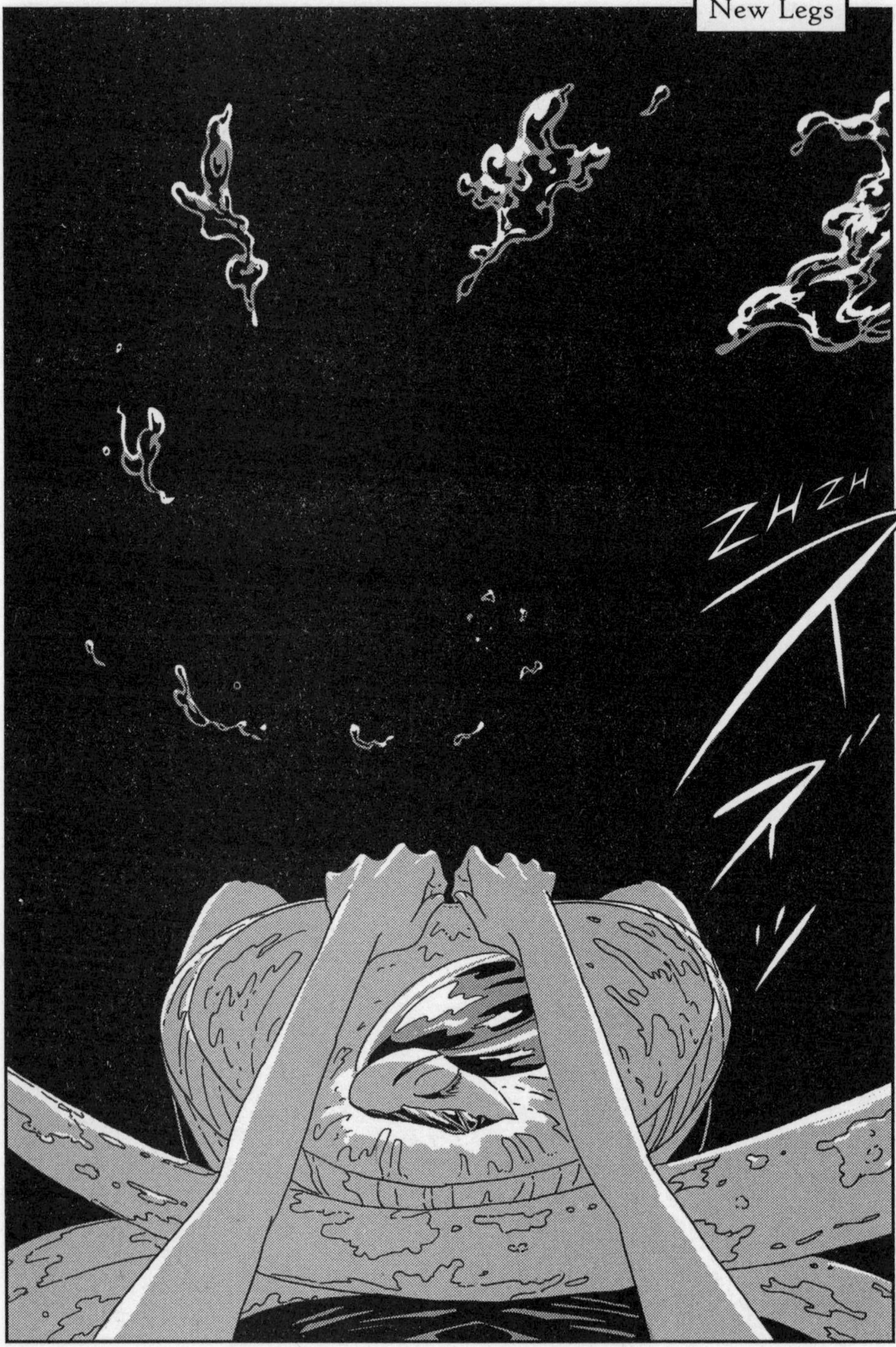
ZHZH

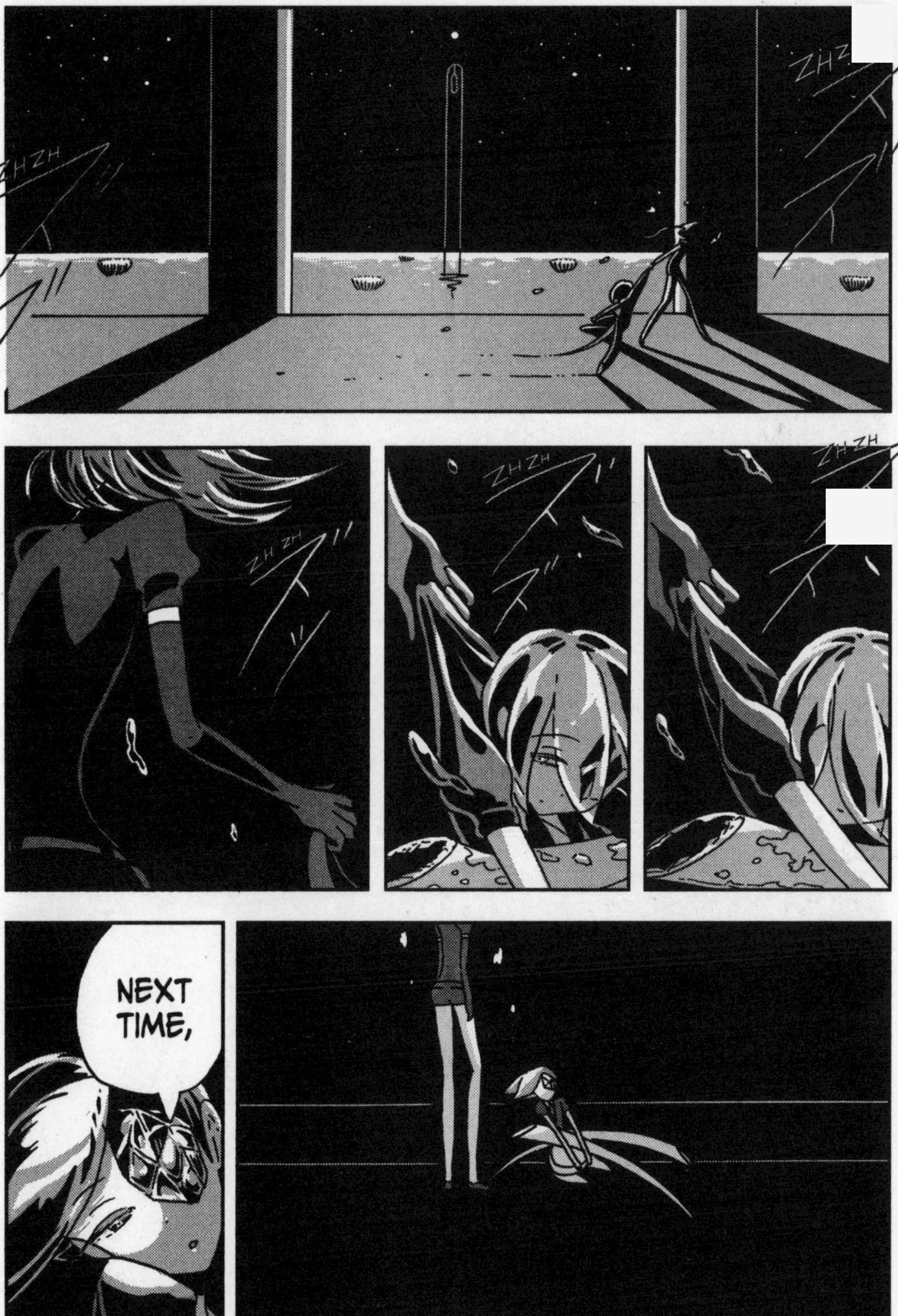
ZHZH
ZHZH
ZHZH
ZHZH
ZHZH
NEXT TIME,

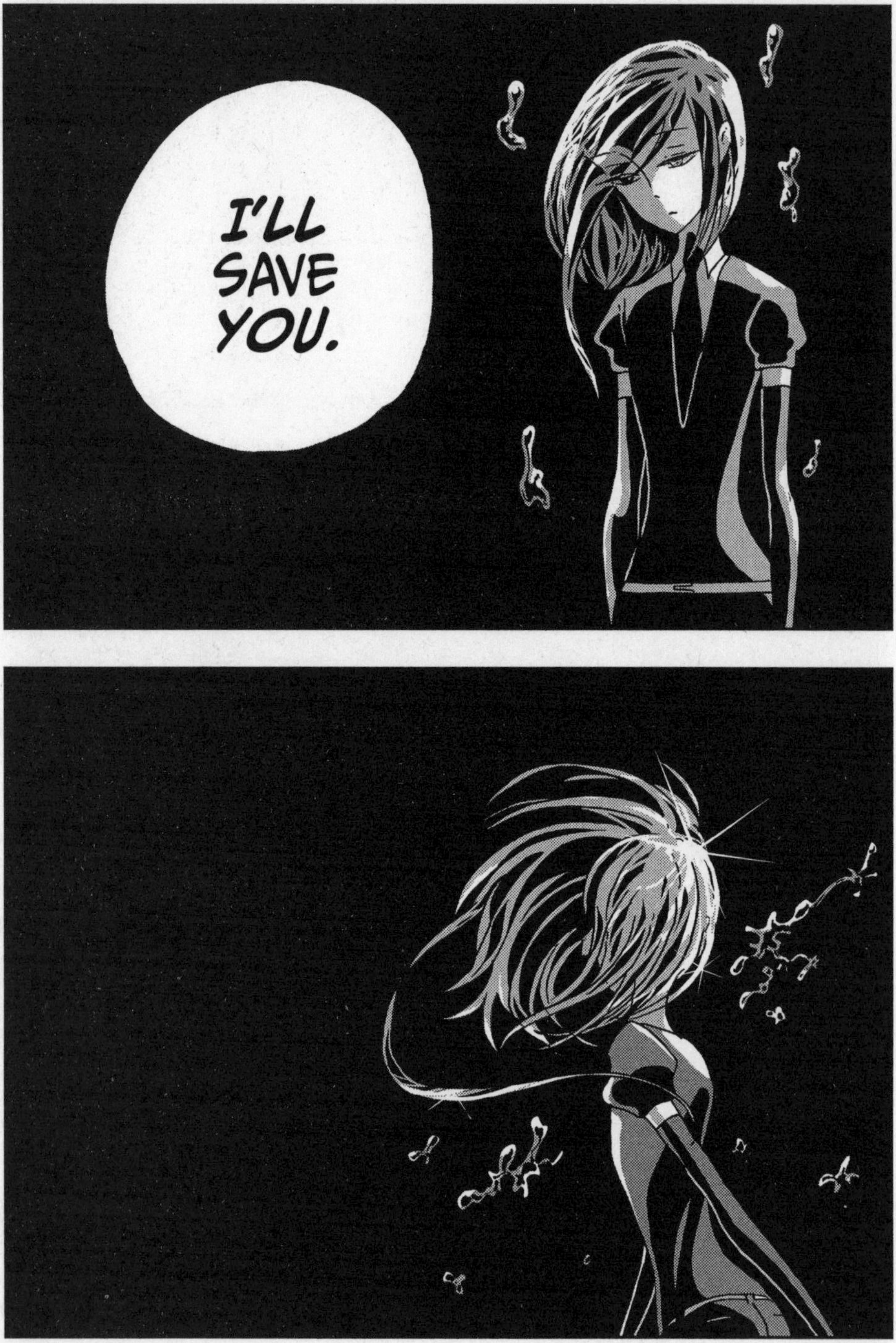
I'LL SAVE YOU.

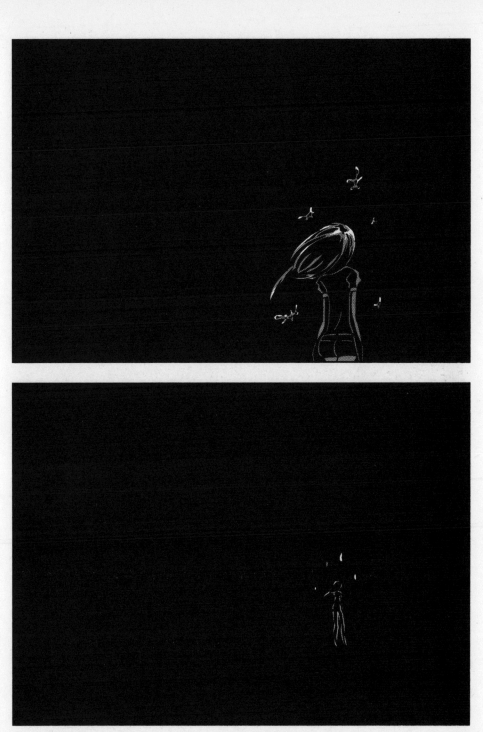

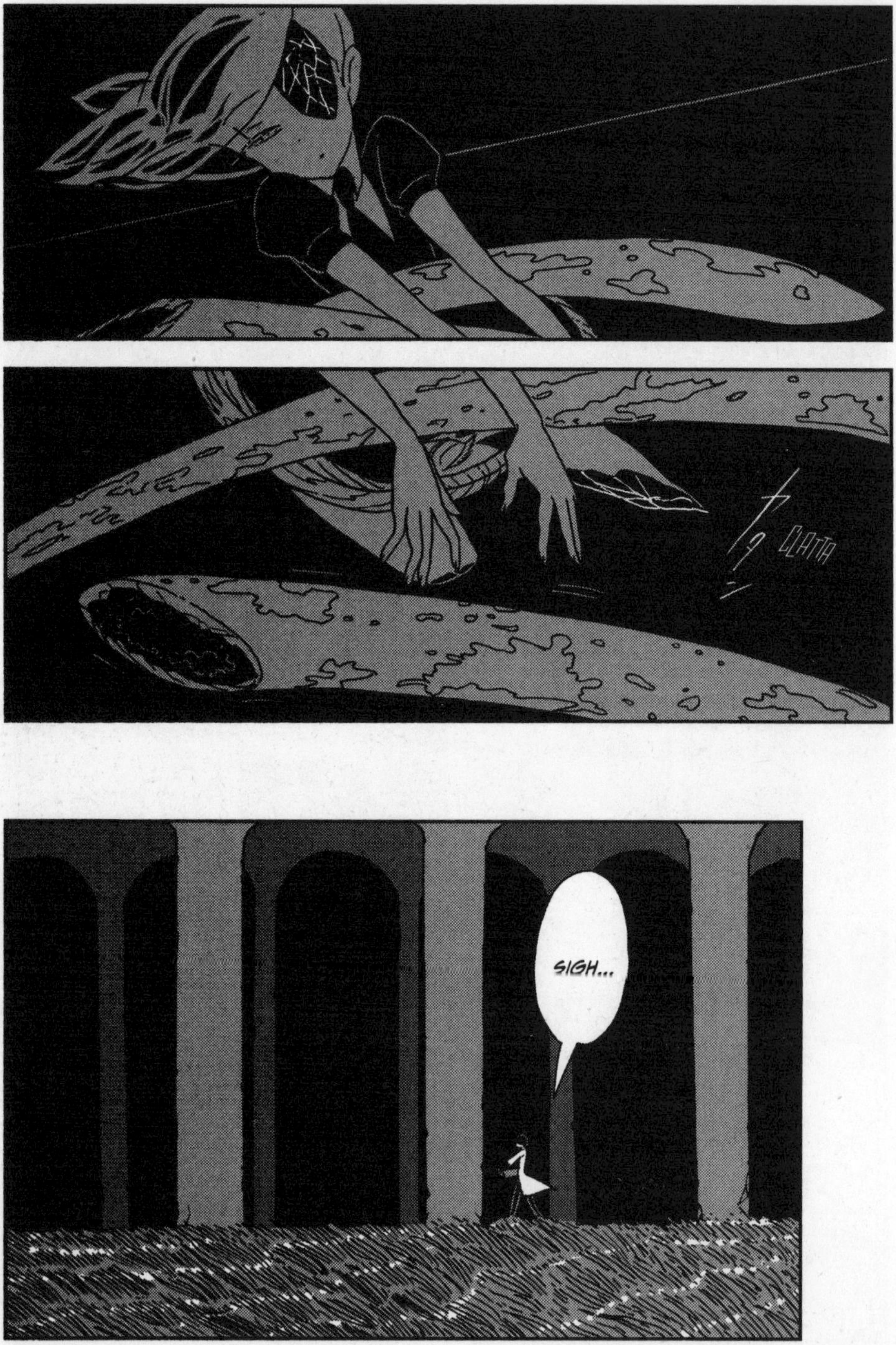
CLATTA
SIGH...

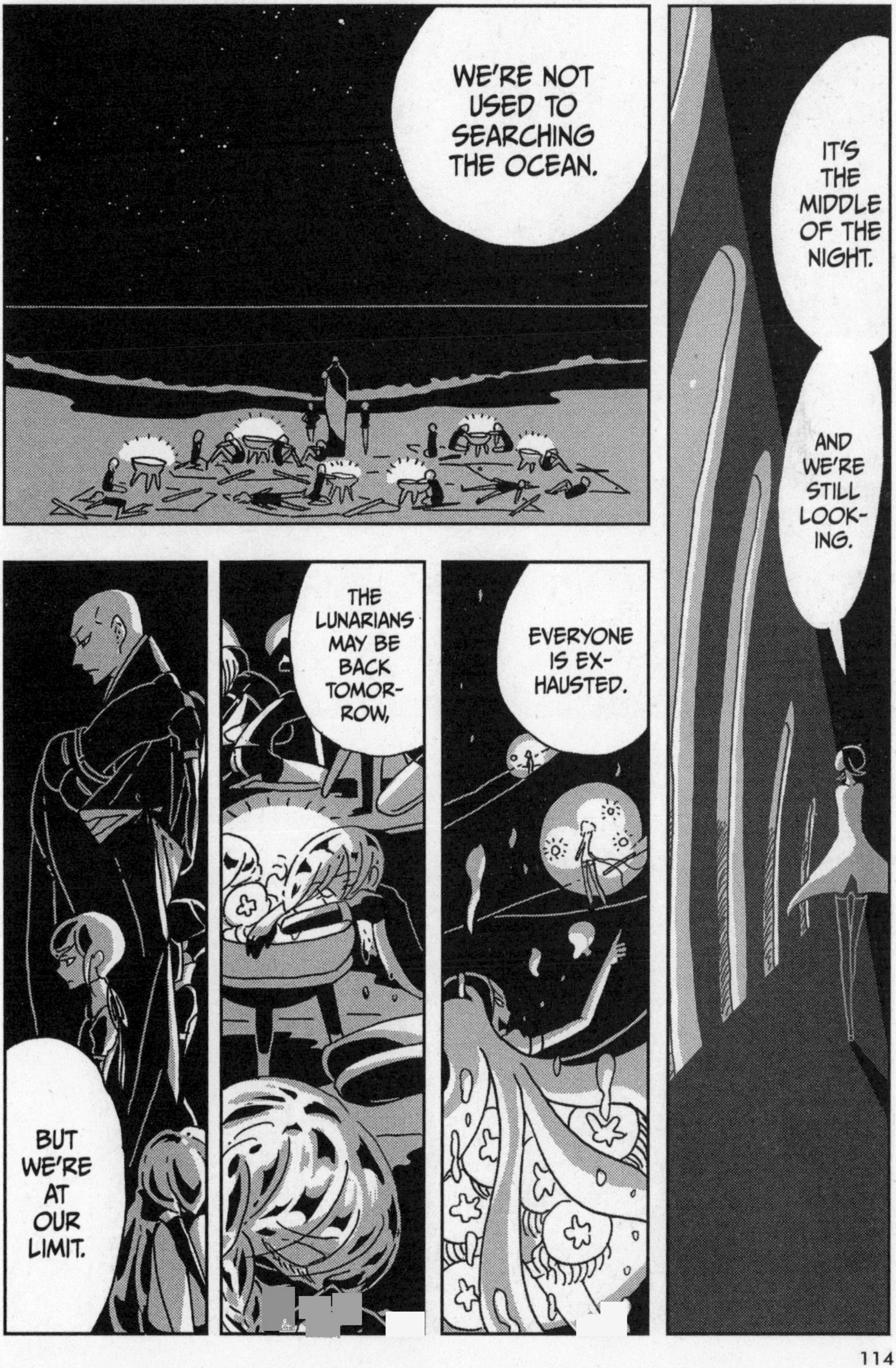
IT'S THE MIDDLE OF THE NIGHT.
AND WE'RE STILL LOOK-ING.
WE'RE NOT USED TO SEARCHING THE OCEAN.
EVERYONE IS EX-HAUSTED.
THE LUNARIANS MAY BE BACK TOMOR-ROW,
BUT WE'RE AT OUR LIMIT.

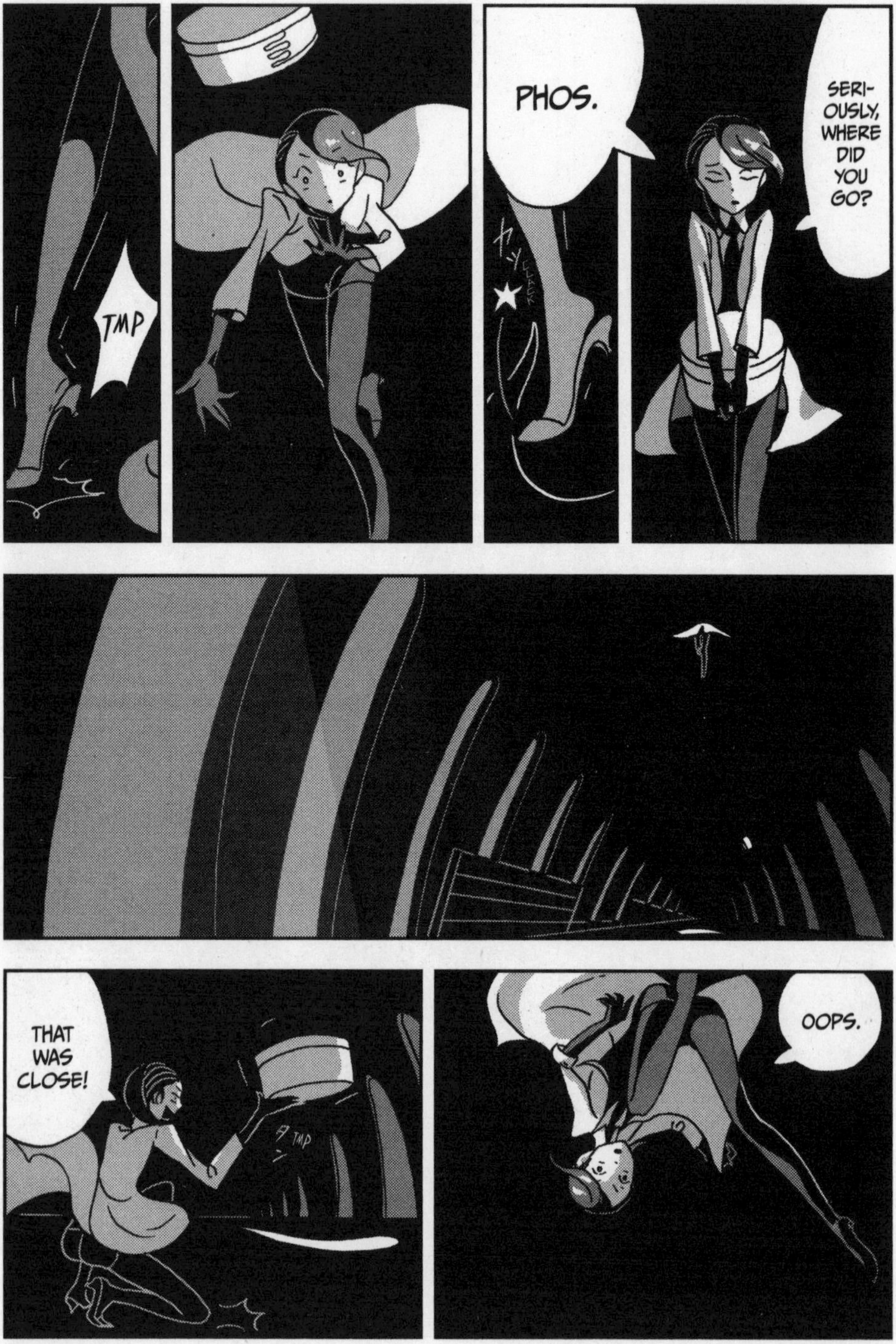
SERI-OUSLY, WHERE DID YOU GO?
PHOS.
CLACK
TMP
OOPS.
THAT WAS CLOSE!
TMP

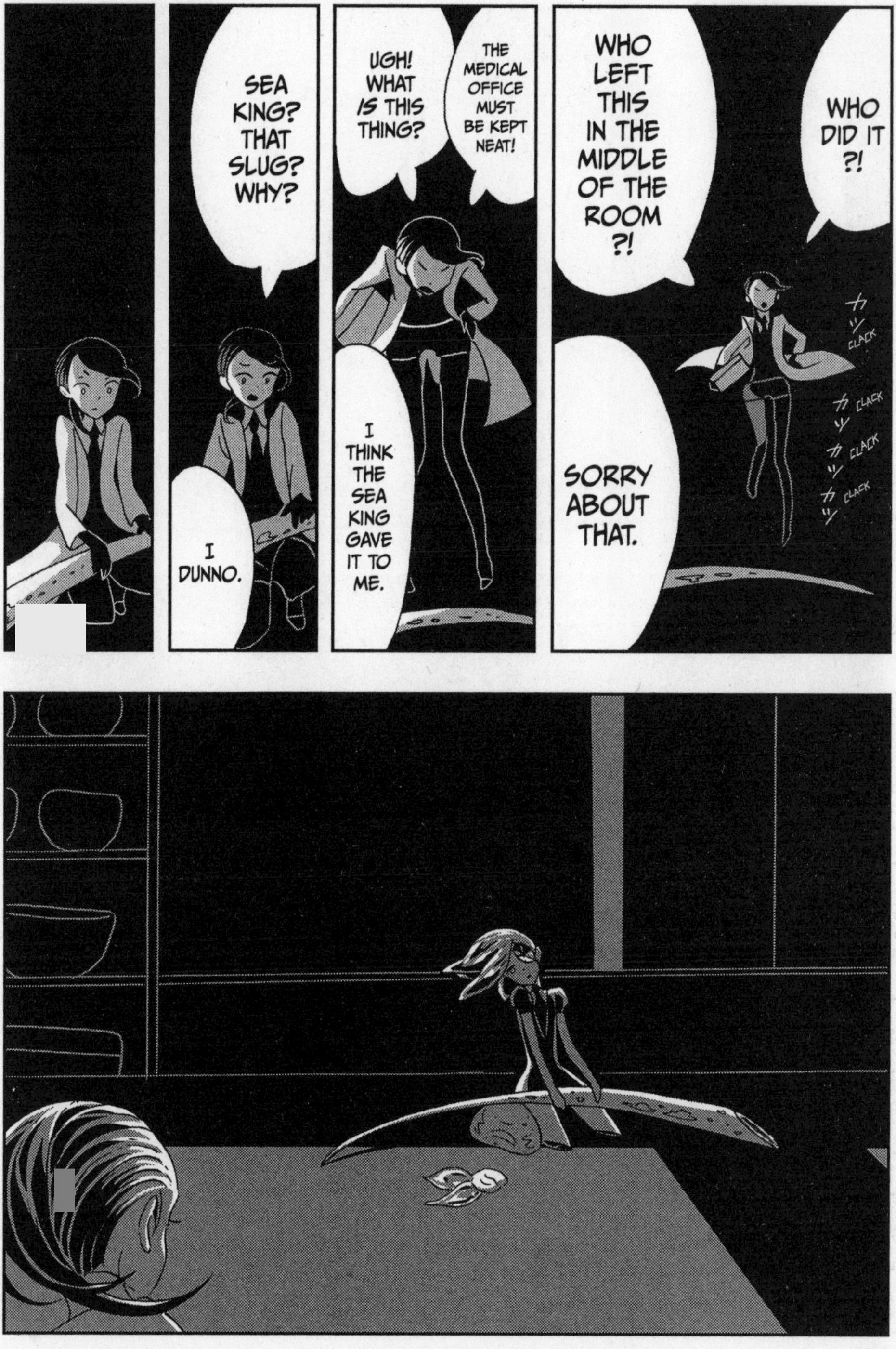
WHO DID IT ?!
WHO LEFT THIS IN THE MIDDLE OF THE ROOM ?!
カツ CLACK
カツ CLACK
カツ CLACK
カツ CLACK
SORRY ABOUT THAT.
THE MEDICAL OFFICE MUST BE KEPT NEAT!
UGH! WHAT IS THIS THING?
I THINK THE SEA KING GAVE IT TO ME.
SEA KING? THAT SLUG? WHY?
I DUNNO.

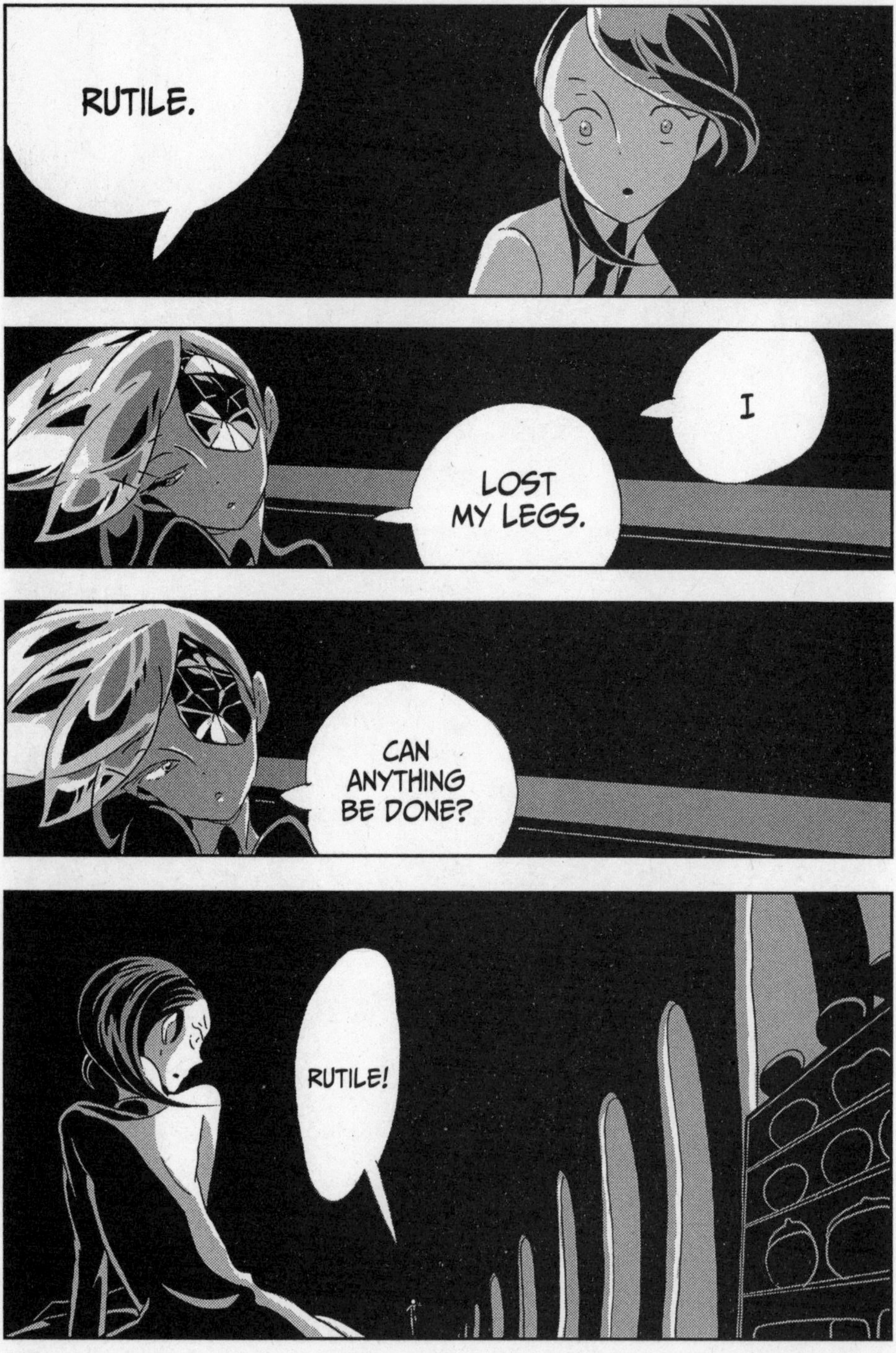
RUTILE.
I
LOST MY LEGS.
CAN ANYTHING BE DONE?
RUTILE!

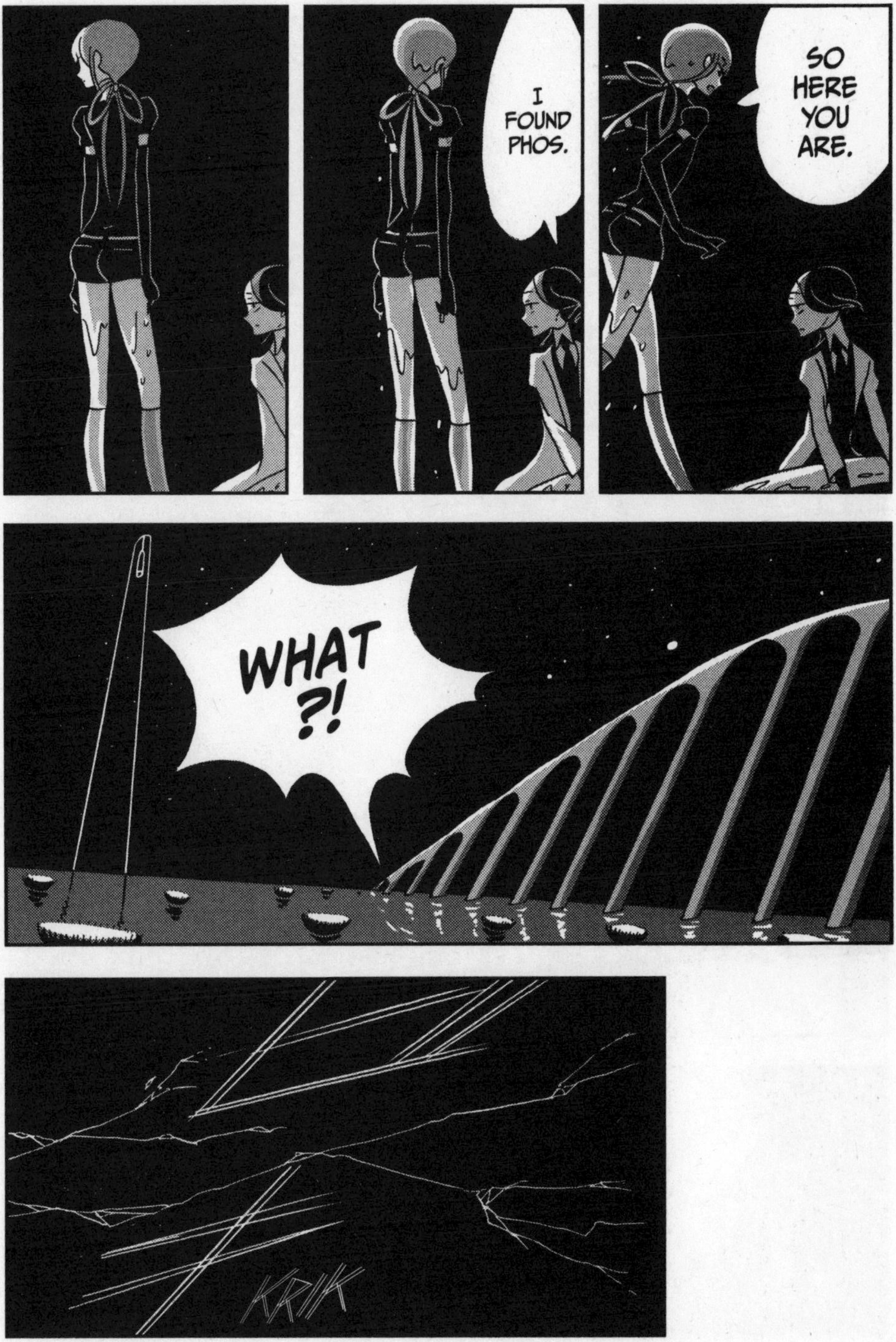

SO HERE YOU ARE.
I FOUND PHOS.
WHAT?!
KRIK

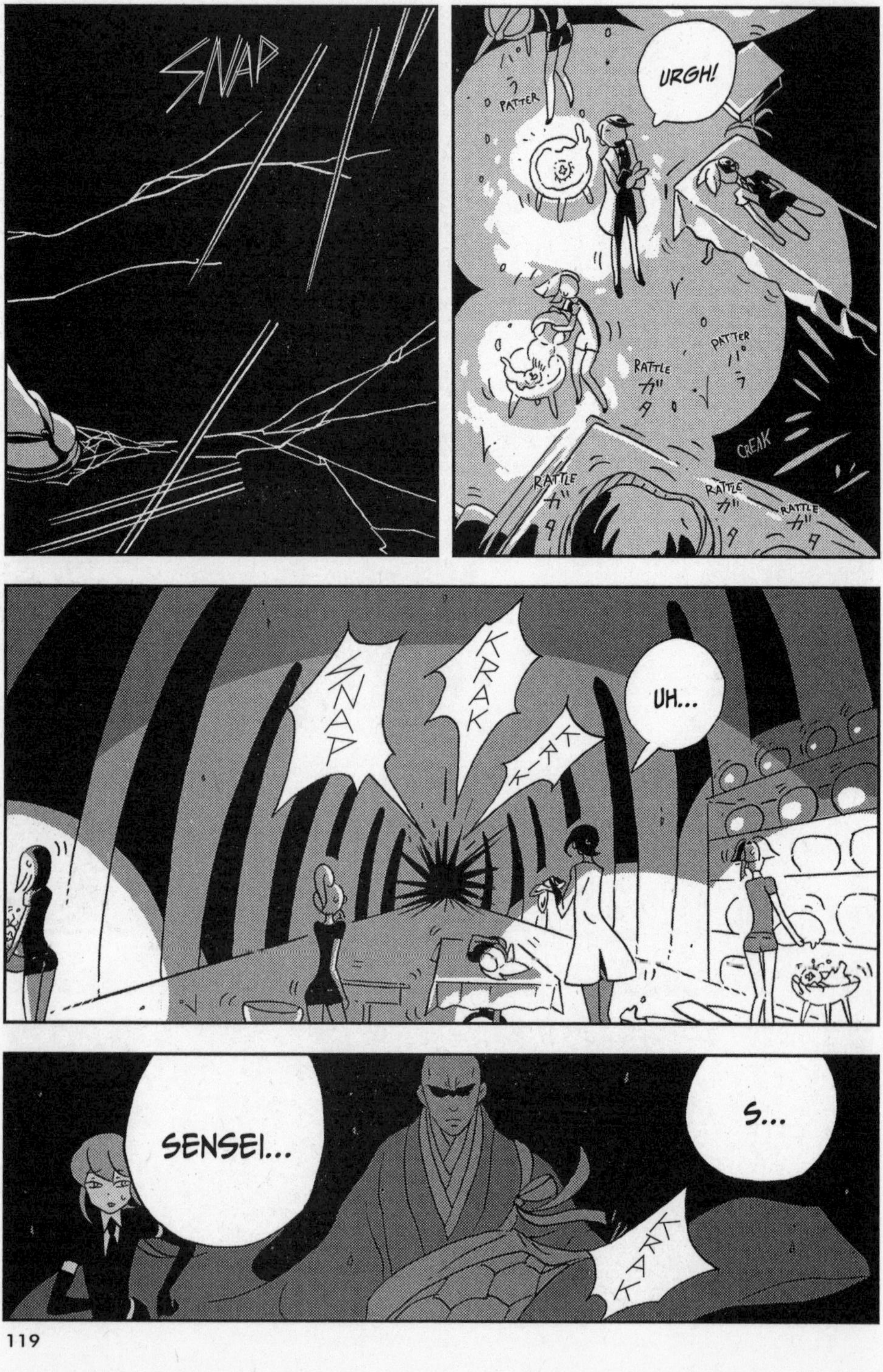
URGH!
PATTER
PATTER
RATTLE
CREAK
RATTLE
RATTLE
RATTLE
SNAP
UH...
KRAK
K-R-K
SNAP
S...
KRAK
SENSEI...

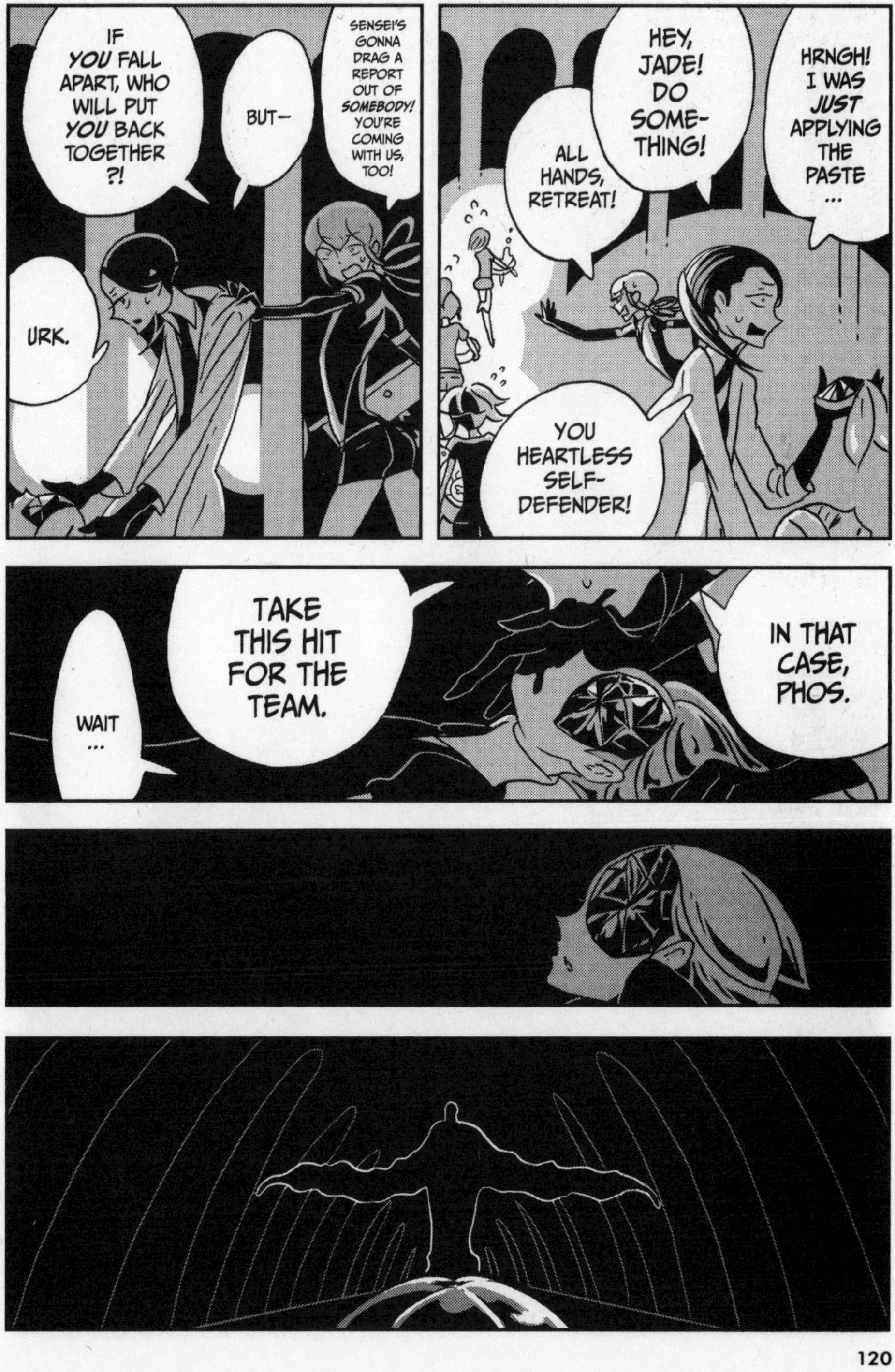
HRNGH! I WAS JUST APPLYING THE PASTE ...
HEY, JADE! DO SOME-THING!
ALL HANDS, RETREAT!
YOU HEARTLESS SELF-DEFENDER!
SENSEI'S GONNA DRAG A REPORT OUT OF SOMEBODY! YOU'RE COMING WITH US, TOO!
BUT—
IF YOU FALL APART, WHO WILL PUT YOU BACK TOGETHER ?!
URK.
IN THAT CASE, PHOS.
TAKE THIS HIT FOR THE TEAM.
WAIT ...

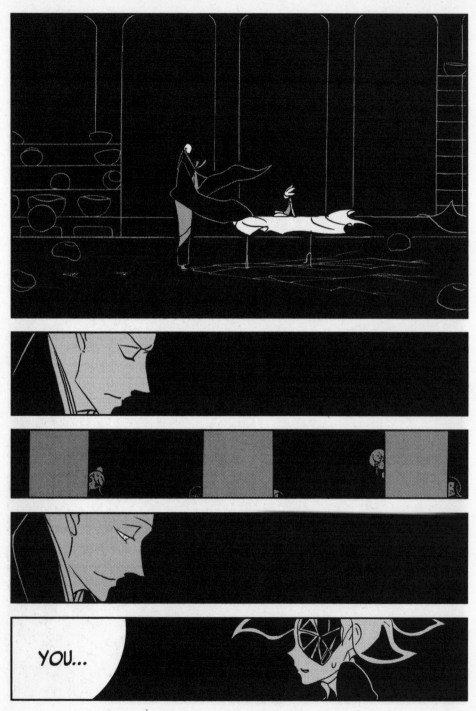

YOU...

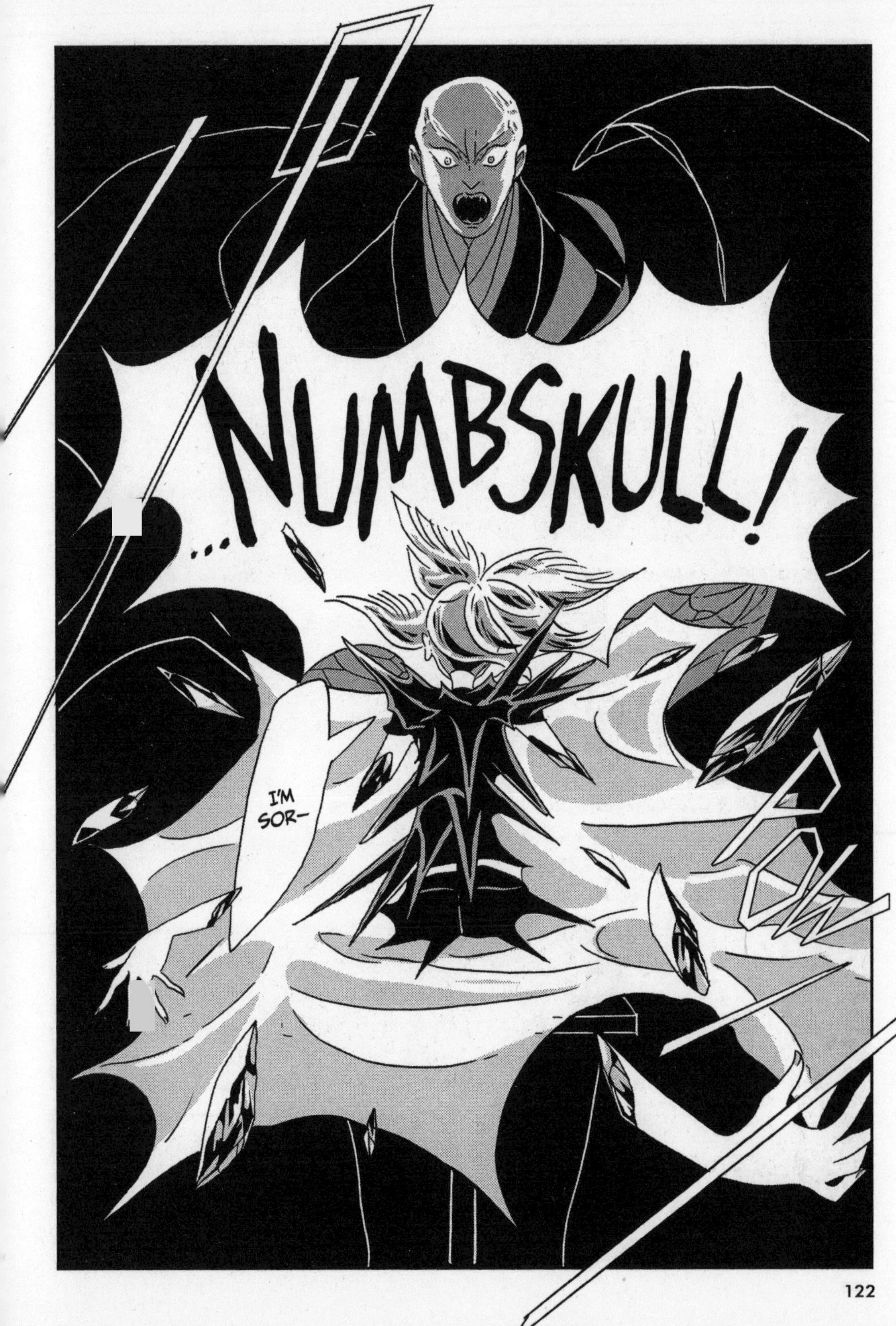
...NUMBSKULL!
I'M SOR—
POW

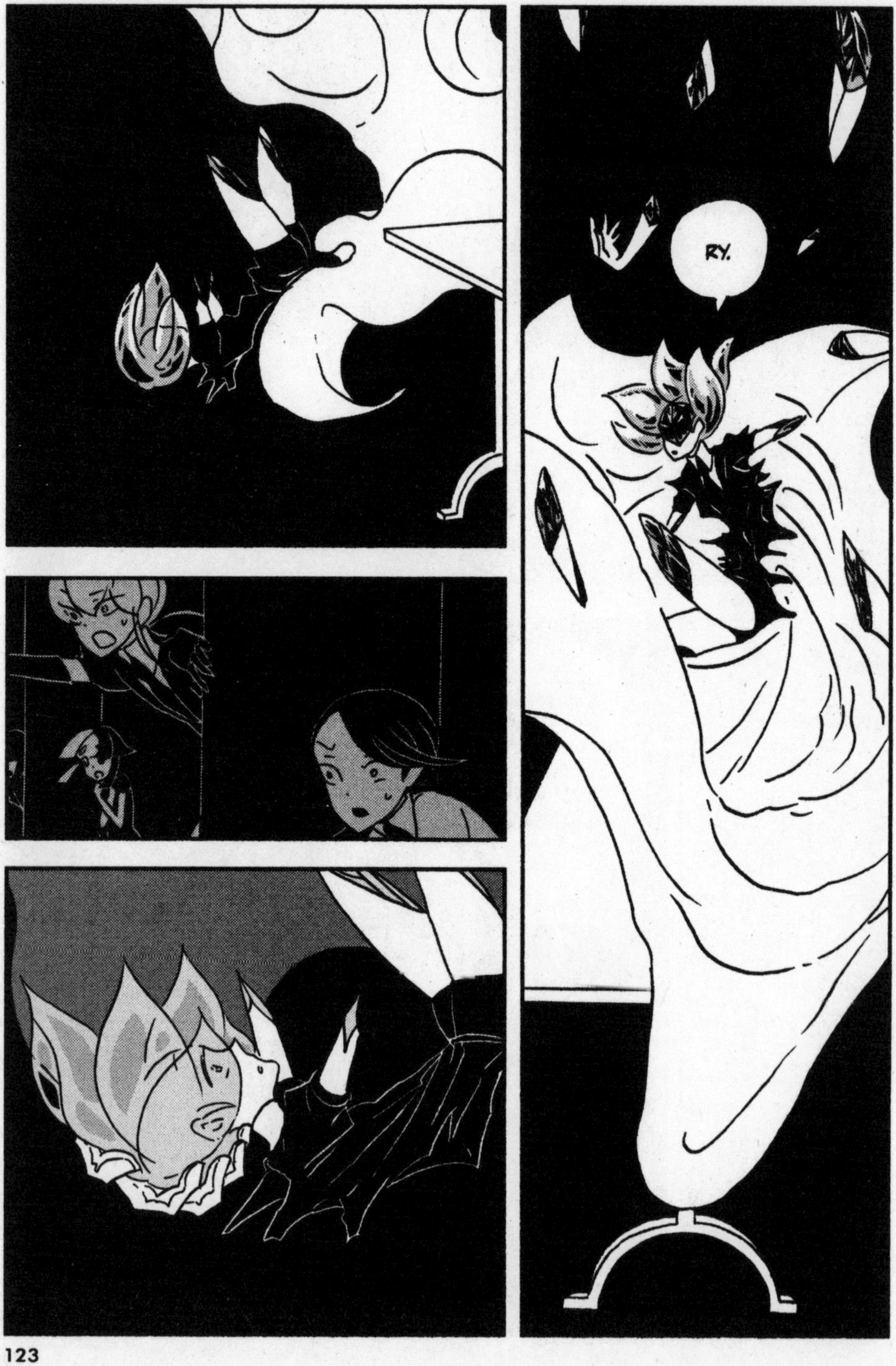
RY.

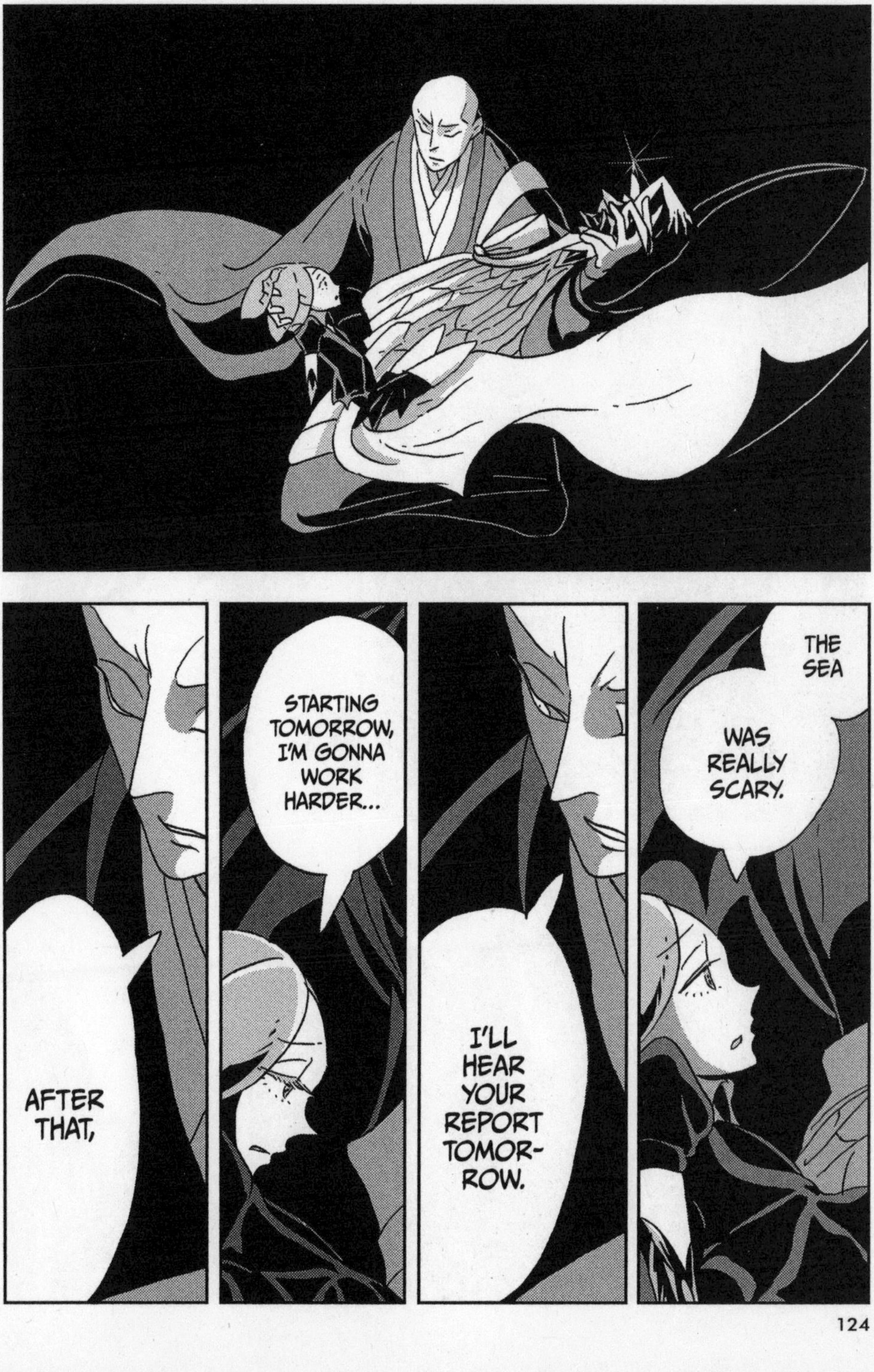
THE SEA WAS REALLY SCARY.
I'LL HEAR YOUR REPORT TOMOR-ROW.
STARTING TOMORROW, I'M GONNA WORK HARDER...
AFTER THAT,

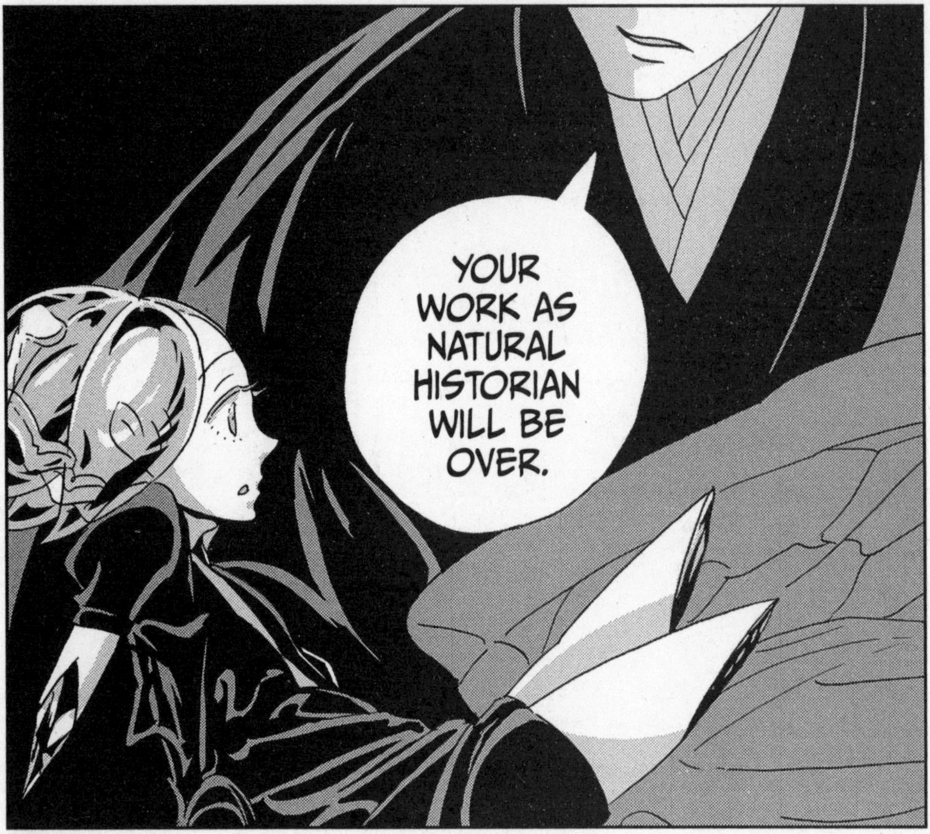
YOUR WORK AS NATURAL HISTORIAN WILL BE OVER.
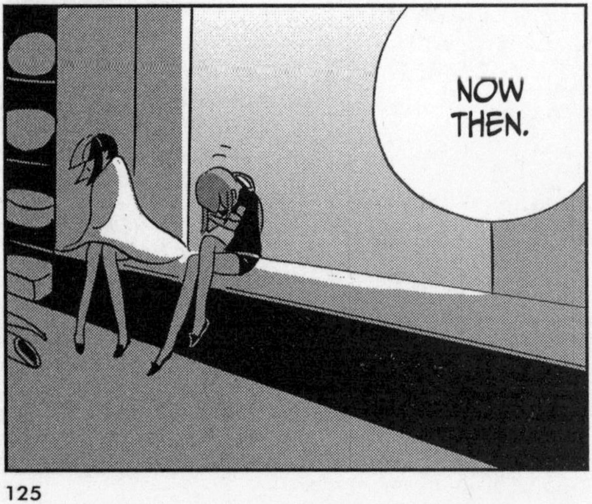
NOW THEN.

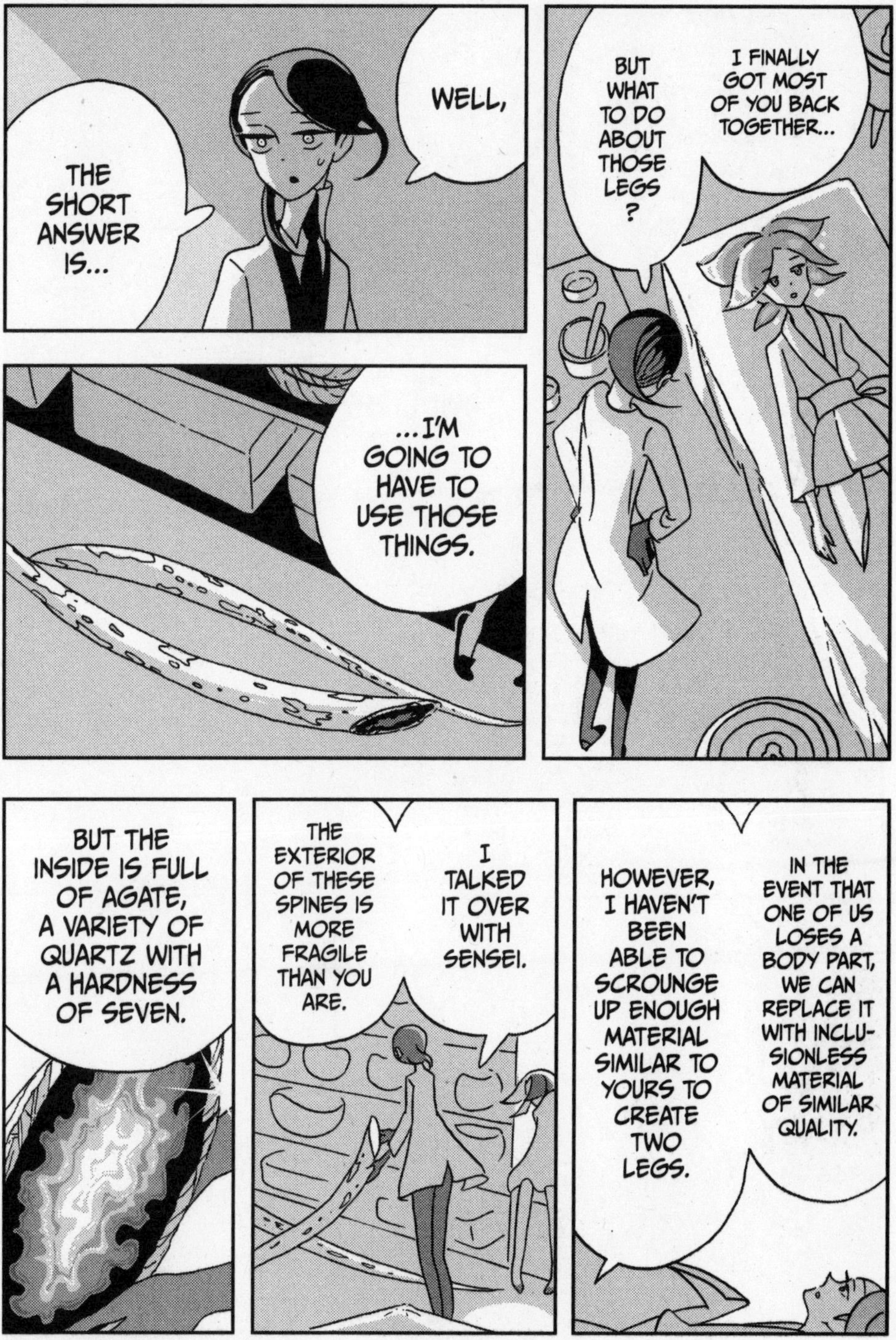

I FINALLY GOT MOST OF YOU BACK TOGETHER...
BUT WHAT TO DO ABOUT THOSE LEGS?
WELL,
THE SHORT ANSWER IS...
...I'M GOING TO HAVE TO USE THOSE THINGS.
IN THE EVENT THAT ONE OF US LOSES A BODY PART, WE CAN REPLACE IT WITH INCLUSIONLESS MATERIAL OF SIMILAR QUALITY.
HOWEVER, I HAVEN'T BEEN ABLE TO SCROUNGE UP ENOUGH MATERIAL SIMILAR TO YOURS TO CREATE TWO LEGS.
I TALKED IT OVER WITH SENSEI.
THE EXTERIOR OF THESE SPINES IS MORE FRAGILE THAN YOU ARE.
BUT THE INSIDE IS FULL OF AGATE, A VARIETY OF QUARTZ WITH A HARDNESS OF SEVEN.

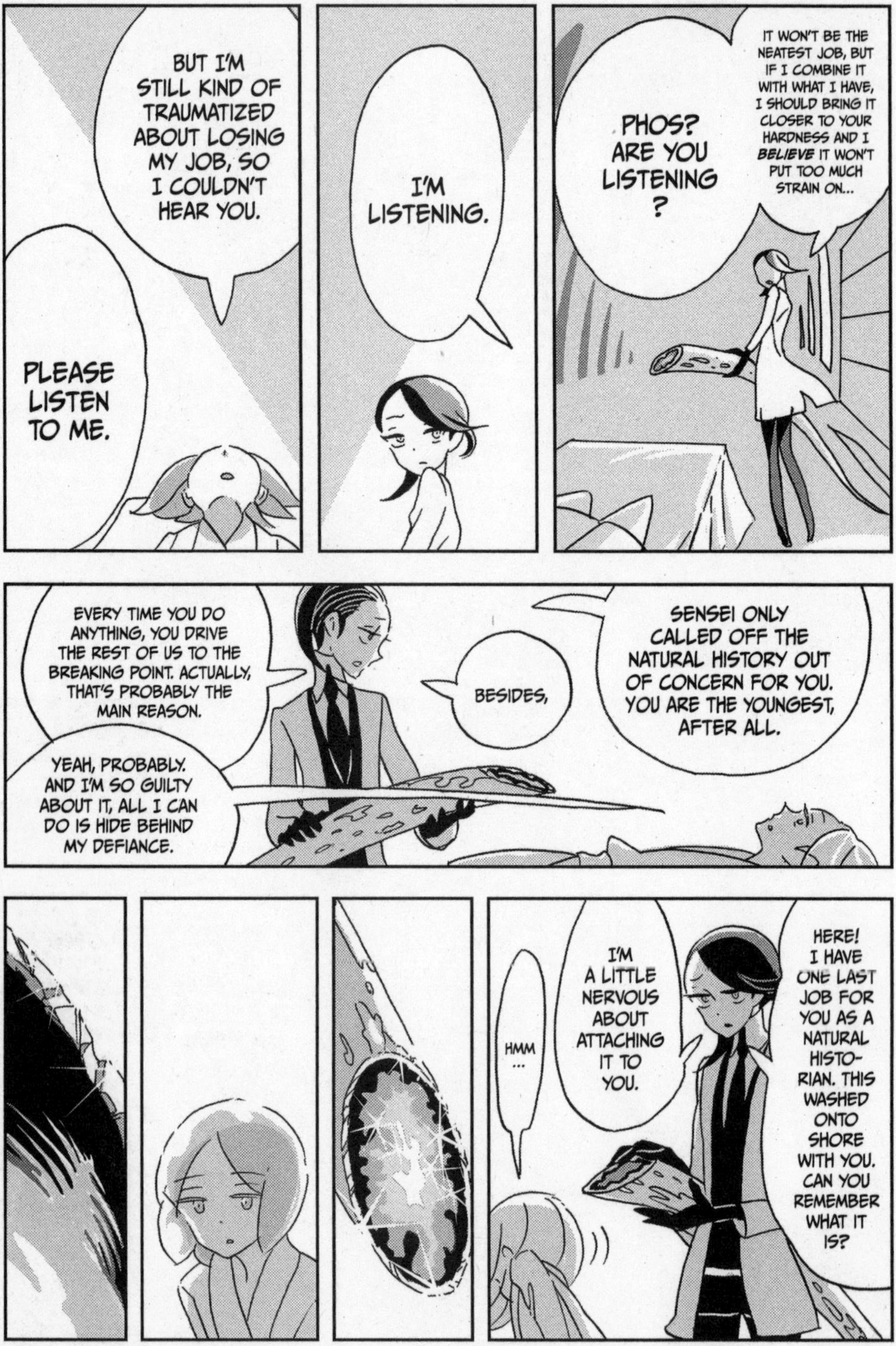
IT WON'T BE THE NEATEST JOB, BUT IF I COMBINE IT WITH WHAT I HAVE, I SHOULD BRING IT CLOSER TO YOUR HARDNESS AND I *BELIEVE* IT WON'T PUT TOO MUCH STRAIN ON...
PHOS? ARE YOU LISTENING?
I'M LISTENING.
BUT I'M STILL KIND OF TRAUMATIZED ABOUT LOSING MY JOB, SO I COULDN'T HEAR YOU.
PLEASE LISTEN TO ME.
SENSEI ONLY CALLED OFF THE NATURAL HISTORY OUT OF CONCERN FOR YOU. YOU ARE THE YOUNGEST, AFTER ALL.
BESIDES,
EVERY TIME YOU DO ANYTHING, YOU DRIVE THE REST OF US TO THE BREAKING POINT. ACTUALLY, THAT'S PROBABLY THE MAIN REASON.
YEAH, PROBABLY. AND I'M SO GUILTY ABOUT IT, ALL I CAN DO IS HIDE BEHIND MY DEFIANCE.
HERE! I HAVE ONE LAST JOB FOR YOU AS A NATURAL HISTO-RIAN. THIS WASHED ONTO SHORE WITH YOU. CAN YOU REMEMBER WHAT IT IS?
I'M A LITTLE NERVOUS ABOUT ATTACHING IT TO YOU.
HMM ...

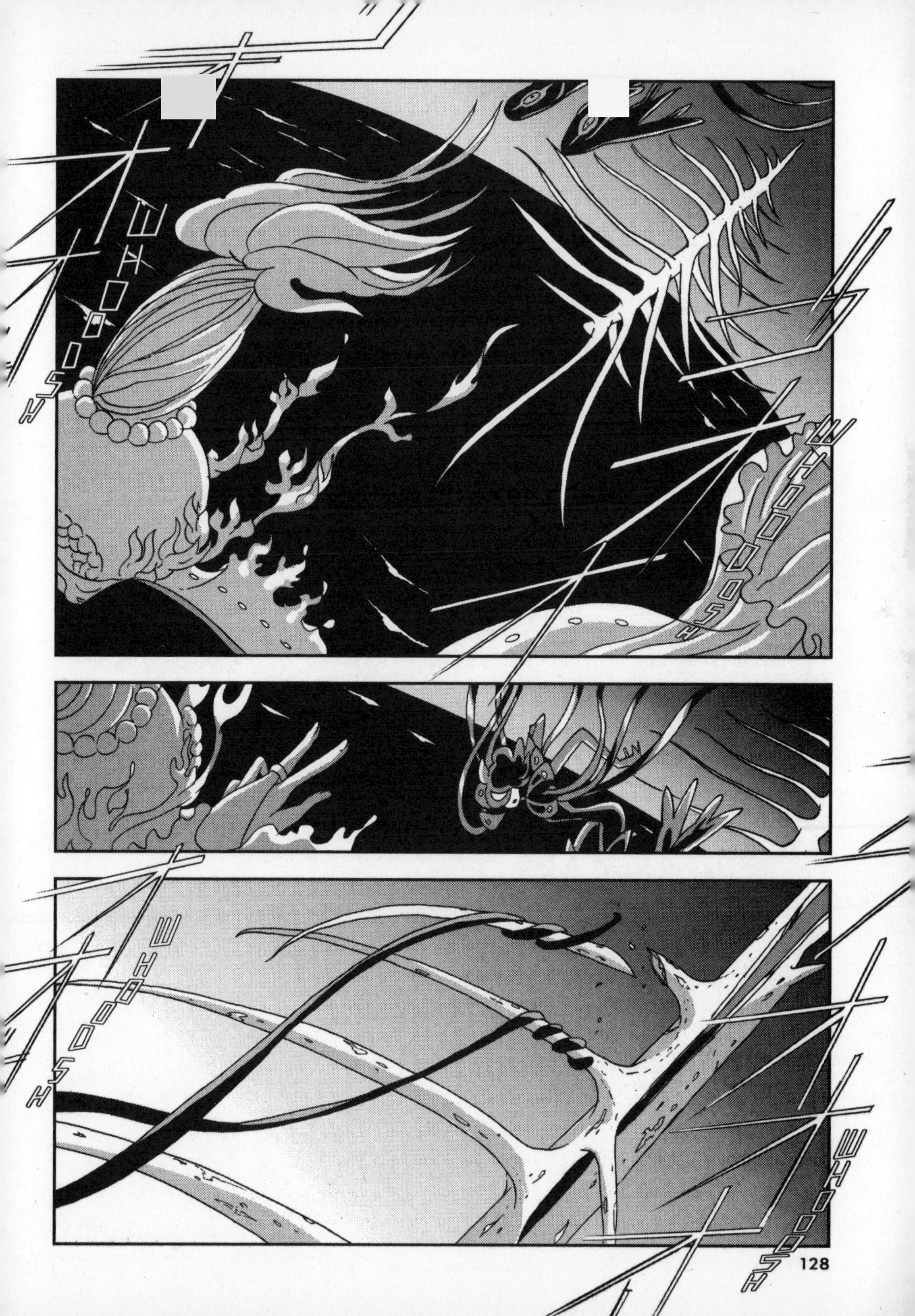
WHOOOOSH
WHOOOOSH
WHOOOOSH
WHOOOOSH

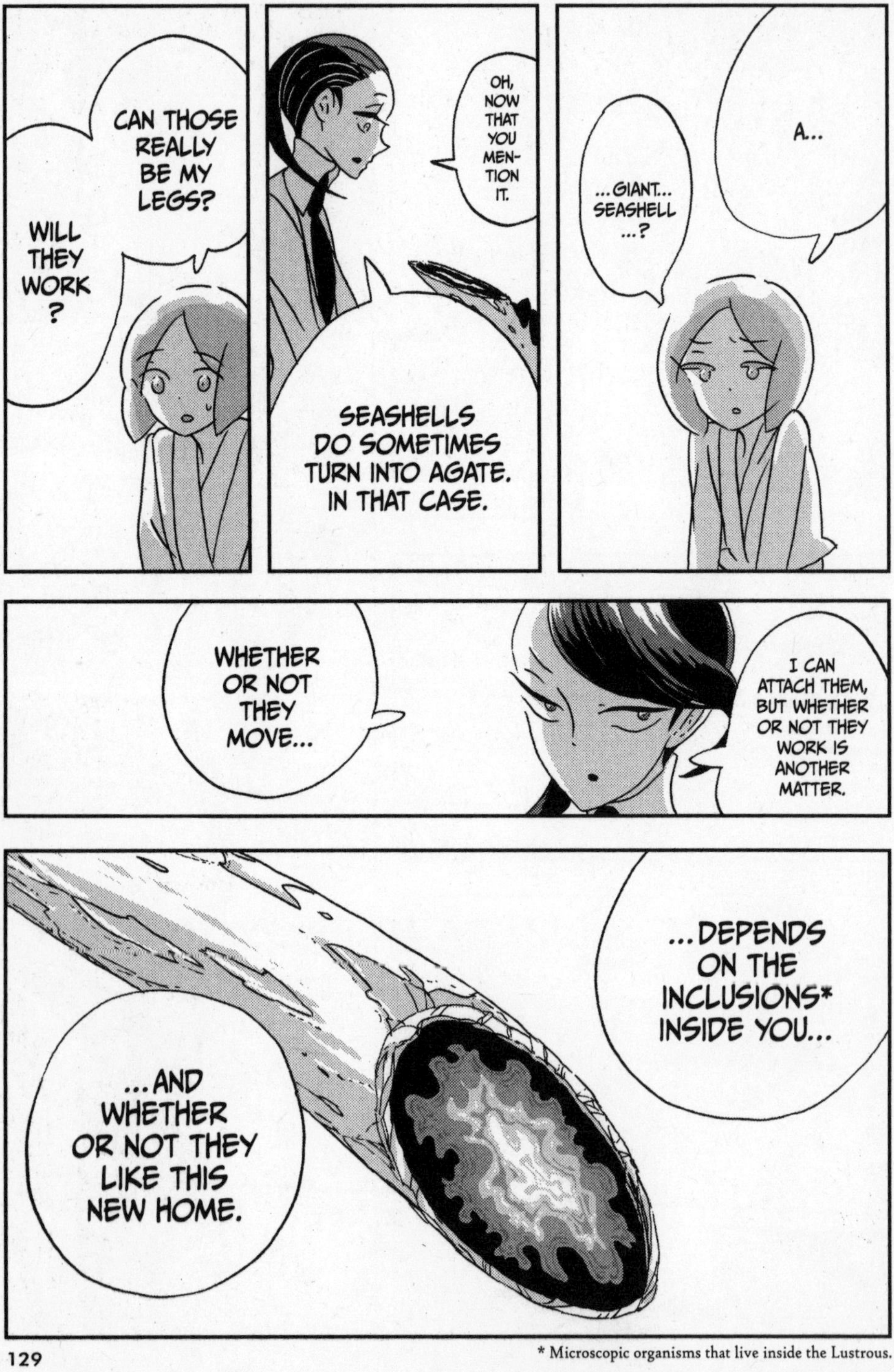
A...
...GIANT... SEASHELL ...?
OH, NOW THAT YOU MEN-TION IT.
SEASHELLS DO SOMETIMES TURN INTO AGATE. IN THAT CASE.
CAN THOSE REALLY BE MY LEGS?
WILL THEY WORK ?
I CAN ATTACH THEM, BUT WHETHER OR NOT THEY WORK IS ANOTHER MATTER.
WHETHER OR NOT THEY MOVE...
...DEPENDS ON THE INCLUSIONS* INSIDE YOU...
...AND WHETHER OR NOT THEY LIKE THIS NEW HOME.

* Microscopic organisms that live inside the Lustrous.

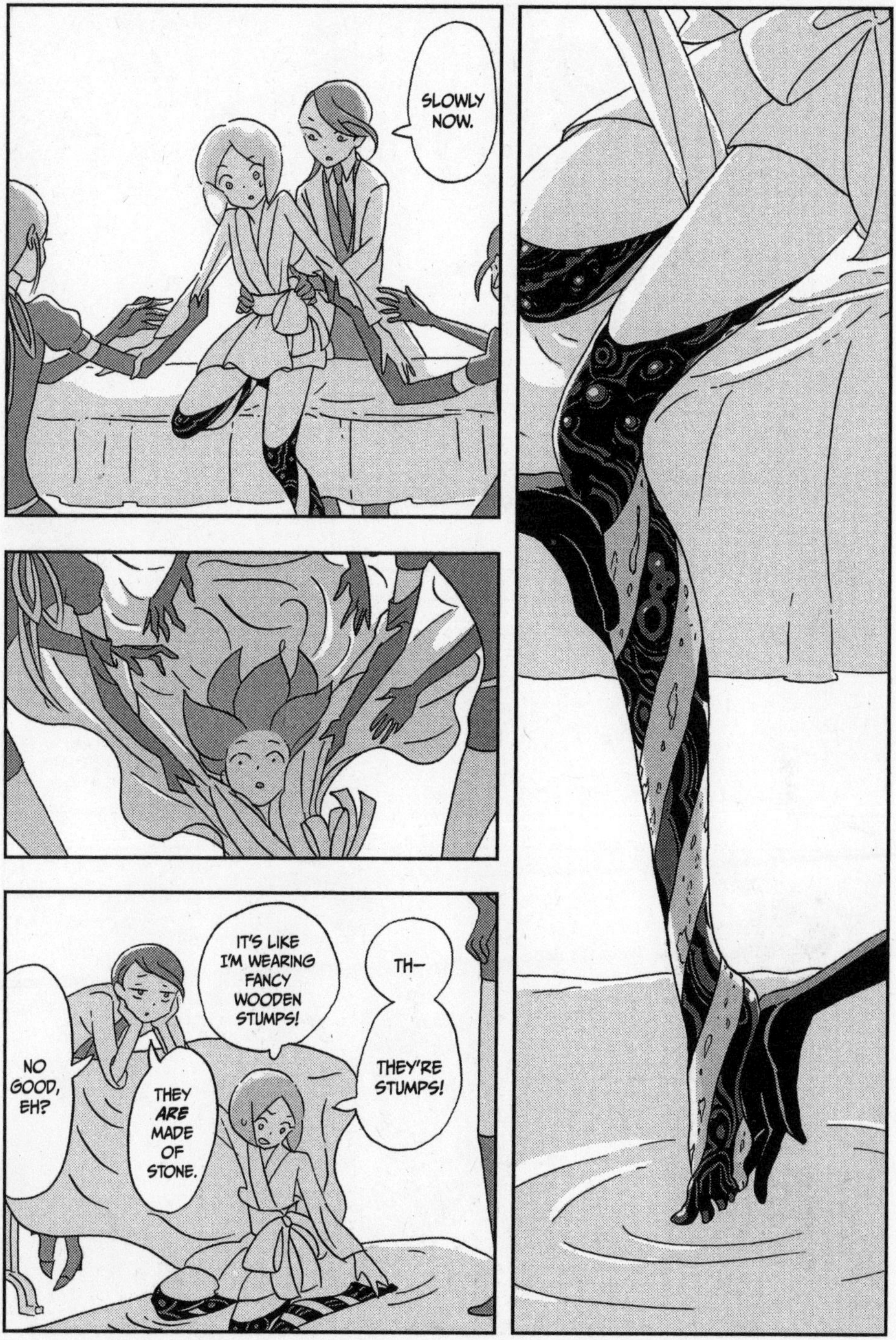
SLOWLY NOW.
TH— THEY'RE STUMPS!
IT'S LIKE I'M WEARING FANCY WOODEN STUMPS!
THEY *ARE* MADE OF STONE.
NO GOOD, EH?

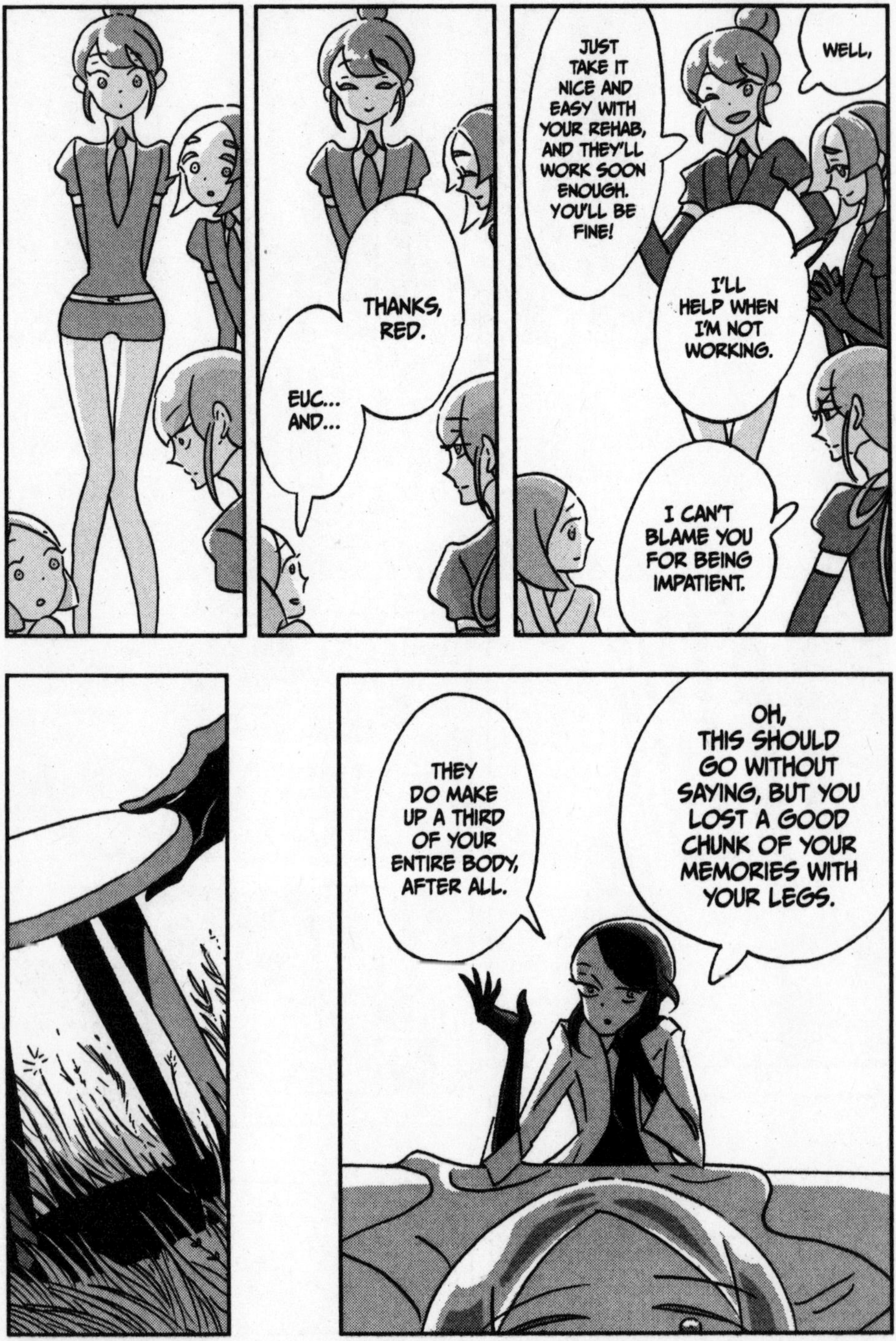
WELL,
JUST TAKE IT NICE AND EASY WITH YOUR REHAB, AND THEY'LL WORK SOON ENOUGH. YOU'LL BE FINE!
I'LL HELP WHEN I'M NOT WORKING.
I CAN'T BLAME YOU FOR BEING IMPATIENT.
THANKS, RED.
EUC... AND...
OH, THIS SHOULD GO WITHOUT SAYING, BUT YOU LOST A GOOD CHUNK OF YOUR MEMORIES WITH YOUR LEGS.
THEY DO MAKE UP A THIRD OF YOUR ENTIRE BODY, AFTER ALL.

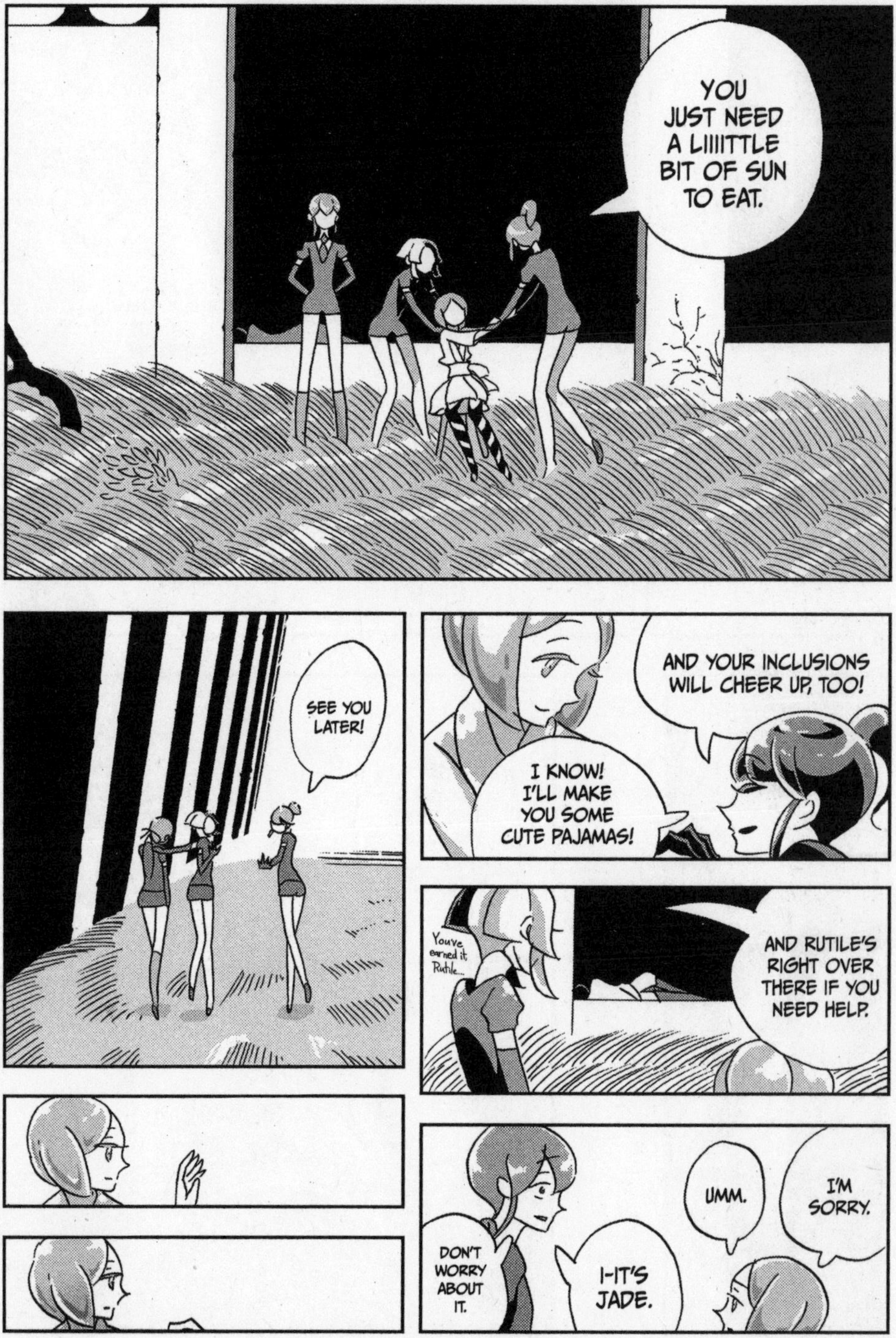
YOU JUST NEED A LIIIITTLE BIT OF SUN TO EAT.
AND YOUR INCLUSIONS WILL CHEER UP, TOO!
I KNOW! I'LL MAKE YOU SOME CUTE PAJAMAS!
AND RUTILE'S RIGHT OVER THERE IF YOU NEED HELP.
You've earned it Rutile...
SEE YOU LATER!
I'M SORRY.
UMM.
I-IT'S JADE.
DON'T WORRY ABOUT IT.

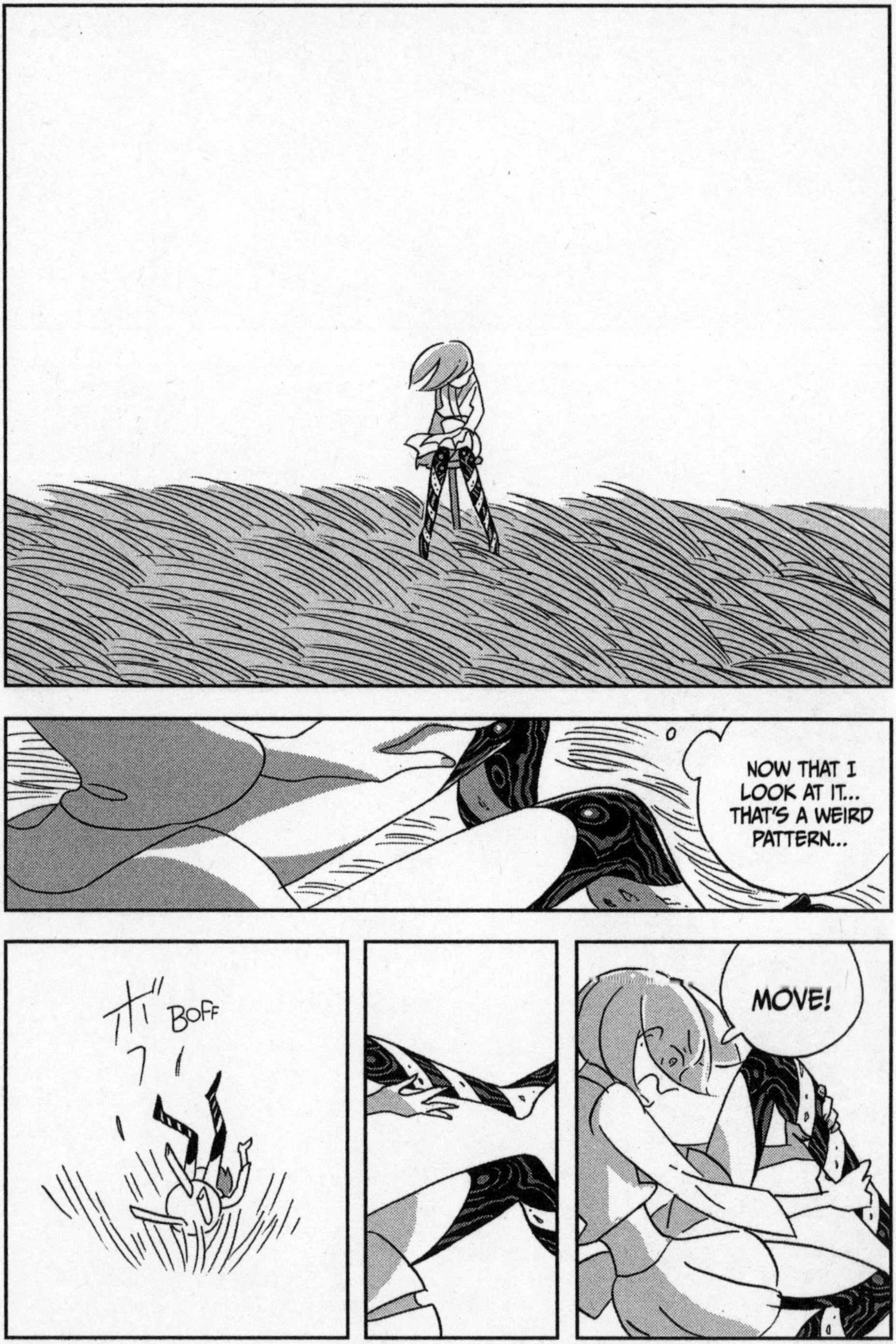
NOW THAT I LOOK AT IT... THAT'S A WEIRD PATTERN...
MOVE!
BOFF

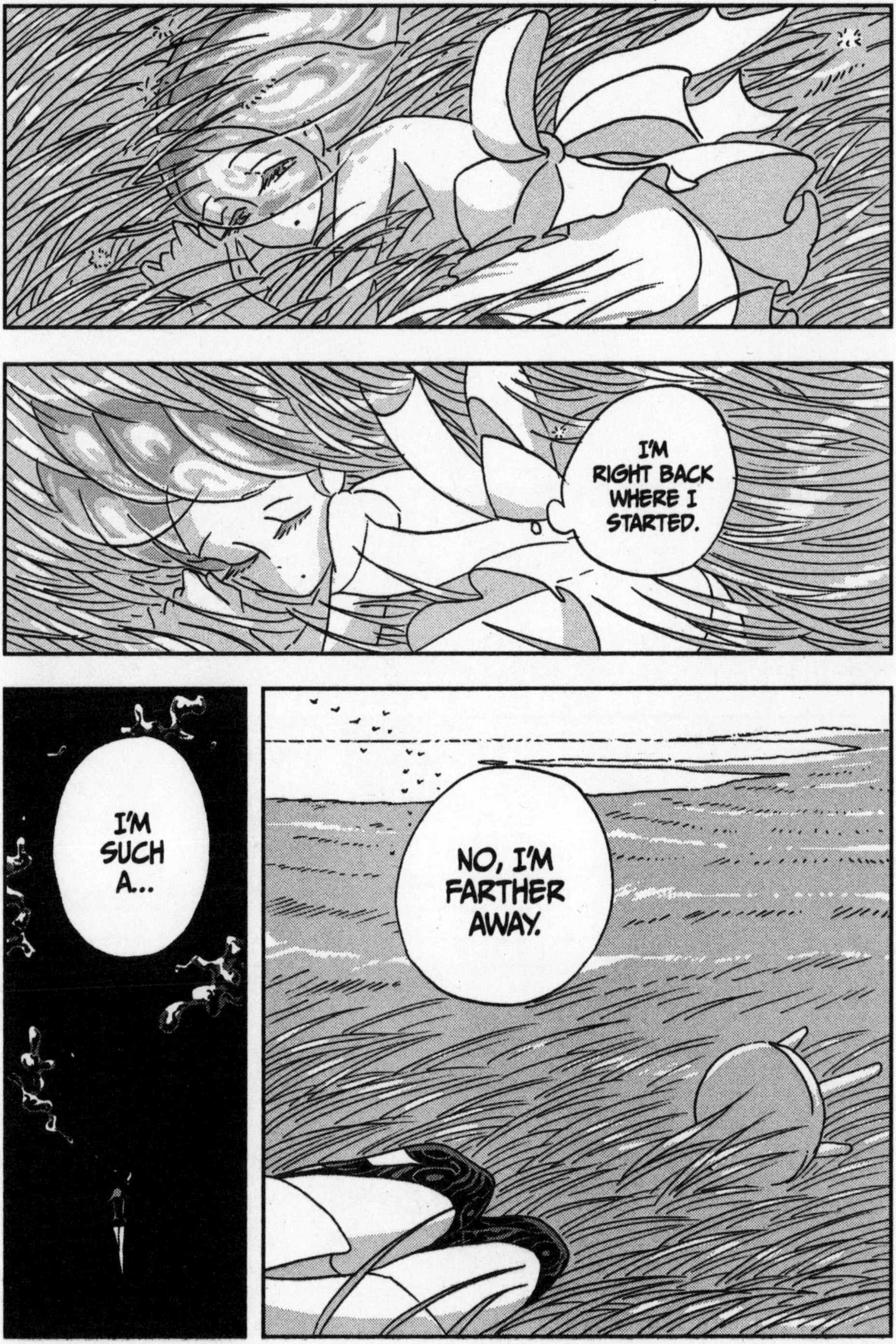
I'M RIGHT BACK WHERE I STARTED.
NO, I'M FARTHER AWAY.
I'M SUCH A...

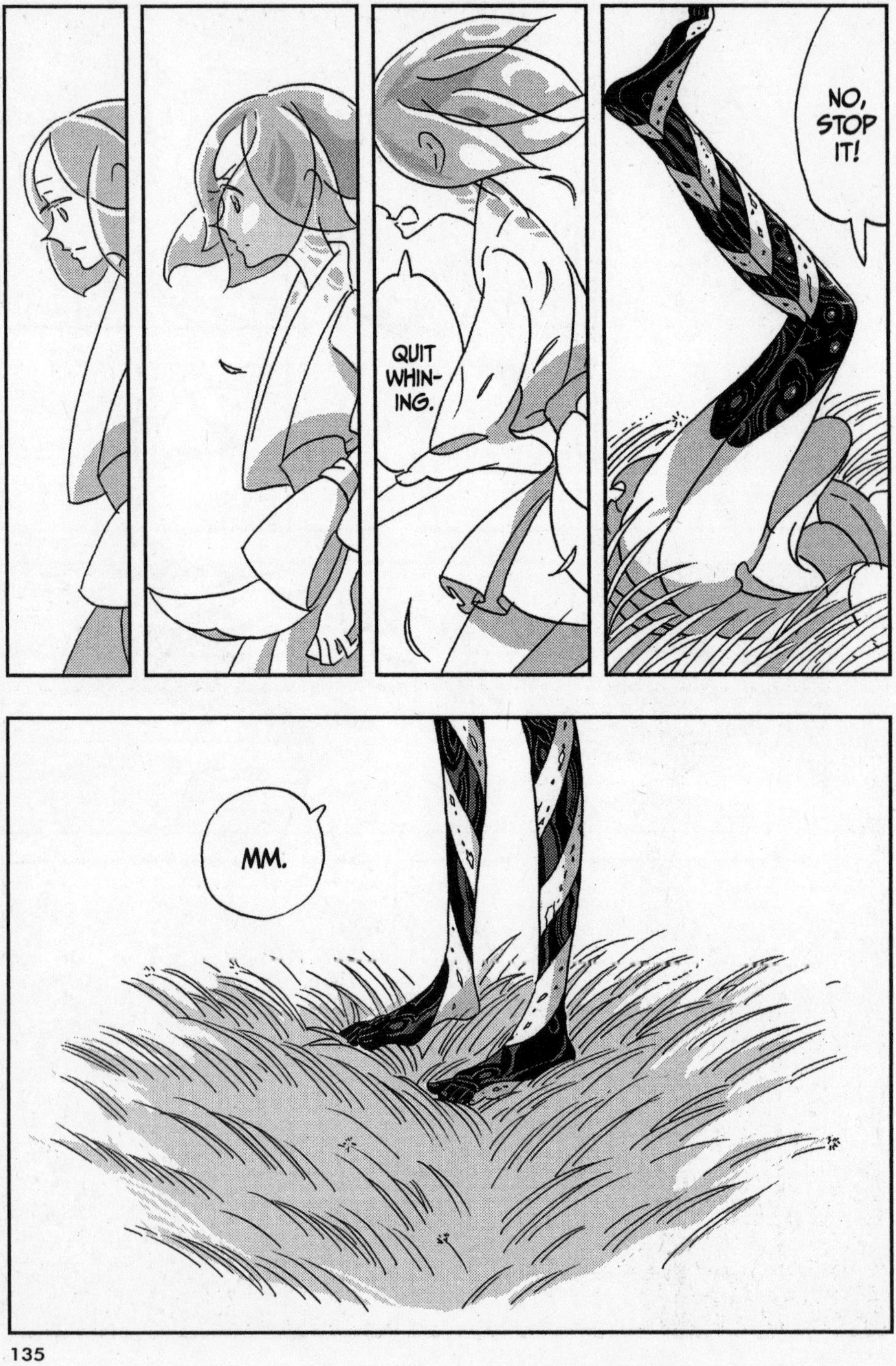
NO, STOP IT!
QUIT WHIN-ING.
MM.

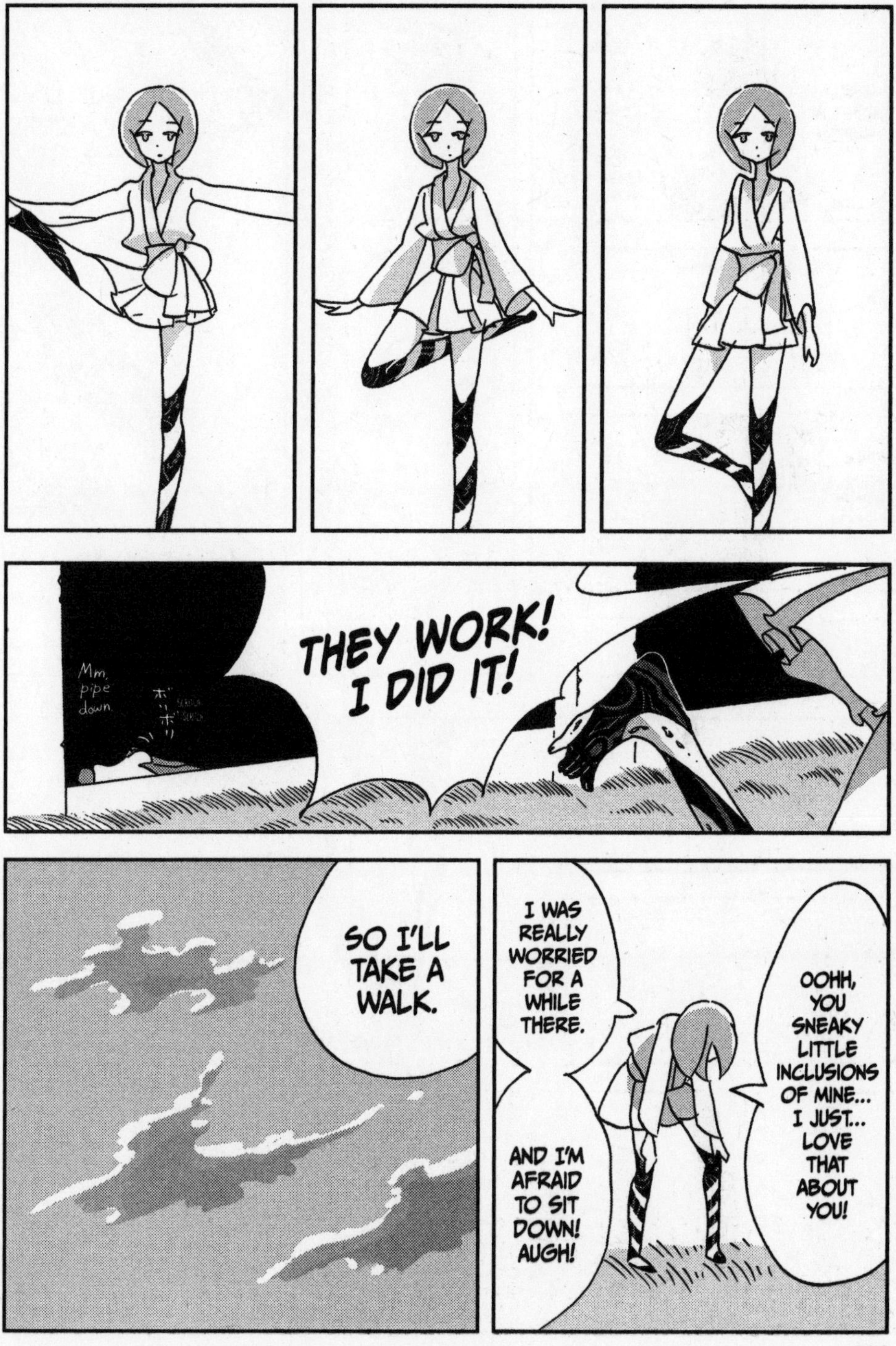
THEY WORK! I DID IT!
ボリボリ
Mm, pipe down.
OOHH, YOU SNEAKY LITTLE INCLUSIONS OF MINE... I JUST... LOVE THAT ABOUT YOU!
I WAS REALLY WORRIED FOR A WHILE THERE.
AND I'M AFRAID TO SIT DOWN! AUGH!
SO I'LL TAKE A WALK.

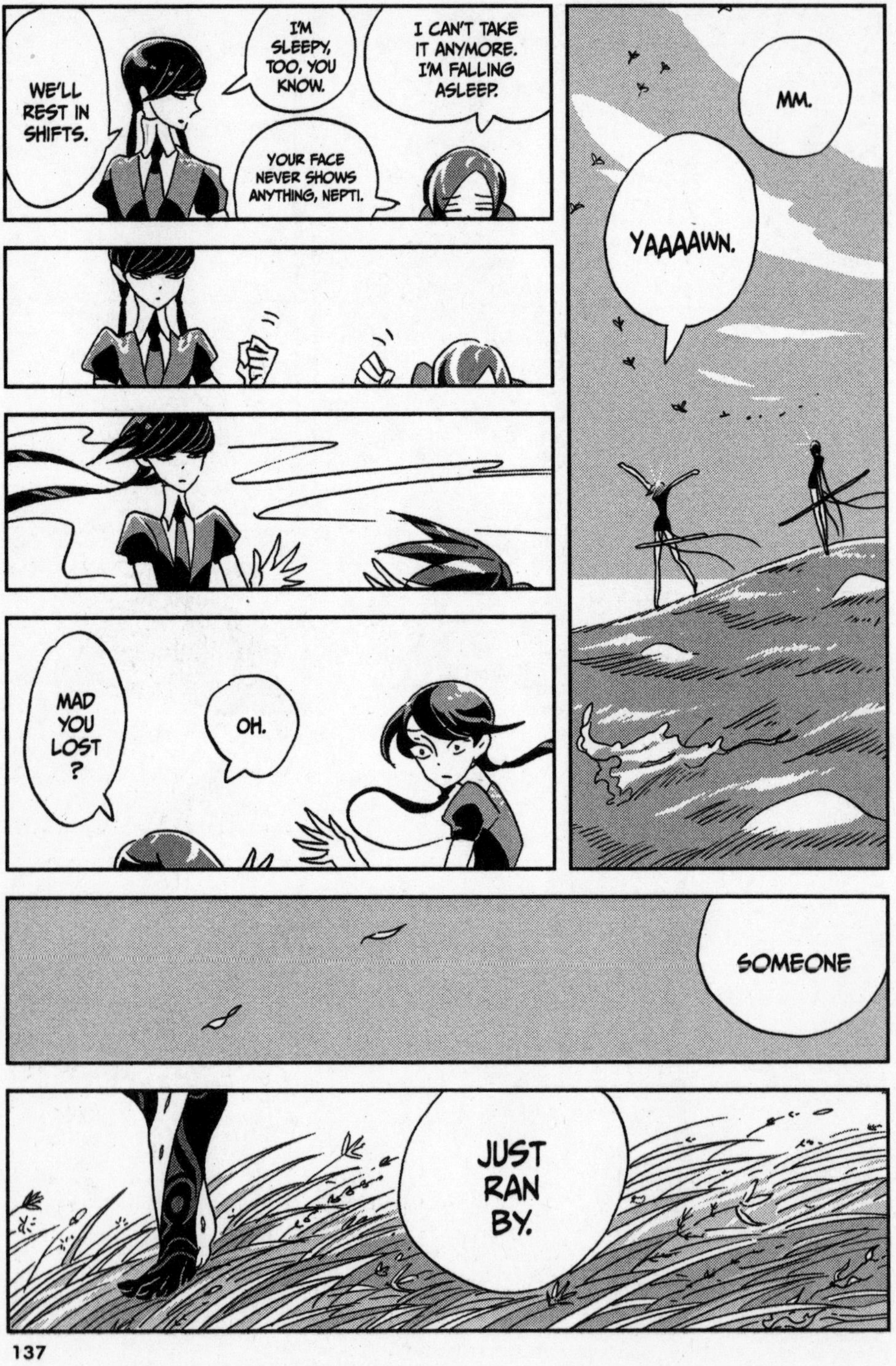
MM.
YAAAAWN.
I CAN'T TAKE IT ANYMORE. I'M FALLING ASLEEP.
I'M SLEEPY, TOO, YOU KNOW.
YOUR FACE NEVER SHOWS ANYTHING, NEPTI.
WE'LL REST IN SHIFTS.
OH.
MAD YOU LOST?
SOMEONE
JUST RAN BY.

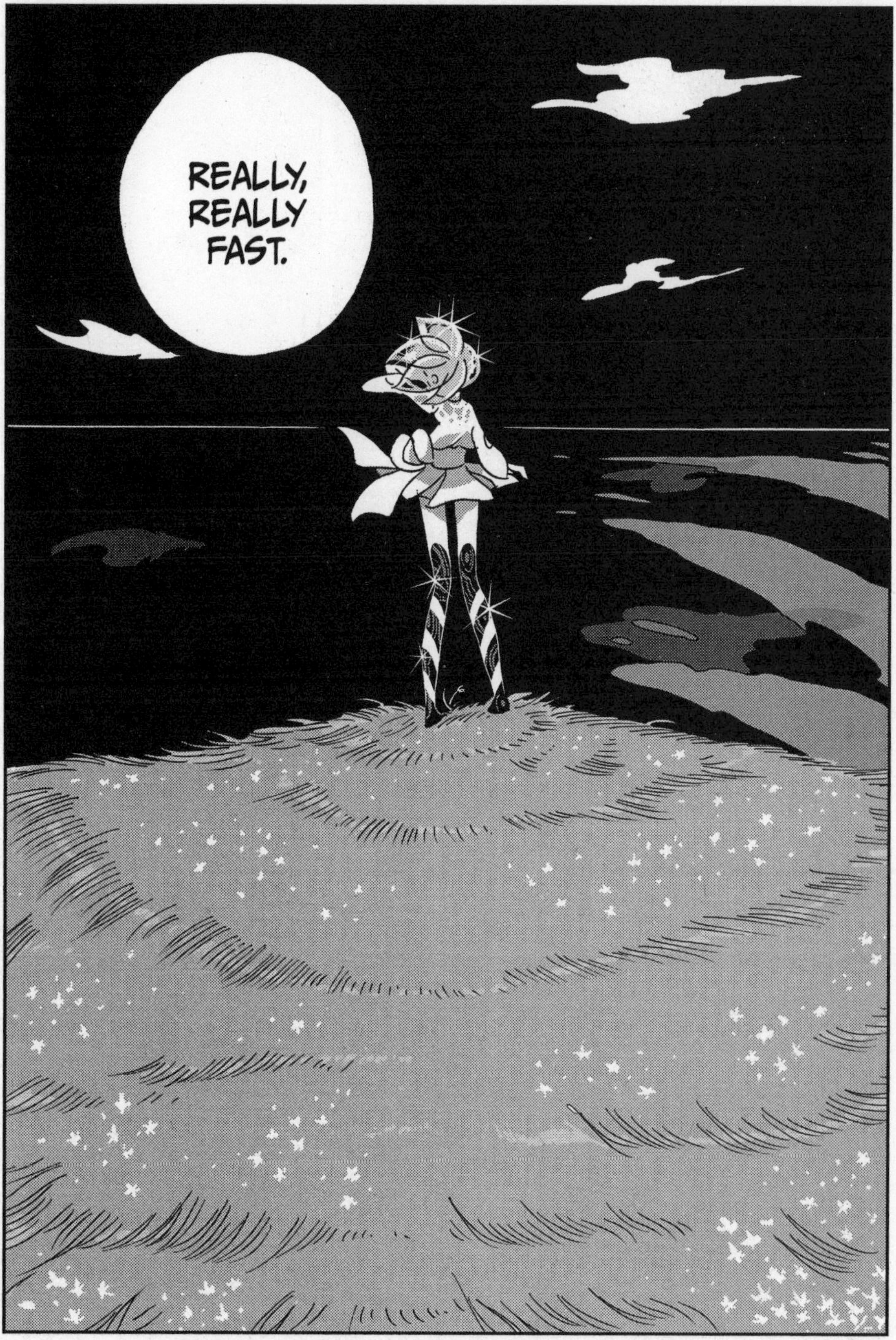
REALLY,
REALLY
FAST.

CHAPTER 12:

Yellow Diamond

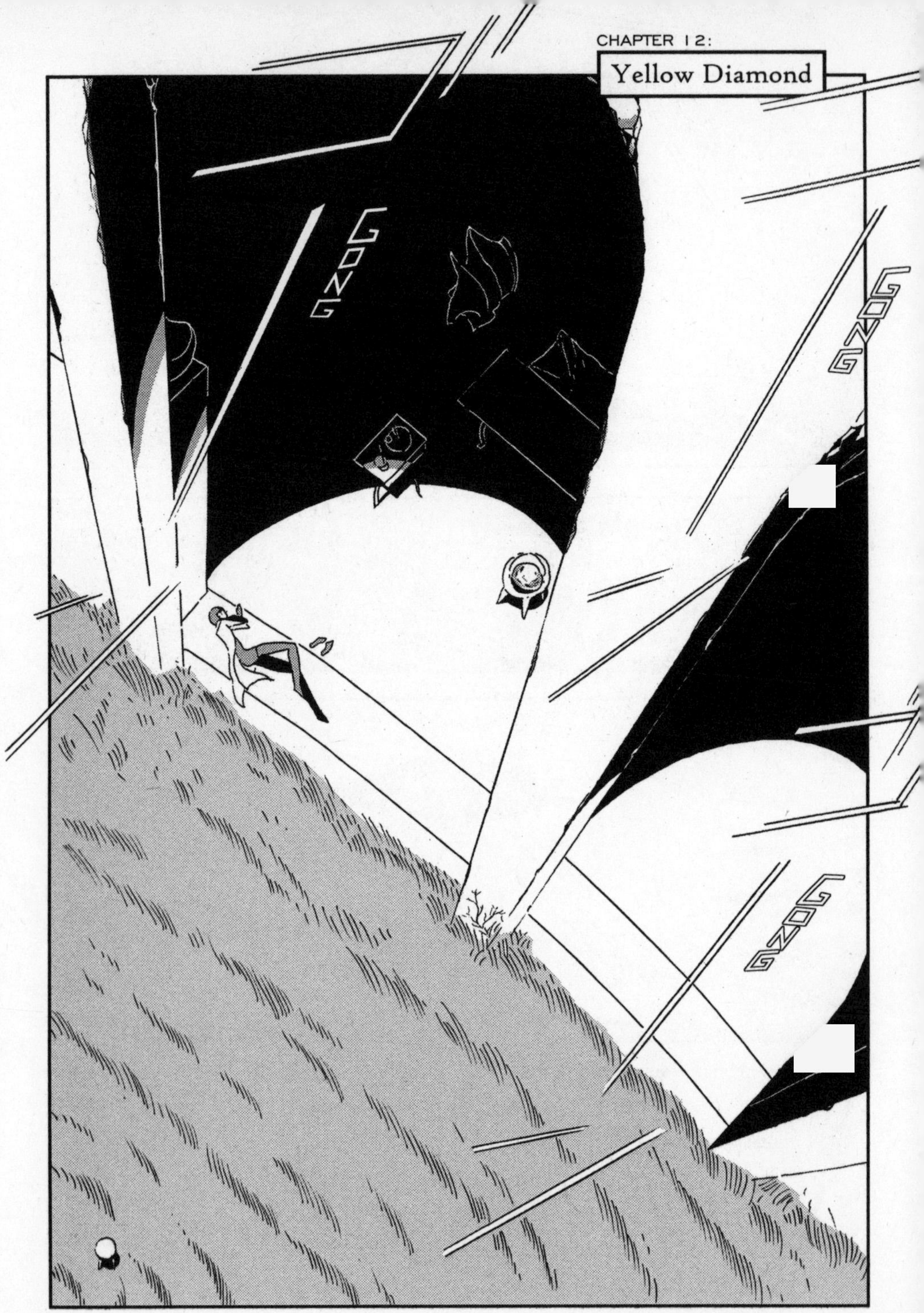
GONG
GONG
GONG

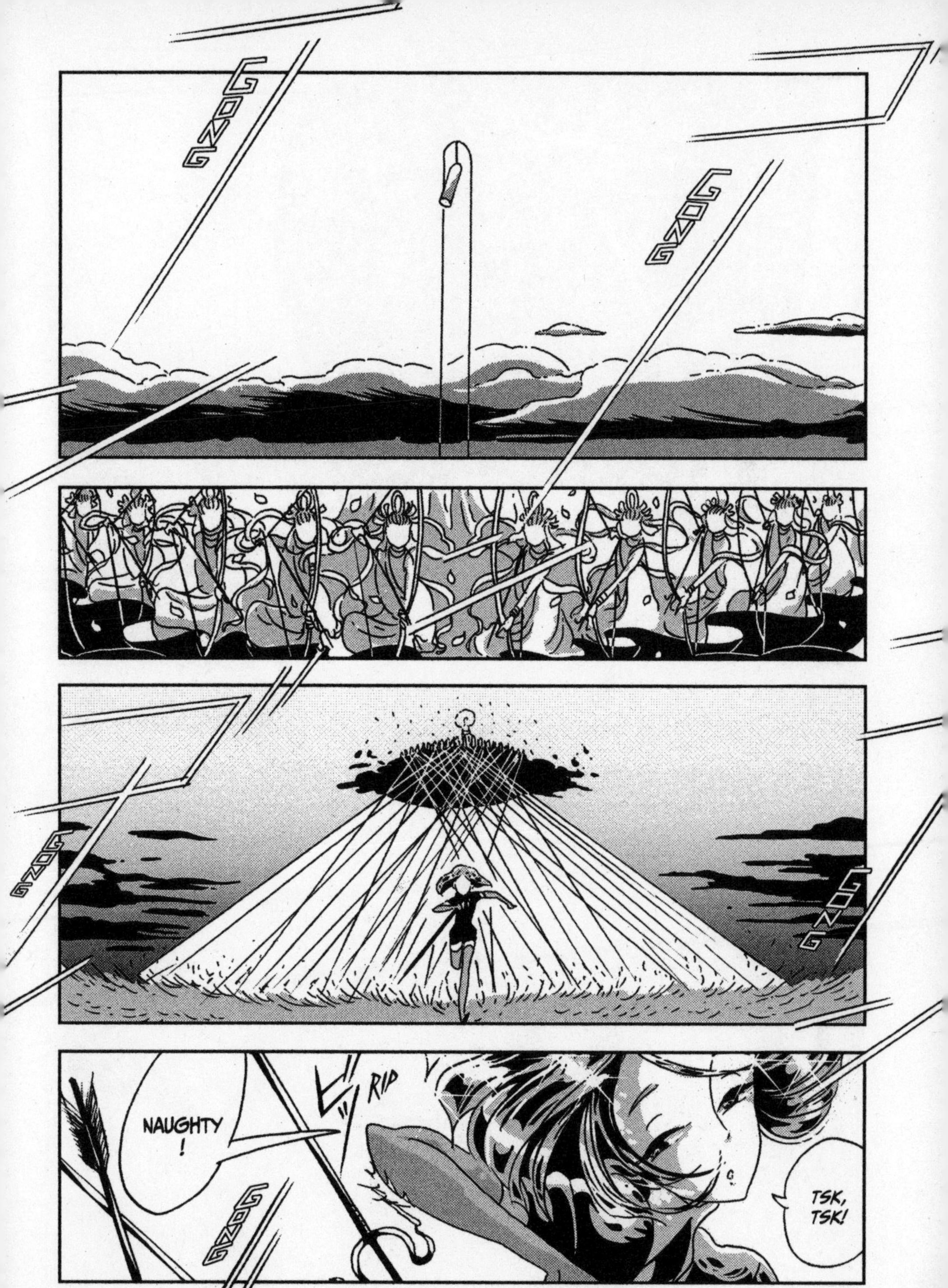
GONG
GONG
GONG
GONG
TSK, TSK!
RIP
NAUGHTY!
GONG

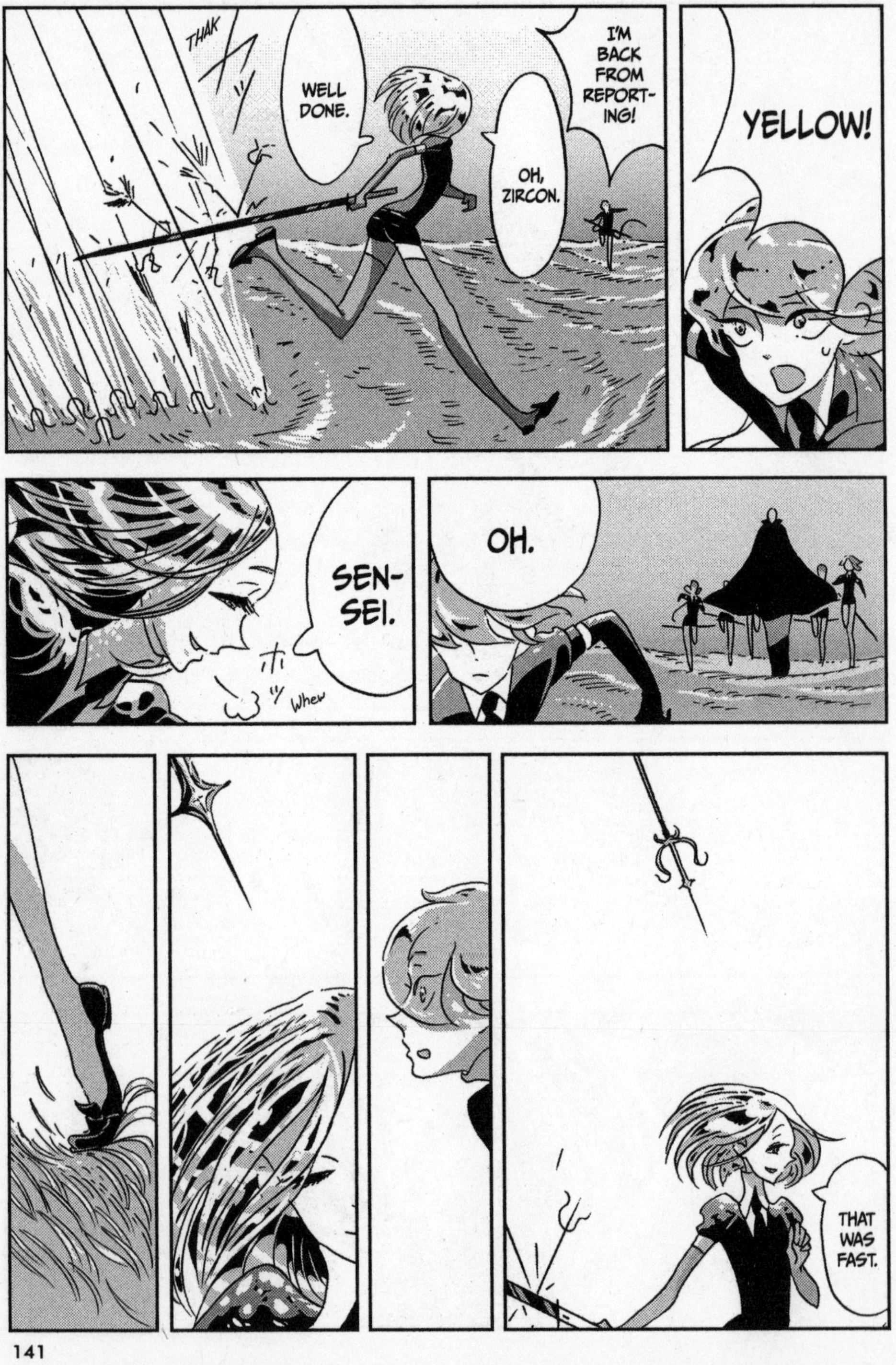
YELLOW!
I'M BACK FROM REPORT-ING!
OH, ZIRCON.
WELL DONE.
THAK
OH.
SEN-SEI.
Whew
THAT WAS FAST.

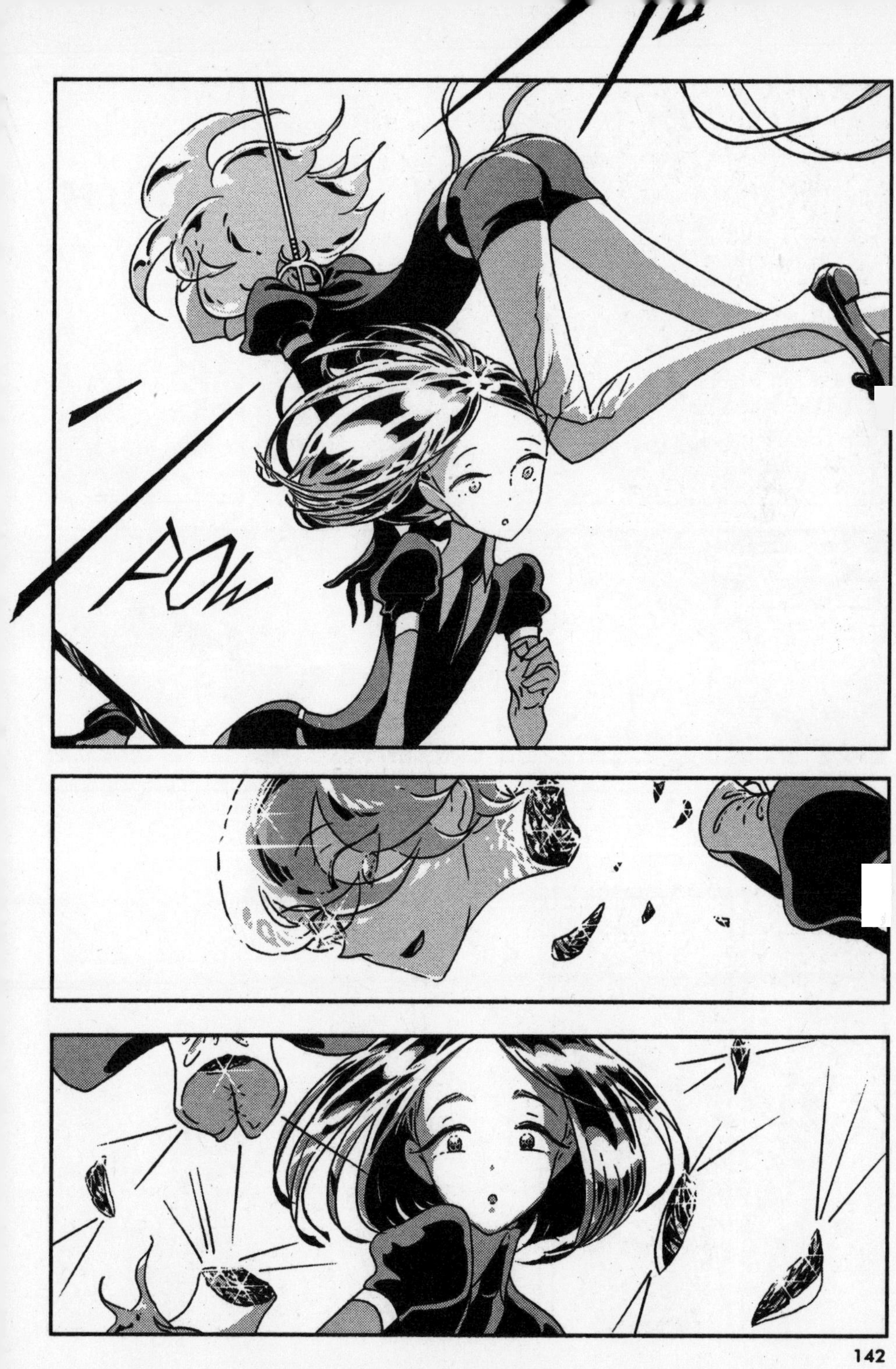
POW

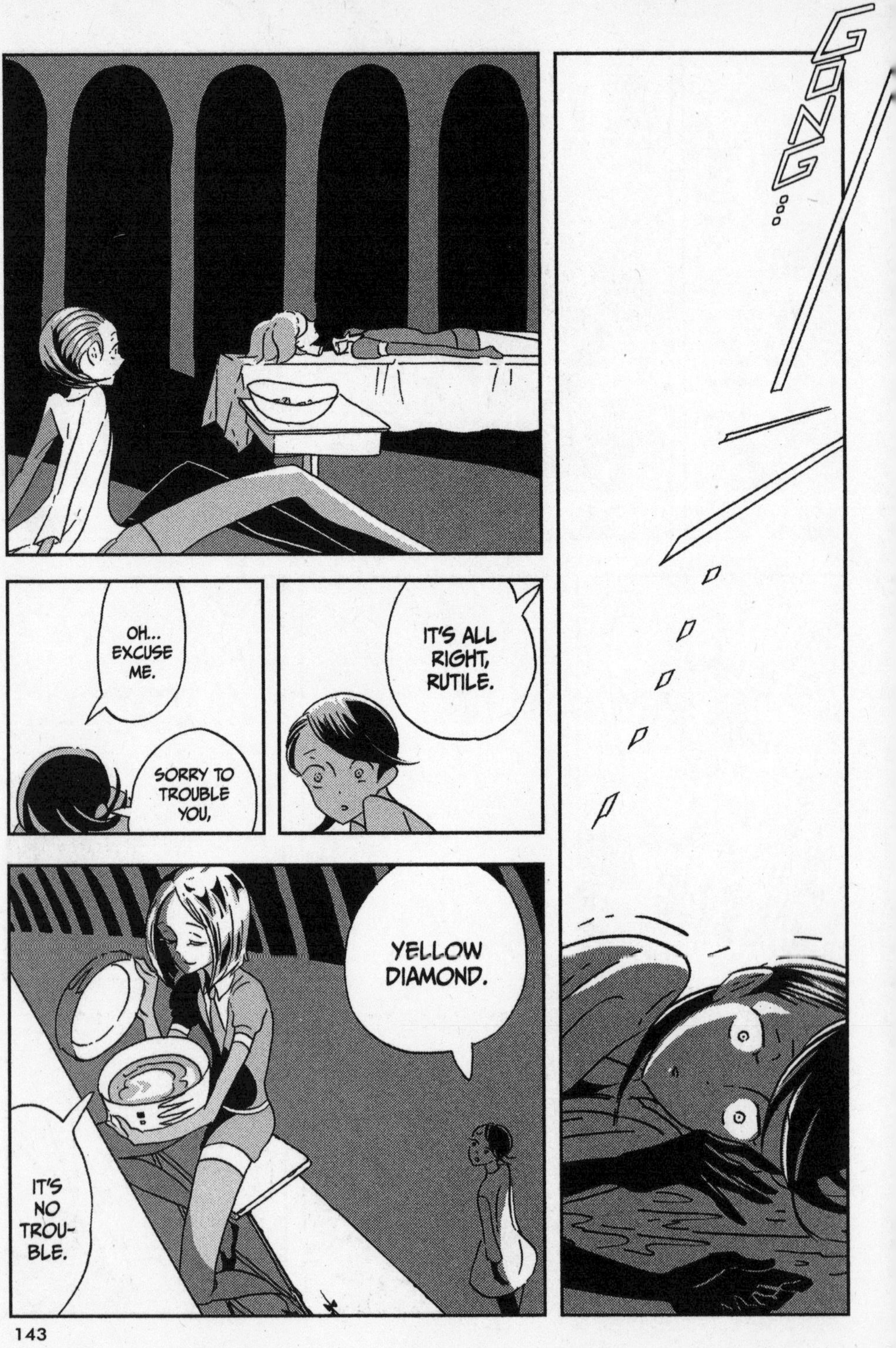
GONG...
IT'S ALL RIGHT, RUTILE.
OH... EXCUSE ME.
SORRY TO TROUBLE YOU,
YELLOW DIAMOND.
IT'S NO TROUBLE.

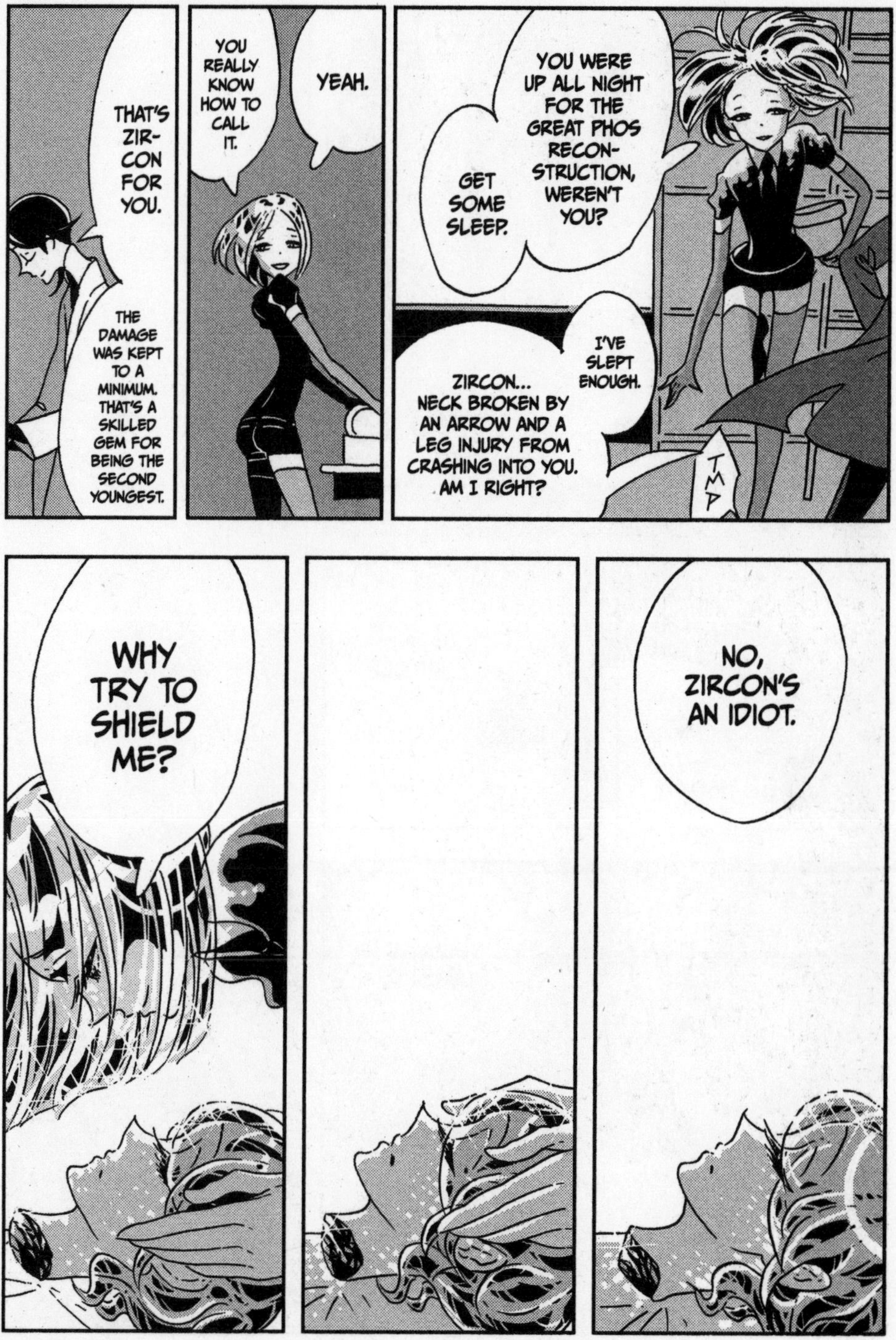
YOU WERE UP ALL NIGHT FOR THE GREAT PHOS RECONSTRUCTION, WEREN'T YOU?
GET SOME SLEEP.
I'VE SLEPT ENOUGH.
ZIRCON... NECK BROKEN BY AN ARROW AND A LEG INJURY FROM CRASHING INTO YOU. AM I RIGHT?
TMP
YEAH.
YOU REALLY KNOW HOW TO CALL IT.
THAT'S ZIRCON FOR YOU.
THE DAMAGE WAS KEPT TO A MINIMUM. THAT'S A SKILLED GEM FOR BEING THE SECOND YOUNGEST.
NO, ZIRCON'S AN IDIOT.
WHY TRY TO SHIELD ME?

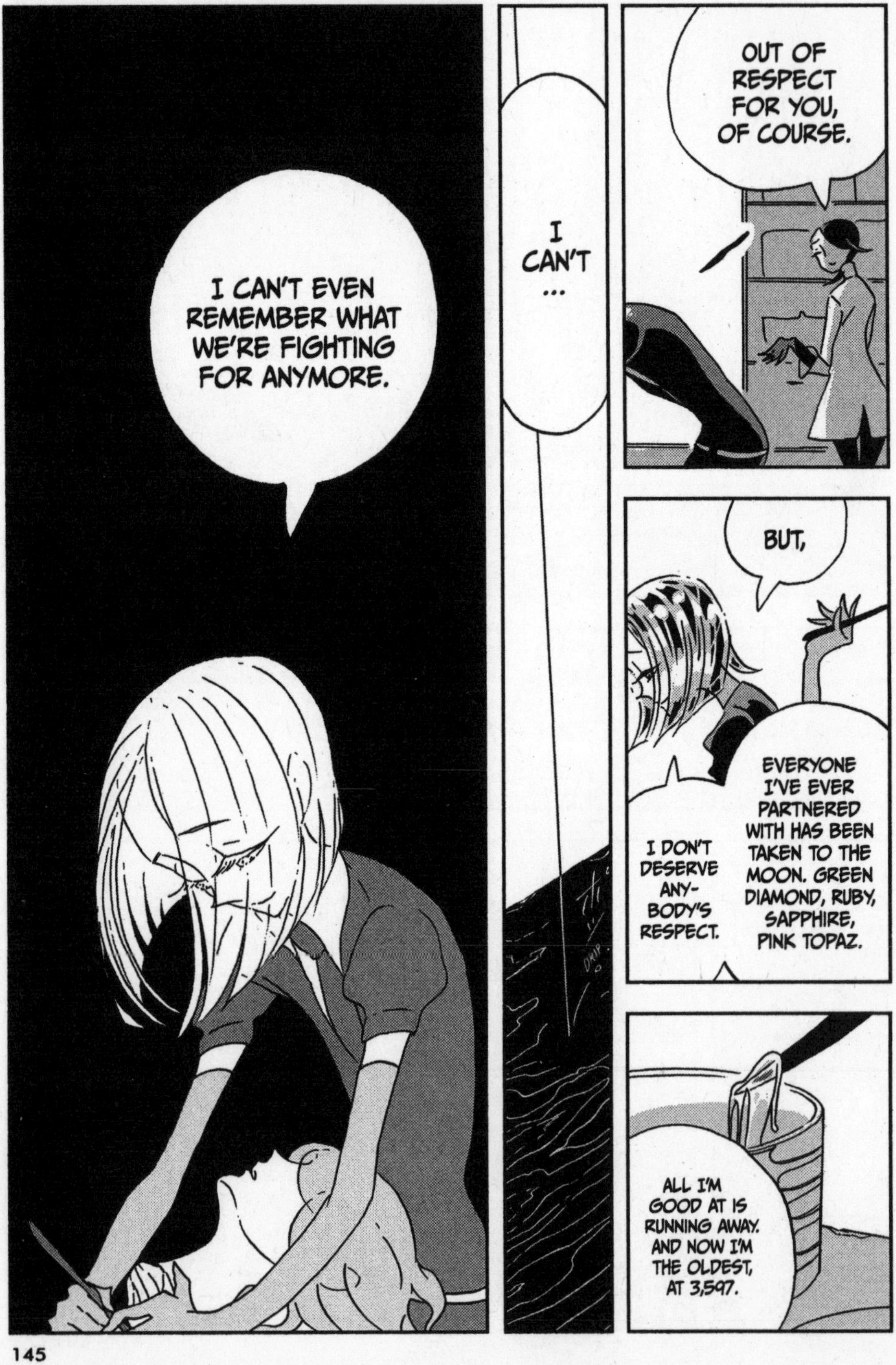
OUT OF RESPECT FOR YOU, OF COURSE.
BUT,
EVERYONE I'VE EVER PARTNERED WITH HAS BEEN TAKEN TO THE MOON. GREEN DIAMOND, RUBY, SAPPHIRE, PINK TOPAZ.
I DON'T DESERVE ANY-BODY'S RESPECT.
ALL I'M GOOD AT IS RUNNING AWAY. AND NOW I'M THE OLDEST, AT 3,597.
I CAN'T ...
I CAN'T EVEN REMEMBER WHAT WE'RE FIGHTING FOR ANYMORE.

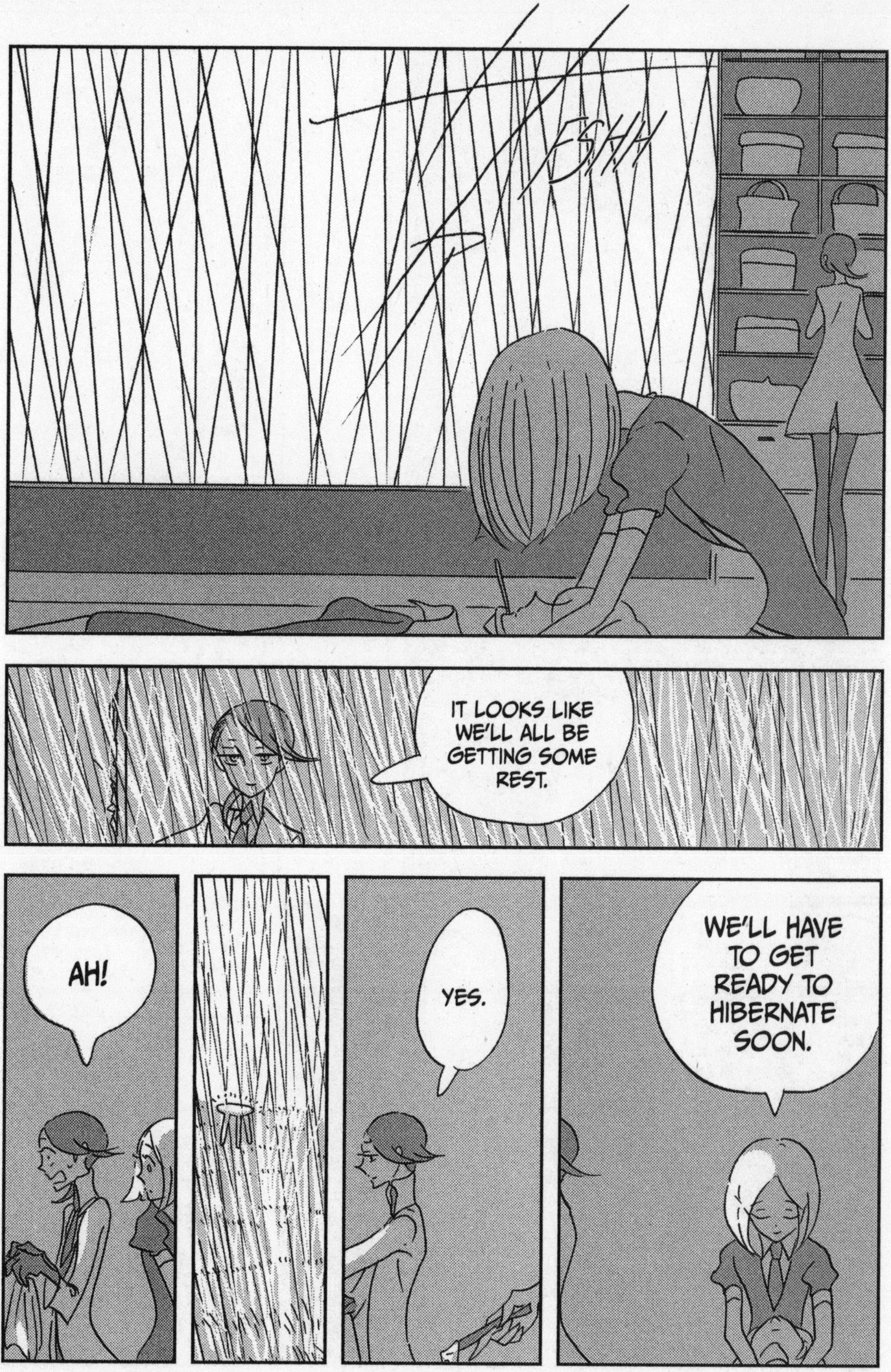
FSHH
IT LOOKS LIKE WE'LL ALL BE GETTING SOME REST.
WE'LL HAVE TO GET READY TO HIBERNATE SOON.
YES.
AH!

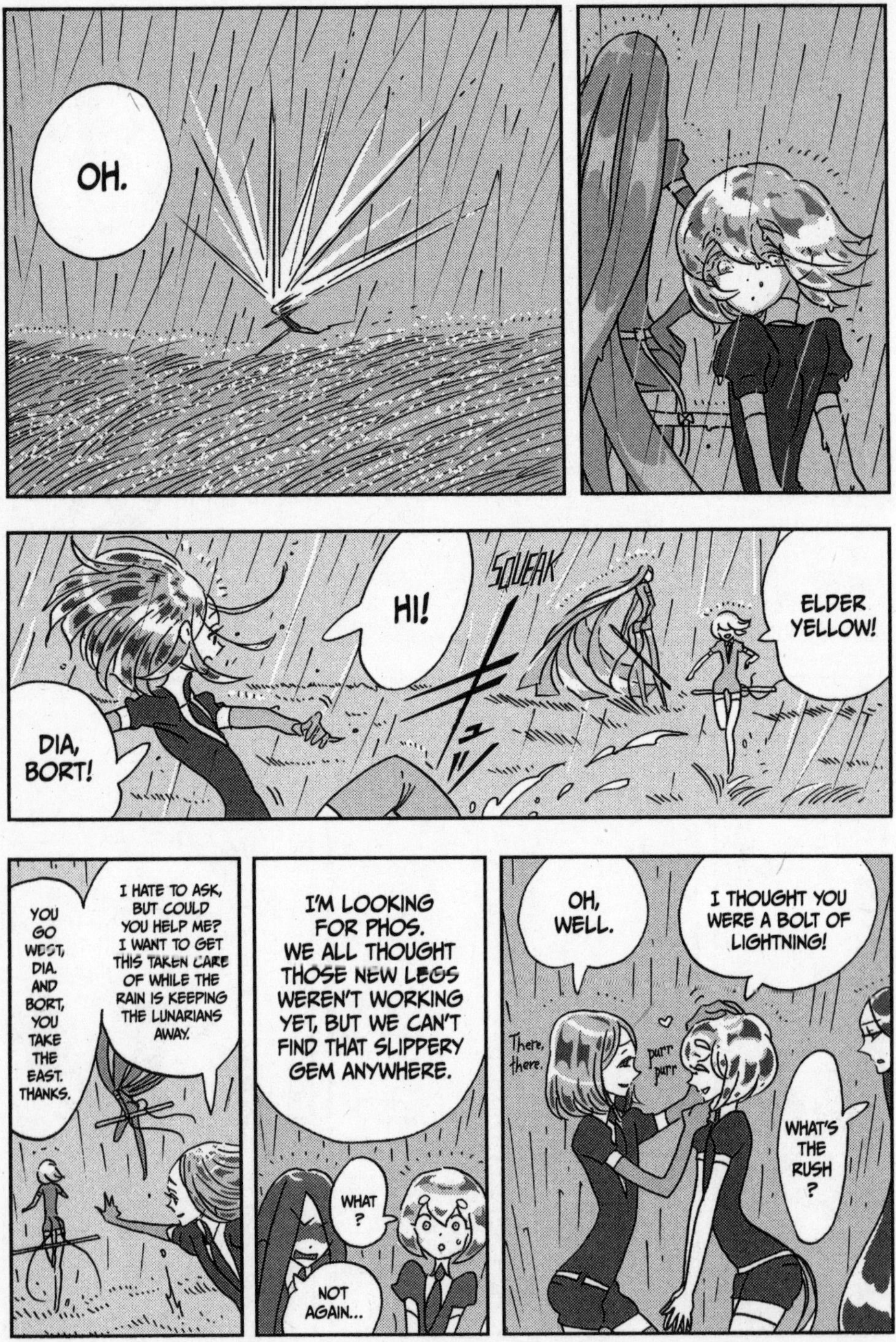
OH.
ELDER YELLOW!
SQUEAK
HI!
DIA, BORT!
I THOUGHT YOU WERE A BOLT OF LIGHTNING!
OH, WELL.
WHAT'S THE RUSH?
purr purr
There, there.
I'M LOOKING FOR PHOS. WE ALL THOUGHT THOSE NEW LEGS WEREN'T WORKING YET, BUT WE CAN'T FIND THAT SLIPPERY GEM ANYWHERE.
WHAT?
NOT AGAIN...
I HATE TO ASK, BUT COULD YOU HELP ME? I WANT TO GET THIS TAKEN CARE OF WHILE THE RAIN IS KEEPING THE LUNARIANS AWAY.
YOU GO WEST, DIA. AND BORT, YOU TAKE THE EAST. THANKS.

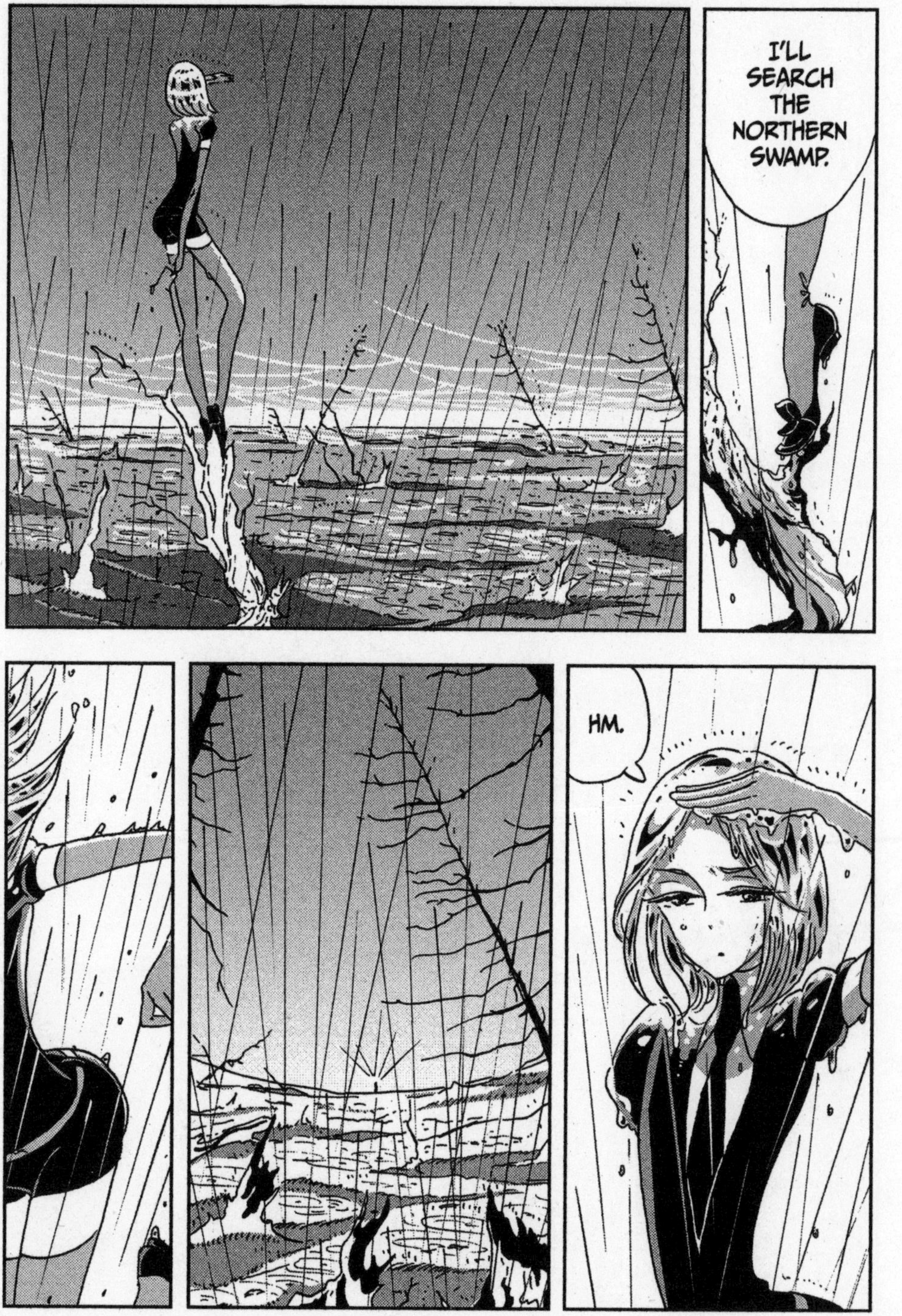
I'LL SEARCH THE NORTHERN SWAMP.
HM.

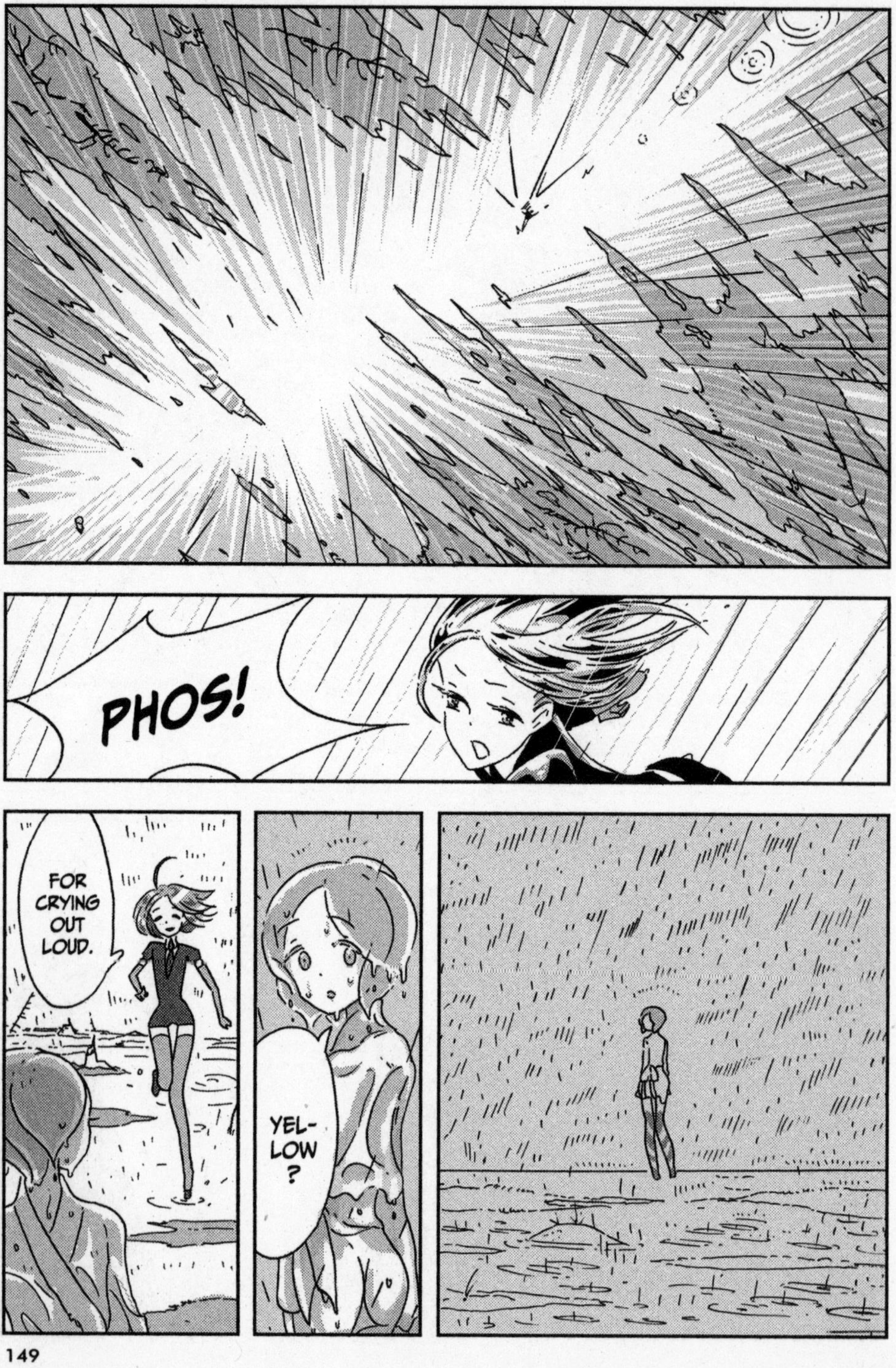
PHOS!
YEL-LOW?
FOR CRYING OUT LOUD.

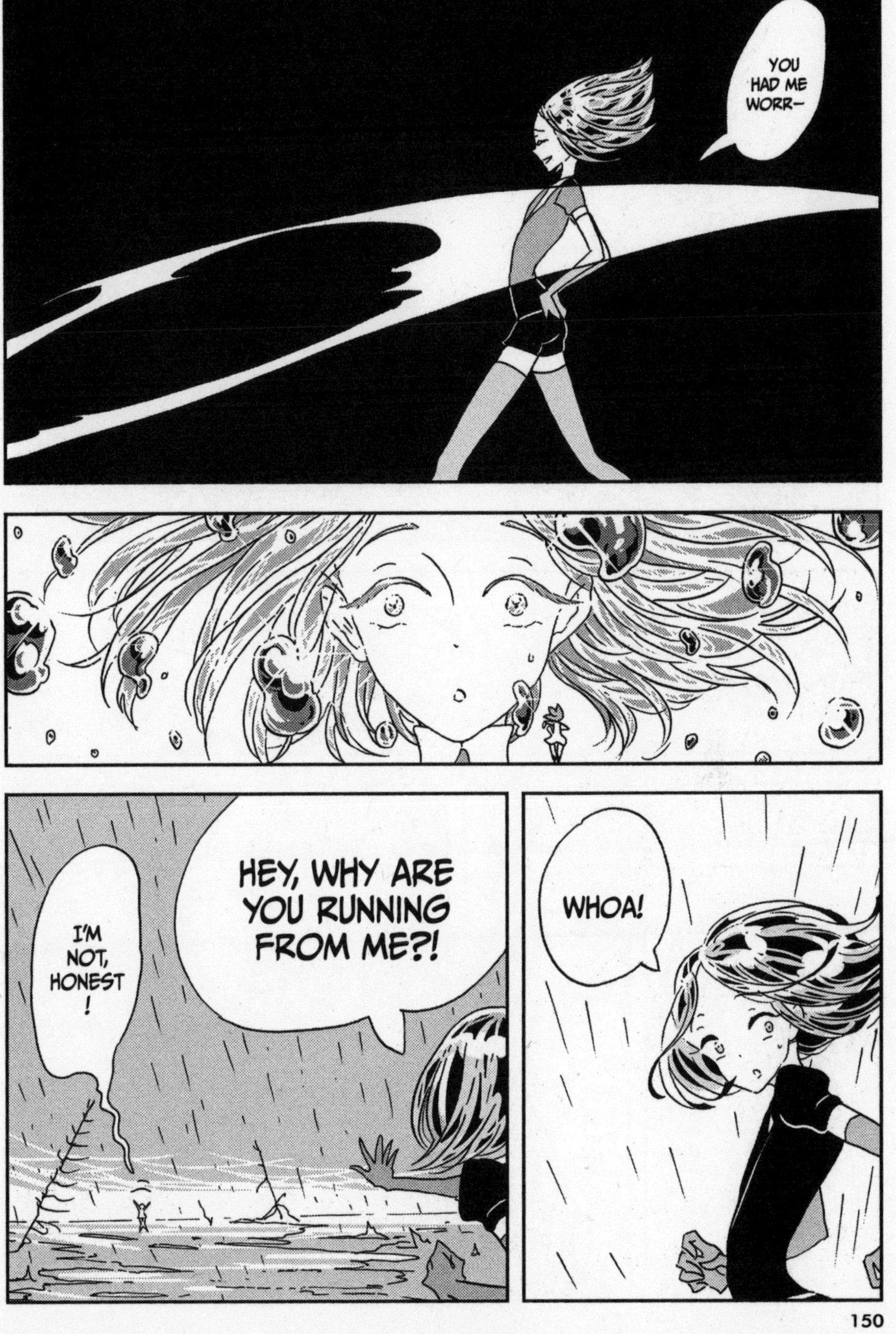
YOU HAD ME WORR—
WHOA!
HEY, WHY ARE YOU RUNNING FROM ME?!
I'M NOT, HONEST!

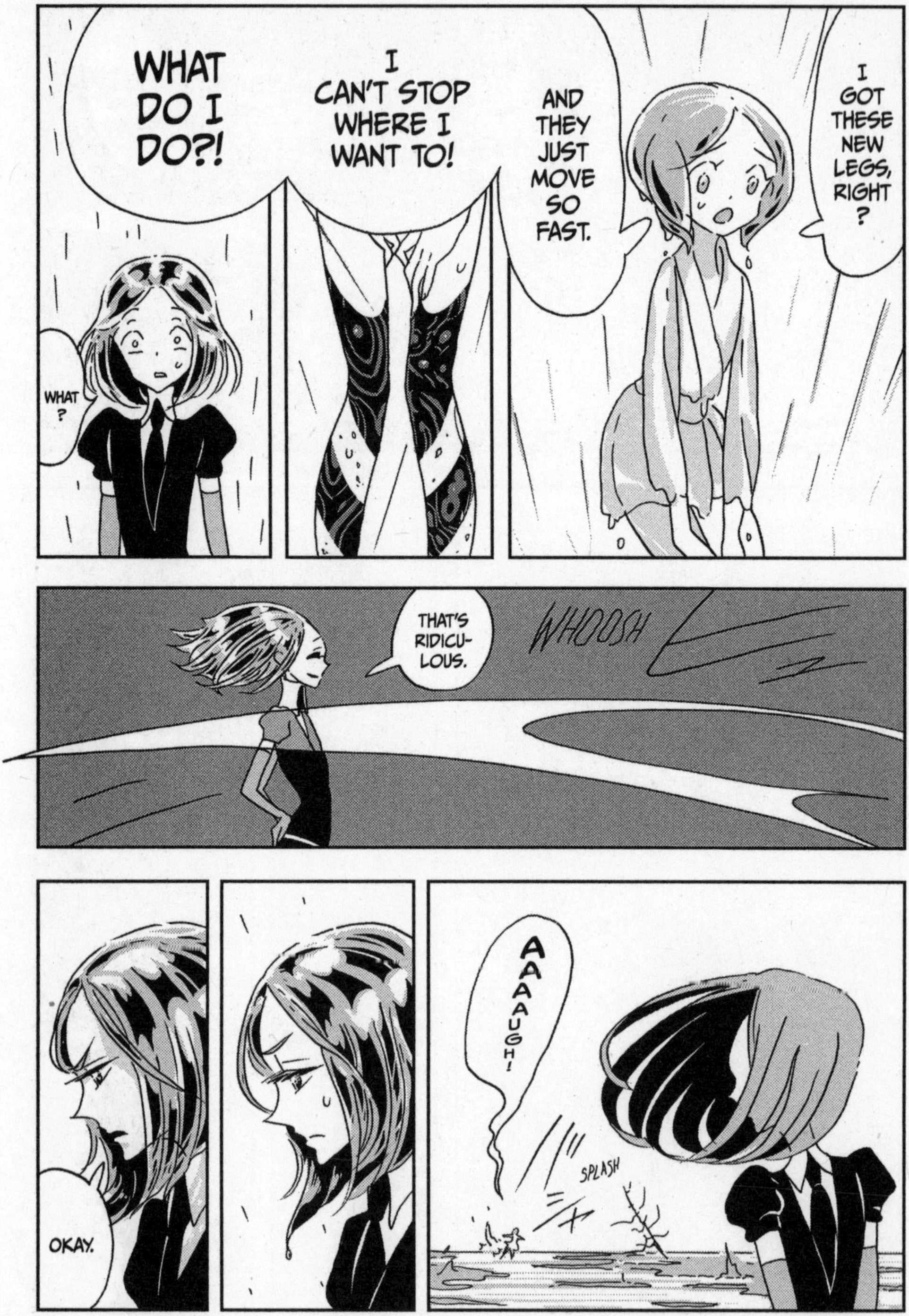
I GOT THESE NEW LEGS, RIGHT?
AND THEY JUST MOVE SO FAST.
I CAN'T STOP WHERE I WANT TO!
WHAT DO I DO?!
WHAT?
WHOOSH
THAT'S RIDICU-LOUS.
AAAAAUGH!
SPLASH
OKAY.

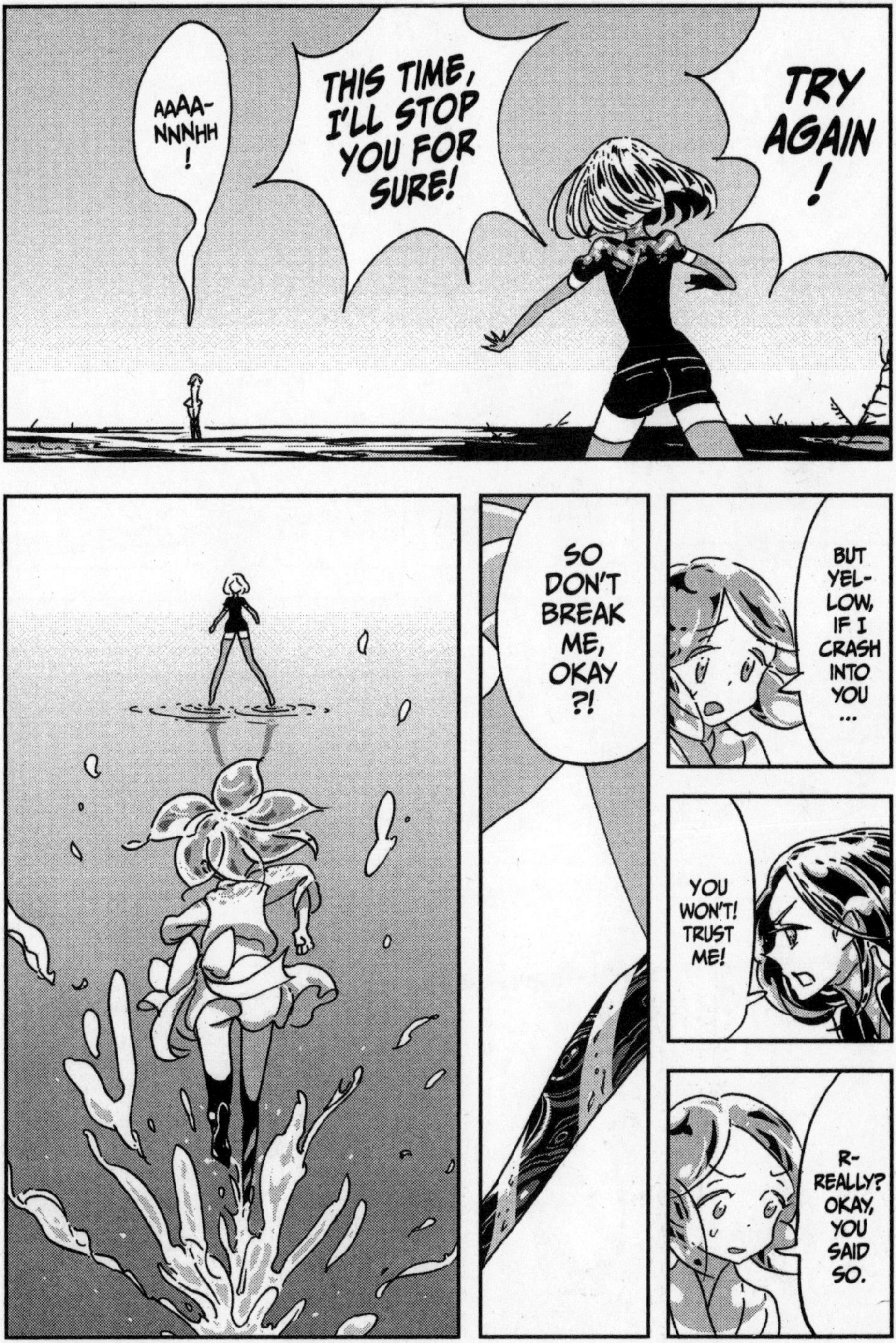
TRY AGAIN!
THIS TIME, I'LL STOP YOU FOR SURE!
AAAA-NNNHH!
BUT YEL-LOW, IF I CRASH INTO YOU...
YOU WON'T! TRUST ME!
R-REALLY? OKAY, YOU SAID SO.
SO DON'T BREAK ME, OKAY?!

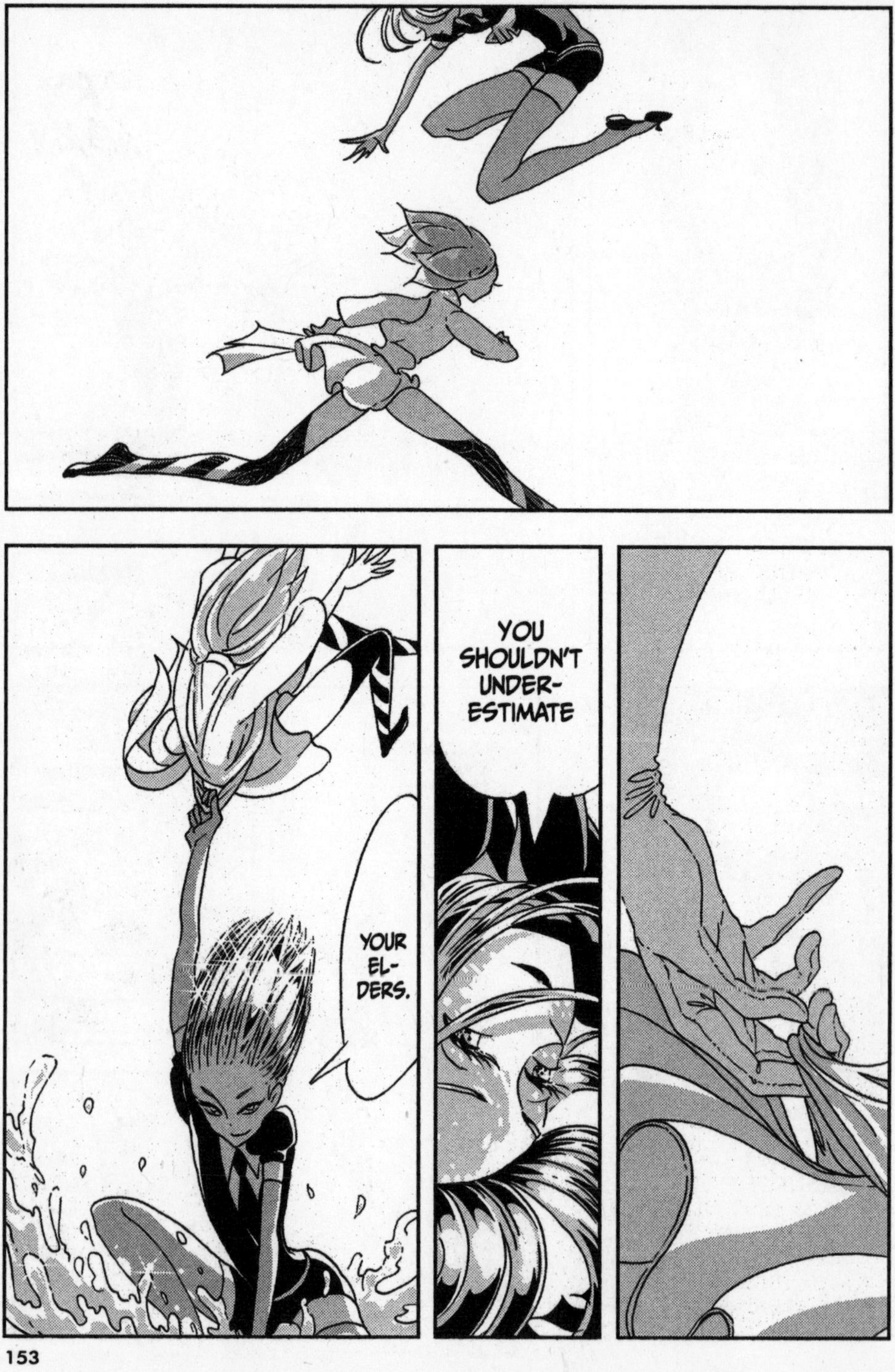
YOU SHOULDN'T UNDER-ESTIMATE
YOUR EL-DERS.

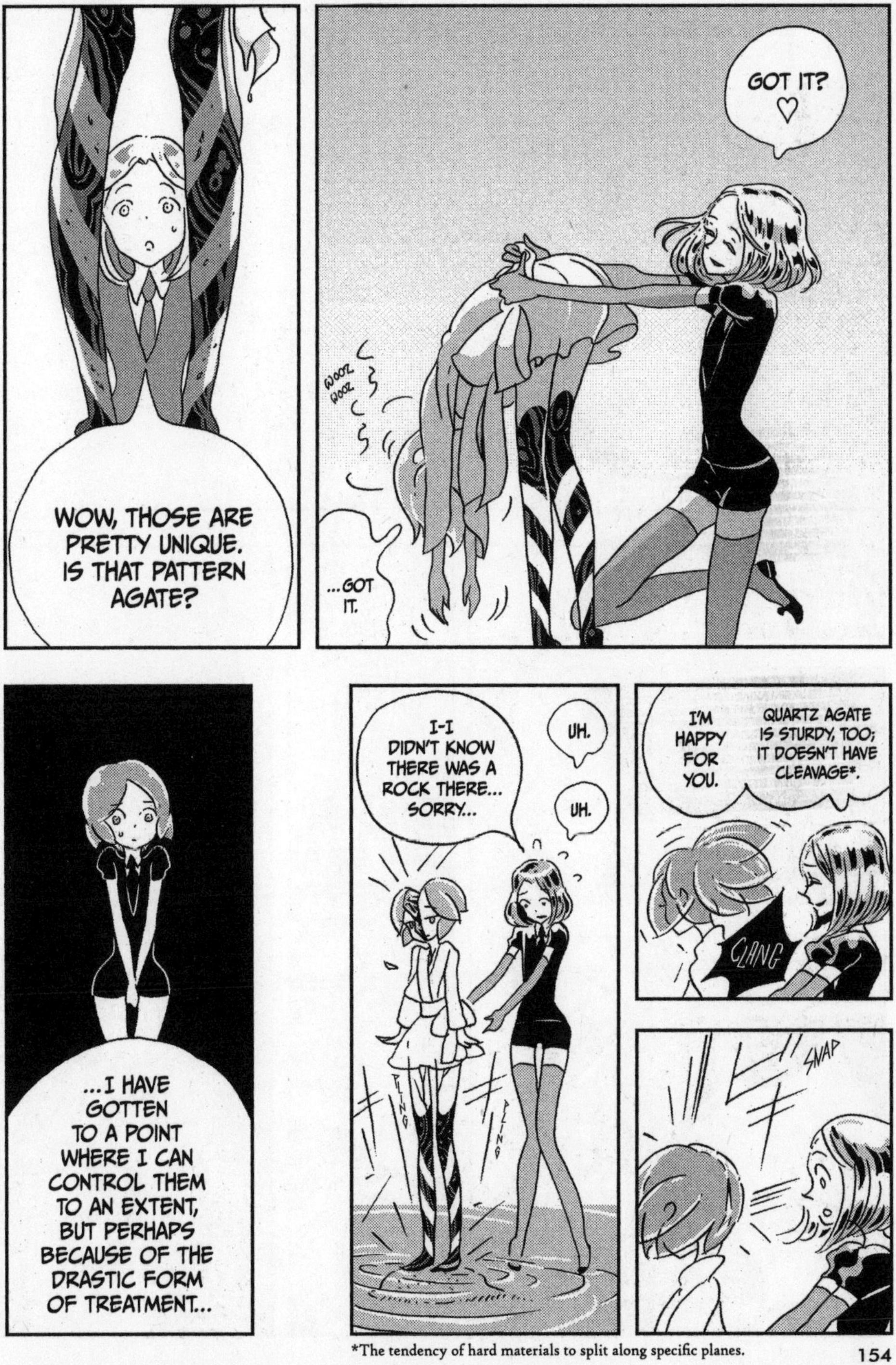
GOT IT? ♡
WOOZ WOOZ
...GOT IT.
WOW, THOSE ARE PRETTY UNIQUE. IS THAT PATTERN AGATE?
QUARTZ AGATE IS STURDY, TOO; IT DOESN'T HAVE CLEAVAGE*.
I'M HAPPY FOR YOU.
CLANG
SNAP
UH.
UH.
I-I DIDN'T KNOW THERE WAS A ROCK THERE... SORRY...
PLING
PLING
...I HAVE GOTTEN TO A POINT WHERE I CAN CONTROL THEM TO AN EXTENT, BUT PERHAPS BECAUSE OF THE DRASTIC FORM OF TREATMENT...

*The tendency of hard materials to split along specific planes.

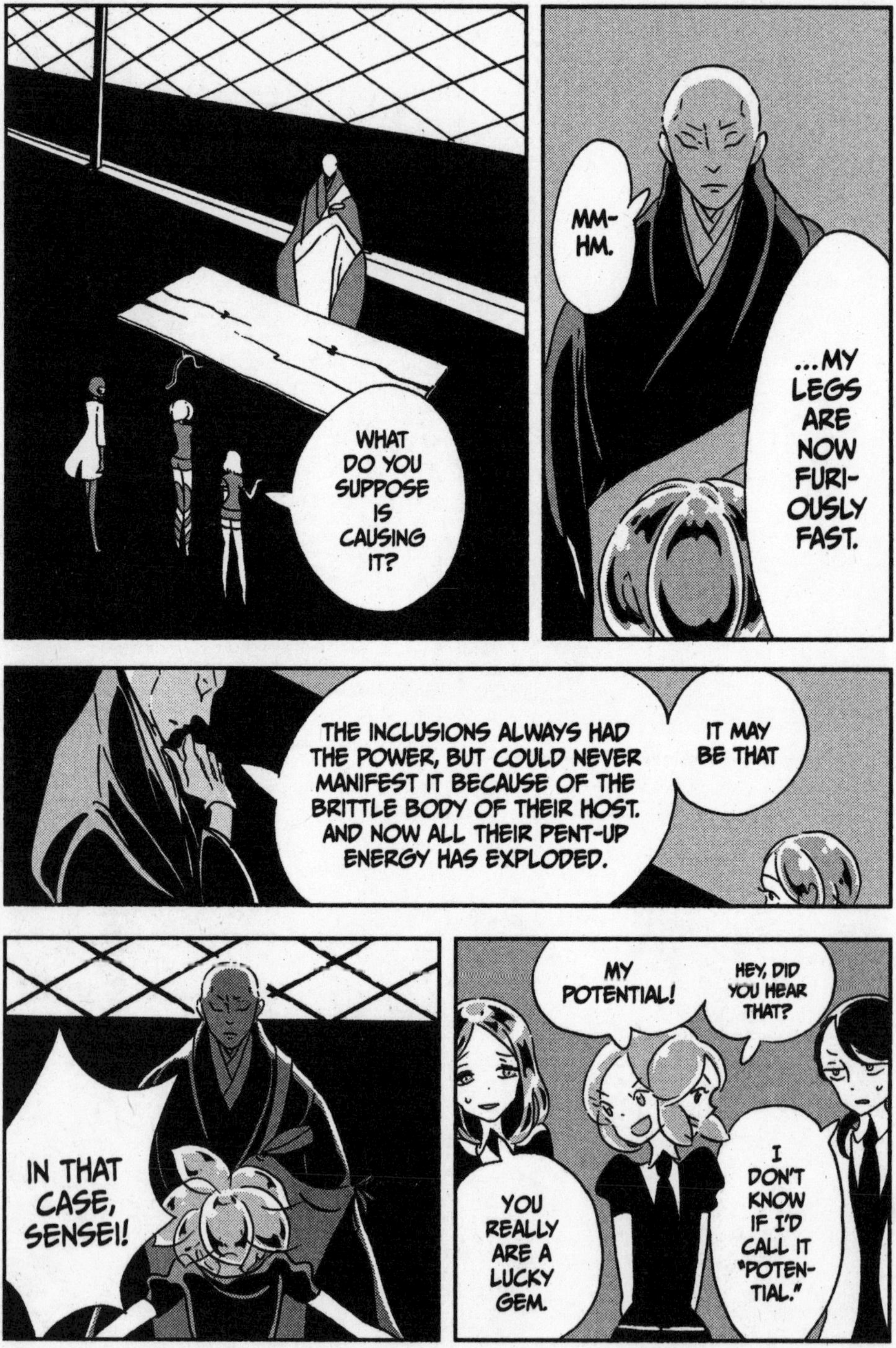
MM-HM.
...MY LEGS ARE NOW FURI-OUSLY FAST.
WHAT DO YOU SUPPOSE IS CAUSING IT?
IT MAY BE THAT
THE INCLUSIONS ALWAYS HAD THE POWER, BUT COULD NEVER MANIFEST IT BECAUSE OF THE BRITTLE BODY OF THEIR HOST. AND NOW ALL THEIR PENT-UP ENERGY HAS EXPLODED.
HEY, DID YOU HEAR THAT?
MY POTENTIAL!
I DON'T KNOW IF I'D CALL IT "POTEN-TIAL."
YOU REALLY ARE A LUCKY GEM.
IN THAT CASE, SENSEI!

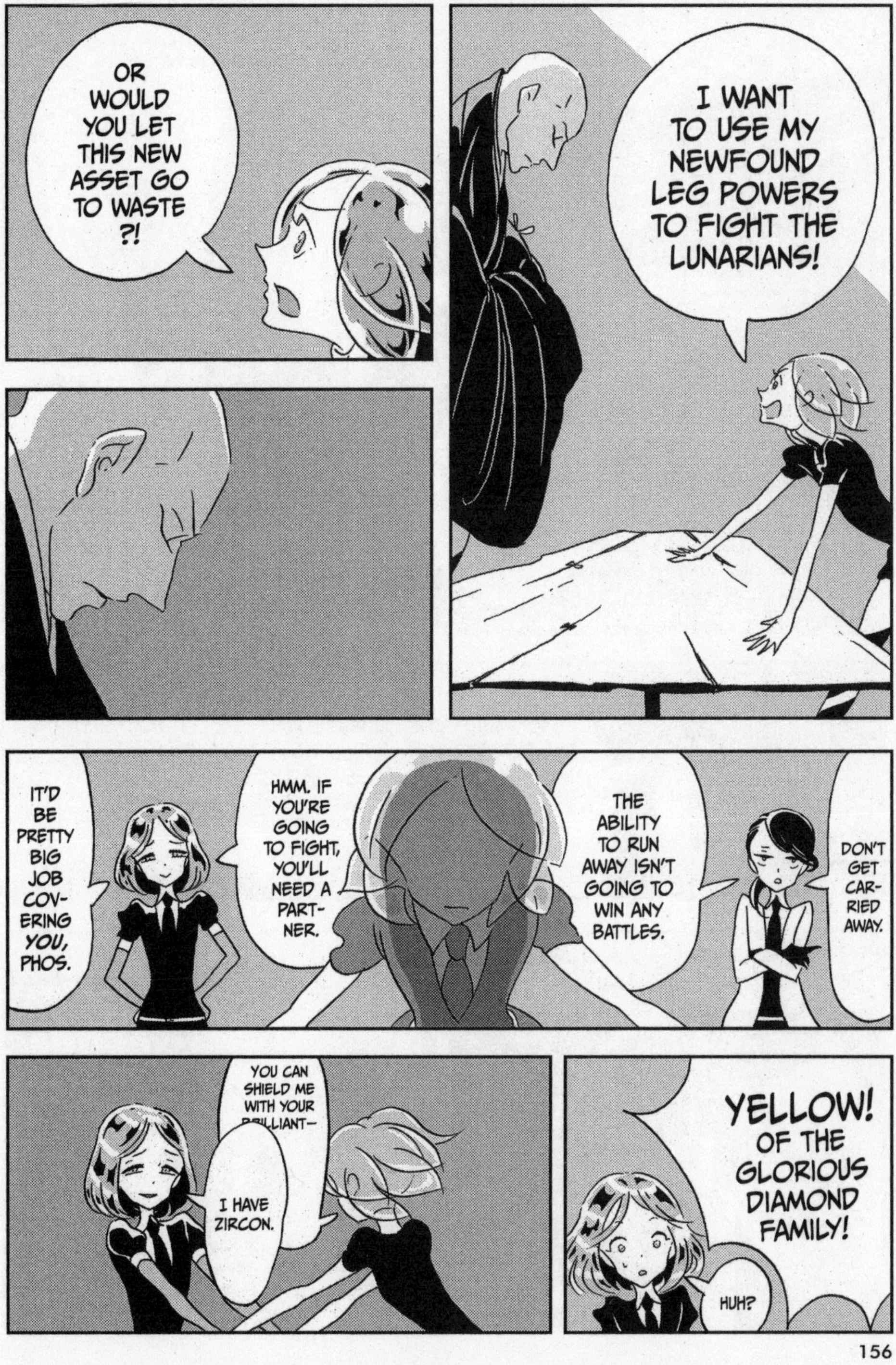
I WANT TO USE MY NEWFOUND LEG POWERS TO FIGHT THE LUNARIANS!
OR WOULD YOU LET THIS NEW ASSET GO TO WASTE ?!
DON'T GET CAR-RIED AWAY.
THE ABILITY TO RUN AWAY ISN'T GOING TO WIN ANY BATTLES.
HMM. IF YOU'RE GOING TO FIGHT, YOU'LL NEED A PART-NER.
IT'D BE PRETTY BIG JOB COV-ERING *YOU*, PHOS.
YELLOW! OF THE GLORIOUS DIAMOND FAMILY!
HUH?
YOU CAN SHIELD ME WITH YOUR BRILLIANT—
I HAVE ZIRCON.

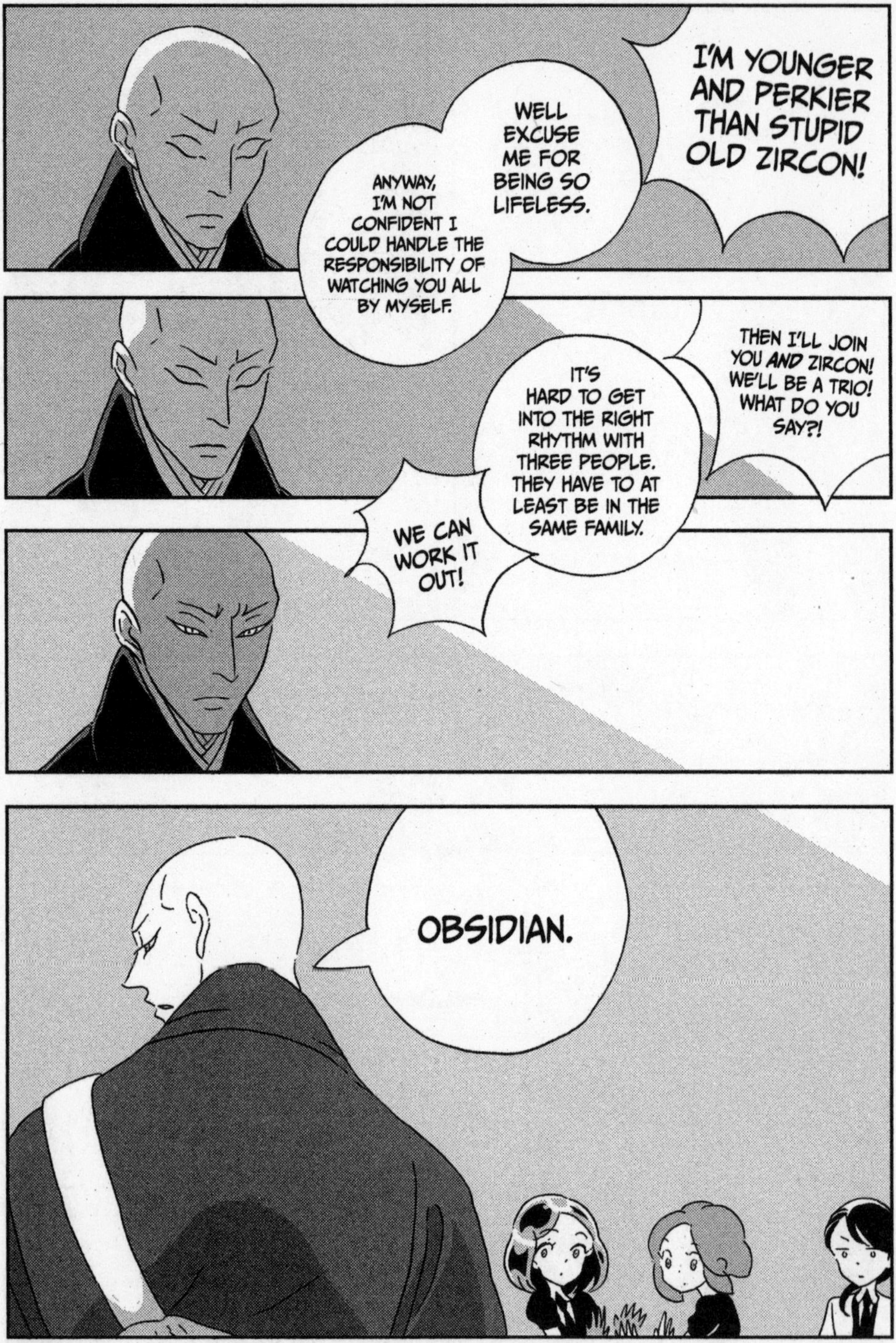
I'M YOUNGER AND PERKIER THAN STUPID OLD ZIRCON!
WELL EXCUSE ME FOR BEING SO LIFELESS.
ANYWAY, I'M NOT CONFIDENT I COULD HANDLE THE RESPONSIBILITY OF WATCHING YOU ALL BY MYSELF.
THEN I'LL JOIN YOU *AND* ZIRCON! WE'LL BE A TRIO! WHAT DO YOU SAY?!
IT'S HARD TO GET INTO THE RIGHT RHYTHM WITH THREE PEOPLE. THEY HAVE TO AT LEAST BE IN THE SAME FAMILY.
WE CAN WORK IT OUT!
OBSIDIAN.

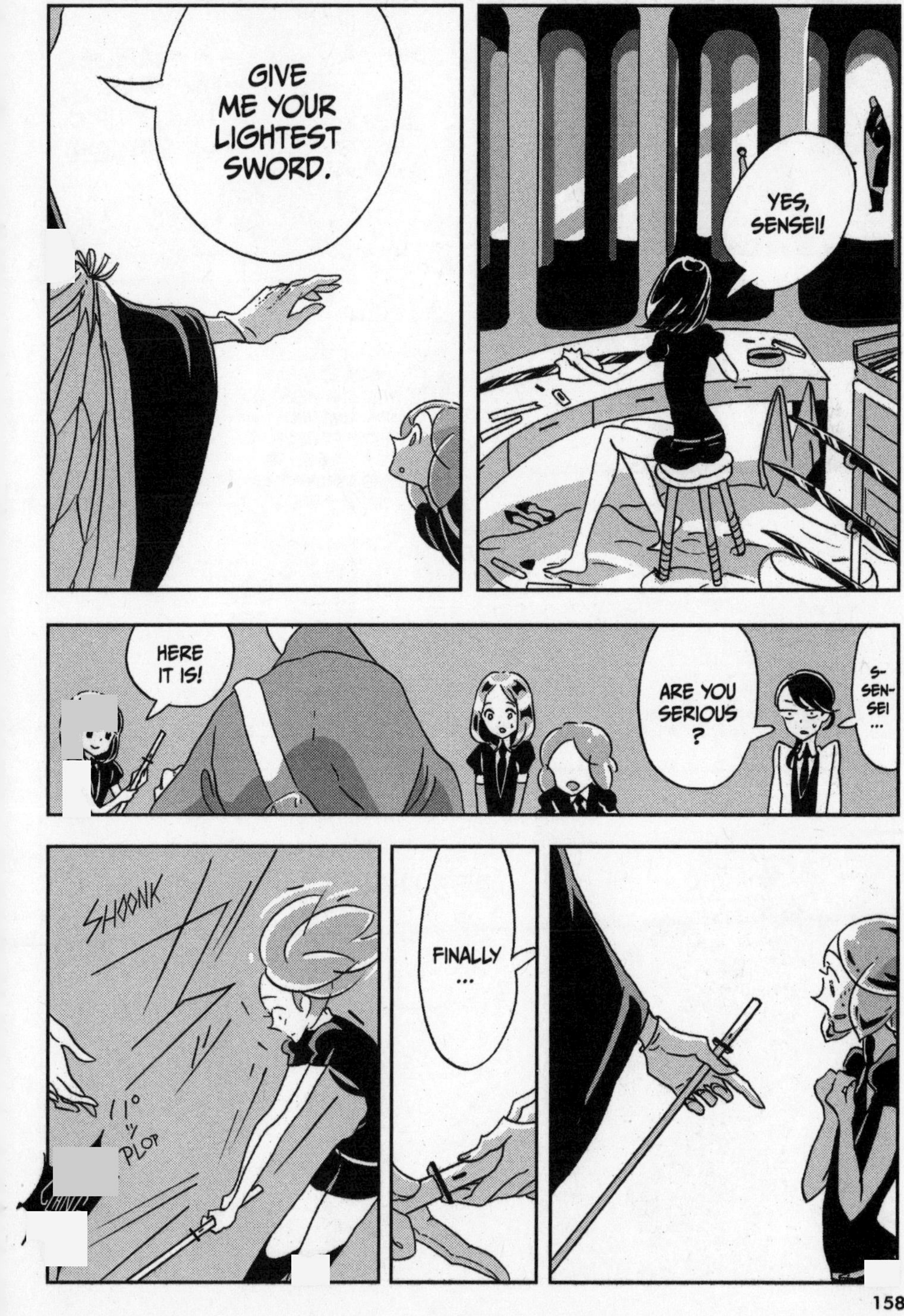
YES, SENSEI!
GIVE ME YOUR LIGHTEST SWORD.
S-SEN-SEI ...
ARE YOU SERIOUS?
HERE IT IS!
FINALLY ...
SHOONK
PLOP

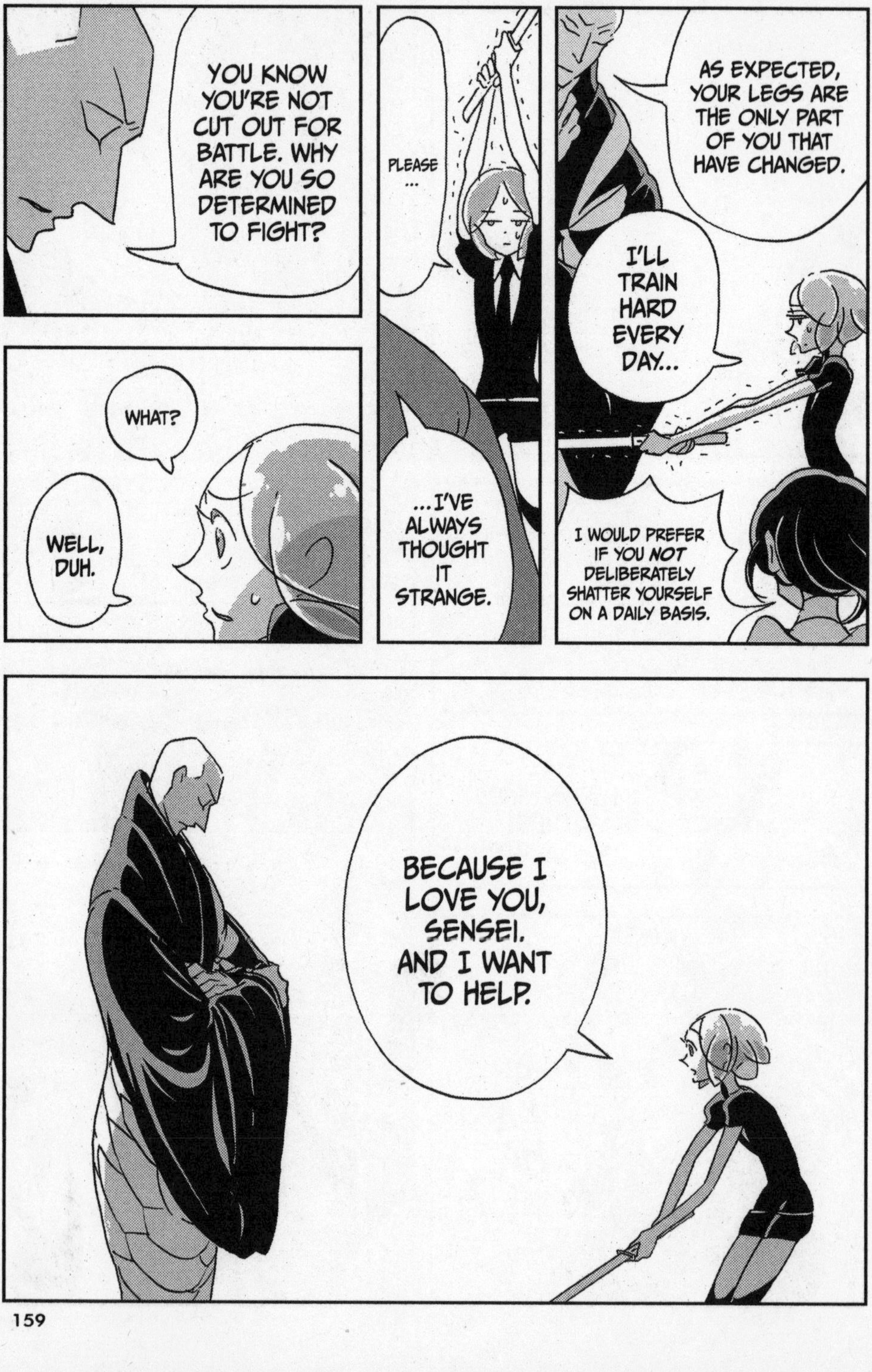
AS EXPECTED, YOUR LEGS ARE THE ONLY PART OF YOU THAT HAVE CHANGED.
I'LL TRAIN HARD EVERY DAY...
I WOULD PREFER IF YOU *NOT* DELIBERATELY SHATTER YOURSELF ON A DAILY BASIS.
PLEASE ...
...I'VE ALWAYS THOUGHT IT STRANGE.
YOU KNOW YOU'RE NOT CUT OUT FOR BATTLE. WHY ARE YOU SO DETERMINED TO FIGHT?
WHAT?
WELL, DUH.
BECAUSE I LOVE YOU, SENSEI. AND I WANT TO HELP.

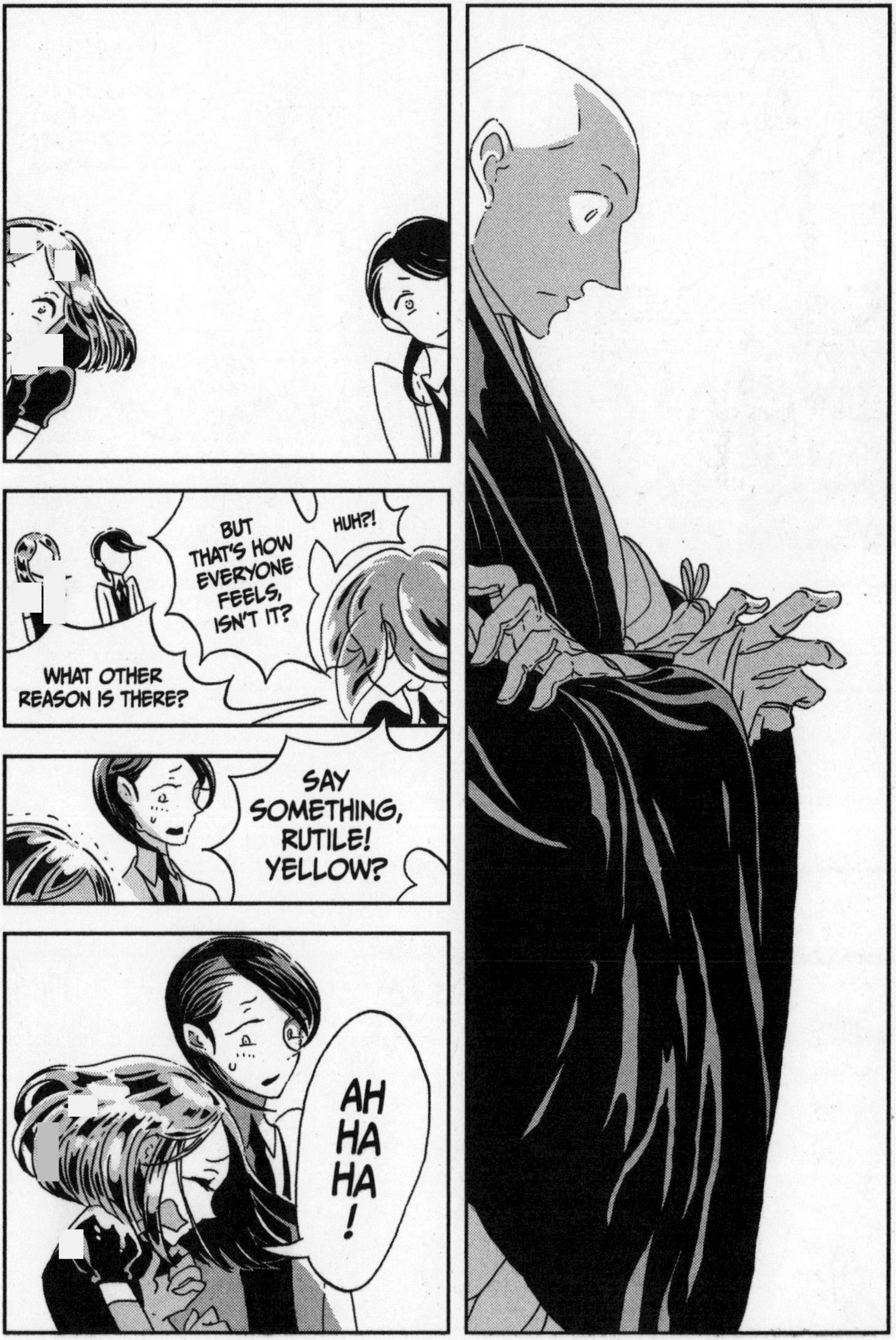
HUH?!
BUT THAT'S HOW EVERYONE FEELS, ISN'T IT?
WHAT OTHER REASON IS THERE?
SAY SOMETHING, RUTILE! YELLOW?
AH HA HA!

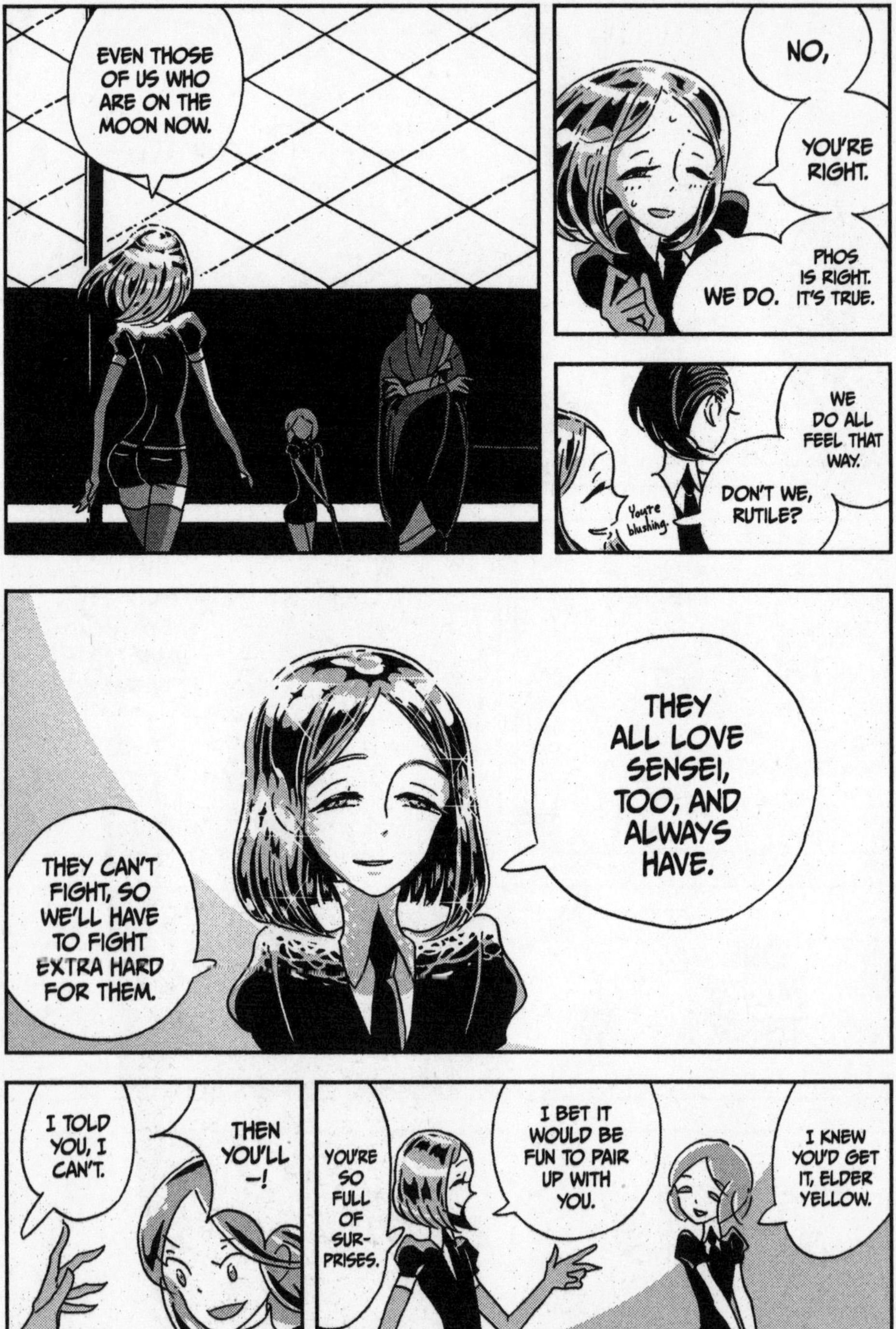
NO,
YOU'RE RIGHT.
PHOS IS RIGHT. IT'S TRUE.
WE DO.
WE DO ALL FEEL THAT WAY.
DON'T WE, RUTILE?
You're blushing.
EVEN THOSE OF US WHO ARE ON THE MOON NOW.
THEY ALL LOVE SENSEI, TOO, AND ALWAYS HAVE.
THEY CAN'T FIGHT, SO WE'LL HAVE TO FIGHT EXTRA HARD FOR THEM.
I KNEW YOU'D GET IT, ELDER YELLOW.
I BET IT WOULD BE FUN TO PAIR UP WITH YOU.
YOU'RE SO FULL OF SUR-PRISES.
THEN YOU'LL —!
I TOLD YOU, I CAN'T.

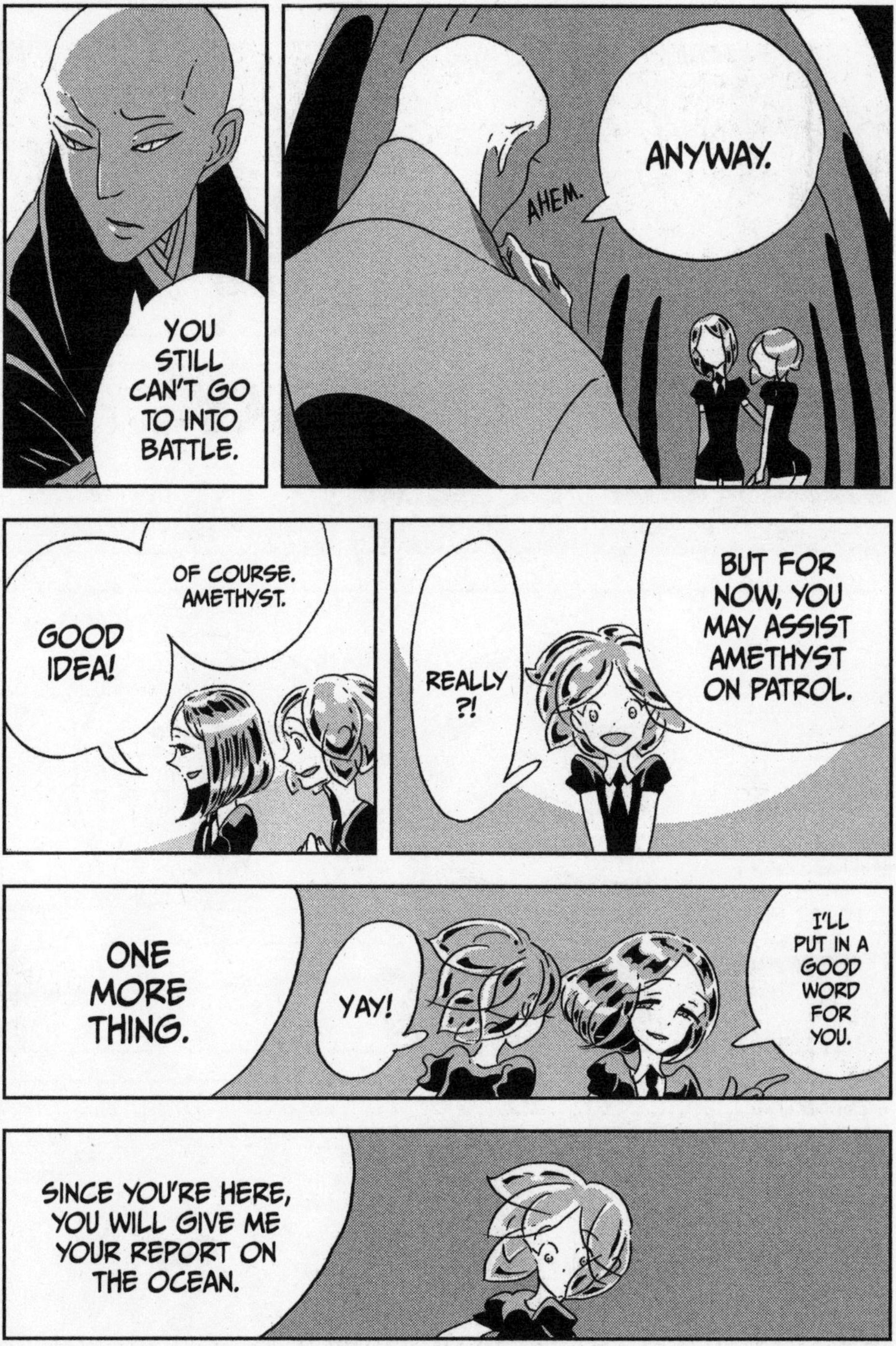
AHEM.
ANYWAY.
YOU STILL CAN'T GO TO INTO BATTLE.
BUT FOR NOW, YOU MAY ASSIST AMETHYST ON PATROL.
REALLY ?!
OF COURSE. AMETHYST.
GOOD IDEA!
I'LL PUT IN A GOOD WORD FOR YOU.
YAY!
ONE MORE THING.
SINCE YOU'RE HERE, YOU WILL GIVE ME YOUR REPORT ON THE OCEAN.

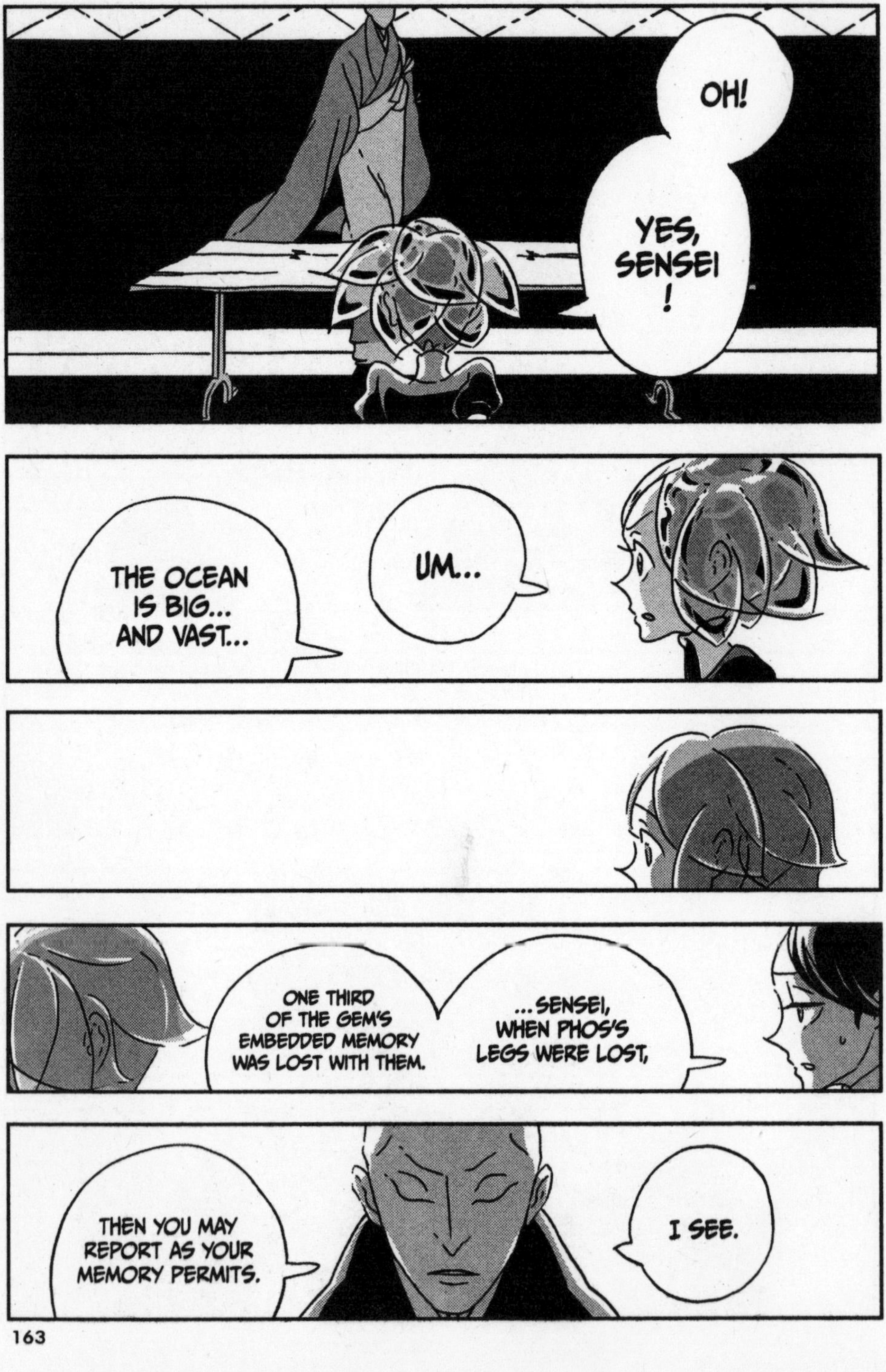
OH!
YES, SENSEI!
UM...
THE OCEAN IS BIG... AND VAST...
...SENSEI, WHEN PHOS'S LEGS WERE LOST,
ONE THIRD OF THE GEM'S EMBEDDED MEMORY WAS LOST WITH THEM.
I SEE.
THEN YOU MAY REPORT AS YOUR MEMORY PERMITS.

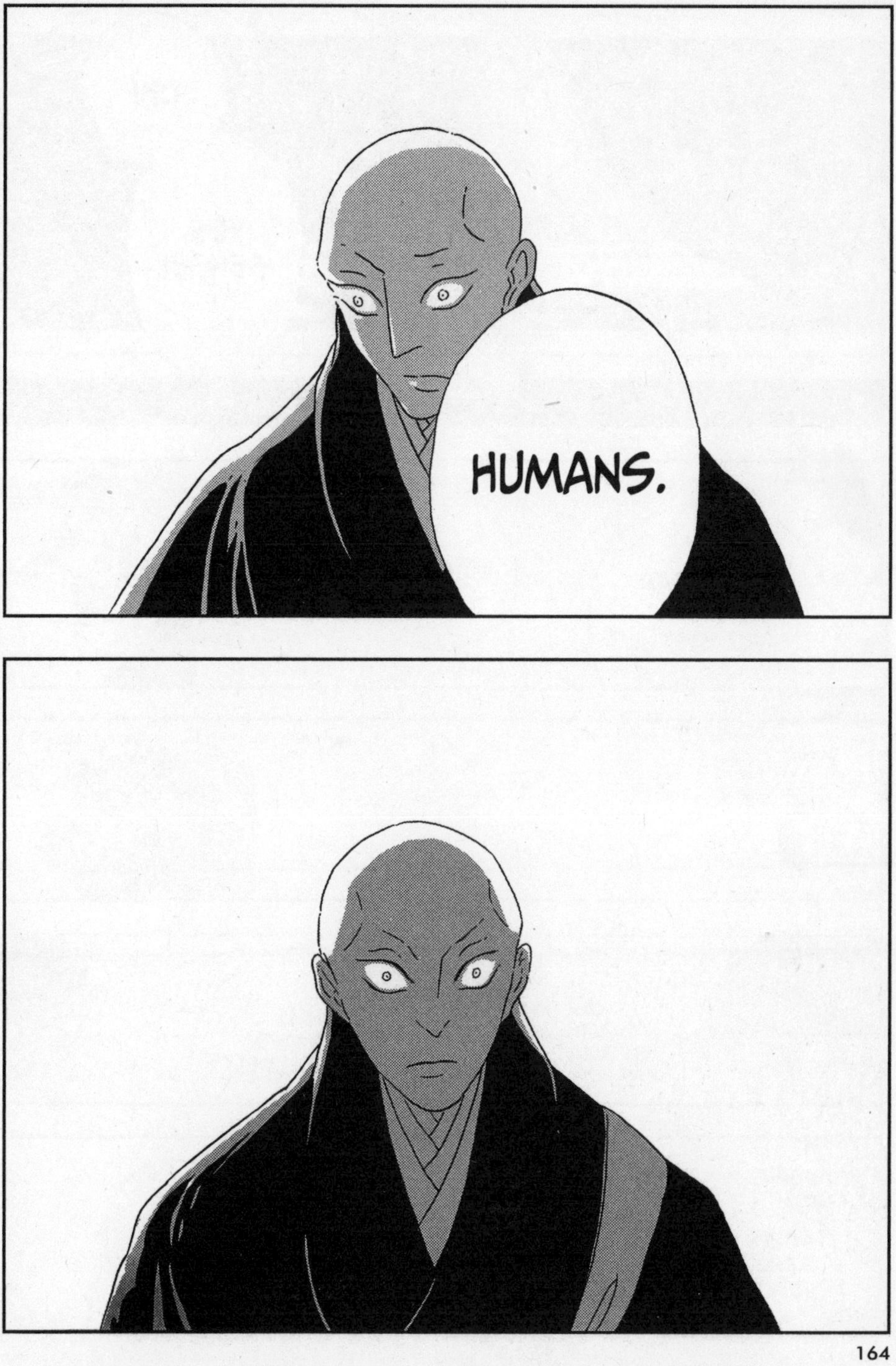
HUMANS.

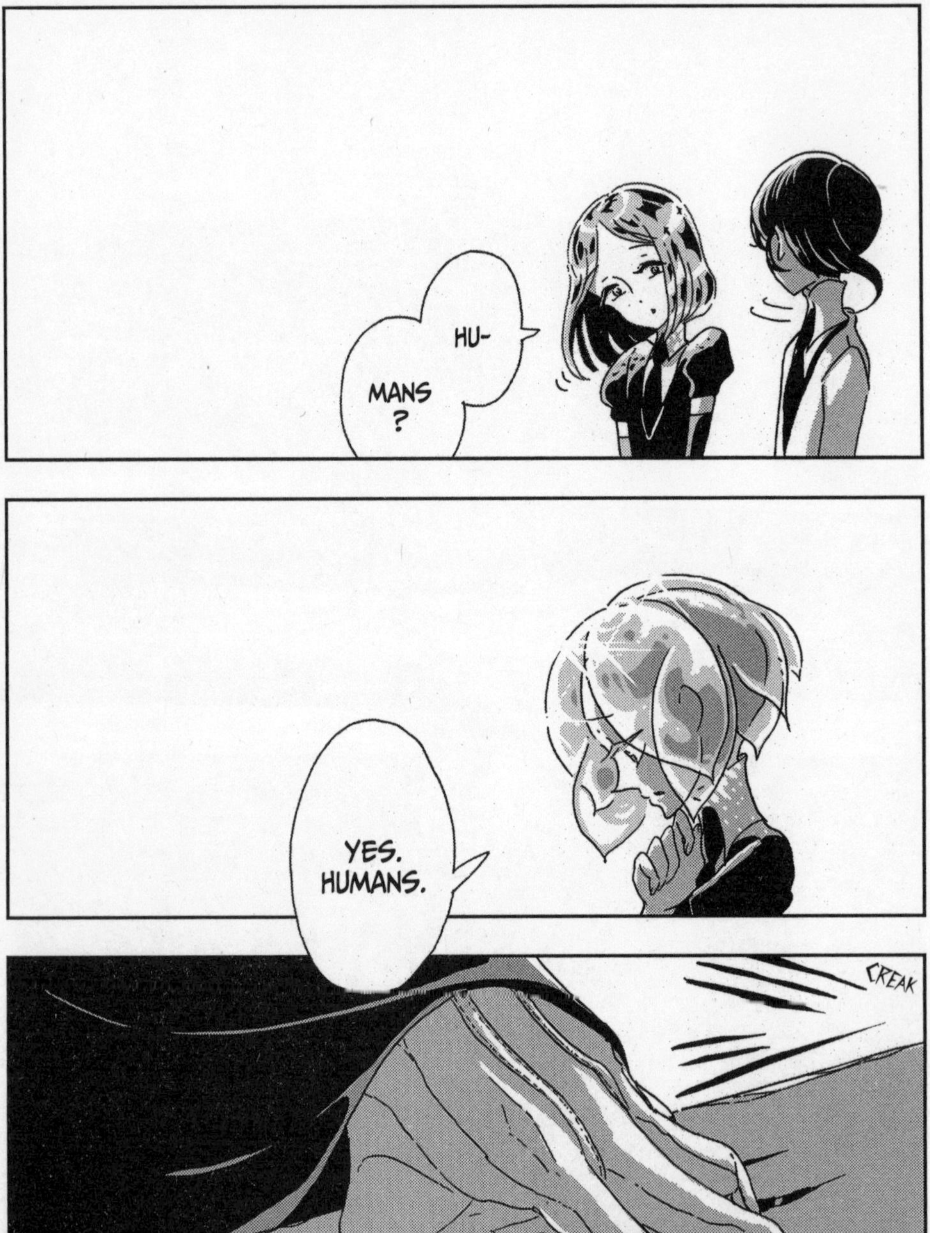
HU-
MANS
?
YES.
HUMANS.
CREAK

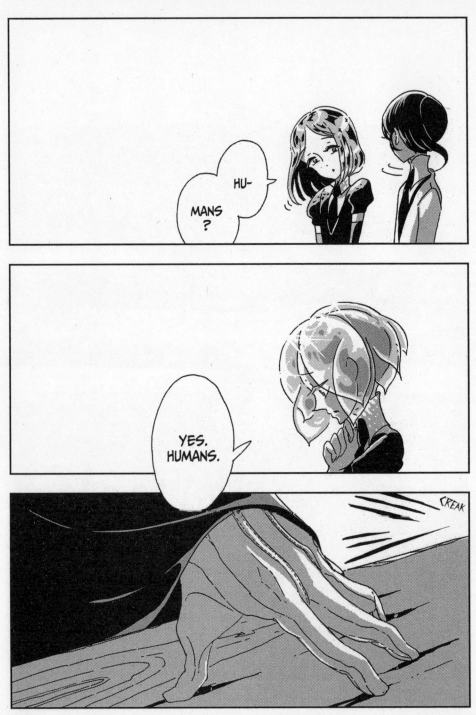

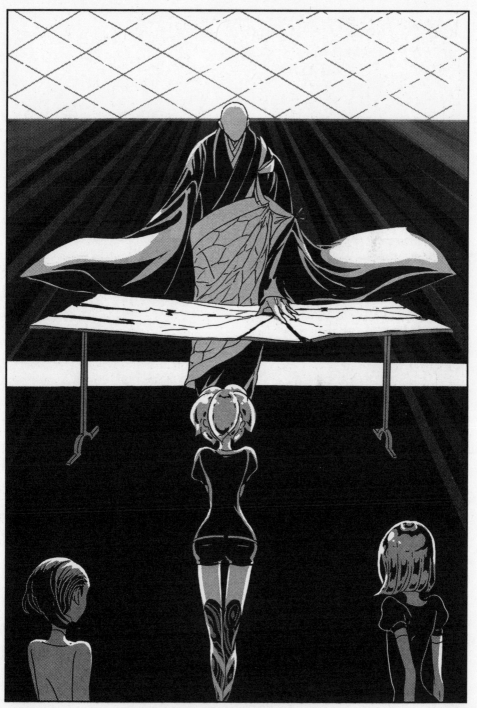

CHAPTER 12: Yellow Diamond END

CHAPTER 13:

Twin Crystals

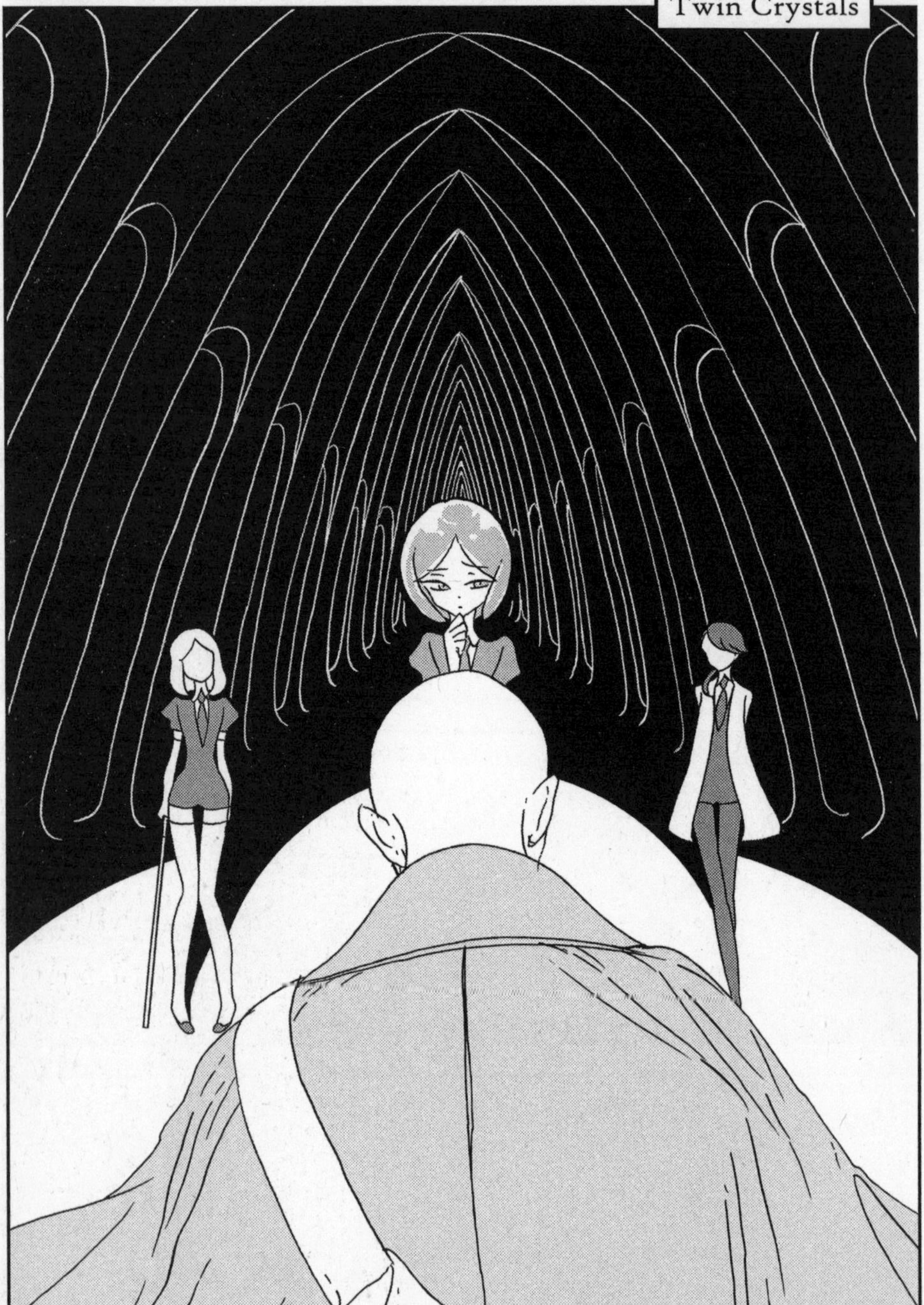

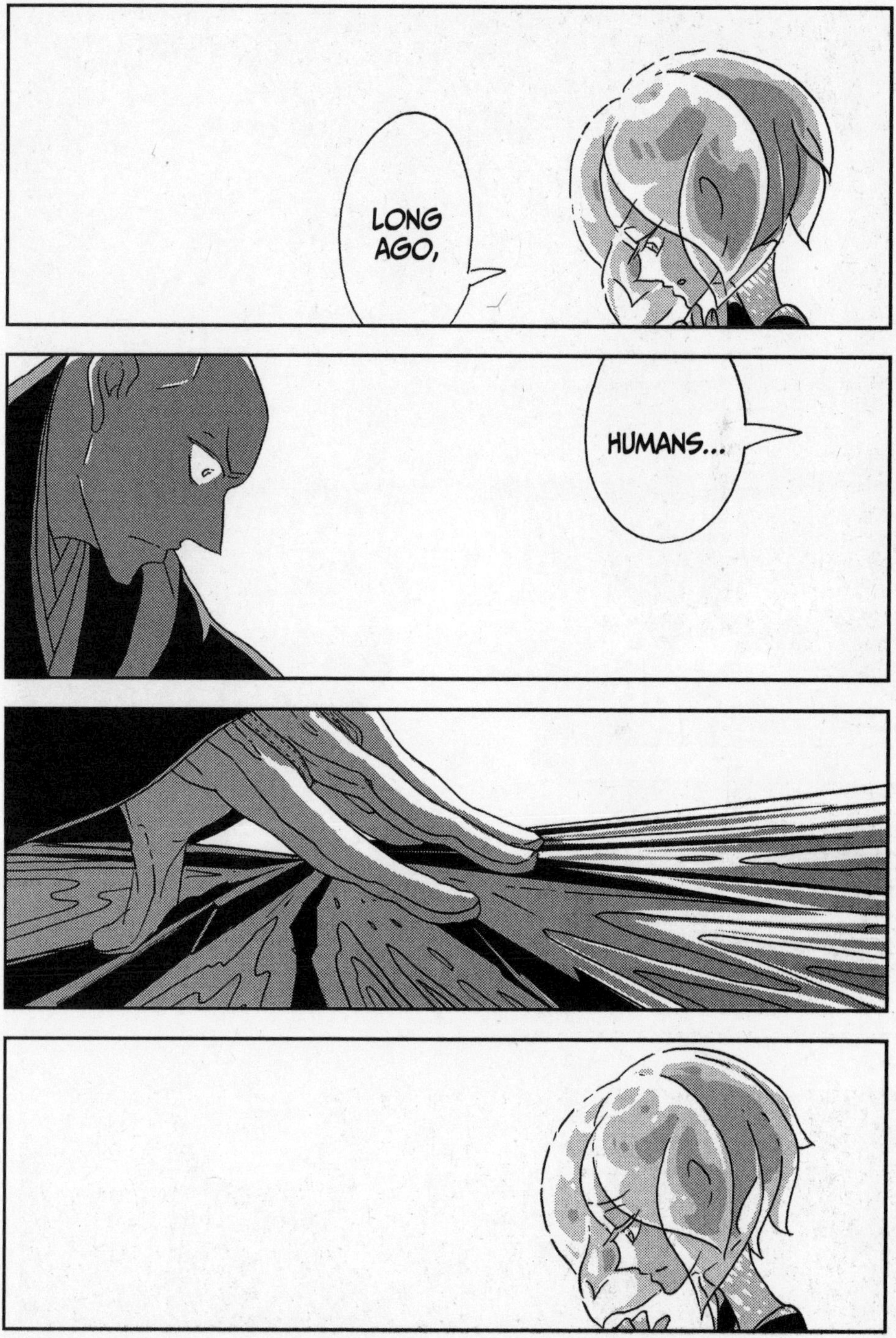
LONG AGO,
HUMANS...

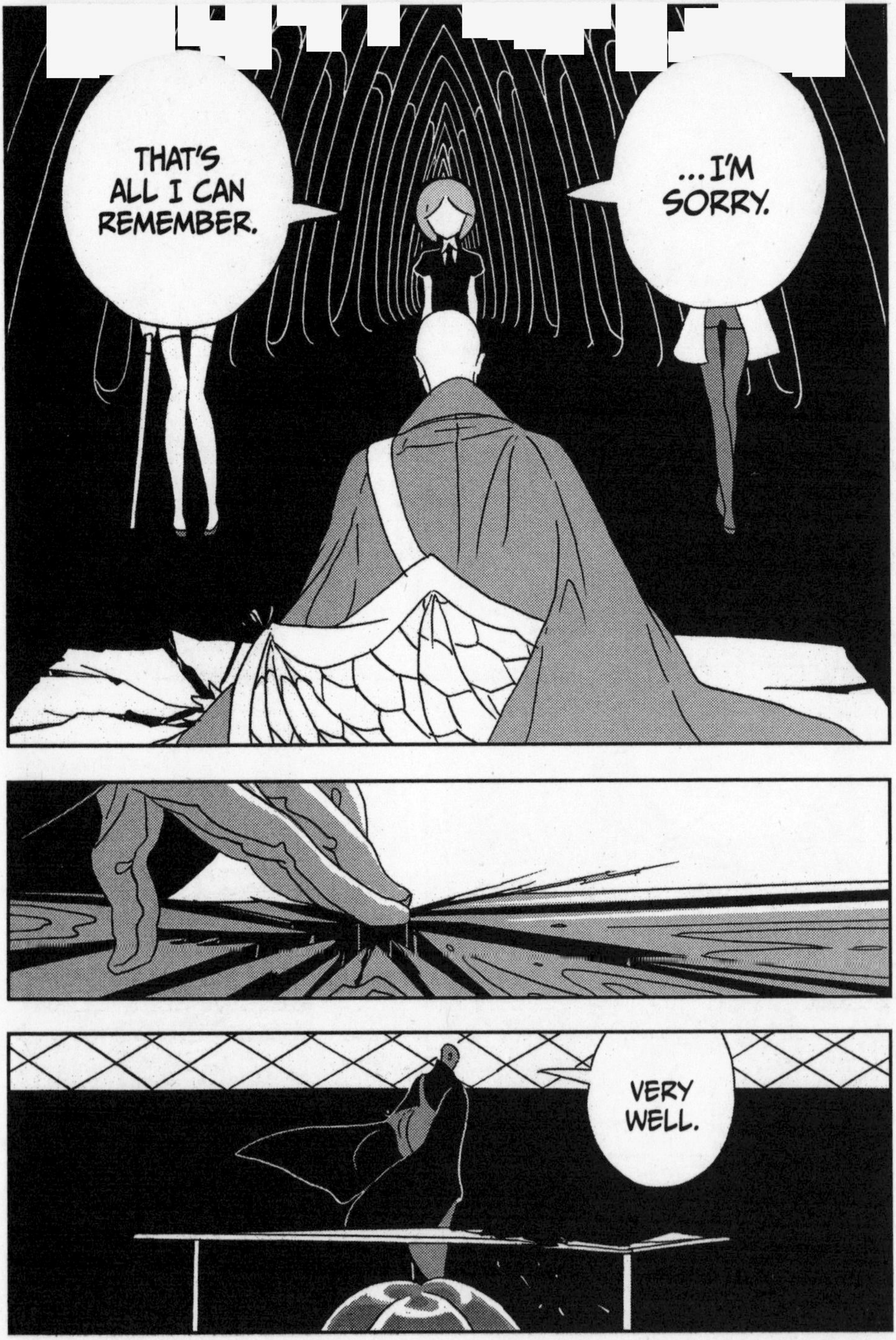
...I'M SORRY.
THAT'S ALL I CAN REMEMBER.
VERY WELL.

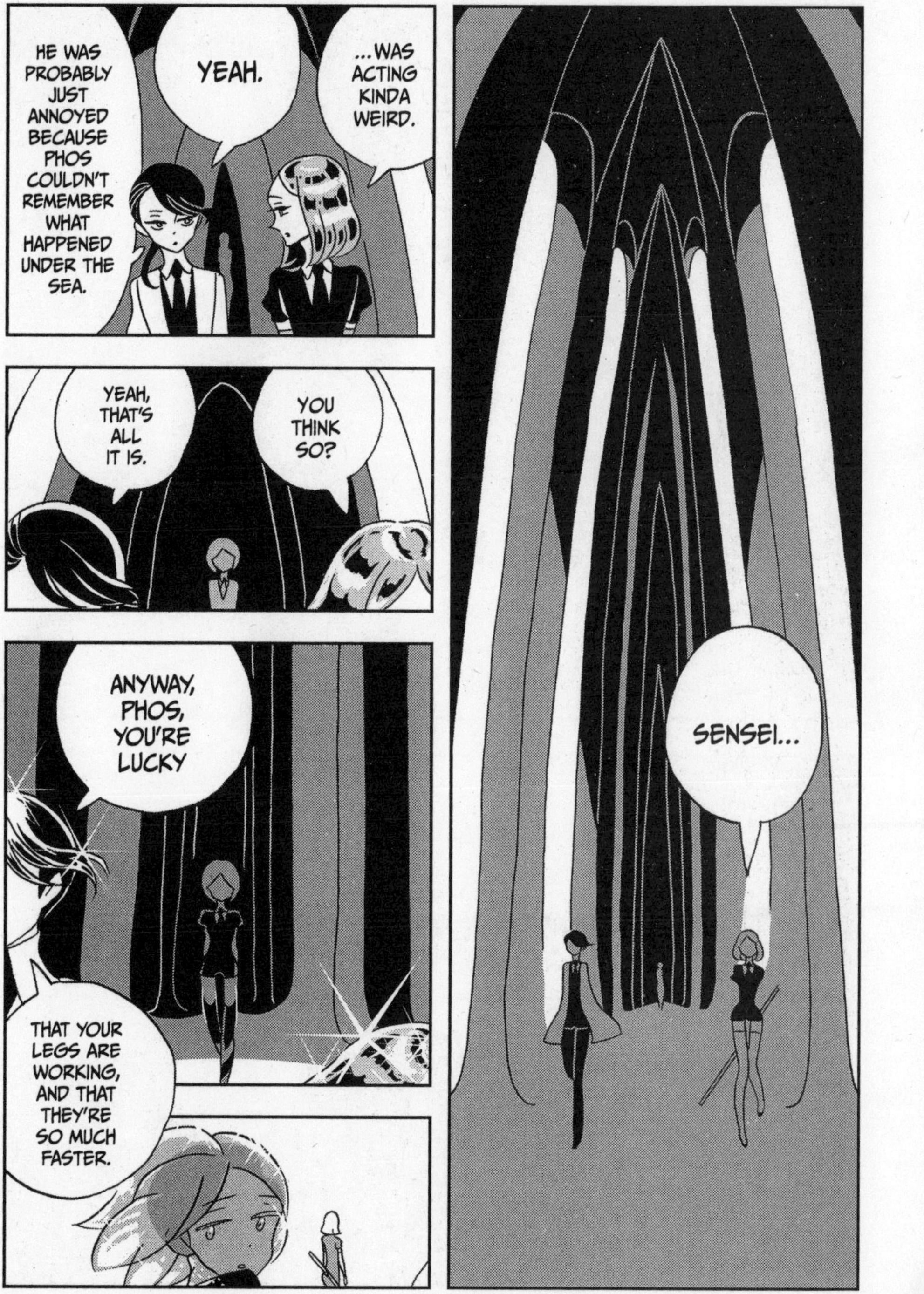
SENSEI...
...WAS ACTING KINDA WEIRD.
YEAH.
HE WAS PROBABLY JUST ANNOYED BECAUSE PHOS COULDN'T REMEMBER WHAT HAPPENED UNDER THE SEA.
YOU THINK SO?
YEAH, THAT'S ALL IT IS.
ANYWAY, PHOS, YOU'RE LUCKY
THAT YOUR LEGS ARE WORKING, AND THAT THEY'RE SO MUCH FASTER.

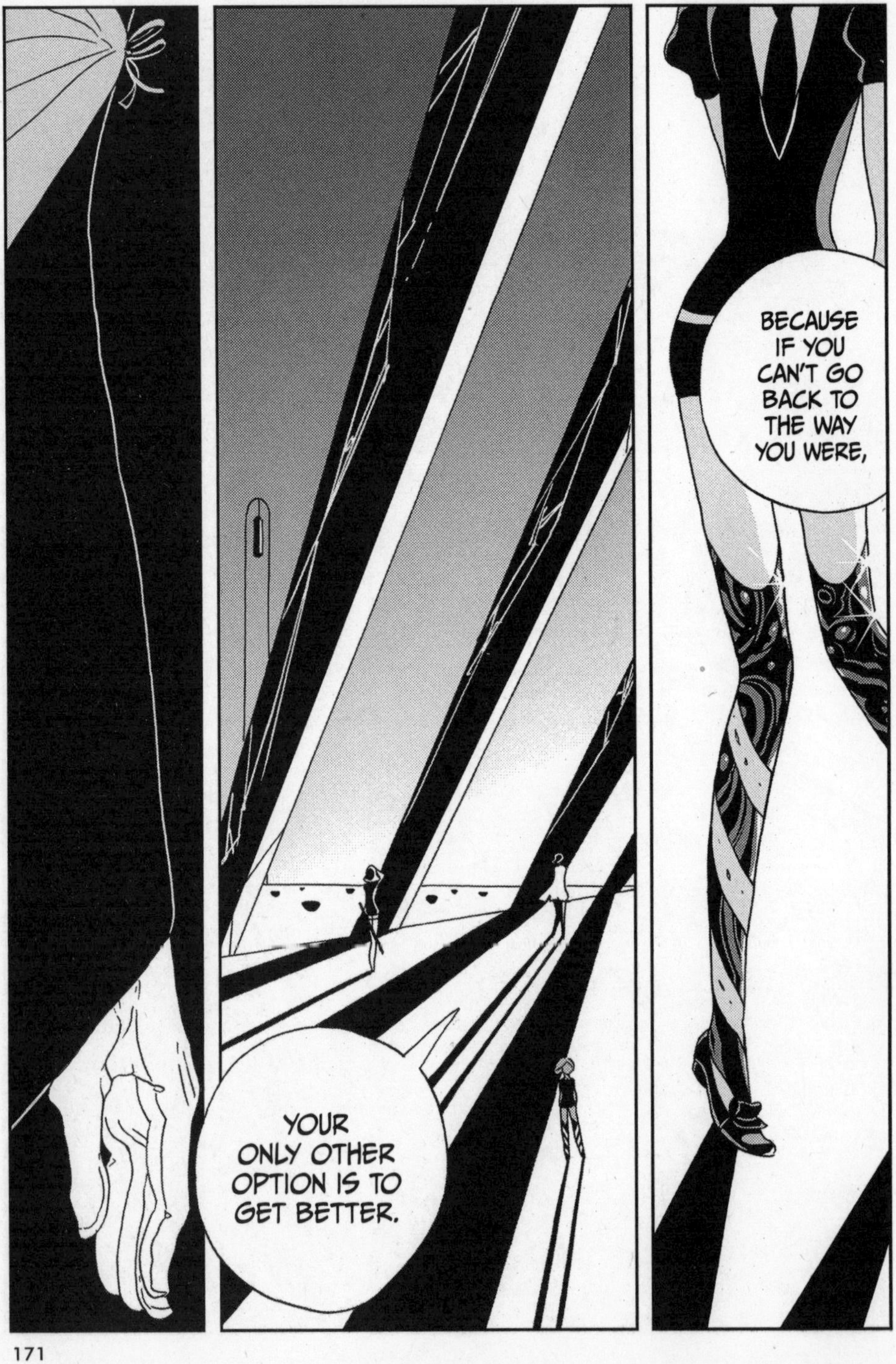
BECAUSE IF YOU CAN'T GO BACK TO THE WAY YOU WERE,
YOUR ONLY OTHER OPTION IS TO GET BETTER.

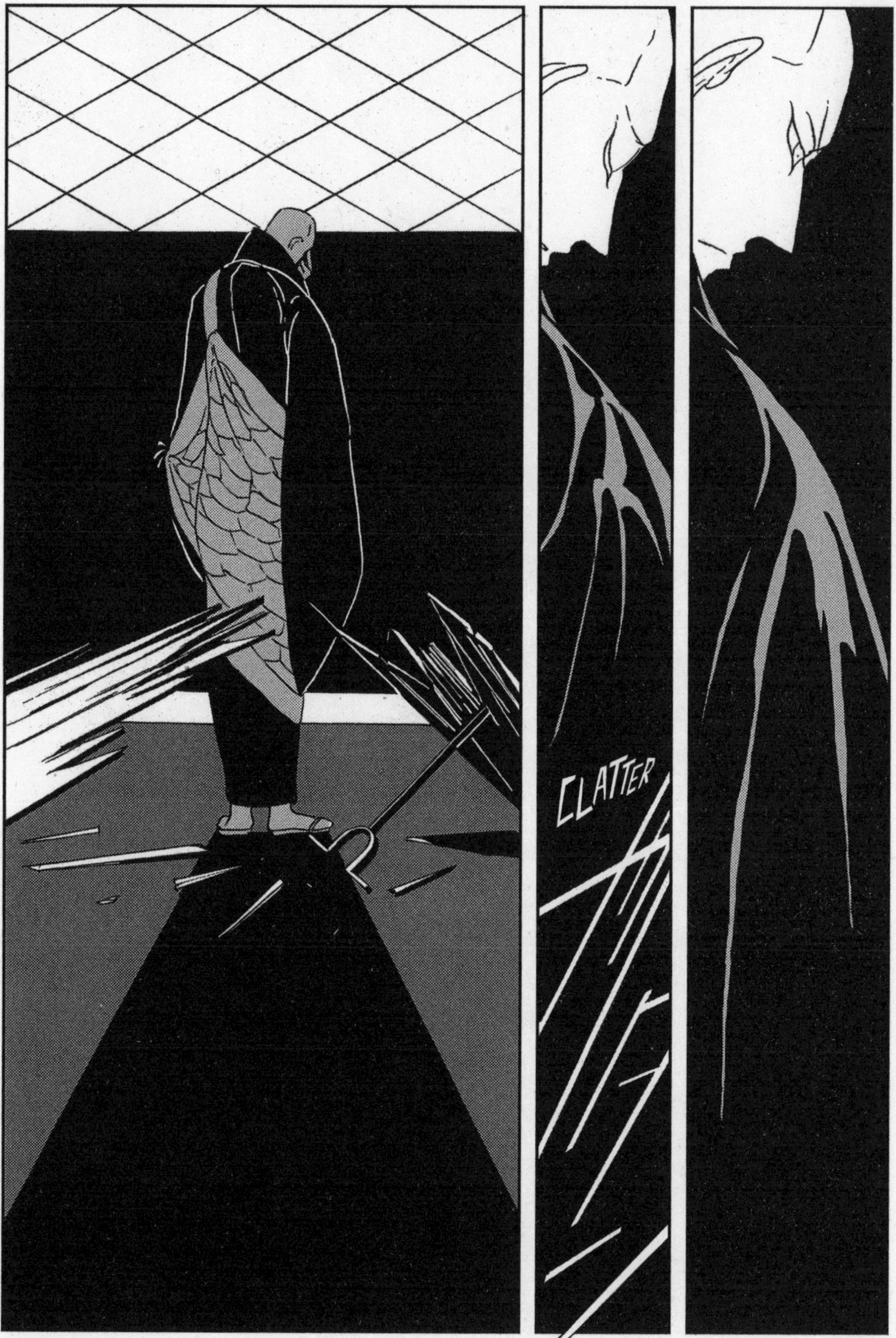
CLATTER

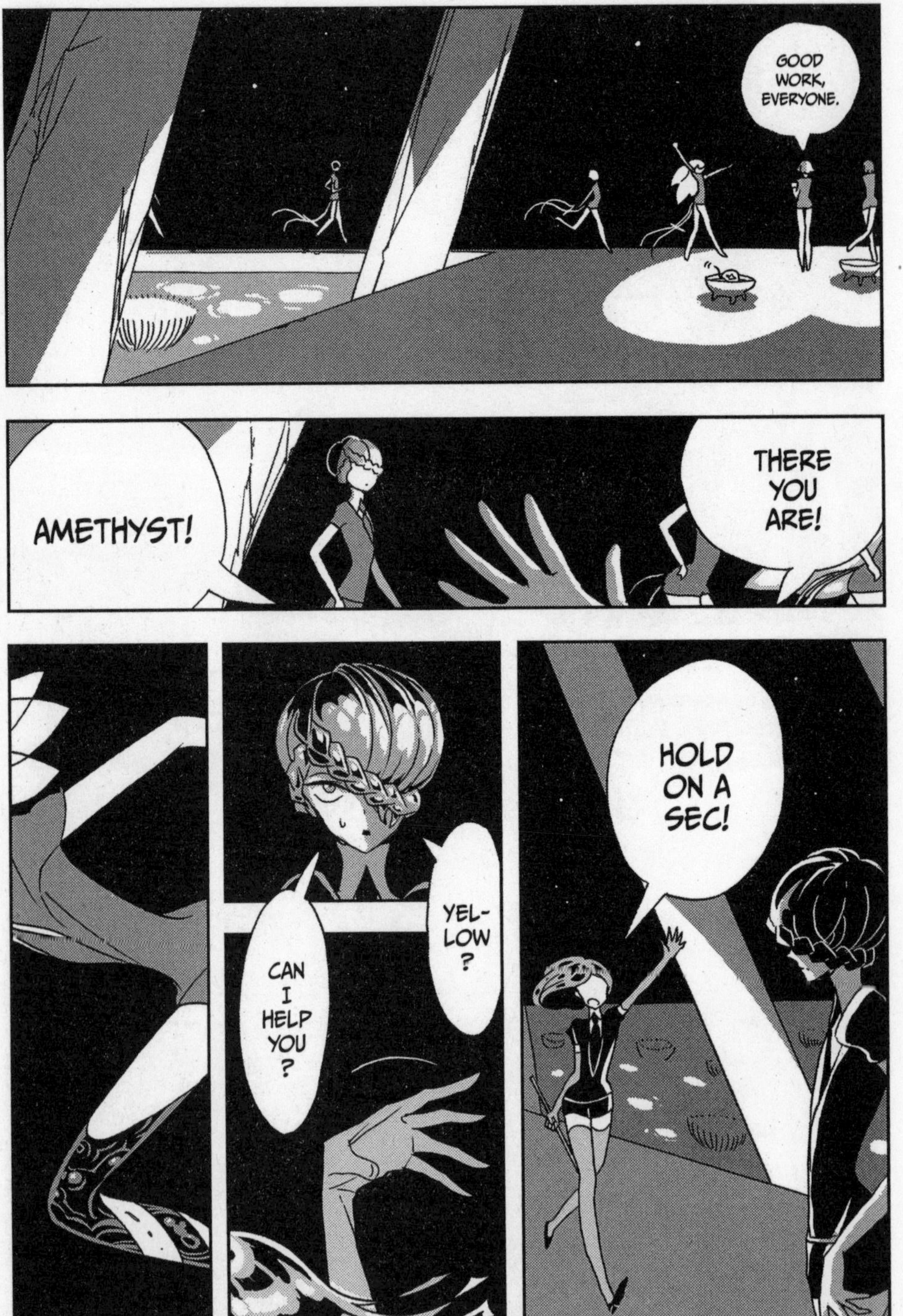
GOOD WORK, EVERYONE.
THERE YOU ARE!
AMETHYST!
HOLD ON A SEC!
YEL-LOW?
CAN I HELP YOU?

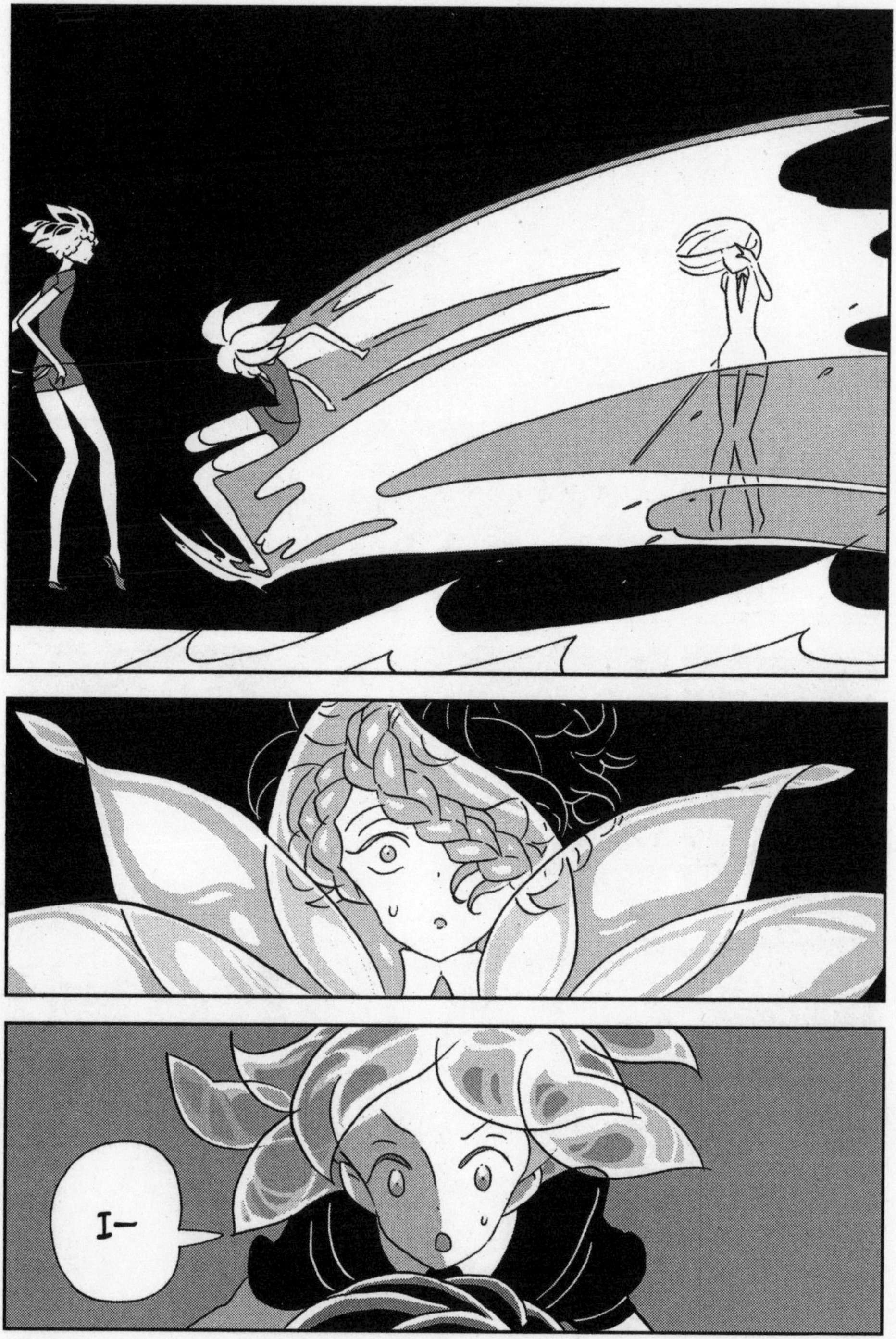
I–

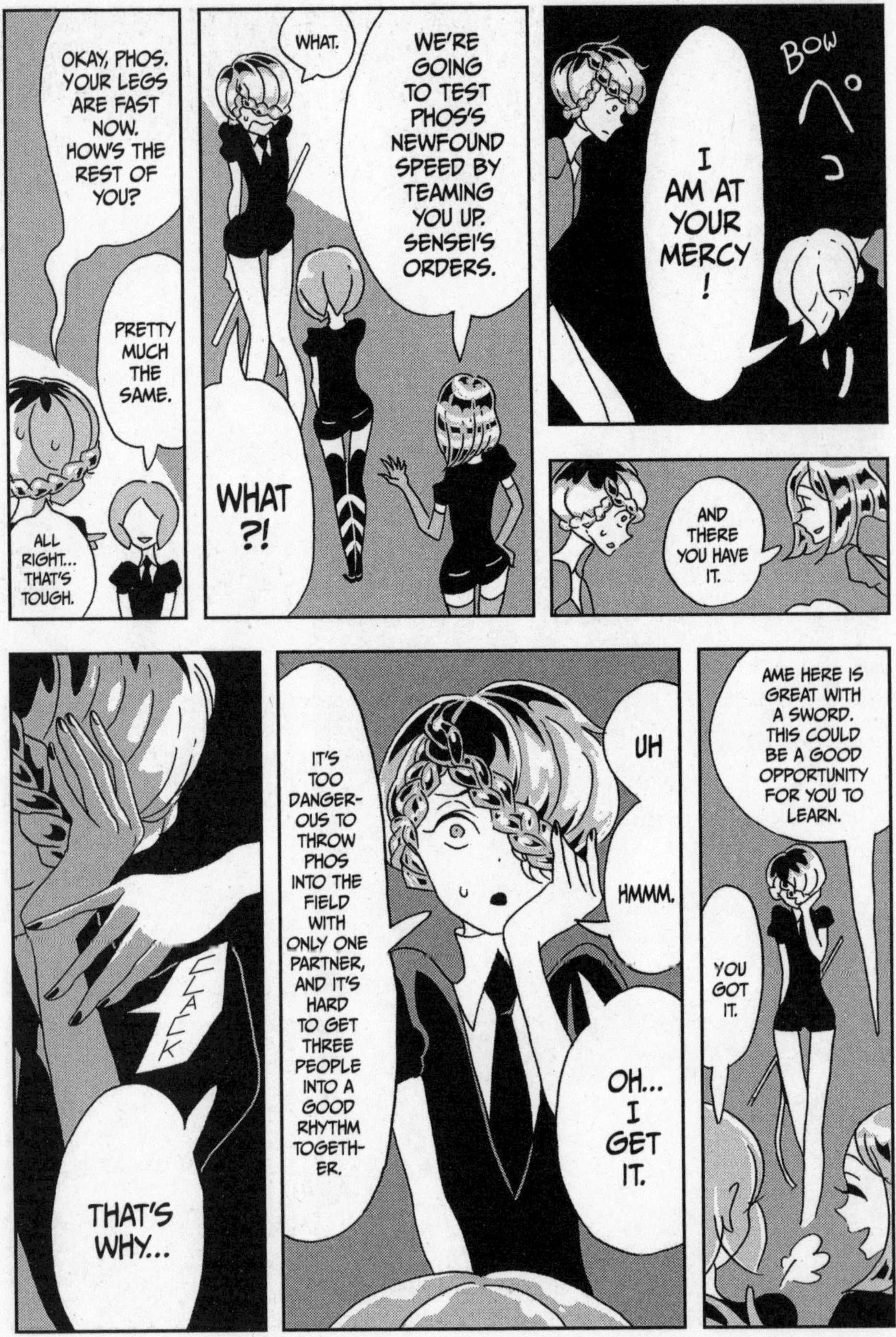
BOW
I AM AT YOUR MERCY!
AND THERE YOU HAVE IT.
WHAT.
WE'RE GOING TO TEST PHOS'S NEWFOUND SPEED BY TEAMING YOU UP. SENSEI'S ORDERS.
WHAT?!
OKAY, PHOS. YOUR LEGS ARE FAST NOW. HOW'S THE REST OF YOU?
PRETTY MUCH THE SAME.
ALL RIGHT... THAT'S TOUGH.
AME HERE IS GREAT WITH A SWORD. THIS COULD BE A GOOD OPPORTUNITY FOR YOU TO LEARN.
YOU GOT IT.
UH
HMMM.
IT'S TOO DANGER-OUS TO THROW PHOS INTO THE FIELD WITH ONLY ONE PARTNER, AND IT'S HARD TO GET THREE PEOPLE INTO A GOOD RHYTHM TOGETH-ER.
OH... I GET IT.
CLACK
THAT'S WHY...

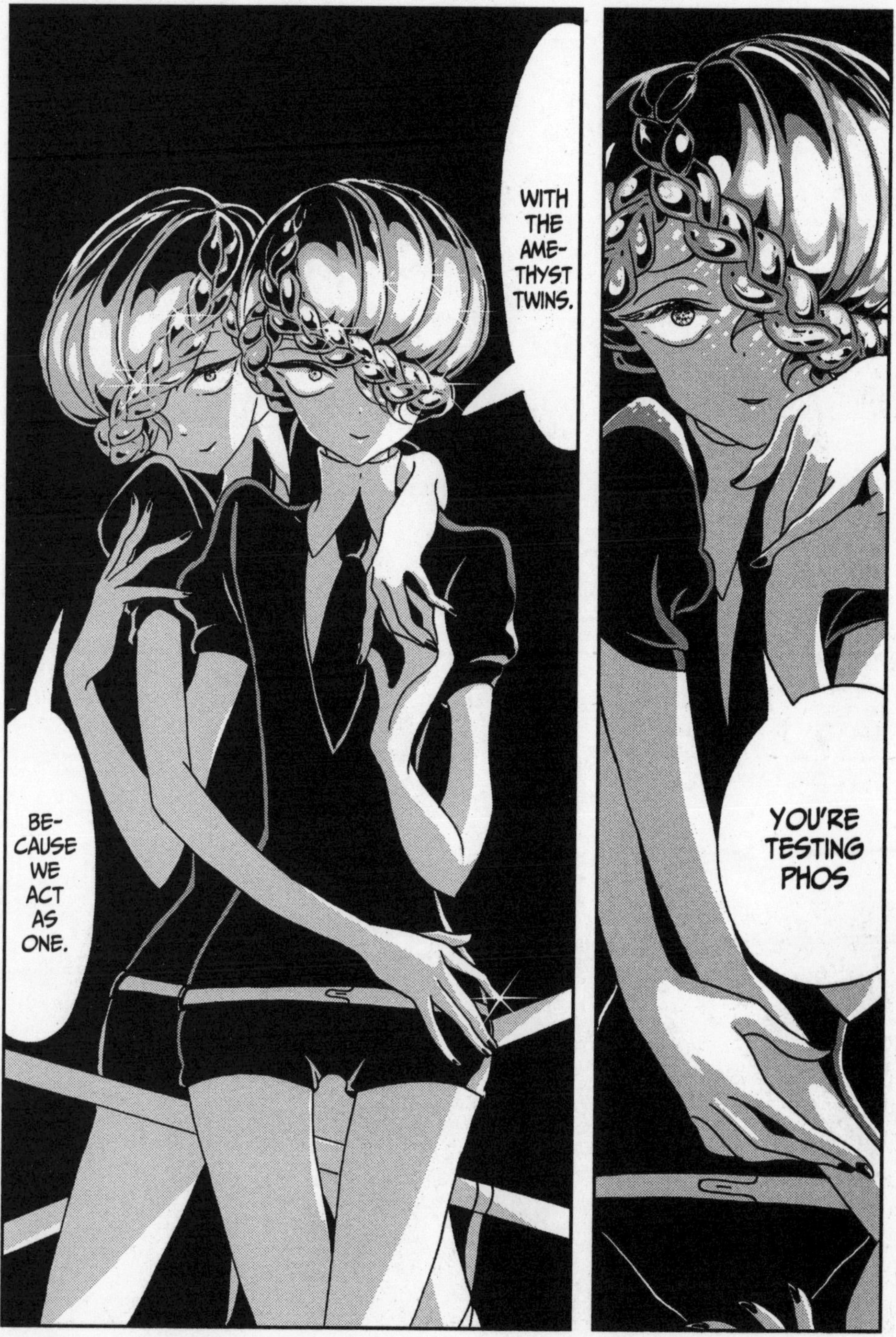
YOU'RE TESTING PHOS
WITH THE AME-THYST TWINS.
BE-CAUSE WE ACT AS ONE.

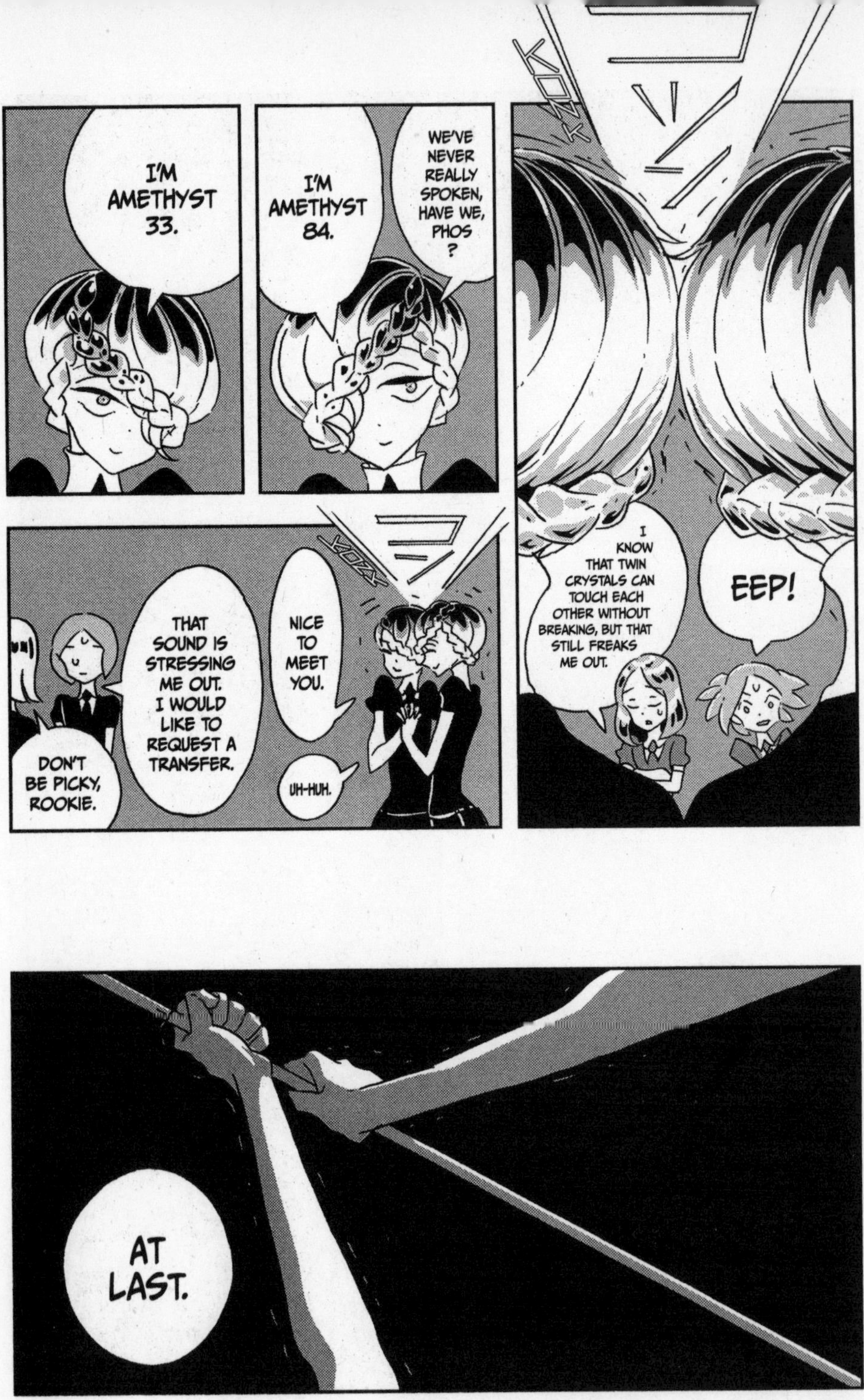
KONK
EEP!
I KNOW THAT TWIN CRYSTALS CAN TOUCH EACH OTHER WITHOUT BREAKING, BUT THAT STILL FREAKS ME OUT.
WE'VE NEVER REALLY SPOKEN, HAVE WE, PHOS?
I'M AMETHYST 84.
I'M AMETHYST 33.
KONK
NICE TO MEET YOU.
UH-HUH.
THAT SOUND IS STRESSING ME OUT. I WOULD LIKE TO REQUEST A TRANSFER.
DON'T BE PICKY, ROOKIE.
AT LAST.

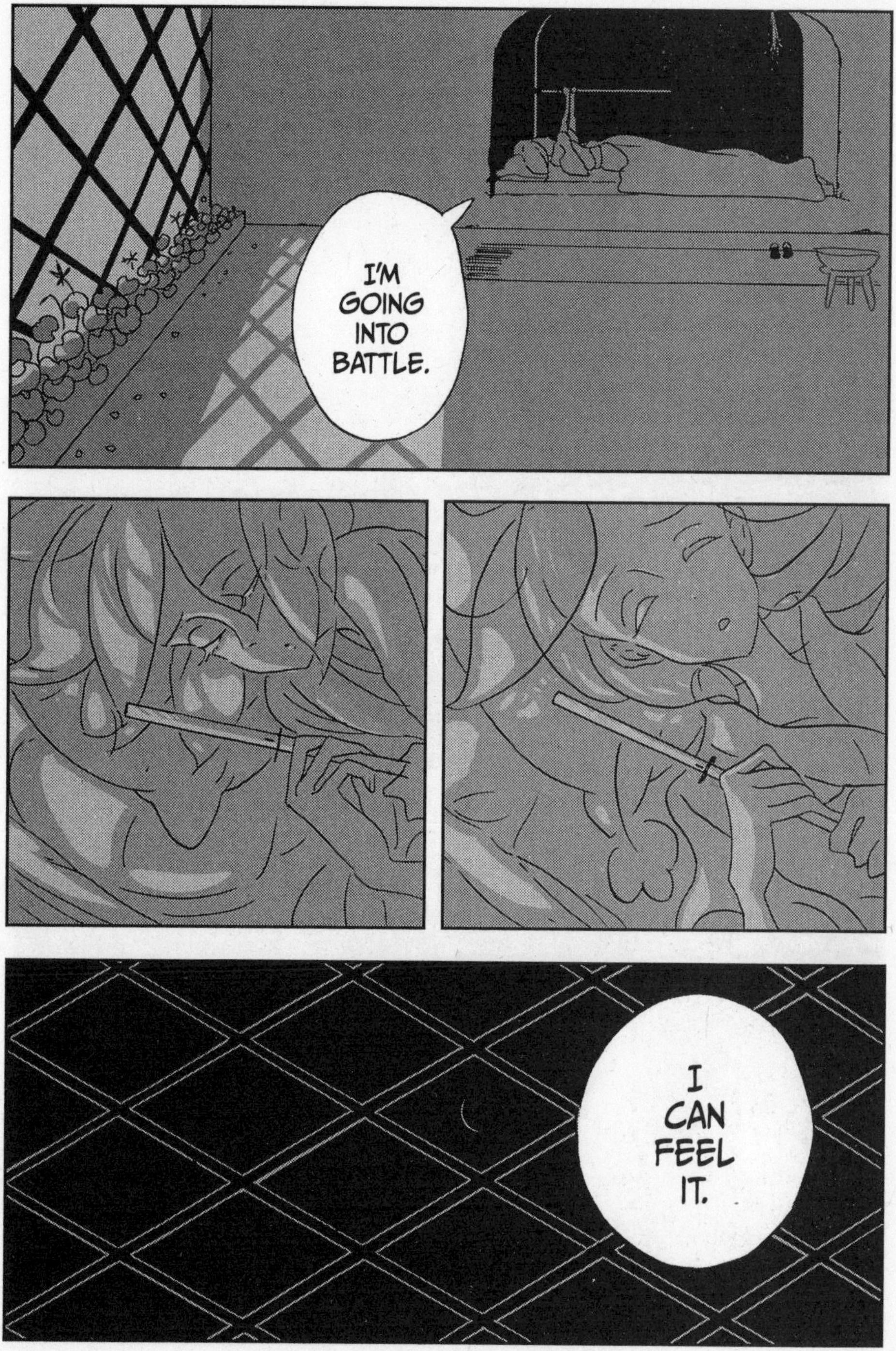
I'M GOING INTO BATTLE.
I CAN FEEL IT.

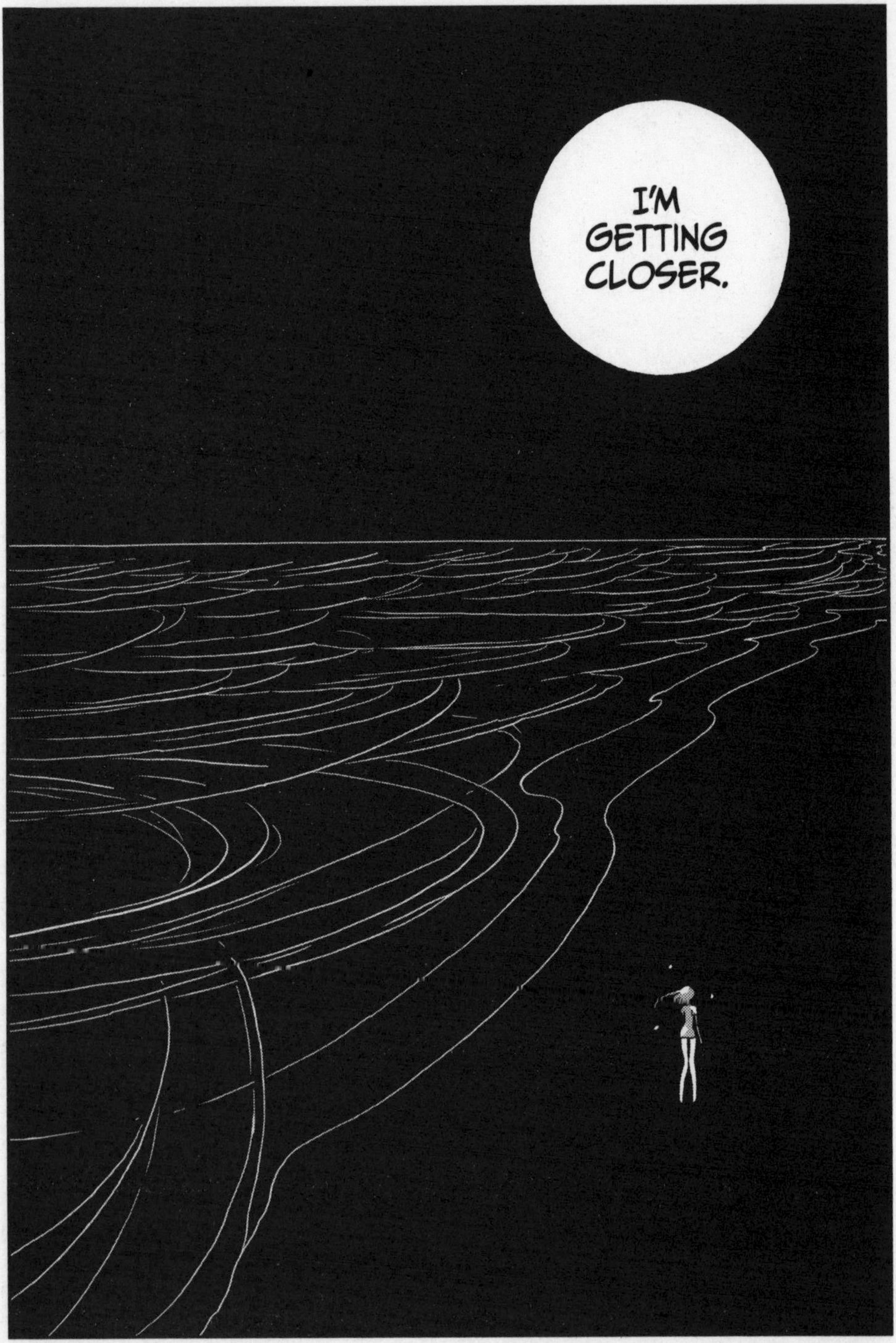
I'M GETTING CLOSER.

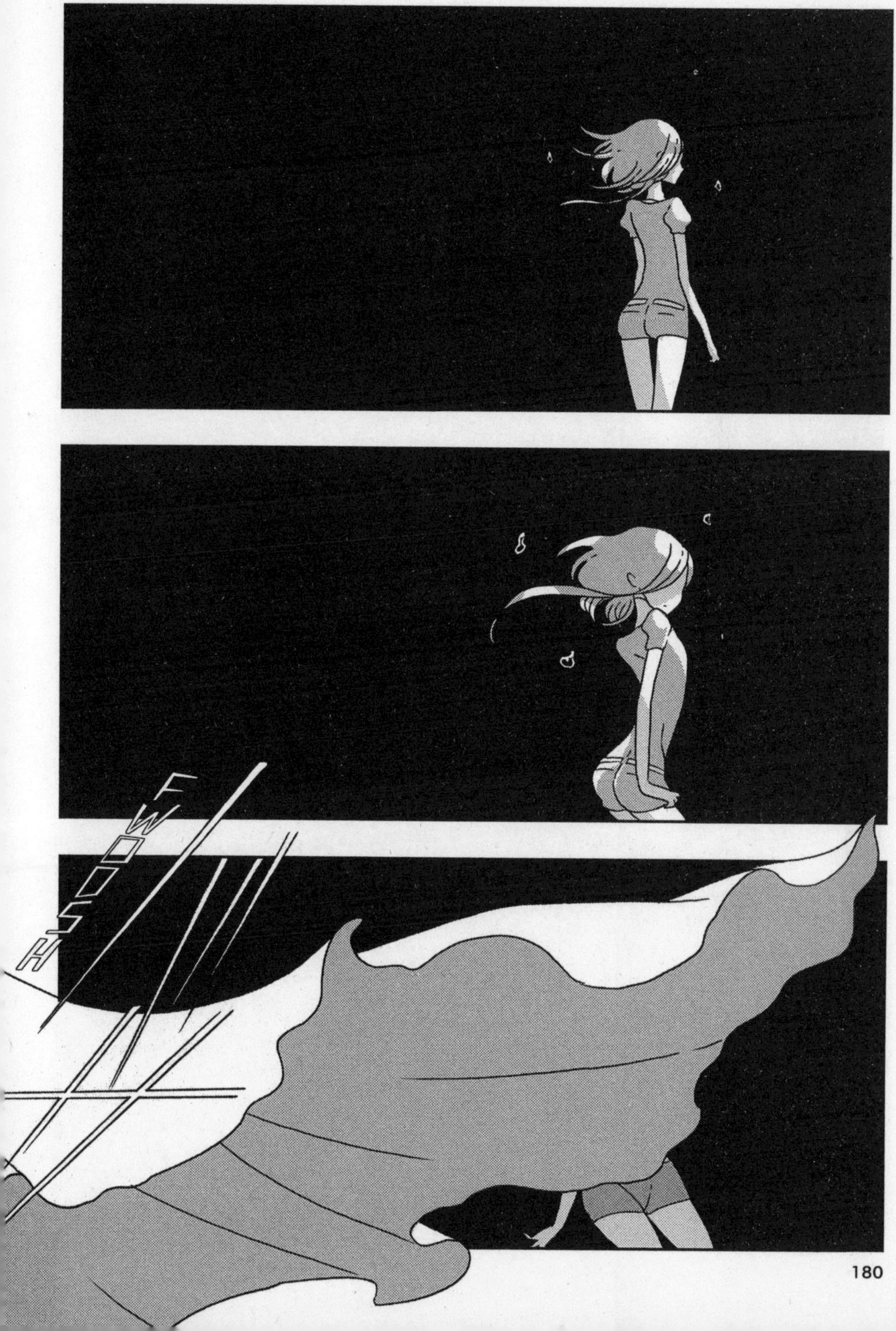
FWOOSH

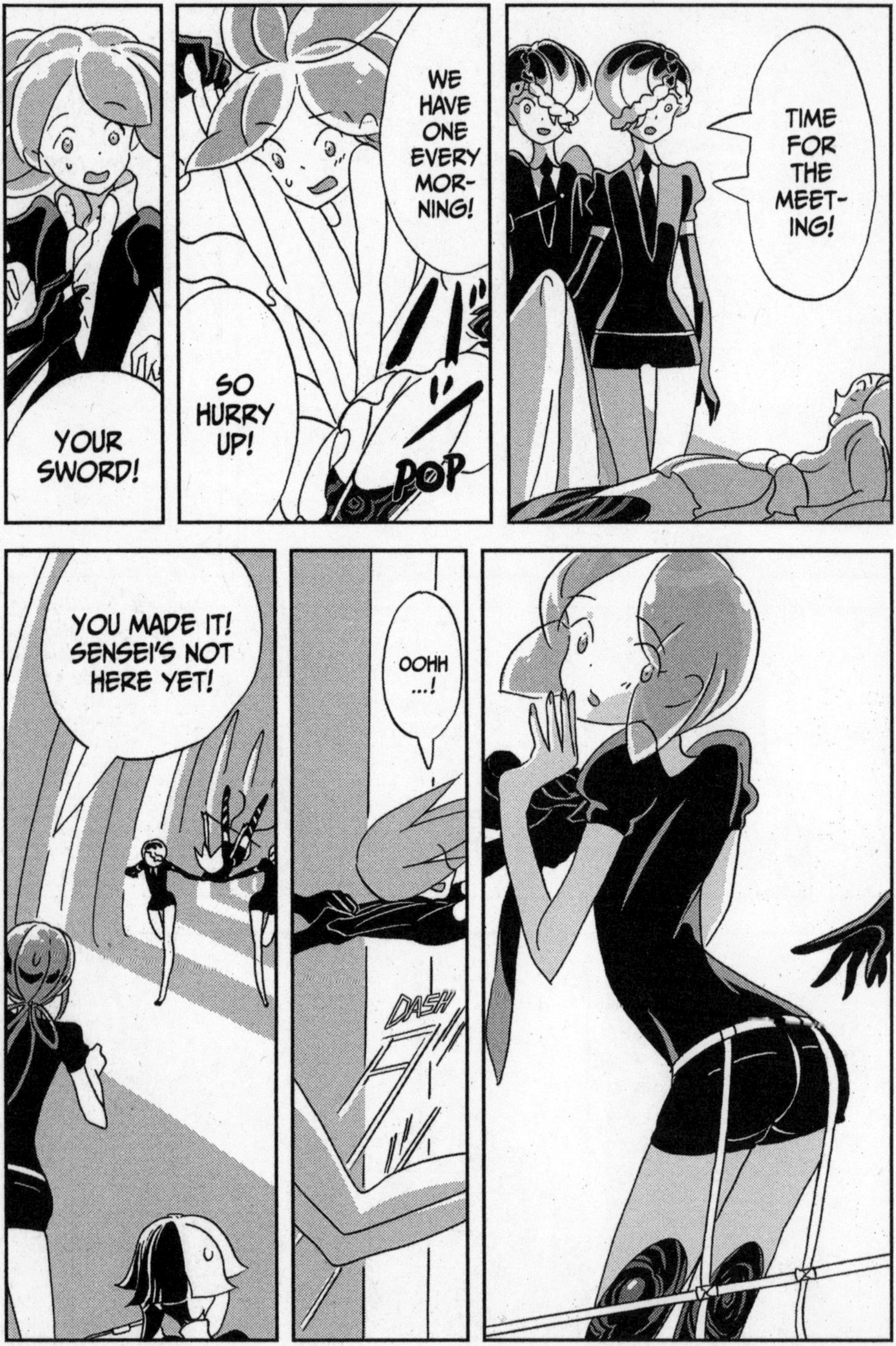
TIME FOR THE MEET-ING!
WE HAVE ONE EVERY MOR-NING!
SO HURRY UP!
POP
YOUR SWORD!
OOHH ...!
DASH
YOU MADE IT! SENSEI'S NOT HERE YET!

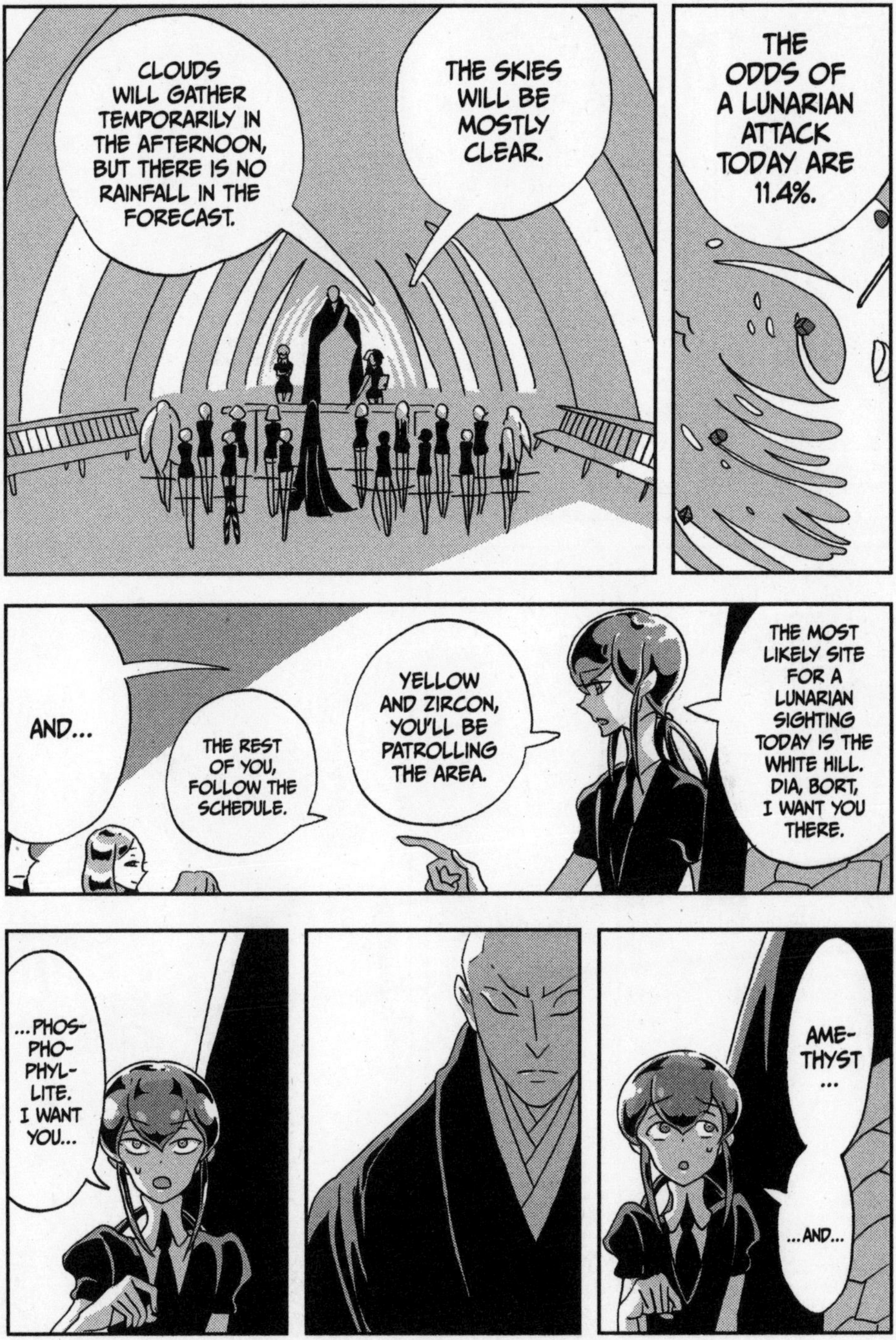
THE ODDS OF A LUNARIAN ATTACK TODAY ARE 11.4%.
THE SKIES WILL BE MOSTLY CLEAR.
CLOUDS WILL GATHER TEMPORARILY IN THE AFTERNOON, BUT THERE IS NO RAINFALL IN THE FORECAST.
THE MOST LIKELY SITE FOR A LUNARIAN SIGHTING TODAY IS THE WHITE HILL. DIA, BORT, I WANT YOU THERE.
YELLOW AND ZIRCON, YOU'LL BE PATROLLING THE AREA.
THE REST OF YOU, FOLLOW THE SCHEDULE.
AND...
AME-THYST...
...AND...
...PHOS-PHO-PHYL-LITE. I WANT YOU...

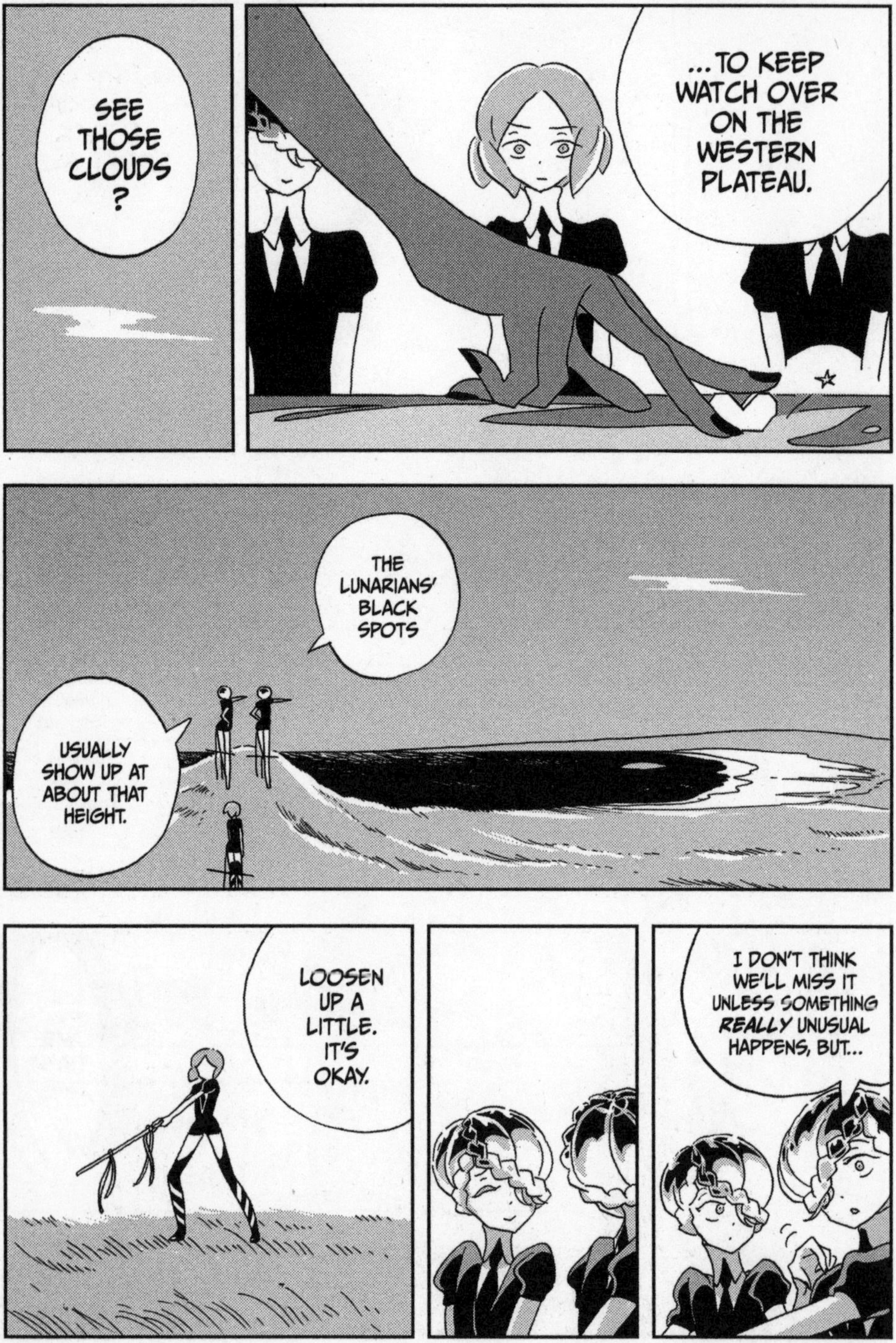
...TO KEEP WATCH OVER ON THE WESTERN PLATEAU.
SEE THOSE CLOUDS ?
THE LUNARIANS' BLACK SPOTS
USUALLY SHOW UP AT ABOUT THAT HEIGHT.
I DON'T THINK WE'LL MISS IT UNLESS SOMETHING *REALLY* UNUSUAL HAPPENS, BUT...
LOOSEN UP A LITTLE. IT'S OKAY.

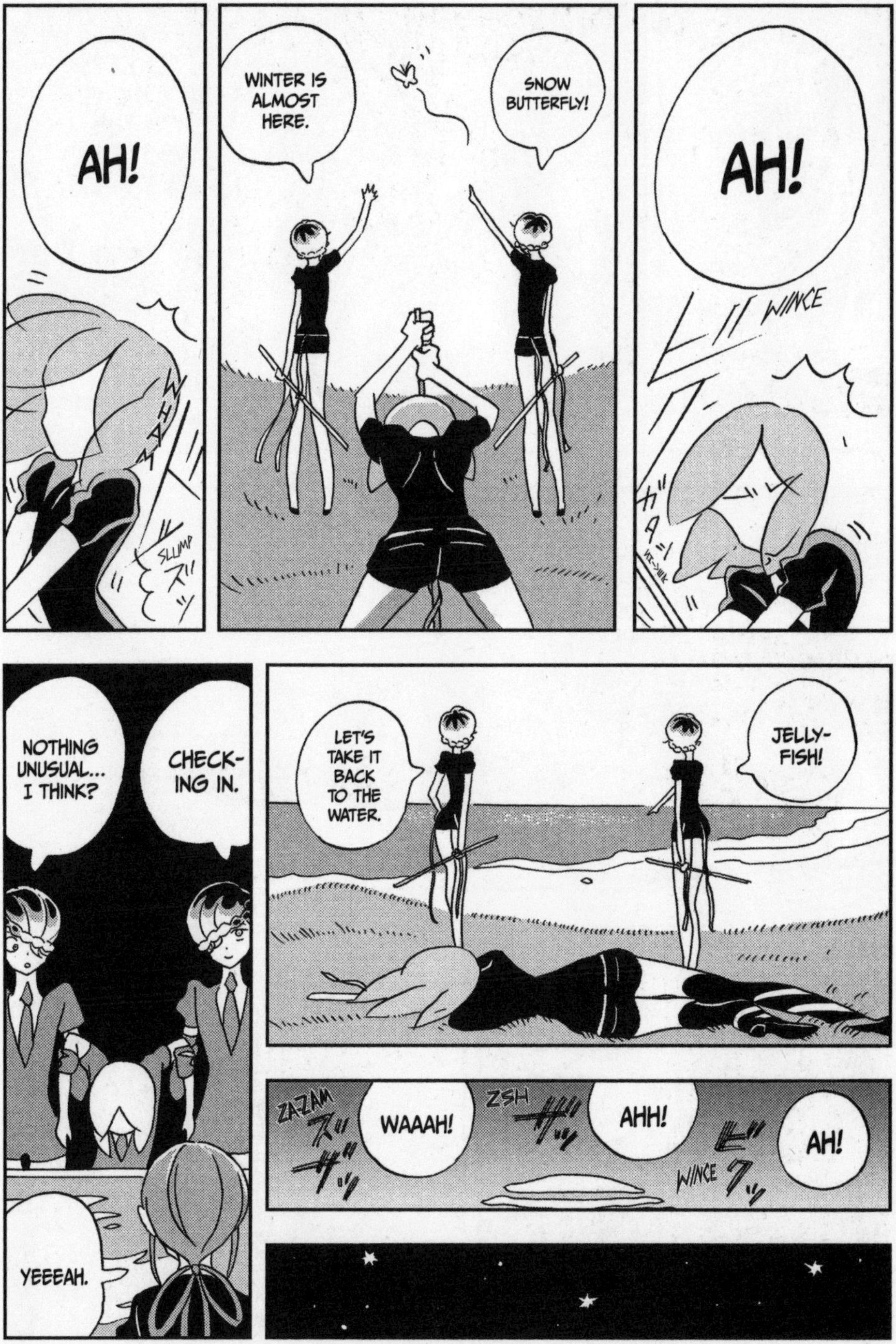
AH!
WINCE
SNOW BUTTERFLY!
WINTER IS ALMOST HERE.
AH!
WHAM
SLUMP
JELLY-FISH!
LET'S TAKE IT BACK TO THE WATER.
AH!
WINCE
AHH!
ZSH
WAAAH!
ZAZAM
CHECK-ING IN.
NOTHING UNUSUAL... I THINK?
YEEEAH.

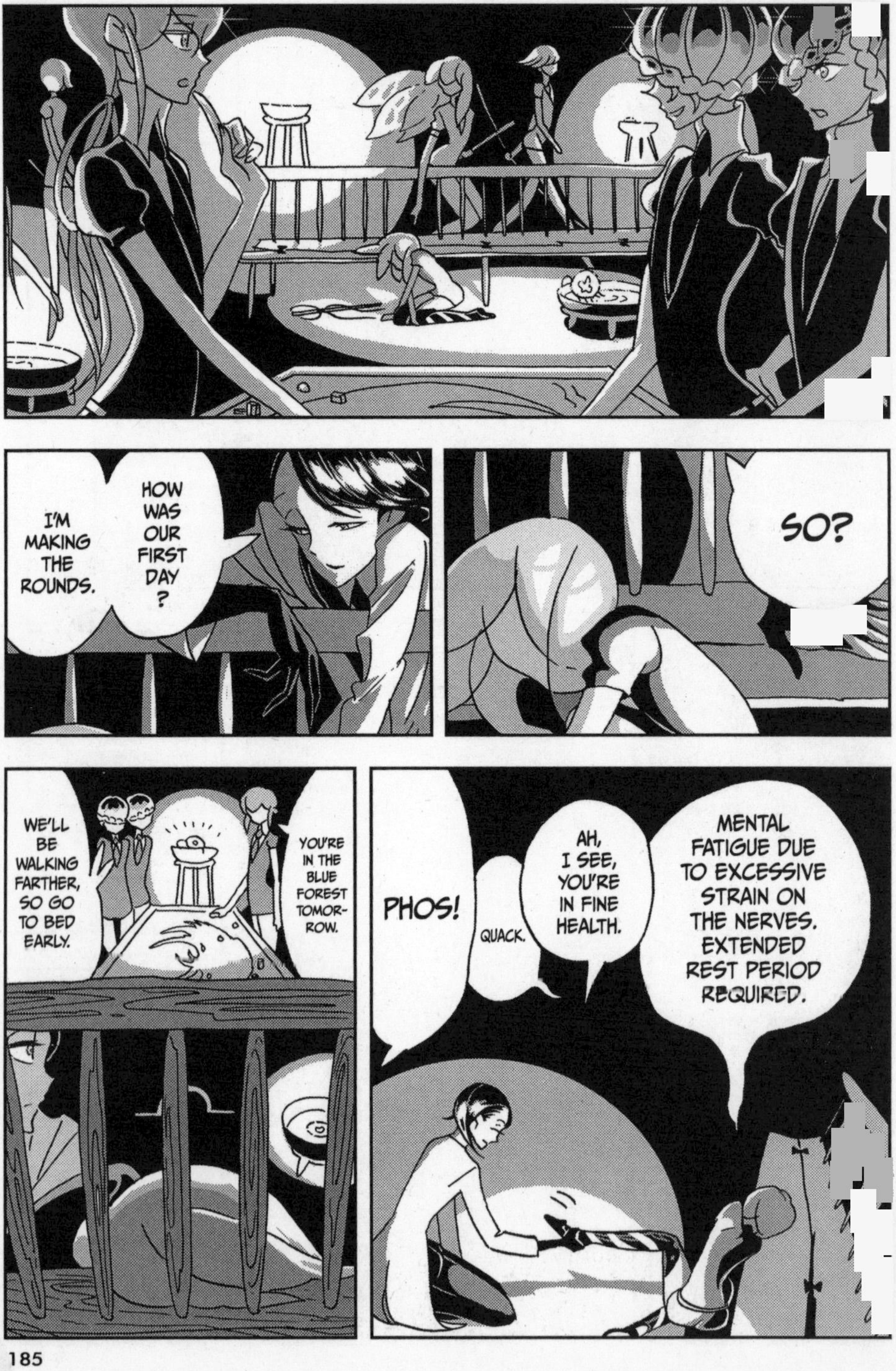
SO?
I'M MAKING THE ROUNDS. HOW WAS OUR FIRST DAY?
MENTAL FATIGUE DUE TO EXCESSIVE STRAIN ON THE NERVES. EXTENDED REST PERIOD REQUIRED.
AH, I SEE, YOU'RE IN FINE HEALTH.
QUACK.
PHOS!
YOU'RE IN THE BLUE FOREST TOMORROW.
WE'LL BE WALKING FARTHER, SO GO TO BED EARLY.

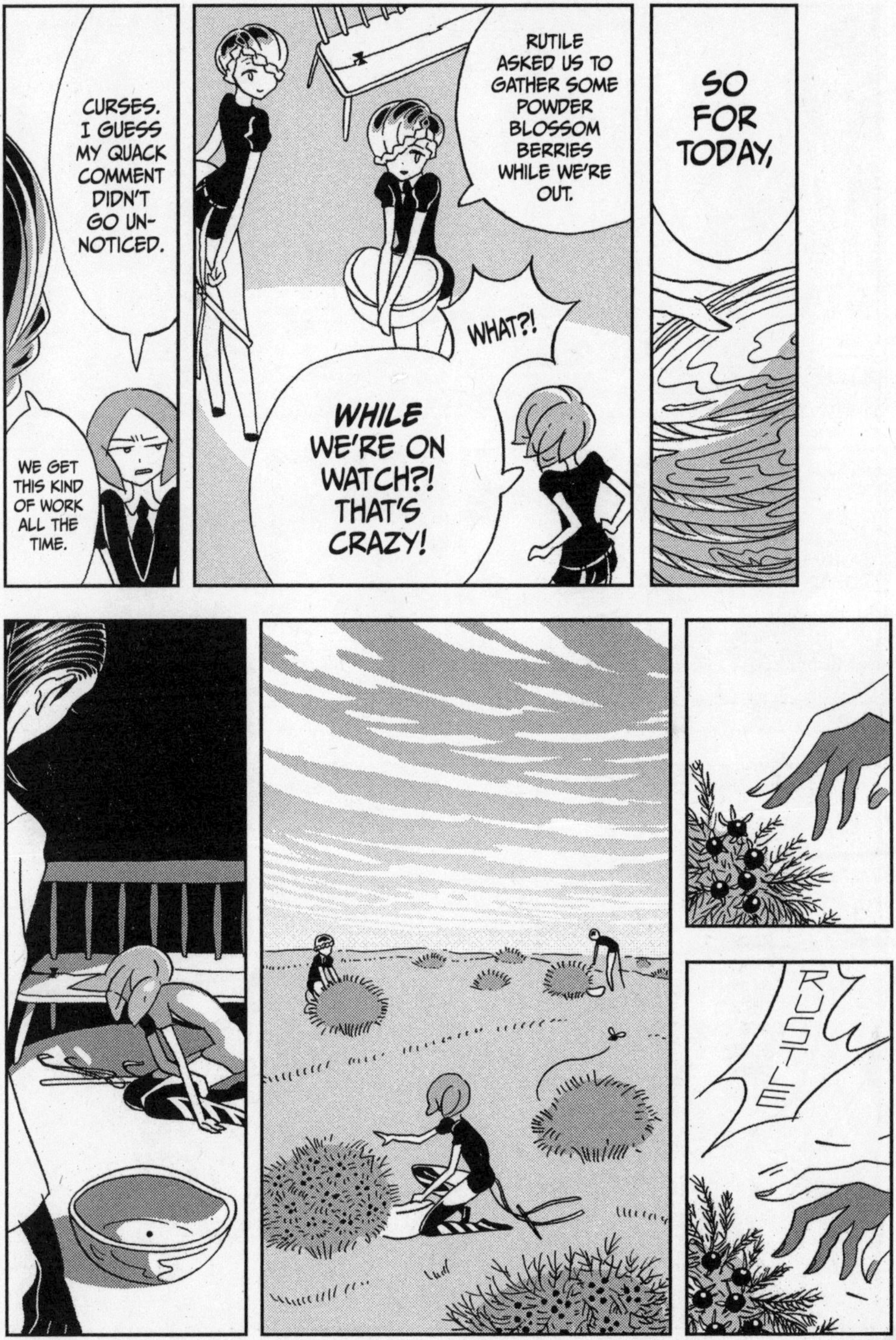
SO FOR TODAY,
RUTILE ASKED US TO GATHER SOME POWDER BLOSSOM BERRIES WHILE WE'RE OUT.
WHAT?!
WHILE WE'RE ON WATCH?! THAT'S CRAZY!
CURSES. I GUESS MY QUACK COMMENT DIDN'T GO UN-NOTICED.
WE GET THIS KIND OF WORK ALL THE TIME.
RUSTLE

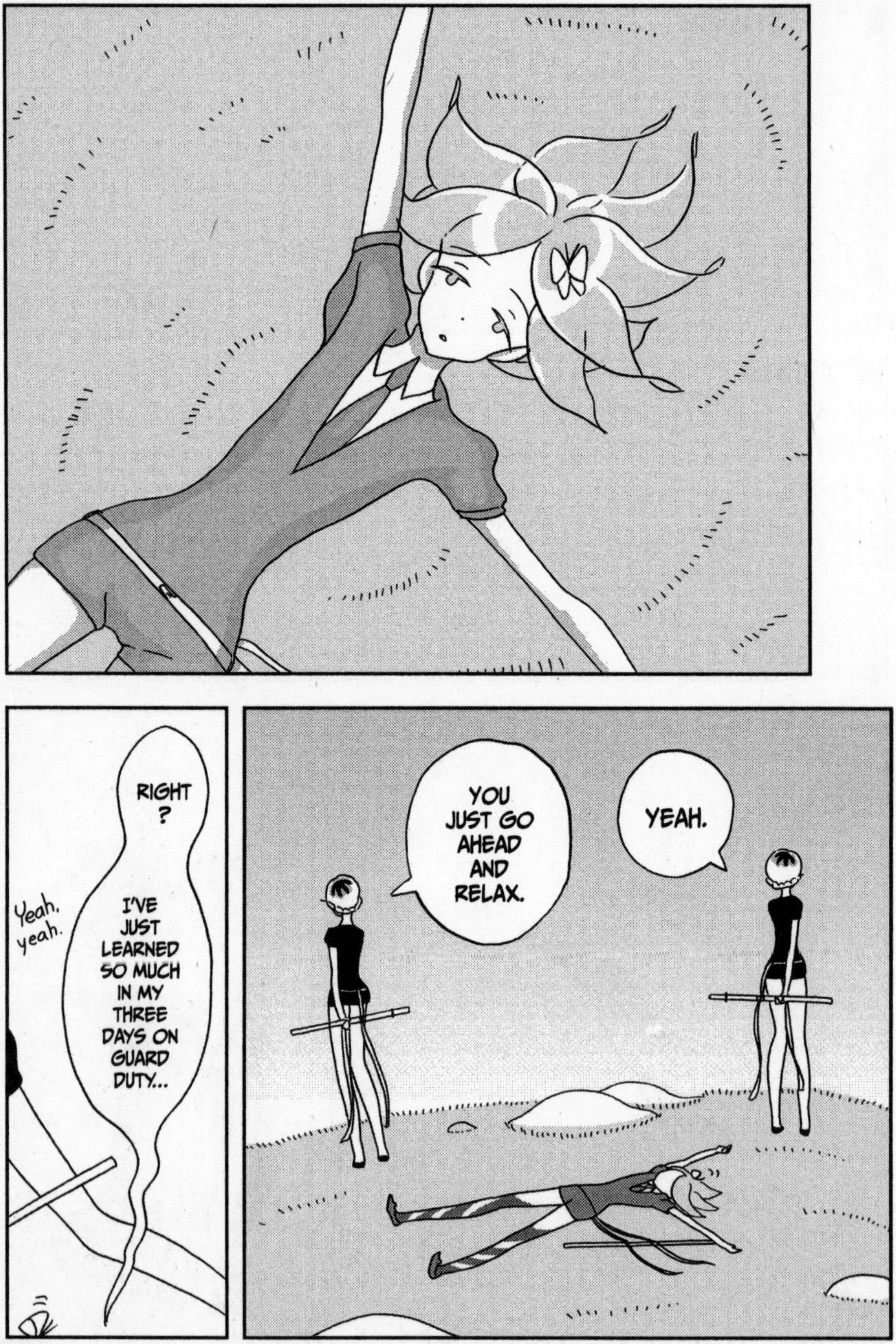
YEAH.
YOU JUST GO AHEAD AND RELAX.
RIGHT? I'VE JUST LEARNED SO MUCH IN MY THREE DAYS ON GUARD DUTY...
Yeah, yeah.

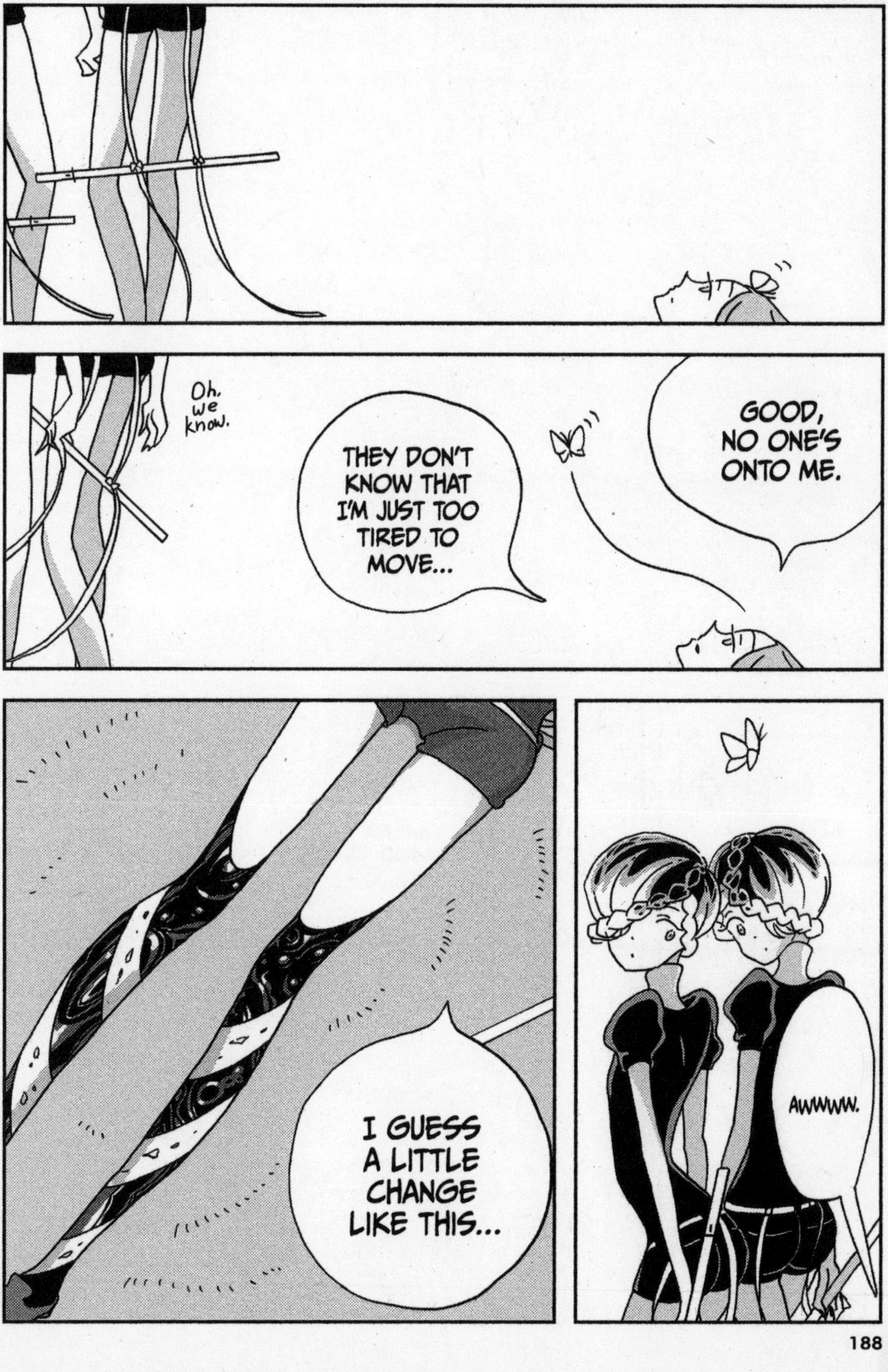
GOOD, NO ONE'S ONTO ME.
THEY DON'T KNOW THAT I'M JUST TOO TIRED TO MOVE...
Oh, we know.
AWWWW.
I GUESS A LITTLE CHANGE LIKE THIS...

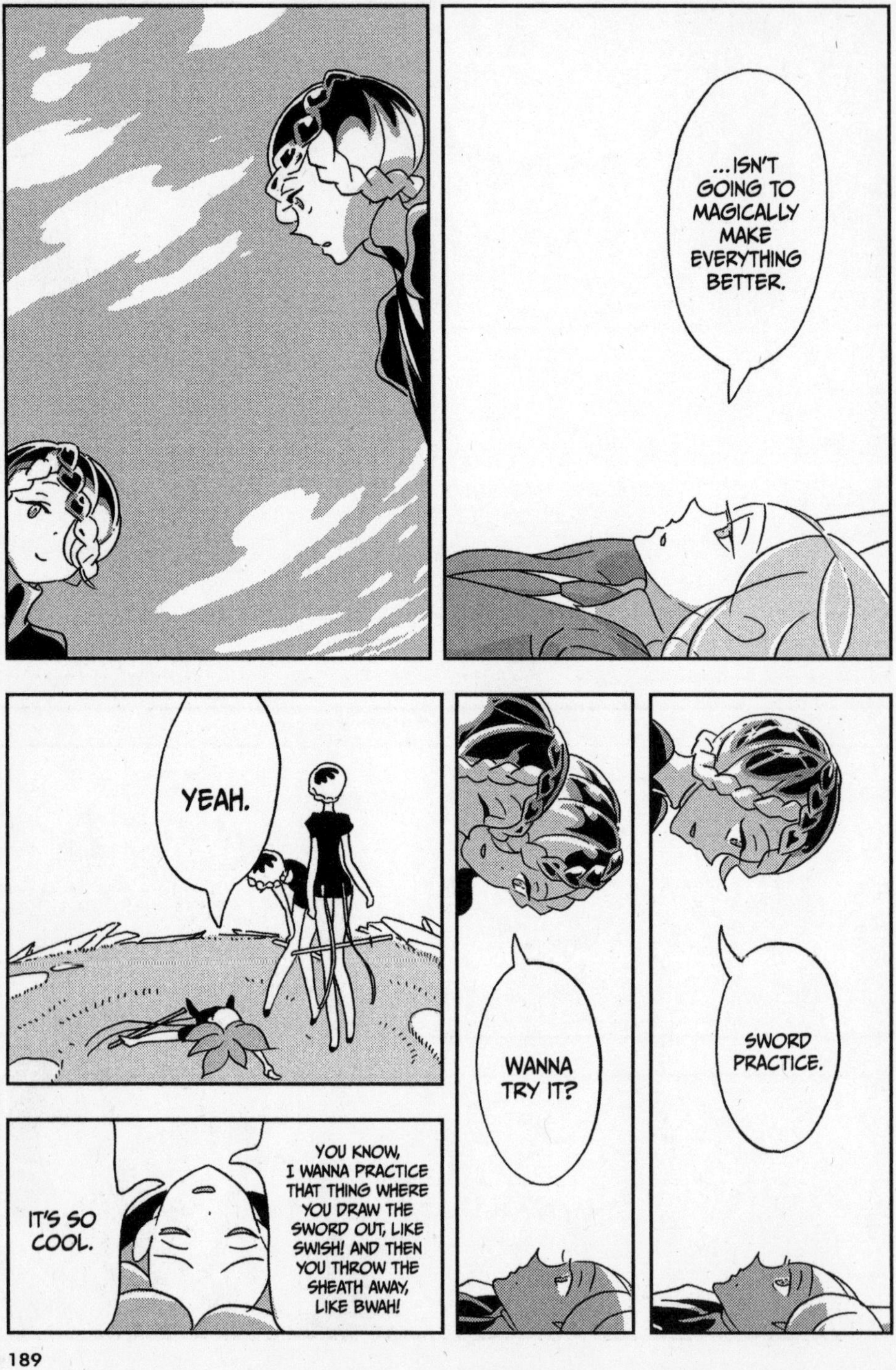
...ISN'T GOING TO MAGICALLY MAKE EVERYTHING BETTER.
SWORD PRACTICE.
WANNA TRY IT?
YEAH.
YOU KNOW, I WANNA PRACTICE THAT THING WHERE YOU DRAW THE SWORD OUT, LIKE SWISH! AND THEN YOU THROW THE SHEATH AWAY, LIKE BWAH!
IT'S SO COOL.

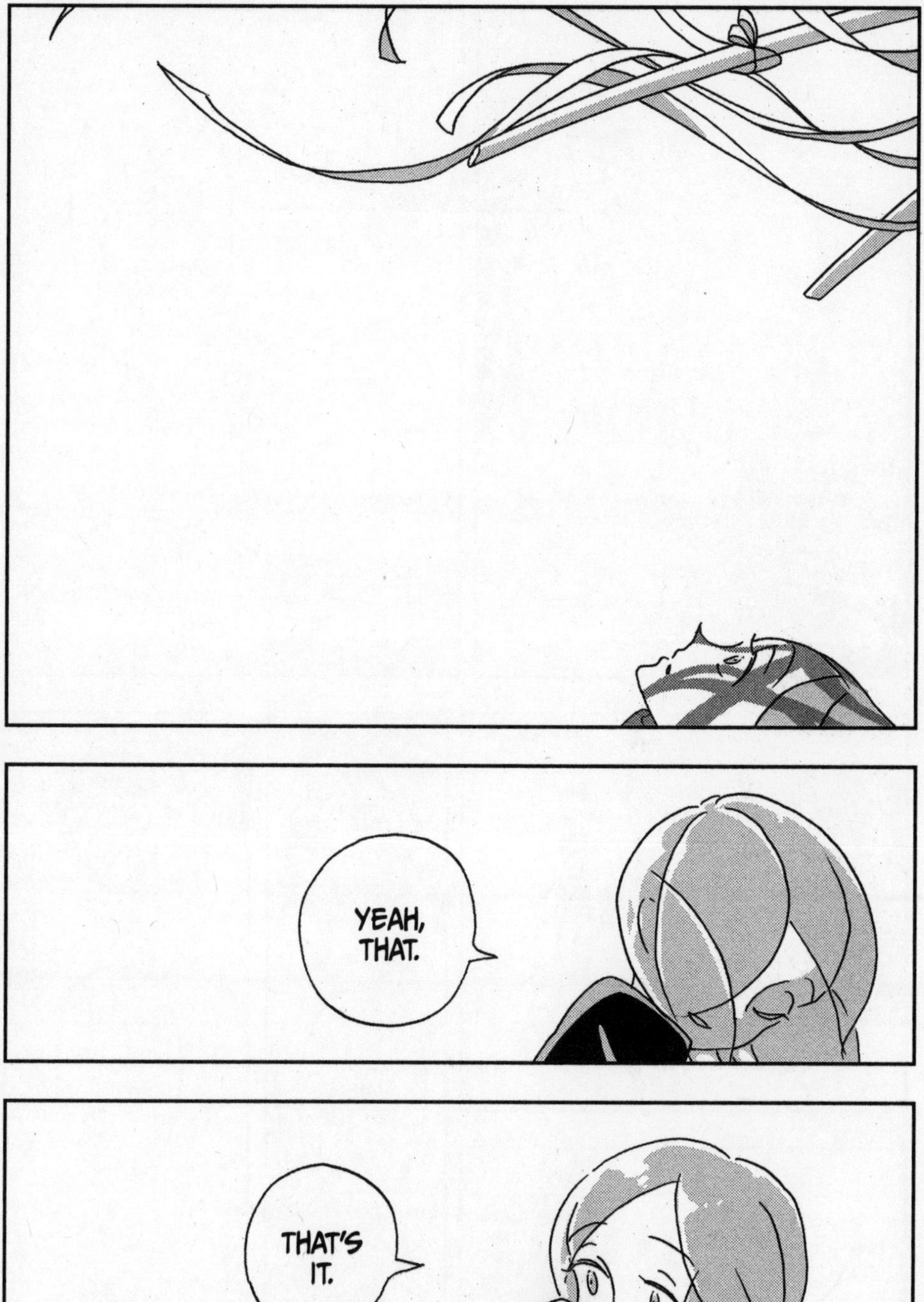
YEAH, THAT.
THAT'S IT.

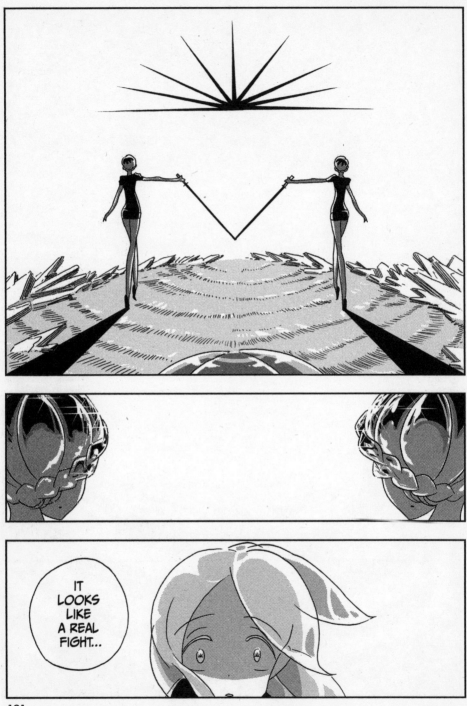

IT LOOKS LIKE A REAL FIGHT...

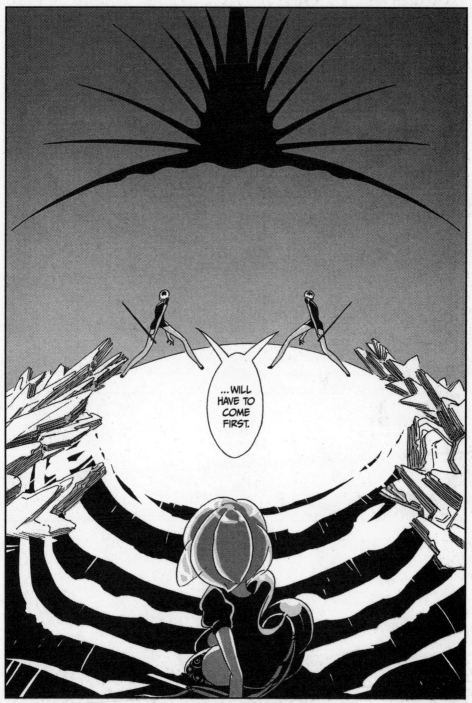

CHAPTER 13: Twin Crystals END

LAND OF THE LATEST FASHION

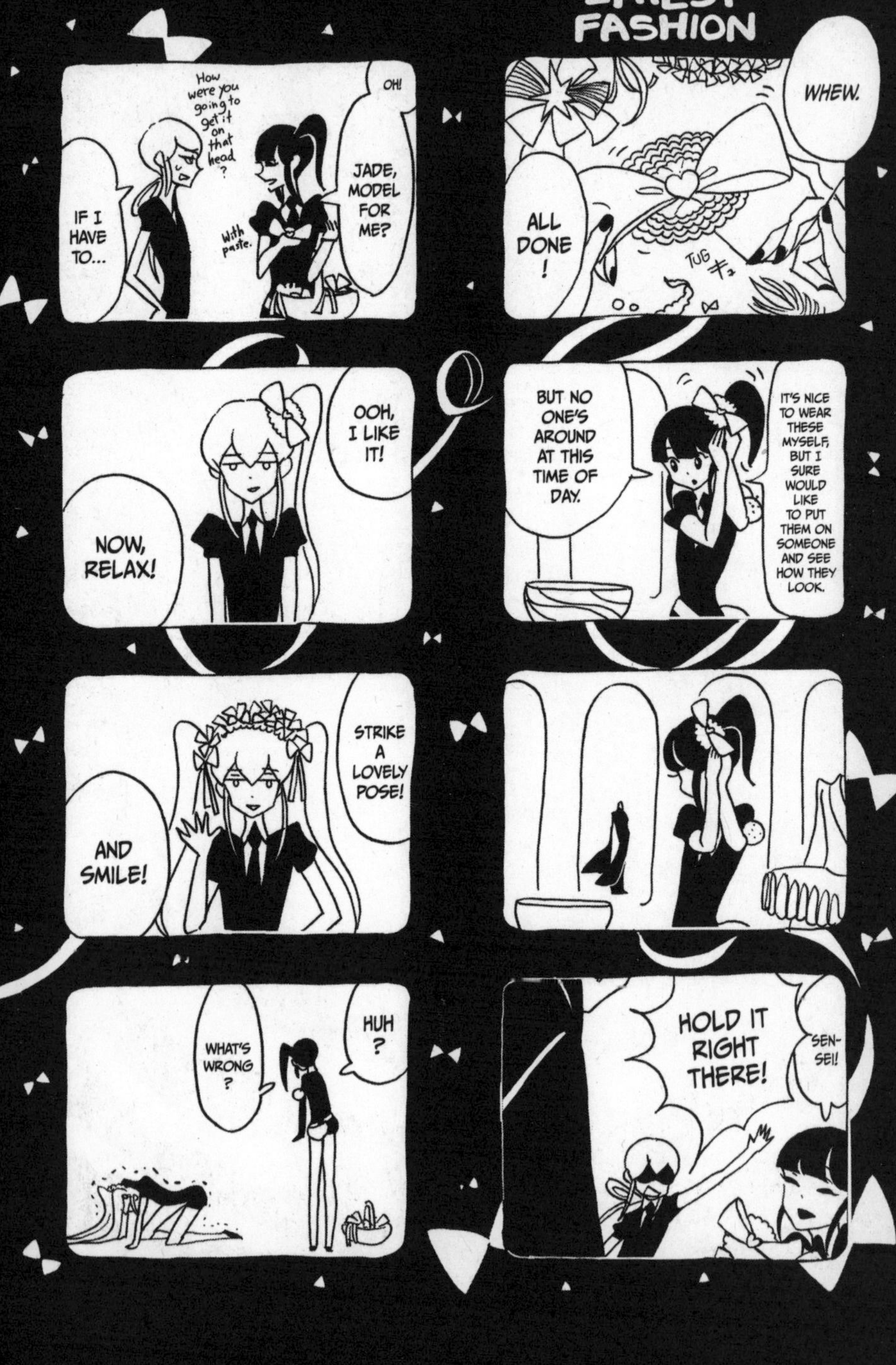
WHEW.
ALL DONE!
TUG
IT'S NICE TO WEAR THESE MYSELF, BUT I SURE WOULD LIKE TO PUT THEM ON SOMEONE AND SEE HOW THEY LOOK.
BUT NO ONE'S AROUND AT THIS TIME OF DAY.
SEN-SEI!
HOLD IT RIGHT THERE!
OH!
How were you going to get it on that head?
JADE, MODEL FOR ME?
With paste.
IF I HAVE TO...
OOH, I LIKE IT!
NOW, RELAX!
STRIKE A LOVELY POSE!
AND SMILE!
HUH?
WHAT'S WRONG?

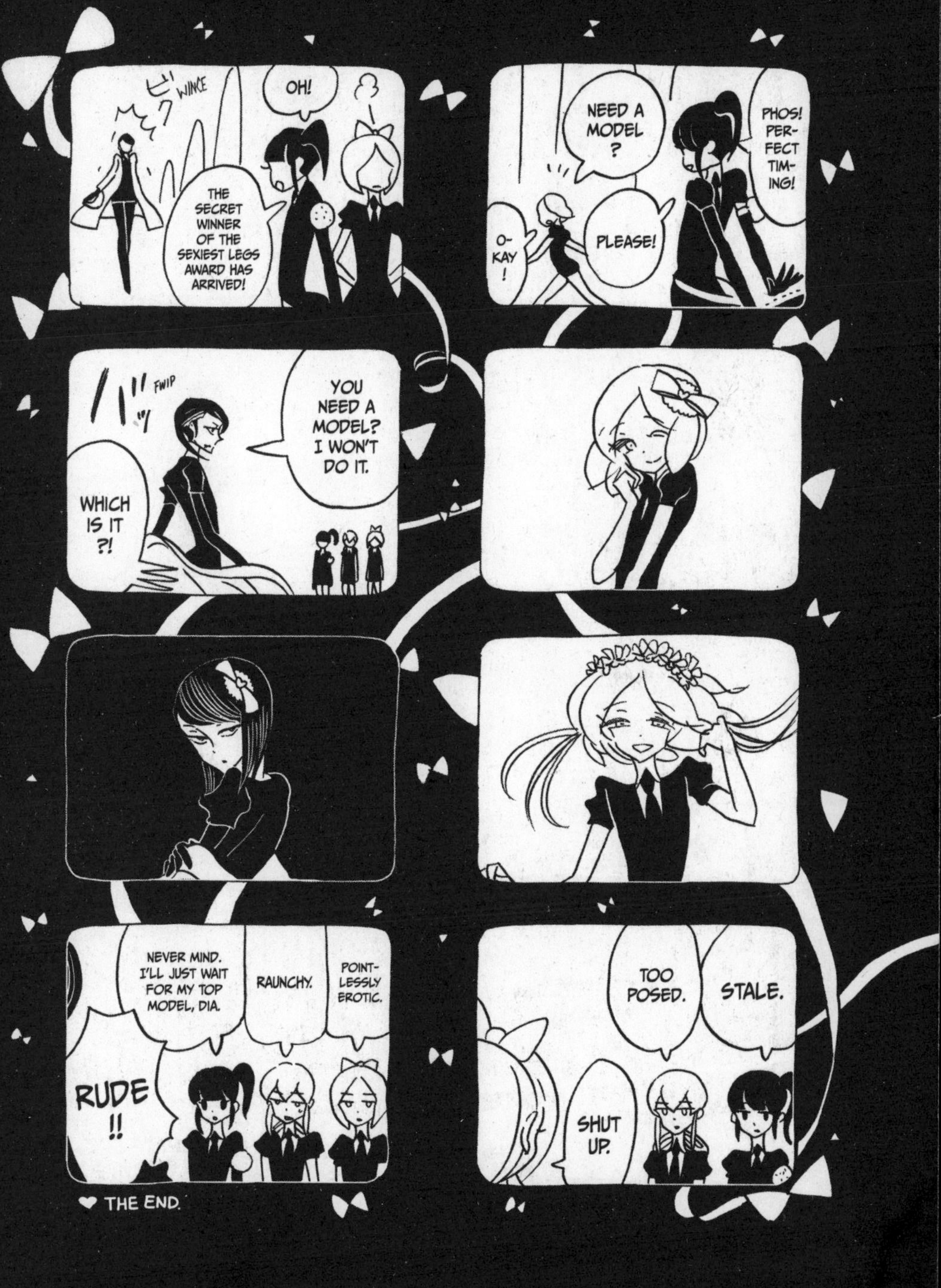
PHOS! PER-FECT TIM-ING!
NEED A MODEL ?
PLEASE!
O-KAY!
OH!
ビク WINCE
THE SECRET WINNER OF THE SEXIEST LEGS AWARD HAS ARRIVED!
YOU NEED A MODEL? I WON'T DO IT.
FWIP
WHICH IS IT ?!
STALE.
TOO POSED.
SHUT UP.
POINT-LESSLY EROTIC.
RAUNCHY.
NEVER MIND. I'LL JUST WAIT FOR MY TOP MODEL, DIA.
RUDE !!
♥ THE END.

TRANSLATION NOTES

VENTRICOSUS AND ACULEATUS *page 80*

The names of these two creatures come from Latin. Ventricosus, the ruler of the Admirabilis race, has a name that fittingly means "corporeal" or "of the flesh." Aculeatus means "prickly" or "barbed," which explains his taste in shell fashion. The reader may reasonably assume that the name Admirabilis is also Latin, and it means "admirable" or "astonishing."

ELDER YELLOW *page 147*

This title is not meant to imply that Yellow Diamond is, for example, a sort of village elder. It is simply used as a term of respect for Yellow Diamond's age as the eldest of the gem family.

84 AND 33 *page 177*

The Amethyst twins must have been formed by a process similar to "crystal twinning," which occurs when two crystals share some of their crystal lattice. There are a few different ways that twinning can occur, and the one that allows the most independence for each twin is Japan Law twinning. In this type of twinning, the crystals grow at an angle of 84 degrees and 33 minutes. Incidentally, this particular angle allows the crystals to form a heart shape.

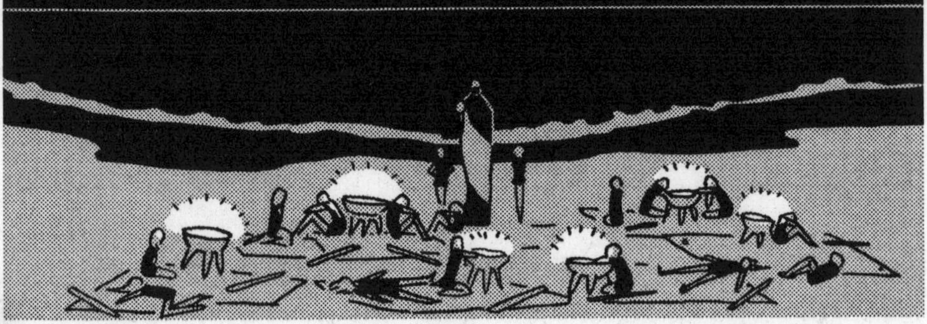

Land of the Lustrous volume 2 is a work of fiction. Names, characters, places, and incidents are the products of the author's imagination or are used fictitiously. Any resemblance to actual events, locales, or persons, living or dead, is entirely coincidental.

A Kodansha Comics Trade Paperback Original.

Published in the United States by Kodansha Comics, an imprint of Kodansha USA Publishing, LLC, New York.

Publication rights for this English edition arranged through Kodansha Ltd., Tokyo.

First published in Japan in 2014 by Kodansha Ltd., Tokyo.

ISBN 978-1-63236-498-2

Printed in the United States of America.

www.kodanshacomics.com

9 8 7 6 5 4 3 2 1

Translator: Alethea Nibley & Athena Nibley
Lettering: Evan Hayden
Editing: Lauren Scanlan
Kodansha Comics edition cover design: Phil Balsman